365 days with Spurgeon

Volume 2

A unique collection of 365 daily readings

from sermons preached

by **Charles Haddon Spurgeon**

from his Metropolitan Tabernacle Pulpit.

Selected and arranged by

Terence Peter Crosby

Day One

© Day One Publications 2002
First printed 2002

Scripture quotations are from the King James Version.

British Library Cataloguing in Publication Data available

ISBN 1 903087 08-2

9 781903 087084

Published by Day One Publications
3 Epsom Business Park, Kiln Lane, Epsom, Surrey KT17 1JF.
☎ 01372 728 300 **FAX** 01372 722 400
e-mail address: sales@dayone.co.uk

Chief Sub-Editor: David Simm
Designed by Steve Devane.

Dedication

To my dear wife Daphne, my 'help meet'
in Christ, who also shares my
interest in Spurgeon

FOREWORD

Charles Haddon Spurgeon aged 30

I am sure I share in the pleasure of many that a second volume of *365 Days with Spurgeon* is now available. All who have seen the first volume will not be surprised that there has been a call for Terence Crosby to go beyond the New Park Street limits of that book and to open up the riches in the Metropolitan Tabernacle Pulpit in the same manner. Dr Crosby has shown himself a thoroughly qualified and wise editor of Spurgeon; he is obviously wholly in sympathy with the material.

Over thirty years ago I produced a small book with the title *The Forgotten Spurgeon*. The fact that it would be absurd to give a book that title today is a reminder how wonderfully Spurgeon's testimony and books have sprung to life again across the world. It is quite possible that he is now being read more widely than ever before. In a well-stocked bookshop in New Zealand, a little while ago, we commented to the owner that although he had a number of old authors there was no Spurgeon to be seen. 'No,' he said, 'that is because they go out as soon as they come in.'

Spurgeon, along with Tyndale, Bunyan and Ryle, is one of the best writers of clear and forceful English. His themes are always fresh because they are always scriptural and we thank God that the prayer which supported his ministry two centuries ago is still being answered. May this book help to introduce him to a yet wider circle!

Iain Murray
Edinburgh

Following the good response to *365 Days with Spurgeon,* based on his New Park Street Pulpit sermons, I have been encouraged to produce this second volume of daily readings, which cover Spurgeon's first six years at the Metropolitan Tabernacle, a period which was immediately followed by its brief closure for renovation work.

In his lifetime Spurgeon published 364 of the sermons he preached in the six year period commencing on 25 March 1861. Of these, 362 have been included in this volume, the two exceptions being those preached on 31 March 1861 (no. 368—the last in the New Park Street Pulpit) and on 24 March 1867 (no. 742—the first of a series of five sermons preached at the Agricultural Hall, Islington during the enforced break while the Metropolitan Tabernacle was closed for renovation work). For the remaining three readings I have used Spurgeon's contributions during the meeting on 11 April 1861 at which The Doctrines of Grace were expounded by five other speakers (nos. 385–388). This was one of the numerous special meetings connected to the opening of the Metropolitan Tabernacle; the other ten related numbers are not represented in this volume, five being addresses by other speakers and five being reports of the various public meetings.

In addition to the opening of the Metropolitan Tabernacle, various points of interest occurred during this period. Volume 7 (which begins as the New Park Street Pulpit and continues as the Metropolitan Tabernacle Pulpit) retains the tiny print used throughout the earlier series; volume 8 (from no. 427) must have been a relief to readers of the sermons, since the tiny print was at last replaced by a larger and clearer print. One of the greatest controversies in Spurgeon's whole life began in 1864 with the preaching of no. 573 against the doctrine of baptismal regeneration; the controversy raged around that sermon together with the follow-up nos. 577, 581 and 591 (all in volume 10). Interestingly it was during this period that Spurgeon dropped the title Rev. from his name on the front page of his sermons, no. 588 being the first to omit it. In response to requests Spurgeon's Scripture readings were mentioned at the end of his sermons from early 1865, starting with no. 623. Very little use has been made of these in this volume, as they are not often directly related to the chosen extract.

As in the previous volume the majority of the readings have been arranged to coincide with the actual dates on which the sermons were preached. Where there is duplication of dates for various reasons, readings have been displaced, as far as possible, to an adjacent day in the same month. About one tenth of the sermons are undated; to provide some thematic continuity and several short topical series, nearly all of these have been allocated to unrepresented dates which come directly before or after readings on related subjects. Each reading indicates Spurgeon's sermon-title and text; on several occasions it has been necessary to abbreviate texts where they are exceptionally long; for the sake of completeness the full texts have still been listed in the Scripture Index. The suggested further readings and footnotes for meditation have been added by the arranger. Once again there has been a minimum of sympathetic updating of the original material to remove antiquated language and terminology. Spurgeon's Scripture quotations (probably from memory) are not always strictly accurate and have been corrected as and when necessary.

In the course of these sermons Spurgeon occasionally mentions contemporary topics of national and international interest; the reader's attention has been drawn to these in footnotes. Of personal and local interest to the compiler has been the Wandsworth connection. From 1857 to 1880 Spurgeon lived at 99 Nightingale Lane, near Wandsworth Common; in the conclusion of no. 472 (preached on the 28 September 1862) he made an appeal in the context of church planting and referred to the outcome of a recuperative walk through Wandsworth which can be more precisely dated to early February 1859. While the passage is unsuitable for a daily reading, the reader may excuse its inclusion here:

'Now, in regard to the particular effort at Wandsworth, for which a collection is to be made. When I was sore sick some three years or more ago, I walked about to recover strength, and walking through the town of Wandsworth, I thought "How few attend a place of worship here. Here are various churches, but there is ample room for one of our own faith and order; something must be done." I thought "If I could start a man here preaching the Word, what good might be done." The next day, some four friends from the town called to see me, one a Baptist, and the three others were desirous of baptism— would I come there and form a Church? We took the large rooms at a tavern, and preaching has been carried on there ever since. Beginning with four, the Church has increased to one hundred and fifty. I have greatly aided the interest by going there continually and preaching and helping to support the minister. Now, a beautiful piece of ground has been taken, and a chapel is to be erected, and I firmly believe there will be a very strong cause raised. We have many rising Churches, but this one has just come to such a point, that a house of prayer is absolutely needed. I should not have asked you for this aid so soon, but the rooms in which they worship are now continually used for concerts on Saturday evenings, and are not altogether agreeable on the Sunday. I would just as soon worship in one place as another, for my own part, but I see various difficulties are now in the way, which a new chapel will remove. I hope you will help them in so doing, help me in the earnest effort of my soul to hold forth the word of life, and to let Christ's kingdom come and his will be done.'

Spurgeon's special enthusiasm for this new fellowship of believers was perhaps due to it having been amongst the very first of many new churches in London promoted by him. His appeal did not fall upon deaf ears; the foundation stone of the new chapel, on the site of the present East Hill Baptist Church in Wandsworth, was laid by Spurgeon himself on 6 October 1862, only eight days later; the new chapel opened on 31 May 1863. It is the compiler's hope and prayer that these daily readings will likewise fall upon good soil and prove to be spiritually fruitful in the lives of all who read them.

Finally I would like to express my thanks again to John Roberts, Steve Devane and all at Day One for their interest, encouragement and involvement in the publication of this volume. Thanks are due to David Simm for his careful editorial eye, and to Dr Digby James for the page layout work and helpful discussions. Gratitude is due to the Evangelical Library, London, for the extended loan of the relevant volumes of the Metropolitan Tabernacle Pulpit.

Terence Peter Crosby
Wandsworth, London

True unity promoted

'Endeavouring to keep the unity of the Spirit in the bond of peace.'
Ephesians 4:3
SUGGESTED FURTHER READING: Romans 15:1–13

Let us cultivate everything that would tend to unity. Are any sick? Let us care for them. Are any suffering? Let us weep with them. Do we know one who has less love than others? Let us have more, so as to make up the deficiency. Do we perceive faults in a brother? Let us admonish him in love and affection. I pray you be peacemakers, everyone. Let us remember that we cannot keep the unity of the Spirit unless we all believe the truth of God. Let us search our Bibles, therefore, and conform our views and sentiments to the teaching of God's Word. Unity in error is unity in ruin. We want unity in the truth of God through the Spirit of God. This let us seek after; let us live near to Christ, for this is the best way of promoting unity. Divisions in churches never begin with those full of love to the Saviour. Cold hearts, unholy lives, inconsistent actions, neglected closets; these are the seeds which sow schisms in the body; but he who lives near to Jesus, wears his likeness and copies his example, will be, wherever he goes, a sacred bond, a holy link to bind the church more closely than ever together. May God give us this, and henceforth let us endeavour to keep the unity of the Spirit in the bond of peace. I commend the text to all believers, to be practised through the coming year. And to those who are not believers, what can I say but that I trust their unity and their peace may be broken for ever, and that they may be led to Christ Jesus to find peace in his death? May faith be given, and then love and grace will follow, so that they may be one with us in Christ Jesus our Lord.

FOR MEDITATION: God alone can create unity between the disunited (Ephesians 2:12–16); we are not expected to manufacture false unity with those who teach another gospel. But neither are we expected to undermine the unity God has already created. Rather we are to work towards its perfection (Ephesians 4:13). What is your track record in this matter? Do you need to make a New Year's resolution?

SERMON NO. 607

A happy Christian

'And the LORD *shall guide thee continually, and satisfy thy soul in drought, and make fat thy bones: and thou shalt be like a watered garden, and like a spring of water, whose waters fail not.' Isaiah 58:11*
SUGGESTED FURTHER READING: Acts 16:6–15

Jehovah shall guide you continually. Notice the word *shall*—'The LORD shall guide thee.' How certain this makes it! How sure it is that God will not forsake us! His precious 'shalls' and 'wills' are better than men's oaths. 'I will never leave thee nor forsake thee; I will never forsake thee.' Then observe that adverb 'continually'. We are not to be guided only sometimes, but we are to have a perpetual monitor; not occasionally to be left to our own understanding, and so to wander, but we are continually to hear the guiding voice of the Great Shepherd; and as we follow close at his heels we shall not err, but be led by a right way to a city to dwell in. You have been, perhaps, in a maze, and you know how difficult it is to find your way to the centre. But sometimes there is one perched aloft who sees the whole of the maze spread out before him like a map, and he calls out to you to turn either to the right or to the left, and if you attend to his directions you soon find the way. Even so the maze of life is only a maze to us, but God can see it all. He who rules over all, looks down upon it as men look down upon a map; and if we will but look to him, and if our communion be constantly kept up we shall never err, but we shall come to the goal of our hopes right speedily by following his voice.

FOR MEDITATION: As in most mazes, we enter the Christian life through one door, the Lord Jesus Christ (John 10:9) and head for one goal—heaven. But wrong paths leading to dead ends will be followed when we fail to obey our guide. We must then turn round, leave the wrong way and seek God for the right way i.e. repent. At times we may not know which path to take or may even find ourselves going round in circles, apparently getting nowhere. We then need to continue to walk by faith, always looking to God for guidance. He is the giver of repentance (2 Timothy 2:25) and faith (Ephesians 2:8) at the start of and throughout the Christian life.

SERMON NO. 736

Suffering and reigning with Jesus

'If we suffer, we shall also reign with him: if we deny him, he also will deny us.' 2 Timothy 2:12

SUGGESTED FURTHER READING: Matthew 10:21–33

What must be the doom of those who deny Christ, when they reach another world? Perhaps some will appear with a sort of hope in their minds, and will come before the judge with 'Lord, Lord, open to me.' 'Who art thou?' saith he. 'Lord, I once took the Lord's Supper—Lord, I was a member of the church, but there came very hard times. My mother bade me give up religion; father was angry; trade went bad; I was so mocked at, I could not stand it. Lord, I fell among evil acquaintances and they tempted me—I could not resist. I was thy servant—I did love thee—I always had love towards thee in my heart, but I could not help it—I denied thee and went to the world again.' What will Jesus say? 'I know thee not, whence thou art.' 'But, Lord, I want thee to be my advocate.' 'I know thee not!' 'But, Lord, I cannot get into heaven unless thou shouldst open the gate—open it for me.' 'I do not know thee; I do not know thee.' 'But, Lord, my name was in the church book.' 'I know thee not—I deny thee.' 'But wilt thou not hear my cries?' 'Thou didst not hear mine—thou didst deny me, and I deny thee.' 'Lord, give me the lowest place in heaven, if I may but enter and escape from wrath to come.' 'No, thou wouldst not brook the lowest place on earth, and thou shalt not enjoy the lowest place here. Thou hadst thy choice, and thou didst choose evil. Keep to thy choice. Thou wast filthy, be thou filthy still. Thou wast unholy, be thou unholy still.'

FOR MEDITATION: God's time for us to reason with him about our sin and disobedience is now (Isaiah 1:18), not on the Day of Judgement. Spurgeon urges you to cry this day mightily unto God, 'Lord, hold me fast, keep me, keep me. Help me to suffer with thee; but do not, do not let me deny thee, lest thou also shouldst deny me.'

A tempted Saviour—our best succour

'For in that he himself hath suffered being tempted, he is able to succour them that are tempted.' Hebrews 2:18
SUGGESTED FURTHER READING: Hebrews 4:14–16

I am certain of this, that when through the deep waters he shall cause you to go, or you are made to pass through furnace after furnace, you cannot want a better rod and staff, nor a better table prepared for you in the wilderness than this my text, 'In that he himself hath suffered being tempted, he is able to succour them that are tempted.' Hang this text up in your house; read it every day; take it before God in prayer every time you bend the knee, and you shall find it to be like the widow's cruse, which failed not, and like her handful of meal, which wasted not: it shall be unto you till the last of December what now it is when we begin to feed upon it in January. Will not my text suit the awakened sinner as well as the saint? There are timid souls here. They cannot say they are saved; yet here is a loophole of comfort here for you, you poor troubled ones that are not yet able to get a hold of Jesus. 'He is able to succour them that are tempted.' Go and tell him you are tempted; tempted, perhaps, to despair; tempted to self-destruction; tempted to go back to your old sins; tempted to think that Christ cannot save you. Go and tell him that he himself has suffered being tempted, and that he is able to succour you. Believe that he will, and he will, for you can never believe anything too much of the love and goodness of my Lord. He will be better than your faith to you. If you can trust him with all your heart to save you, he will do it; if you believe he is able to put away your sin, he will do it.

FOR MEDITATION: Of all who have lived on earth the Lord Jesus Christ had the greatest experience possible of exposure to temptation, but was the one and only total stranger to sin. In this dual capacity he is uniquely and ideally qualified to help us in our ongoing conflicts with both temptation and sin (Hebrews 4:15). Are you one of those who seek his help?

SERMON NO. 487

A psalm for the New Year

'But grow in grace and in the knowledge of our Lord and Saviour Jesus Christ. To him be glory both now and for ever. Amen.' 2 Peter 3:18
SUGGESTED FURTHER READING: Philippians 3:8–16

My beloved brethren in the Lord Jesus, we must see to it that we ripen in the knowledge of him. O that this year we may know more of him in his divine nature, and in his human relationship to us; in his finished work, in his death, in his resurrection, in his present glorious intercession, and in his future royal advent. To know more of Christ in his work is, I think, a blessed means of enabling us to work more for Christ. We must study to know more of Christ also in his character—in that divine compound of every perfection, faith, zeal, deference to his Father's will, courage, meekness and love. He was the Lion of the tribe of Judah, and yet the man upon whom the dove descended in the waters of baptism. Let us thirst to know him of whom even his enemies said, 'Never man spake like this man,' and his unrighteous judge said, 'I find no fault in him.' Above all, let us long to know Christ in his person. This year endeavour to make a better acquaintance with the crucified one. Study his hands and his feet; abide hard by the cross, and let the sponge, the vinegar and the nails, be subjects of your devout attention. This year seek to penetrate into his very heart, and to search those deep far-reaching caverns of his unknown love, that love which can never find a rival, and can never know a parallel. If you can add to this a knowledge of his sufferings, you will do well. O if you can grow in the knowledge of fellowship—if you shall this year drink of his cup, and be baptised with his baptism—if you shall this year abide in him and he in you—blessed shall you be.

FOR MEDITATION: As a child the Lord Jesus Christ grew—in strength, in wisdom, in stature and in favour with God and man (Luke 2:40,52). Those who have become God's children by faith in the Lord Jesus Christ need to do exactly the same.

SERMON NO. 427

Good cheer for the New Year

'The eyes of the LORD thy God are always upon it, from the beginning of the year even unto the end of the year.' Deuteronomy 11:12
SUGGESTED FURTHER READING: Job 23:1–17

Imagine that you and I have to live all the year without the eyes of God upon us, not finding a moment from the beginning of the year to the end of the year in which we perceive the Lord to be caring for us or to be waiting to be gracious to us. Imagine that there is none to whom we may appeal beyond our own fellow creatures for help. O miserable supposition! We have come to the opening of the year, and we have to get through it somehow, we must stumble through January, go muddling through the winter, groaning through the spring, sweating through the summer, fainting through the autumn, and grovelling on to another Christmas, and no God to help us. But I will suppose this in the case of you sinners. You know you have been living for twenty, or thirty, or forty years without God, without prayer, without trust, without hope, yet I should not wonder that if I were solemnly to tell you that God would not let you pray during the next year, and would not help you if you did pray, I should not wonder if you were greatly startled at it. Though I believe that the Lord will hear you from the beginning of the year to the end of the year, though I believe that he will watch over you and bless you if you seek him, yet I fear that the most of you are despising his care, living without fellowship with him; and so you are without God, without Christ, without hope, and will be so from the beginning of the year to the end of the year.

FOR MEDITATION: This was Spurgeon's position before his conversion on 6 January 1850. If you are not yet a Christian, this will remain your position until you are converted. But if you never are converted, this is what your condition will be throughout eternity—only it will be infinitely worse—for ever without hope and without God (Ephesians 2:12).

SERMON NO. 728

Unity in Christ

'Neither pray I for these alone, but for them also which shall believe on me through their word; that they all may be one; as thou, Father, art in me, and I in thee, that they also may be one in us: that the world may believe that thou hast sent me.' John 17:20–21
SUGGESTED FURTHER READING: Ephesians 4:4–16

If you would promote the unity of Christ's church, look after his lost sheep, seek out wandering souls. If you ask what is to be your word, the answer is in the text—it is to be concerning Christ. They are to believe in him. Every soul that believes in Christ is built into the great gospel unity in its measure, and you will never see the church as a whole while there is one soul left unsaved for whom the Saviour shed his precious blood. Go out and teach his Word! Tell out the doctrines of grace as he has given you ability. Hold up Christ before the eyes of men, and you will be the means in God's hand of bringing them to believe in him, and so the church shall be built up and made one. Here is work for the beginning of the year; here is work till the end of the year. Do not sit down and scheme and plot and plan how this denomination may melt into the other; you leave that alone. Your business is to go and 'tell to sinners round what a dear Saviour you have found', for that is God's way of using you to complete the unity of his Church. Unless these be saved, the Church is not perfect. That is a wonderful text, 'That they without us should not be made perfect.' That is to say, saints in heaven cannot be perfect unless we get there. What! the blessed saints in heaven not perfect except the rest of believers come there? So the Scripture tells us, for they would be a part of the body and not a whole body; they cannot be perfect as a flock unless the rest of the sheep come there.

FOR MEDITATION: God's instrument for furthering and completing true unity is spiritual—the ongoing addition of souls to his kingdom through the proclamation of Christ crucified. Man's instrument for promoting organisational unity is political and carnal. Unity, just like the new birth, is 'not of blood, nor of the will of the flesh, nor of the will of man, but of God' (John 1:13).

SERMON NO. 668

A discourse for a revival season

'Behold the voice of the cry of the daughter of my people because of them that dwell in a far country: Is not the LORD in Zion? is not her king in her?'
Jeremiah 8:19
SUGGESTED FURTHER READING: Luke 11:5-13

Our prayers, poor as they are, are the prayers of God's own people, and therefore they must be heard. You will say, 'Is that a right argument?' O, yes it is. 'If ye then, being evil, know how to give good gifts unto your children.' Remember that is how Christ puts it. You are the Lord's children, therefore he will hear you. If you were strangers it might be a different thing. Our prayers might very readily be pulled to pieces by critics, but our Father will not criticise them, because they are the cries of his own children. I do not think we set such store by believers' prayers as we ought to do. Would you let your child constantly cry to you and not answer him? I know you would not. Put it differently: would you let your own brother plead with you and not grant him his desire if you could grant it? You have not a brother's heart if you would. Or I will touch you more closely. We love our wives—if your wife should ask for anything that would be for her good, and you could give it, would you refuse it? Husband, would you refuse it? You are no husband if you did. Look at Christ, the husband of the church, do you think he will refuse the cry of his own spouse? What, shall his own dear bride come before him, and embrace his feet, and say, 'I will not let thee go except thou bless me;' and shall he who has espoused her unto himself in faithfulness, say to her, 'I have bidden thee seek me, but I will not be found of thee; I have commanded thee to knock, but the door shall not be opened; I have told thee to ask, but thou shalt not receive'? O, slander not my loving Lord, because 'he feels at his heart all our sighs and our groans.'

FOR MEDITATION: Spurgeon's references to loving family relationships, probably prompted by the fact that this was his 9th wedding anniversary, remind us that Christians have a heavenly friend who sticks closer than father (Luke 11:11-13), mother (Isaiah 49:15), brother (Proverbs 18:24), husband and wife.

SERMON NO. 608

No illusion

'And wist not that it was true which was done by the angel; but thought he saw a vision.' Acts 12:9

SUGGESTED FURTHER READING: Habakkuk 2:1–4

Peter's case was put into God's hands. The company that met at the house of Mary, the mother of Mark, were appealing to the great Advocate. If any man be in prison, 'we have an advocate with the Father, Jesus Christ the righteous.' With their humble prayers and tears they were pleading for their brother, whose valuable life they could ill afford to spare, for the infant church needed the apostles at least for a season. I think I hear them pleading one after the other—'Lord, remember Peter! Thou knowest how we love him; our desires go up for him. Let not Peter be slain! Oh, take not thou the prop from under us! Remove not the pillar from the wall, nor the stone from its place.' The Lord has heard their cries. Peter's cause is in his hand. He will interfere in due time. The assurance that prayer is heard is the earnest that prayer will be answered. The petition is accepted, though no answer has yet been received. Well, we can leave it there. But see, brethren, Peter has been lying in prison the whole week. The feast of unleavened bread is over, it is the last night—the last night! The evening has crept on; the dark hours have set in; it is midnight. The sun will soon be rising—in a few more hours—and then where is Peter? Lord, if thou do not interfere, where is Peter? If thou come not now to help him his blood shall make the populace of Jerusalem glad while they gloat and delight in his slaughter! Yes, but just at that last and darkest hour of the night, God's opportunity overtook man's extremity. A light shone in the dungeon. Peter was awakened. God never is before his time; nor is he ever too late; he comes just when he is needed.

FOR MEDITATION: Many of our problems and much false doctrine (e.g. evolution, the mass, instant sanctification, purgatory and annihilation) illustrate the fact that God's thoughts and ways are higher than ours (Isaiah 55:8–9); the human heart displays a strong resistance to God's time scales and speeds (2 Peter 3:8–9). Sometimes his apparent delays and slowness to act test our faith to its limits (John 11:6,21,32,39).

A desperate case—how to meet it

'Then came the disciples to Jesus apart, and said, Why could not we cast him out? And Jesus said unto them, Because of your unbelief: for verily I say unto you, If ye have faith as a grain of mustard seed, ye shall say unto this mountain, Remove hence to yonder place; and it shall remove: and nothing shall be impossible unto you. Howbeit this kind goeth not out but by prayer and fasting.' Matthew 17:19–21
SUGGESTED FURTHER READING: Matthew 6:16–18

There are those who watch unto prayer, wait before the Lord, seek his face, and exercise patience till they get an audience. Such disciples continue in their retirement until they have that experience of access for which they crave. And what is fasting for? That seems the difficult point. It is evidently accessory to the peculiar continuance in prayer, practised often by our Lord, and advised by him to his disciples. Not a kind of religious observance, in itself meritorious, but a habit, when associated with the exercise of prayer, unquestionably helpful. I am not sure whether we have not lost a very great blessing in the Christian church by giving up fasting. It was said there was superstition in it; but, as an old divine says, we had better have a spoonful of superstition than a basin full of gluttony. Martin Luther, whose body, like some others, was of a gross tendency, felt as some of us do, that in our flesh there dwelleth no good thing, in another sense than the apostle meant it; and he used to fast frequently. He says his flesh was wont to grumble dreadfully at abstinence, but fast he would, for he found that when he was fasting, it quickened his praying. There is a treatise by an old Puritan, called, 'The soul-fattening institution of fasting.' and he gives us his own experience that during a fast he has felt more intense eagerness of soul in prayer than he had ever done at any other time. Some of you, dear friends, may get to the boiling-point in prayer without fasting. I am sure that others cannot.

FOR MEDITATION: Jesus said 'when' not 'if you fast' (Matthew 6:16). In Scripture, fasting seems to have been reserved for special times: disaster (Judges 20:26; 2 Samuel 1:12); danger (Ezra 8:23; Esther 4:3,16); disease (2 Samuel 12:21–23; Psalm 35:13) and decision (Acts 13:2–3; 14:23). Are we missing out on something?

SERMON NO. 549

Cheer for the faint-hearted

'But his wife said unto him, If the LORD were pleased to kill us, he would not have received a burnt offering and a meat offering at our hands, neither would he have shewed us all these things, nor would as at this time have told us such things as these.' Judges 13:23
SUGGESTED FURTHER READING: 1 Peter 2:9–11

About five days after I first found Christ, when my joy had been such that I could have danced for very mirth at the thought that Christ was mine, on a sudden I fell into a sad fit of despondency. I will tell you why. When I first believed in Christ, I am not sure that I thought the devil was dead, but certainly I had a kind of notion that he was so mortally wounded he could not disturb me. And then I certainly fancied that the corruption of my nature had received its death blow. I felt persuaded that it would never sprout again. I was going to be perfect—I fully calculated upon it—and lo, I found an intruder I had not reckoned upon, an evil heart of unbelief in departing from the living God. So I went to that same Primitive Methodist chapel where I first received peace with God, through the simple preaching of the Word. The text happened to be 'O wretched man that I am! who shall deliver me from the body of this death?' 'There,' I thought 'that's a text for me.' I had got as far as that—in the middle of that very sentiment—when the minister began by saying, 'Paul was not a believer when he said this.' Well now I knew I was a believer, and it seemed to me from the context that Paul must have been a believer too. Now I am sure he was. The man went on to say, that no child of God ever did feel any conflict within. So I took up my hat and left the place.

FOR MEDITATION: This appears to have been on 11 January 1850. The very same people who have helped us can soon become a hindrance to us (Matthew 16:16–23; James 3:1–2). God is always a help in the Christian's time of need (Hebrews 4:16).

A cure for care

'Casting all your care upon him; for he careth for you.' 1 Peter 5:7
SUGGESTED FURTHER READING: Jonah 4:6–11

Believe in a universal providence; the Lord cares for ants and angels, for worms and for worlds; he cares for cherubim and for sparrows, for seraphim and for insects. Cast your care on him, he that calls the stars by their names, and leads them out by numbers, by their hosts. 'Why sayest thou, O Jacob, and thinkest O Israel, my way is passed over from God and he has utterly forgotten me?' Let his universal providence cheer you. Think next of his particular providence over all the saints. 'Precious shall their blood be in his sight.' 'Precious in the sight of the Lord is the death of his saints.' 'We know that all things work together for good to them that love God, to them who are the called according to his purpose.' While he is the Saviour of all men, he is specially the Saviour of them that believe. Let that cheer and comfort you, that special providence which watches over the chosen. 'The angel of the LORD encampeth round about them that fear him.' And then, let the thought of his special love *to you* be the very essence of your comfort. 'I will never leave *thee*, nor forsake *thee*.' God says that as much to you, as he said it to any saint of old. 'Fear not, I am thy shield, and thy exceeding great reward.' O I would beloved, that the Holy Spirit would make you feel the promise as being spoken to *you*; out of this vast assembly forget the rest and only think of yourself, for the promises are unto you, meant for you. O grasp them. It is ill to get into a way of reading Scripture for the whole church, read it for yourselves, and specially hear the Master say to you, 'Let not *your* heart be troubled: ye believe in God, believe also in me.'

FOR MEDITATION: While we should not be so preoccupied with ourselves that we are unable to see the wood for the trees, there is also the danger of neglect or ingratitude resulting from a failure to see the trees for the wood. 'They made me the keeper of the vineyards; but mine own vineyard have I not kept.' (Song of Solomon 1:6). Never forget how personal the Saviour is— 'who loved me, and gave himself for me' (Galatians 2:20).

SERMON NO. 428

Cheering words and solemn warnings

'*Say ye to the righteous, that it shall be well with him: for they shall eat the fruit of their doings.*' *Isaiah 3:10*
SUGGESTED FURTHER READING: Psalm 37:16–40

'Say ye to the righteous, that it shall be well with him,' from the beginning of the year to the end of the year, from the rising of the sun unto the going down of the same, from the first gatherings of evening shadows until the day-star shines. It shall be well with him when, like Samuel, God calls him from the bed of his childhood; it shall be well with him when, like David in his old age, he is stayed up in the bed to conclude his life with a song of praise; it shall be well with him if, like Solomon, he shall abound in wealth, and well with him if like Lazarus he shall lie upon a dunghill and the dogs shall lick his sores; it shall be well with him, if like Job he washes his feet with oil and his steps with butter, if the princes are before him bowing their heads, and the great ones of the earth do him obeisance; but it shall be equally well with him if, like Job in his trial, he sits down to scrape himself with a potsherd, his children gone, his wife bidding him curse his God, his friends become miserable comforters to him, and himself left alone; it shall be well, always well. The text evidently means that it is well with the righteous at all times alike, and never otherwise than well; because no time is mentioned, no season is excluded, and all time is intended.

'What cheering words are these!
Their sweetness who can tell?
In time, and to eternal days,
'Tis with the righteous well.

'Tis well when joys arise,
'Tis well when sorrows flow,
'Tis well when darkness veils the skies,
And strong temptations blow.'

FOR MEDITATION: We become righteous only as the result of trusting in the Lord Jesus Christ and what he has done for us (Romans 5:19). It is bound to be well with the righteous at all times and in all circumstances because 'He hath done all things well' (Mark 7:37).

The ravens' cry

'He giveth to the beast his food, and to the young ravens which cry.' Psalm
147:9
SUGGESTED FURTHER READING: Revelation 8:1–4

Never a sinner prays truly without Christ praying at the same time. You
cannot see nor hear him, but never does Jesus stir the depths of your soul by
his Spirit without his soul being stirred too. O sinner! your prayer when it
comes before God is a very different thing from what it is when it issues forth
from you. Sometimes poor people come to us with petitions which they wish
to send to some company or great personage. They bring the petition and
ask us to have it presented for them. It is very badly spelt, very strangely
written, and we can but just make out what they mean; but still there is
enough to let us know what they want. First of all we make out a fair copy
for them, and then, having stated their case, we put our own name at the
bottom, and if we have any interest, of course they get what they desire
through the power of the name signed at the foot of the petition. This is just
what the Lord Jesus Christ does with our poor prayers. He makes a fair copy
of them, stamps them with the seal of his own atoning blood, puts his own
name at the foot, and thus they go up to God's throne. It is your prayer, but it
is his prayer too, and it is the fact of its being his prayer that makes it prevail.
Now, this is a sledgehammer argument: if the ravens prevail when they cry
all alone, if their poor chattering brings them what they want of themselves,
how much more shall the plaintive petitions of the poor trembling sinner
prevail who can say, 'For Jesus' sake,' and who can clench all his own
arguments with the blessed plea, 'The Lord Jesus Christ deserves it; O Lord,
give it to me for his sake.'

FOR MEDITATION: To say 'For Jesus' sake' or 'In Jesus' name' at the end of
prayer is not supposed to be regarded as the done thing or as a magic
formula. It is a humble confession that we do not deserve an audience with
God, but a confident profession of faith in the only one who does (John
14:13–14; 15:16; 16:23–24).

SERMON NO. 672

Knowledge commended

'But the people that do know their God shall be strong, and do exploits. And they that understand among the people shall instruct many.' Daniel 11:32–33

SUGGESTED FURTHER READING: Ezra 7:1–10

Search the Scriptures. Do not merely read them—search them; look out the parallel passages; collate them; try to get the meaning of the Spirit upon any one truth by looking to all the texts which refer to it. Read the Bible consecutively: do not merely read a verse here and there—that is not fair. You would never know anything about John Bunyan's *Pilgrim's Progress* if you opened it every morning and read six lines in any part and then shut it up again; you must read it all through if you want to know anything about it. Get those books, say Mark or John; read Mark right through from beginning to end; do not stop with two or three verses, or a chapter, but try to know what Mark is aiming at. It is not fair to Paul to take his epistle to the Romans and read one chapter: we are obliged to do it in public service; but if you want to get at Paul's meaning, read the whole epistle through as you would another letter. Read the Bible in a commonsense way. Pray after you have read it as much as you like. When you are reading it, if you come to a knotty point, do not skip it. You all have some Christian friend who knows more than you do; go to him and try to get the thing explained. Above all, when you have read any passage, and do understand it, act it out, and ask the Spirit of God to burn the meaning into your conscience till it is written on the fleshy tables of your heart.

FOR MEDITATION: Daily readings should supplement Bible study, not replace it. Have you ever tried to read the Bible in a year? There are reading schemes to help you. It may be hard work, especially the first time, but many have been so blessed that they have resolved to read the whole Bible every year. But beware of it becoming an academic exercise. Note Ezra's example—his desire was to study God's word, to do it and to teach it—in that order (Ezra 7:10). His aim was not to practise what he preached, but to preach what he practised!

Frost and thaw

'He giveth snow like wool: he scattereth the hoarfrost like ashes. He casteth forth his ice like morsels: who can stand before his cold? He sendeth out his word, and melteth them: he causeth his wind to blow, and the waters flow.' Psalm 147:16–18

SUGGESTED FURTHER READING: Psalm 19:1–6

A man puts his hand into a woolpack and throws out the wool; God giveth snow as easily as that. 'He giveth snow like wool.' A man stands upon a heap of ashes, takes up a handful, throws them into the air, and they fall around. 'He scattereth the hoarfrost like ashes'—just as easily. There are wondrous marvels of nature in ice and snow; those who have looked at the crystals, and examined their marvellous beauty, must have been astonished at the inimitable skill displayed in them. 'He casteth forth his ice like morsels'—just as easily as we cast crumbs of bread outside the window to the robins during these wintry days. When the rivers are hard frozen, and the earth held in iron chains, then the melting of the whole—how is that done? Not by the lighting of innumerable fires or the sending of electric shocks from huge batteries through the interior of the earth—no; 'He sendeth out his word, and melteth them: he causeth his wind to blow, and the waters flow'. The whole matter is accomplished with a word and a breath. See the magnificent ease with which God accomplishes all his purposes in nature! If you and I have any great thing to do, what puffing and panting, what straining and tugging there must be; and even the great engineers, who perform great things by machinery, must make much noise and stir about it. It is not so with the Almighty One. Here is this our world spinning round every day in four-and-twenty hours, and yet it does not make so much noise as a humming-top. If I enter a factory I hear a deafening din, but God's great wheels revolve without noise or friction: all the divine work is simply, easily, and beautifully managed.

FOR MEDITATION: God doesn't need to make a lot of noise to speak to us (1 Kings 19:11–12); but we sometimes make too much noise to hear him and need to quieten down (Psalm 46:10).

SERMON NO. 670

Winnowing time

'What is the chaff to the wheat? saith the LORD.*' Jeremiah 23:28*
SUGGESTED FURTHER READING: Jude 1–4

Watch and pray, as a Christian church, each one of you as members of it, that we may not be allowed to flatter ourselves with a nominal increase, unless it be a real increase from God, for 'what is the chaff to the wheat?' Suppose the report should be that there are so many added to the church, but suppose that they are not added to the Lord now, nor found in Christ hereafter? We have done these people serious damage by, as it were, endorsing their pretensions to Christianity when they have no real claim to it. We may have helped their delusion, we may have rocked the cradle of delusive slumber into which they have fallen, and out of which they will never wake until they open their eyes in hell. 'What is the chaff to the wheat?' I wish that such a text as this would go whistling through some of the churches! I would like to hear of its being preached from every pulpit in London, and I would pray the Holy Spirit to apply it to the conscience of every hearer. Your admission into the church by infant sprinkling, or by confirmation, or by the right hand of fellowship, or by believers' immersion, all go for nothing unless you have been admitted into union with Christ. Your sitting at the Lord's table; coming often to holy communion; being found regularly occupying your place in public worship; joining in the solemn hymn; bending with others in earnest prayers—these things are all nothing, and less than nothing and mockery, unless your heart has been renewed. Unless you have the Spirit of Christ you are none of his. 'Ye must be born again.'

FOR MEDITATION: Those who are members of local churches without being members of Christ's body have been placed in a position of extremely dangerous false assurance and are unequally yoked with converted church members. It is kinder and wiser to refuse to admit such to membership rather than to give them the benefit of the doubt. A challenge to their false hopes will probably do more to bring them to their spiritual senses (Acts 8:13–24).

Broad rivers and streams

'Look upon Zion ... thine eyes shall see Jerusalem ... there the glorious LORD *will be unto us a place of broad rivers and streams; wherein shall go no galley with oars, neither shall gallant ship pass thereby. For the* LORD *is our judge, the* LORD *is our lawgiver, the* LORD *is our king; he will save us.'* Isaiah 33:20–22

SUGGESTED FURTHER READING: Exodus 14:10–31

In 1588, when the Armada sailed towards Britain, God blew with his winds and all Spain's mighty hosts were broken, and God's favoured isle was free. We were doubtless spared the horrors of war under Napoleon because of the Channel. It was especially so in the old times of ancient warfare; then a narrow trench was almost as useful as a broad channel would be now, for they had no ready means of crossing, though on old Assyrian sculptures we see galleys with oars crossing over rivers, and we have one or two sculptures, I believe, in the British Museum, of the Assyrian king turning the river into another channel so that he might the more easily take the city. But still, rivers were for a defence. O beloved, what a defence is God to his church! Ah, the devil cannot cross this broad river of God. Between me and you, O fiend of hell, is my God. Do remember this, Christian; between you and your arch-enemy is your God; Satan has to stand on the other side, and how he wishes he could dry up that stream, but God is omnipotent. How he wishes he could change the current, but fear not, for God abides immutably the same. How he wishes he could get at you and me; but only once let us get safe landed in Zion, we may look over its walls across the broad rivers and streams, and remember that we are out of gunshot of the enemy so far as our spiritual existence is concerned. He cannot destroy us; worry us he may; for we are such timid souls, but kill he cannot, for God, even our mighty God keeps us safe beyond all possibility of destruction.

FOR MEDITATION: Others may have assumed the title 'Defender of the Faith' or even undermined it—'Defender of faith'—but God is the true and everlasting defender of his people (Psalm 5:11; 20:1; 59:1; Isaiah 31:5; 37:35; 38:6; Zechariah 12:8).

Grace exalted—boasting excluded

'Where is boasting then? It is excluded. By what law? of works? Nay: but by the law of faith.' Romans 3:27
SUGGESTED FURTHER READING: Galatians 3:1–14

There are two ways by which man might have been for ever blessed. The one was by works: 'This do and thou shalt live; be obedient and receive the reward.' The other plan was: 'Receive grace and blessedness as the free gift of God; stand as a guilty sinner having no merit, and as a rebellious sinner deserving the very reverse of goodness, but stand there and receive all thy good things, simply, wholly, and alone of the free love and sovereign mercy of God.' Now, the Lord has not chosen the system of works. The word 'law', as used twice in the text, is employed, it is believed by many commentators, out of compliment to the Jews, who were so fond of the word, that their antagonism might not be aroused; but it means here, as elsewhere in Scripture, plan, system, method. There were two plans, two systems, two methods, two spirits,—the plan of works and the plan of grace. God has once for all utterly refused the plan of merit and of works, and has chosen to bless men only, and entirely through the plan, or method, or law of faith. This indeed is the bottom of theology, and he who can understand this clearly, it seems to me, can never be very heterodox; orthodoxy must surely follow, and the right teaching of God must be understood when we once for all are able to discriminate with accuracy between that which is of man— works, and that which is of God—faith, and grace received by faith. Now the plan of salvation by works is impossible for us.

FOR MEDITATION: There are still two basic ideas of salvation—God's way of sending the Lord Jesus Christ down to earth to lift to heaven all who trust in his death on the cross (John 3:16); and man's way of trying to climb heavenwards by some other route, even though the Lord Jesus Christ is the only way back to God (John 14:6). Which path are you on—the one called 'God's way' or the one called 'My way'? They lead to different places (Matthew 7:13–14).

SERMON NO. 429

Let not your hearts be troubled

'Let not your heart be troubled: ye believe in God, believe also in me.'
John 14:1
SUGGESTED FURTHER READING: John 16:1–15

Let me say it ought to be a great deal easier for you and me to live above heart trouble than it was to the apostles; I mean easier than it was to the apostles at the time when the Saviour spoke to them and for forty days afterwards. You say, 'How was that?' Because you have three things which they had not. You have *experience* of many past troubles out of which you have been delivered. They had only been converted at the outside three years; they had not known much trouble, for Jesus in the flesh had dwelt among them to screen off troubles from them. Some of you have been converted thirty—forty—what if I say sixty years, and you have had abundance of trouble—you have not been screened from it. Now all this experience ought to make it easier for you to say, 'My heart shall not be troubled.' Again, you have received *the Holy Spirit*, and they had not. The Holy Spirit was not given, as you remember, until the day of Pentecost. His direct government in the church was not required while Christ was here. You have the Spirit, the Comforter, to abide with you for ever; surely you ought to be less distracted than they were. Thirdly, you have the whole of *Scripture*, they had but a part. They certainly had not the richest Scriptures of all, for they had not the evangelists nor any of the New Testament, and having, as we have, all that store of promise and comfort, we ought surely to find it no hard work to obey the sweet precept, 'Let not your heart be troubled.'

FOR MEDITATION: Have you ever wished you had been a contemporary of the Lord Jesus Christ and an eyewitness of his life on earth? That would have been an experience to be valued and never to be forgotten (John 1:14; 2 Peter 1:16–18; 1 John 1:1–3). However, he pronounced a particular blessing upon those of us who have trusted in him without having seen him (John 20:29). We too are able to love him and experience great joy in the midst of trials and temptations (1 Peter 1:6–8).

The reward of the righteous

'*Then shall the King say unto them on his right hand, Come...inherit the kingdom...for I was an hungred, and ye gave me meat: I was thirsty, and ye gave me drink: I was a stranger, and ye took me in: naked, and ye clothed me: I was sick, and ye visited me: I was in prison, and ye came unto me.*' *Matthew 25:34–36*
SUGGESTED FURTHER READING: Luke 6:32–36

The Duke of Burgundy was waited upon by a very loyal subject, who brought him a very large root which he had grown. He was a very poor man indeed, but simply as a loyal offering he brought to his prince the largest his little garden produced. The prince was so pleased with the man's evident loyalty and affection that he gave him a very large sum. The steward thought, 'Well, I see this pays; this man has got fifty pounds for his large root, I think I shall make the duke a present.' So he bought a horse, and he presented it: the duke, like a wise man, quietly accepted the horse, and gave the greedy steward nothing. So you say, 'Well, here is a Christian, and he gets rewarded. He has been giving to the poor, helping the Lord's church, and see he is saved; the thing pays, I shall make a little investment.' Yes, but you see the steward gave the horse out of very great love to himself, and therefore had no return; and if you perform deeds of charity with the idea of getting to heaven by them, it is yourself that you are feeding and clothing; all your virtue is not virtue, it is rank selfishness, and Christ will never accept it; you will never hear him say, 'Thank you' for it. You served yourself, and no reward is due. You must first come to the Lord Jesus Christ, and look to him to save you; you will for ever renounce all idea of doing anything to save yourself, and being saved, you will be able to give to the poor without selfishness mixing with your motive.

FOR MEDITATION: There is great gain in godliness with contentment, but regarding godliness as a means towards gain and gain as a motive for being godly is a sure mark of ungodliness (1 Timothy 6:5–6).

SERMON NO. 671

Zechariah's vision of Joshua the High Priest

'And he shewed me Joshua the high priest standing before the angel of the LORD, *and Satan standing at his right hand to resist him. And the* LORD *said unto Satan, The* LORD *rebuke thee, O Satan … is not this a brand plucked out of the fire?' Zechariah 3:1–2*
SUGGESTED FURTHER READING: Hebrews 13:10–16

Who are the priests? Why, every humble man and woman that knows the power of Jesus Christ in his own soul, to purge and cleanse him from dead works, is appointed to serve as a priest unto God. I say every humble man and every humble woman too, for in Christ Jesus there is neither male nor female, but we are all one in him. We offer prayer unto God, knowing that it ascends to heaven like sweet odours before the throne; we offer praise, believing that 'whoso offereth praise, glorifieth God.' Jesus has made us priests and kings unto God, and even here upon earth we exercise the priesthood of consecrated living and hallowed service, and hope to exercise it till the Lord shall come. When I see Joshua the high priest, I do but see a picture of each and every child of God, who has been made nigh by the blood of Christ, and has been taught to minister in holy things, and enter into that which is within the veil. But observe where this High Priest is: he is said to be 'standing before the angel of the Lord,' that is, standing to minister. This should be the perpetual position of every true believer. I have no business on the bed of sloth; I have no right to be wandering abroad after private business; I can claim no time which I may set apart for my own follies, or to my own aggrandisement. My true position as a Christian is to be always ministering to God, always standing before his altar. Do I hear you ask how this can be, with your farms and with your merchandise? Know you not, brethren, that whether you eat, or drink, or whatsoever you do, you may do it all to the glory of God?

FOR MEDITATION: Our Great High Priest has completed his one sacrifice for our salvation and has sat down (Hebrews 10:12). Our sacrifices in his service are to be continual and in all our walks of life (Hebrews 13:15–16) and require us to stand against the enemy (Ephesians 6:11,13–14).

The Gospel's power in a Christian's life

'Only let your conversation be as it becometh the gospel of Christ.'
Philippians 1:27
SUGGESTED FURTHER READING: Titus 3:1–8

The word 'conversation' does not merely mean our talk and converse one with another, but the whole course of our life and behaviour in the world. The Greek word signifies the actions and the privileges of citizenship, and we are to let our whole citizenship, our actions as citizens of the new Jerusalem, be such as 'becometh the gospel of Christ.' Observe, dear friends, the difference between the exhortations of the legalists and those of the gospel. He who would have you perfect in the flesh, exhorts you to work that you may be saved, that you may accomplish a meritorious righteousness of your own, and so may be accepted before God. But he who is taught in the doctrines of grace, urges you to holiness for quite another reason. He believes that you are saved, since you believe in the Lord Jesus Christ, and he speaks to as many as are saved in Jesus, and then he asks them to make their actions conformable to their position; he only seeks what he may reasonably expect to receive; 'Let your conversation be such as becometh the gospel of Christ. You have been saved by it, you profess to glory in it, you desire to extend it; let then your conversation be such as becometh it.' The one, you perceive, bids you to work that you may enter heaven by your working; the other exhorts you to labour because heaven is yours as the gift of divine grace, and he would have you act as one who is 'made meet to be a partaker of the inheritance of the saints in light.'

FOR MEDITATION: If you call the Lord Jesus Christ your Lord and Saviour and God your Father, does your lifestyle fit in with his character (1 Peter 1:14–17)? Would any aspects of your life be more appropriate for an atheist or for somebody following a false god?

Faith and life

'Whereby are given unto us exceeding great and precious promises: that by these ye might be partakers of the divine nature, having escaped the corruption that is in the world through lust.' 2 Peter 1:4
SUGGESTED FURTHER READING: Colossians 3:1–10

Rejoice in this, brethren, you are made partakers of the divine nature, and all these promises are given to you in order that you may show this forth among the sons of men, that you are like God, and not like ordinary men; that you are different now from what flesh and blood would make you, having been made participators of the nature of God. The other result which follows is this, 'Having escaped the corruption that is in the world through lust.' Ah, beloved, it were ill that a man who is alive should dwell in corruption. 'Why seek ye the living among the dead?' said the angel to Magdalene. Should the living dwell among the dead? Should divine life be found amongst the corruptions of worldly lusts? A member of Christ's body found intoxicated in the streets, or lying, or blaspheming, or dishonest! God forbid. Shall I take the members of Christ, and make them members of a harlot? How can I drink the cup of the Lord, and drink the cup of Belial? How can it be possible that I can have life, and yet dwell in the foul tomb of the world's lusts? Surely, brethren, from these open lusts and sins you have escaped: have you also escaped from the more secret and more delusive temptations of Satan? O, have you come forth from the lust of pride? Have you escaped from laziness? Have you clean escaped from carnal security? Are you seeking day by day to live above worldliness, the love of the things of the world, and the ensnaring greed which they nourish? Remember, it is for this that you have been enriched with the treasures of God.

FOR MEDITATION: Never treat evangelism as an excuse for worldly behaviour. We must meet unconverted people, but what will make an impression upon them is the fact that we have been transformed by the grace of God. This should be seen both positively (Matthew 5:16) and negatively (1 Peter 4:3–4).

Gracious renewal

'Renew a right spirit within me.' Psalm 51:10
SUGGESTED FURTHER READING: 2 Thessalonians 2:13–15

Let us be moved today to renew our covenant with Christ, or rather to ask him to renew our spirit, because every covenant transaction binds us to it. You believe in the doctrine of election. We do not blush to preach it, and you love to hear it. What does election mean? It means that God has chosen you; very well, if it be so, then you will acknowledge it anew today, by choosing his way and word. You believe in a special and efficacious redemption, that you were redeemed from among men; very well, then you are not your own, you are bought with a price. You believe in effectual calling; you know that you were called out; if it be so, recognise your distinction and separateness as a sacred people set apart by God. You believe that this distinction in you is perpetual, for you will persevere to the end: if you are to be God's for ever, be his today. And are you not looking for a heaven from which selfishness shall be banished? Are you not expecting a heaven where glory shall consist in being wholly absorbed in Christ? Well then, this day, by all that is coming, as well as by all that is past, let your soul be bound as with cords that cannot be broken to the altar of your God. Backsliders, you that have gone astray, pray this prayer today. He bids you pray it, and he will therefore answer it. The text in the margin reads 'renew a constant spirit within me.' You have been froward, wayward, unstable, fickle. Poor backslider, he has put this prayer here for you—'Renew a constant spirit within me.'

FOR MEDITATION: While inward spiritual renewal is an ongoing process in the Christian life (2 Corinthians 4:16), it is not to be taken for granted—we are commanded to have our minds renewed (Romans 12:2: Ephesians 4:23). Our part in the process of renewal is to wait upon the Lord (Isaiah 40:31; 41:1).

A secret and yet no secret

'A garden enclosed is my sister, my spouse; a spring shut up, a fountain sealed.' 'A fountain of gardens, a well of living waters, and streams from Lebanon.' Song of Solomon 4:12,15
SUGGESTED FURTHER READING: Philippians 2:12–16

The believer has three principles, the body, the soul, and the indwelling spirit, which is none other than the Holy Spirit of God abiding in the faithful continually. Just such a relationship as the soul bears to the body does the spirit bear to the soul; for as the body without the soul is dead, so the soul without the spirit is dead in trespasses and sins; as the body without the soul is dead naturally, so the soul without the spirit is dead spiritually. And, contrary to the general teaching of modern theologians, we do insist upon it that the Spirit of God not only renovates the faculties which were there already, but does actually implant a new principle—that he does not merely set to rights a machinery which had before gone awry, but implants a new life which could not have been there. It is not a waking up of dormant faculties—it is the infusion of a supernatural spirit to which the natural heart is an utter stranger. Now, we think the first verse, to a great extent, sets forth the secret and mysterious work of the Holy Spirit in the creation of the new man in the soul. Into this secret no eye of man can look. The inner life in the Christian may well be compared to an enclosed garden—to a spring shut up—to a fountain sealed. But the second verse sets forth the manifest effects of grace, for no sooner is that life given than it begins to show itself. No sooner is the mystery of righteousness in the heart, than, like the mystery of iniquity, it 'doth already work.' It cannot lie still; it cannot be idle; it must not rest; but, as God is ever active, so this God-like principle is active too; thus you have a picture of the outer life, proceeding from the inner.

FOR MEDITATION: Whenever God does a work on the inside, it will result in works on the outside. Otherwise the obvious conclusion is that it is not a work of God in the first place. 'As the body without the spirit is dead, so faith without works is dead also.' (James 2:26) Saving faith is a secret and yet no secret.

SERMON NO. 431

The heart—a den of evil

'For out of the heart proceed evil thoughts, murders, adulteries, fornications, thefts, false witness, blasphemies.' Matthew *15:19*
SUGGESTED FURTHER READING: Psalm 58:1–6

Your child will have evil thoughts without your sending him to a diabolical infant school; children who have been brought up in the midst of honesty, will be found guilty of little thefts early enough in life. False witness, which is one form of lying, is so common, that perhaps to find a tongue which never did bear false witness would be to find a tongue that never spoke. Is this caused by education or by nature? It is so common a thing that even when the ear has heard nothing but the most rigid truth, children learn to lie and men commonly do lie and love to tell an evil tale against their fellow men whether it be true or not, bearing false witness with an avidity which is perfectly shocking. Is this a matter of education, or is it a depraved heart? Some men will wilfully invent a slanderous lie, knowing that they need not take any special care of their offspring, for they may lay it in the street and the first passer-by will take it up and nurse it, and the lie will be carried in triumph round the world; whereas a piece of truth which would have done honour to a good man's character, will be left to be forgotten till God shall remember it at the day of judgment. You never need educate any man into sin. The serpent is scarcely born before it rears itself and begins to hiss. The young lion may be nurtured in your parlour, but it will develop ere long the same thirst for blood as if it were in the forest. So is it with man; he sins as naturally as the young lion seeks for blood, or the young serpent stores up venom.

FOR MEDITATION: Adam and Eve were created sinless in God's image (Genesis 1:27; 5:1); they became sinners and as the result of disobedience Adam's children were born sinful in his image (Genesis 5:3). Everybody since has sinned as the result of being born a sinner—except for the Son of God who was born in the likeness of sinful flesh i.e. in real, but sinless, flesh. Are you trusting in him alone as the one who was punished in his own flesh for your sin (Romans 8:3)?

SERMON NO. 732

Secret sins driven out by stinging hornets

'Moreover the LORD thy God will send the hornet among them, until they that are left, and hide themselves from thee, be destroyed.' Deuteronomy 7:20
SUGGESTED FURTHER READING: Psalm 19:7–14

John Bunyan in The Holy War very wisely describes the town of Mansoul after it had been taken by Prince Immanuel. The Prince rode to the Castle called the Heart and took possession of it, and the whole city became his; but there were certain Diabolonians, followers of Diabolus, who never quitted the town. They could not be seen in the streets, but lurked about in certain old dens and caves. Some of them got impudent enough even to hire themselves out for servants to the men of Mansoul under other names. There was Mr Covetousness, who was called Mr Prudent Thrifty, and there was Mr Lasciviousness, who was called Mr Harmless Mirth. They took other names, and still lived there, much to the annoyance of the town of Mansoul, skulking about in holes and corners, and only coming out on dark days, when they could do mischief and serve Diabolus. Now in all of us, however watchful we may be, though we may set Mr Pry Well to listen at the door, and he may watch; and my Lord Mayor, Mr Understanding, be very careful to search all these out, yet there will remain much hidden sin. I think we ought always to pray to God to forgive us sins that we do not know anything about. Perhaps the sins which you and I confess are not the tenth of what we really do commit. Our eyes are not sufficiently opened to know of the heinousness of our own sin. It is possible that God in mercy suffers us to be somewhat blind to the abominable accursedness of sin. He gives us enough of it to make us hate it, but not enough to drive us absolutely to despair. Our sin is exceedingly sinful.

FOR MEDITATION: 'Be sure your sin will find you out.' (Numbers 32:23) Be also sure that you will never find out all your sins. Even if you could, you could never make yourself right before God. He alone knows the extent of the wickedness of your heart (Jeremiah 17:9); only God the Son could shed his blood and cleanse you from all unrighteousness (1 John 1:7,9).

Jesus washing his disciples' feet

'Then cometh he to Simon Peter: and Peter saith unto him, Lord, dost thou wash my feet?' John 13:6
SUGGESTED FURTHER READING: Philemon 4–20

The Scottish Baptists were accustomed to wash the saints' feet literally; I dare say it would not do some of the saints much hurt; but still it never was intended for us to carry out literally the example of the Saviour; there is a spiritual meaning here, and what he means is this. If there be any deed of kindness or love that we can do for the very meanest and most obscure of God's people, we ought to be willing to do it—to be servants to God's servants—to feel like Abigail did, when she said to David, 'Let thine handmaid be a servant to wash the feet of the servants of my lord.' Abigail became David's wife; but yet she felt she was not worthy even to wash his servants' feet. That must be our spirit. Do you know a brother who is rather angry in temper, and he wants a kind word said to him, and some one says, 'I will not speak to any such person as he is'? Do it—do it, my dear brother; go and wash his feet! Do you know one who has gone astray? Some one says, 'I would not like to be seen in association with him.' My dear friend, you are spiritual; go and restore such a one in the spirit of meekness. Wash his feet! There is another riding the high horse; he is very very proud. One says, 'I am not going to humble myself to him.' My dear brother, go to him, and wash his feet! Whenever there is a child of God who has any defilement upon him, and you are able to point it out and rid him of it, submit to any degradation, put yourself in any position, sooner than that child of God should be the subject of sin.

FOR MEDITATION: The New Testament gives Christians many instructions about their mutual behaviour towards one another. Check yourself against these commands: 1. In general—love; have peace; be likeminded; care. 2. In attitude—be subject; esteem better; prefer; forbear; forgive; be kind; consider; receive. 3. In speech—exhort; comfort; edify; greet; teach; admonish; confess; pray. 4. In action—bear burdens; serve; minister; use hospitality. Whose 'feet' are you 'washing' (John 13:14)?

SERMON NO. 612

A voice from the Hartley Colliery

'If a man die, shall he live again?' Job 14:14
SUGGESTED FURTHER READING: 1 Samuel 28:3–16

What would any of us who fear God think, if we were once in heaven? Would not the very suggestion of return, though it were to the most faithful spouse and best-beloved children, be a cruelty? What, bring back again to battle the victor who wears the crown? What, bring me back again to pain and sorrow, to temptation, and to sin? No. Blessed be God, that all the wishes of friends shall not accomplish this, for we shall be 'Far from this world of grief and sin.'

This world is not so lovely as to tempt us away from heaven. Here we are strangers and foreigners; here we have no abiding city; but we seek one to come. There is one wilderness, but we bless God there are not two. There is one Jordan to be crossed, but there is not another. There is one season when we must walk by faith and not by sight, and be fed with manna from heaven; but blessed be God there is not another, for after that comes the Canaan— the rest which remaineth for the people of God. What man among you, immersed in the cares of business, would desire two lives? Who, that is tired today with the world's noise, and vexed with its temptations, who that has come from a bed of sickness, who that is conscious of sin, would wish to leave the haven when once it is reached? As well might galley-slave long to return to his oar, or captive to his dungeon!

FOR MEDITATION: The story of the rich man and Lazarus (Luke 16:19–31) teaches plainly that, for sinner or saint, there is no way back from eternity. Longing for such a return is therefore fruitless, no matter how loved anyone has been. We should seek to be delivered from such desires.

N.B. This sermon was preached on the occasion of the Hartley Colliery disaster in which some 200 miners were killed. Several of them were Christians.

Do you know him?

'That I may know him.' Philippians 3:10
SUGGESTED FURTHER READING: Acts 8:9–24

Let me warn you of second-hand spirituality; it is a rotten soul-deceiving deception. Beware of all esteeming yourself according to the thoughts of others, or you will be ruined. Another man's opinion of me may have great influence over me. I have heard of a man in perfectly good health killed by the opinion of others. Several of his friends had foolishly agreed to play him a practical trick; whereupon one of them met him and said, 'How ill you look this morning.' He did not feel so; he was very much surprised at the remark. When he met the next, who said to him, 'Oh! dear, how bad you look,' he began to think there might be something in it; and as he turned smart round the corner, a third person said to him, 'What a sight you are! How altered from what you used to be!' He went home ill, he took to his bed and died. So goes the story, and I should not marvel if it really did occur. Now, if such might be the effect of persuasion and supposed belief in the sickness of a man, how much more readily may men be persuaded into the idea of spiritual health! A believer meets you, and by his treatment seems to say, 'I welcome you as a dear brother'—and means it too. You are baptised, and you are received into church fellowship, and so everybody thinks that you must be a follower of Christ; and yet you may not know him. O I do pray you, do not be satisfied with being persuaded into something like an assurance that you are in him, but do know him—know him for yourself.

FOR MEDITATION: We should all take it for granted that by nature we are all hell-deserving sinners. None of us have any right to take it for granted that we are heaven-bound saints. Even with the kindest of motives, spiritual flattery is a killer. For God to wound us by telling us the awful truth about ourselves is an amazing offer of friendship (Proverbs 27:6), a merciful warning to flee from the wrath to come by trusting in Christ crucified (2 Corinthians 5:19–21).

SERMON NO. 552

Nominal Christians—real infidels

'If I say the truth, why do ye not believe me?' John 8:46
SUGGESTED FURTHER READING: Mark 1:1–15

The claims of Jesus of Nazareth are briefly stated by Peter, 'Repent ye therefore, and be converted, that your sins may be blotted out, when the times of refreshing shall come from the presence of the Lord.' He demands *repentance*; that is, a change of mind—the changing of your mind with reference to sin, caring no more for its pleasures, despising it and turning away from it: a change of mind with regard to holiness; seeking your happiness in it: a change of mind with regard to Christ himself, so that you shall no longer look upon him as without form or comeliness, but as a most precious Saviour, such as you need. Sinner, Christ demands of you that you should take your ornaments of self-righteousness from yourself, and wrap yourself in the sackcloth of humiliation, and cast the ashes of penitence upon your head, and cry, 'Unclean! unclean! unclean!' Moreover, he requires *faith* of you. 'Repent ye and believe the gospel.' 'This is the commandment that ye believe on Jesus Christ whom God hath sent.' The Jews said, 'What shall we do that we may do the work of God?' Christ said, 'This is the work of God, that ye believe on Jesus Christ whom he hath sent.' He demands that faith which will accept him to be the sole cleanser from sin, and so to be sole possessor, as he is sole redeemer, of the heart. Friend, you believe that no less a person than the Son of God thus bids you look upon him and be saved; you believe that the Son of God was nailed to the cross, and that out of love to you he demands that you forsake the sin which will destroy you, and believe in his blood which will cleanse you. Does Jesus thus speak? Are these demands the hard inventions of a tyrannical priesthood, or the mild and tender claims of love?

FOR MEDITATION: The Lord Jesus Christ commanded such repentance and faith in him at the start of his ministry (Mark 1:15); his apostles continued to combine the same two gospel commands (Acts 20:21). They have never been withdrawn. Have you obeyed them? If not, 'What doth the Lord require of thee?' (Micah 6:8)

SERMON NO. 492

Life in earnest

'He did it with all his heart and prospered.' 2 Chronicles 31:21
SUGGESTED FURTHER READING: Joshua 14:6–14

Look around you; who are the most useful men in the Christian church today? The men who do what they undertake for God with all their hearts. Where is the preacher whom God blesses by the conversion of hundreds in a year? Is he a sleepy, prosaic soul? Does he confine himself within narrow limits? Does he speak sleepy words to a slumbering congregation? We know it is not so, but where God is pleased to assemble a congregation it is, whatever it may not be, a proof that there has been earnestness in the preacher. Who are the most successful Sunday school teachers? The most learned? Every superintendent will tell you it is not so. The most talented? The most wealthy? No; they who are the most zealous; the men whose hearts are on fire; those are the men who honour Christ. Who among you today is doing the most for your Master's kingdom? I will tell you. Lend me a spiritual thermometer by which I may try the heat of your heart, and I will tell you the amount of your success. If your hearts be cold towards God, I am sure you are doing nothing though you may pretend to do it, but if you can say, 'Lord, my soul is all on flame with an agony of desire to do good to the souls of men,' then you are doing good, and God is blessing you as he did Hezekiah, who did it with all his heart and prospered. Feeling that very many Christians are not Christians with all their hearts, and that perhaps some of you have only given Jesus Christ a dull, cobwebby corner of your hearts, instead of bidding him sit at the head of the table and reign upon the throne: fearing that we are all in danger of getting into a Laodicean lukewarm state, I wish to stir you up.

FOR MEDITATION: While we must avoid zeal without knowledge (Romans 10:2), it is not in God's purposes for us to be satisfied with the possession of knowledge without zeal (Titus 2:14). Do you seek to do with all your might whatever your hand finds to do (Ecclesiastes 9:10)?

Unstaggering faith

'And being not weak in faith, he considered not his own body now dead, when he was about an hundred years old, neither yet the deadness of Sarah's womb: he staggered not at the promise of God through unbelief; but was strong in faith, giving glory to God.' Romans 4:19–20
SUGGESTED FURTHER READING: Exodus 5:22–6:13

If your heart has been set upon any special object in prayer, if you have an express promise for it, you must not be staggered if the object of your desire be farther off now than when you first began to pray. If even after months of supplication the thing should seem more difficult now of attainment than ever it was, wait at the mercy seat in the full persuasion that although God may take his time, and that time may not be your time, yet he must and will redeem his promise when the fulness of time has come. If you have prayed for the salvation of your child, or husband, or friend, and that person has grown worse instead of better, do not cease praying. If that dear little one has become more obstinate, and that husband more profane even, still God must be held to his word; and if you have the faith to challenge his attributes of faithfulness and power, assuredly he never did and never will let your prayers fall fruitless to the ground; and I repeat the word, that you may be sure to bear that away with you, let not the fact that the answer seems farther off than ever be any discouragement to you. Remember that to trust God in the light is nothing, but to trust him in the dark—that is faith. To rest upon God when everything witnesses with God—that is nothing; but to believe God when everything gives him the lie—that is faith. To believe that all shall go well when outward providences blow softly is any fool's play, but to believe that it must and shall be well when storms and tempests are round about you, and you are blown farther and farther from the harbour of your desire—this is a work of grace.

FOR MEDITATION: The assumption that smooth progress indicates God's favour and that trouble is a mark of his displeasure is not a safe one. Our circumstances often prove the opposite to be true (Luke 6:20–26).

The mighty arm

'Thou hast a mighty arm: strong is thy hand, and high is thy right hand.'
Psalm 89:13
SUGGESTED FURTHER READING: Genesis 1:1–2:3

Remember the mighty power of God in creation. Man wants something to work upon: give him material, and with cunning instruments he straightway makes for himself a vessel; but God began with nothing; and by his word alone made all things out of nothing. 'He spake, and it was done: he commanded, and it stood fast.' Darkness and chaos lay in the way before him, but these soon gave place to the excellence of his might when he said, 'Let there be light, and there was light.' 'In six days the Lord made the heavens and the earth, and all the hosts of them.' How rapid was that work, and yet how perfect, how gloriously complete! Now, Christian, I want you to draw living water out of this well. The God who in the old creation did all this, can he not work today? He made the world out of nothing, can he not make new creatures without the aid of human will? His word fashioned the creation of old, and his word can work marvels still. Spoken by whomsoever he pleases to send, his word shall be as potent now as in primeval days. There may be darkness and confusion in the sinner's soul; a word shall remove all, and swift and quick, requiring not even six days. God can make new creatures in this house of prayer and throughout this city. The Lord has but to will it with his omnipotent will, and the sinner becomes a saint. O let creation encourage you to expect a new creation!

FOR MEDITATION: Every Christian is a new creation (2 Corinthians 5:17); God applies the same principles to his 'new creations' as he did during his original act of creation i.e. he gives them new life (Genesis 2:7; Ephesians 2:1), a new likeness (Genesis 1:26–27; Ephesians 4:24), new light to be separate from darkness (Genesis 1:3–4,6–7,14–18; 2 Corinthians 4:6; 6:14–18), new love (Genesis 2:18,21–22; Ephesians 2:14–16) and new labours (Genesis 1:22,28; 2:15; Ephesians 2:10). Are you one of God's new creations in Christ Jesus?

SERMON NO. 674

The strong one driven out by a stronger one

'When a strong man armed keepeth his palace, his goods are in peace: but when a stronger than he shall come upon him, and overcome him, he ... divideth his spoils ... When the unclean spirit is gone out of a man...'
Luke 11:21–24
SUGGESTED FURTHER READING: 1 Thessalonians 5:1–10

So long as you are content with the world, and with the prince who governs it, you will go on, on, on, to your own destruction. Satan does with men as the sirens are fabled to have done with mariners; they sat upon the rocks and chanted lays so harmonious that no mariner, who once caught the sound, could ever resist the impulse to steer his ship towards them, so each vessel voyaging that way was wrecked upon the rocks through their disastrous, but enchanting strain. Such is Satan's voice; he lures to eternal ruin with the sweetest strains of infernal minstrelsy. This is the dulcet note 'Peace, peace.' O sinner, if you were not a fool, you would stop your ears to this treacherous lay. For ever blessed be that sovereign grace which has saved us from the enchantments of this destroyer. The tenant of the heart is called 'an unclean spirit.' He is unclean, notwithstanding all the peace he gives you. Flatter not yourself to the contrary. He is ever the same, unchanged, unchangeable. Perhaps you tell me that you are not subject to any uncleanness; you do not drink, nor swear, nor lie; but remember, it is unclean not to be reconciled to God; it is unclean to be a stranger to Christ; it is unclean to disobey God who created you; and above all it is unclean not to love the Redeemer, whose most precious blood has delivered his people from their sins. At his best the devil is no better than a devil, and the heart in which he dwells is no better than a den for a traitor to hide in.

FOR MEDITATION: Sin affects every part of our being; even what we regard as our good points are unclean in God's sight (Isaiah 64:6). We remain unclean until we trust in the blood of the Lord Jesus Christ to cleanse us from all sin (1 John 1:7).

SERMON NO. 613

Consider before you fight

'What king, going to make war against another king, sitteth not down first, and consulteth whether he be able with ten thousand to meet him that cometh against him with twenty thousand? Or else, while the other is yet a great way off, he sendeth an ambassage, and desireth conditions of peace.' Luke 14:31-32
SUGGESTED FURTHER READING: Judges 16:4-22

You may be enticed by friends who will be very pressing. You can give up sin just now, but you do not know who may be the tempter at some future time. If *she* should allure you, who has tempted so well before. If *he* should speak. He! the very word has wakened up your recollection; if he should speak as he alone can speak, and look as only he can look, can you then resist, and stand out? That witching voice, that fascinating eye! O how many souls have been damned for what men call love! O that they had but a little true love of themselves and others, and would not thus pander to the prince of hell. But alas, while the cup itself looks sweet, there is to be added to it the hand that holds it out. It is not so easy to contend with Satan when he employs the service of some one whom you esteem highly, and love with all your heart. Remember the case of Solomon whose wisdom was marvellous, but who was enticed by his wives, and fell a prey into the hands of the evil one. It needs a spirit like the Master's, to be able to say, 'Get thee behind me, Satan,' to the tempter, when he has the appearance of one of your best loved friends. The devil is a crafty being, and if he cannot force the door, he will try and get the key which fits the wards of the lock, and, by the means of our tenderest love and affections, will make a way for himself into our hearts; you will find it no easy task therefore to contend with him.

FOR MEDITATION: Even our nearest and dearest are sinners and possible sources of temptation to us (Deuteronomy 13:6); if we expect too much from them, they will let us down sooner or later. It is far better to reserve our true confidence for God himself (Psalm 118:8-9; Micah 7:5-7).

Election no discouragement to seeking souls

'I will be gracious upon whom I will be gracious, and will show mercy upon whom I will show mercy.' Exodus 33:19
SUGGESTED FURTHER READING: Romans 9:14–26

Our opponents put the case thus: suppose a father should condemn some of his children to extreme misery, and make others supremely happy, out of his own arbitrary will, would it be right and just? Would it not be brutal and detestable? My answer is, of course, it would; it would be detestable in the highest degree, and far, very far be it from us to impute such a course of action to the Judge of all the earth. But the case stated is not at all the one under consideration, but one as opposite from it as light from darkness. Sinful man is not now in the position of a well-deserving or innocent child, neither does God occupy the place of a complacent parent. We will suppose another case far nearer the mark, indeed, it is no supposition, but an exact description of the whole matter. A number of criminals, guilty of the most aggravated and detestable crimes, are righteously condemned to die, and die they must, unless the king shall exercise the prerogative vested in him, and give them a free pardon. If for good and sufficient reasons, known only to himself, the king chooses to forgive a certain number, and to leave the rest for execution, is there anything cruel or unrighteous here? If, by some wise means, the ends of justice can be even better answered by the sparing of the pardoned ones, than by their condemnation, while at the same time, the punishment of some tends to honour the justice of the lawgiver, who shall dare to find fault? None, I venture to say, but those who are the enemies of the state and of the king. And so may we well ask, 'Is there unrighteousness with God? God forbid.'

FOR MEDITATION: Our accusations of injustice against God arise from mistaken assumptions. Against the Lord Jesus Christ the Jews argued that they were all free and children of God (John 8:33,41); whereas the truth is that by nature they and we are all slaves of sin and children of the devil (John 8:34,44). What should amaze us is not that God would punish us for our sin, but that he chooses to have mercy upon any of us at all!

SERMON NO. 553

Gethsemane

'And being in an agony he prayed more earnestly: and his sweat was as it were great drops of blood falling down to the ground.' Luke 22:44
SUGGESTED FURTHER READING: Mark 14:32–42

Behold the Saviour's unutterable woe. The emotions of that dolorous night are expressed by several words in Scripture. John describes him as saying four days before his passion, 'Now is my soul troubled;' as he marked the gathering clouds he hardly knew where to turn himself, and cried out 'What shall I say?' Matthew writes of him, 'he began to be sorrowful and very heavy.' Upon the word *ademonein* translated 'very heavy,' Goodwin remarks that there was a distraction in the Saviour's agony since the root of the word signifies 'separated from the people—men in distraction, being separated from mankind.' What a thought, my brethren, that our blessed Lord should be driven to the very verge of distraction by the intensity of his anguish. Matthew represents the Saviour himself as saying 'My soul is exceeding sorrowful, even unto death.' Here the word *perilupos* means encompassed, encircled, overwhelmed with grief. 'He was plunged head and ears in sorrow and had no breathing-hole,' is the strong expression of Goodwin. Mark records that he began to be sore amazed, and to be very heavy. In this case *thambeisthai*, with the prefix *ek*, shows extremity of amazement, like that of Moses when he did exceedingly fear and quake. Luke uses the strong language of my text—'being in an agony.' These expressions are quite sufficient to show that the grief of the Saviour was of the most extraordinary character, well justifying the prophetic exclamation 'Behold and see if there be any sorrow like unto my sorrow which is done unto me.'

FOR MEDITATION: The instruments we associate with the shedding of Christ's blood were wielded by men—the scourge, crown of thorns, nails and spear (John 19:1–2,18,34). The fact that he sweat 'great drops of blood' in Gethsemane before any man could lay a finger on him gives us an important glimpse behind the scenes—his life was not taken from him by men; it was given by him for men (John 10:17–18).

SERMON NO. 493

Threefold sanctification

'Sanctified by God the Father.' Jude 1
'Sanctified in Christ Jesus.' 1 Corinthians 1:2
'Through sanctification of the Spirit.' 1 Peter 1:2
SUGGESTED FURTHER READING: 1 Thessalonians 3:11–4:8

We may without the slightest mistake speak of sanctification as the work of the Spirit, yet we must take heed that we do not view it as if the Father and the Son had no part therein. It is correct to speak of sanctification as the work of the Father, of the Spirit, and of the Son. Jehovah says, 'Let us make man in our image, after our likeness,' and thus 'we are his workmanship, created in Christ Jesus unto good works, which God hath before ordained that we should walk in them.' My brethren, I beg you to notice and carefully consider the value which God sets upon real holiness, since the Trinity is represented as co-working to produce a church without 'spot, or wrinkle, or any such thing.' Holiness is the architectural plan upon which God builds up his living temple. We read in Scripture of the 'beauties of holiness;' nothing is beautiful before God but that which is holy. All the glory of Lucifer, that son of the morning, could not screen him from divine abhorrence when he had defiled himself by sin. 'Holy, Holy, Holy,'—the continual cry of cherubim is the loftiest song that creature can offer, and the noblest that the divine Being can accept. See then, he counts holiness to be his choice treasure. It is as the seal upon his heart, and as the signet upon his right hand. I pray you who profess to be followers of Christ, set a high value upon purity of life and godliness of conversation. Value the blood of Christ as the foundation of your hope, but never speak disparagingly of the work of the Spirit.

FOR MEDITATION: Some overemphasise the work of the Holy Spirit so much that they appear to worship him alone as a unity. Others in reaction seem to overlook the work of the Holy Spirit so much that they appear to worship only the Father and Son as a duality. Real Trinitarians give due honour to all three persons of the Godhead. Something is seriously wrong if any one is belittled or omitted (John 5:23; Acts 19:2).

The dawn of revival, or prayer speedily answered

'At the beginning of thy supplications the commandment came forth, and I am come to shew thee; for thou art greatly beloved.' Daniel 9:23
SUGGESTED FURTHER READING: Luke 18:1–8

To multiply expressions such as 'O Lord! O Lord! O Lord!' may not always be right. There may be much sin in such repetitions, amounting to taking God's name in vain. But it is not so with Daniel. His repetitions are forced from the depths of his soul, 'O Lord, hear; O Lord, forgive; O Lord, hearken and do.' These are the volcanic eruptions of a soul on fire, heaving terribly. It is just the man's soul wanting relief. Jesus himself, when he prayed most vehemently, prayed three times, using the same words. Variety of expression sometimes shows that the mind is not altogether absorbed in the object, but is still able to consider the mode of its utterance; but when the heart becomes entirely swallowed up in the desire it cannot stay to polish and fashion its words, it seizes upon any expressions nearest to hand, and with these it continues its entreaties. So long as God understands it, the troubled mind has no anxiety about its modes of speech. Daniel here, with what the old divines would have called multiplied ingeminations [repetitions], groans himself upward till he gains the summit of his desires. To what shall I liken the pleadings of the man greatly beloved? It seems to me as though he thundered and lightened at the gate of heaven. He stood there before God and said to him, 'O thou Most High, thou hast brought me to this river Ulai [see Daniel 8:2,16] as thou didst Jacob to the Jabbok, and with thee all night I mean to stay and wrestle till the break of day. I cannot, will not let thee go except thou bless me.' No prayer is at all likely to bring down an immediate answer if it be not a fervent prayer. 'The effectual fervent prayer of a righteous man availeth much;' but if it be not fervent we cannot expect to find it effectual or prevalent. We must get rid of the icicles that hang about our lips.

FOR MEDITATION: Repetition in prayer is not wrong in itself. What we must avoid is vain repetition (Matthew 6:7). Contrast the wild and vain repetition of the prophets of Baal (1 Kings 18:26–29) with the meaningful and heartfelt repetition of Elijah's brief prayer which God answered (1 Kings 18:36–39).

SERMON NO. 734

Spring in the heart

'Thou blessest the springing thereof.' Psalm 65:10
SUGGESTED FURTHER READING: Revelation 2:1–7

God is blessing the springing thereof. In looking back upon my own 'springing,' I sometimes think God blessed me then in a way in which I desire he would bless me now. An apple tree when loaded with apples is a very comely sight; but give me, for beauty, the apple tree in bloom. The whole world does not present a more lovely sight than an apple blossom. Painters have declared that there is nothing in the whole world to excel it in beauty. Now, a full-grown Christian laden with fruit is a blessed sight, but still there is a blessedness, a peculiar blessedness about the young Christian in bloom. Let me just tell you what I think that blessedness is. You have probably now a greater tenderness about sin than some professors who have known the Lord for years; they might wish that they felt your tenderness of conscience. You have now a graver sense of duty, and a more solemn fear of the neglect of it than some who have known the Lord for years; and you have a greater zeal than many. You are now doing your first works for God, and burning with your first love; nothing is too hot for you or too hard for you. To go to a sermon, now—no matter what weather it may be—seems to you to be an imperative necessity; you would go over hedge and ditch to hear the Word. But some who are of older growth want soft cushions to sit upon; they cannot stand in the aisle now as they used to do, everybody must be particularly polite when they come in, or they care not to worship at all.

FOR MEDITATION: The believer is the apple of God's eye (Psalm 17:8; Zechariah 2:8); what kind of apple tree would you be in God's eye? One that still produces pleasing fruit (Song of Solomon 7:8) or one that has withered away (Joel 1:12)?

SERMON NO. 675

For Christ's sake

'For Christ's sake.' Ephesians 4:32
SUGGESTED FURTHER READING: Colossians 3:17–4:1

What have we done? Preached a few times, but with how little fire; prayed at certain seasons, but with what little passion; talked now and then to sinners, but with what half-heartedness; given to the cause of Christ, but seldom given till we denied ourselves and made a real sacrifice; believed in God at times, but with what unbelief mixed with our faith; loved Christ, but with what cold, stolid hearts. 'For Christ's sake.' Do you feel the power of it? Then let it be like a rushing mighty wind to your soul to sweep out the clouds of your worldliness, and clear away the mists of sin. 'For Christ's sake;' be this the tongue of fire that shall sit on every one of you: 'for Christ's sake;' be this the divine rapture, the heavenly inspiration to bear you aloft from earth, the divine spirit that shall make us bold as lions and swift as eagles in our Lord's service. How much owest thou unto my Lord? Has he ever done anything for thee? Has he forgiven thy sins? Has he covered thee with a robe of righteousness? Has he set thy feet upon a rock? Has he established thy goings? Has he prepared heaven for thee? Has he prepared thee for heaven? Has he written thy name in his book of life? Has he given thee countless blessings? Has he a store of mercies which eye hath not seen nor ear heard? Then do something for Christ worthy of his love. Wake up from natural sleepiness, and this very day, before the sun goes down, do something in some way by which you shall prove that you feel the power of that divine motive, 'for Christ's sake.'

FOR MEDITATION: For our sakes the Lord Jesus Christ became poor and was made sin (2 Corinthians 8:9; 5:21); we didn't give him a motive. God supplied one himself—his undeserved love. 'For Christ's sake' should be a powerful motive for our prayers (Romans 15:30), readiness to be treated as fools (1 Corinthians 4:10), service (2 Corinthians 4:5), willingness to suffer hardship (2 Corinthians 12:10; Philippians 1:29), civil obedience (1 Peter 2:13) and gospel ministry (3 John 7). What are you prepared to do for his sake?

SERMON NO. 614

Life eternal

'And I give unto them eternal life; and they shall never perish, neither shall any man pluck them out of my hand.' John 10:28
SUGGESTED FURTHER READING: Isaiah 49:14–16

'They shall *never* perish.' There is a way of explaining away everything, I suppose, but I really do not know how the opponents of the perseverance of God's saints will get over this text. They may do with it as they will, but I shall still believe what I find here, that I shall never perish if I am one of Christ's people. If I perish, then Christ will not have kept his promise; but I know he must abide faithful to his word. 'He is not a man that he should lie, nor the son of man that he should repent.' Every soul that rests on the atoning sacrifice is safe, and safe for ever; 'they shall *never* perish.'

Then comes the third sentence, in which we have a position guaranteed—'in Christ's hand.' It is to be in a place of honour: we are the ring he wears on his finger. It is a place of love: 'I have graven thee upon the palms of my hands; thy walls are continually before me.' It is a place of power: his right hand encloses all his people. It is a place of property: Christ holds his people; 'all the saints are in thy hand.' It is a place of discretion: we are yielded up to Christ, and Christ wields a discretionary government over us. It is a place of guidance, a place of protection: as sheep are said to be in the hand of the shepherd, so are we in the hand of Christ. As arrows in the hand of a mighty man, to be used by him, as jewels in the hand of the bride to be her ornament, so are we in the hand of Christ.

FOR MEDITATION: If our trust in him is genuine, the Lord Jesus Christ has promised that we will never thirst (John 4:14), never hunger (John 6:35) and never taste death (John 8:51–52; 11:26), in other words that we will never perish. However, there will be no protection for those whose faith is not genuine; on the Day of Judgement he will say to them 'I never knew you: depart from me,' despite all that they claim to have done in his name (Matthew 7:21–23). Which kind of 'never' applies to you?

SERMON NO. 726

Enduring to the end

'He that endureth to the end shall be saved.' Matthew 10:22
SUGGESTED FURTHER READING: 1 John 2:18–25

You do not find in Scripture many cases of young people going astray. You do find believers sinning, but they were mostly getting old men. There is Noah—no youth. There is Lot, when drunken—no child. There is David with Bathsheba—no young man in the heat of passion. There is Peter denying his Lord—no boy at the time. These were men of experience and knowledge and wisdom. 'Let him that thinketh he standeth, take heed lest he fall.' With sorrow do we remember one whom, years ago, we heard pray among us, and sweetly too; esteemed and trusted by us all. I remember a dear brother saying very kindly, but not too wisely, 'If he is not a child of God, I am not.' But what did he, my brethren, to our shame and sorrow, but go aside to the very worst and foulest of sins. But this is the badge of a true child of God: that a man endures to the end; and if a man does not hold on, but slinks back to his old master, and wears again the Satanic yoke, there is sure proof that he has never come out of the spiritual Egypt through Jesus Christ, and has never obtained that eternal life which cannot die, because it is born of God. I have thus then, dear friends, said enough to prove, I think, beyond dispute, that the true badge of the Christian is perseverance, and that without it, no man has proved himself to be a child of God.

FOR MEDITATION: The perseverance of the saints is not a theoretical concept; the fact that we are God's children can only be proved by practice. It is a bad sign when those professing to be Christians will not endure, for example, affliction (Mark 4:17) or sound doctrine (2 Timothy 4:3). Our endurance in the Christian faith points to a glorious future (2 Thessalonians 1:4–5; James 1:12).

N.B. This sermon was preached after the death of Spurgeon's grandfather, James Spurgeon, on 12 February 1864 at the age of 87. He had endured 'to the end as a minister of Christ,' said Spurgeon in a glowing tribute.

The betrayal

'But Jesus said unto him, Judas, betrayest thou the Son of man with a kiss?' Luke 22:48
SUGGESTED FURTHER READING: 1 Timothy 6:6–10

I do solemnly believe, that of all hypocrites, those are the persons of whom there is the least hope whose god is their money. You may reclaim a fallen Christian, who has given way to vice, may loathe his lust, and return from it; but I fear that the cases in which a man who is cankered with covetousness has ever been saved, are so few that they might be written on your finger nail. This is a sin which the world does not rebuke. God knows what thunders I have launched out against men who are all for this world, and yet pretend to be Christ's followers; but they always say, 'It is not for me.' What I should call stark naked covetousness, they call prudence, discretion, economy, and so on; and actions which I would scorn to spit upon they will do, and think their hands quite clean after they have done them, and still sit as God's people sit, and hear as God's people hear, and think that after they have sold Christ for paltry gain, they will go to heaven. O souls, beware most of all of greed! It is not money, nor the lack of money, but the love of money which is the root of all evil. It is not getting it; it is not even keeping it; it is loving it; it is making it your god; it is looking at that as the main chance, and not considering the cause of Christ, nor the truth of Christ, nor the holy life of Christ, but being ready to sacrifice everything for gains' sake. O such men make giants in sin; their damnation shall be sure and just.

FOR MEDITATION: Covetousness usually appears in the New Testament's lists of scandalous behaviour (Mark 7:22; Romans 1:29; 1 Corinthians 5:10–11; 6:10; Ephesians 5:3,5; Colossians 3:5; 2 Timothy 3:2). Beware of it (Luke 12:15). Judas didn't. His response to missing out on a small fortune (John 12:3–6) was to betray the Lord Jesus Christ for financial gain (Matthew 26:6–16); it proved to be his own ruin (Matthew 27:3–5; 1 Timothy 6:9). 'Thou shalt not covet' (Exodus 20:17).

Obtaining promises

'Who through faith...obtained promises.' Hebrews 11:33
SUGGESTED FURTHER READING: Matthew 7:7–11

There are three ways of 'obtaining the promise.' Many of them only need the outstretched hand to grasp them; you may go with believing faith at once and take the promise—'Ask and ye shall receive.' There are many of the promises so readily attainable, that if you are in Christ you may see them fulfilled by simply believing them. Believe them to be true, and you shall have what they promise you. Some of God's promises are like cheques; you present them at the counter and the cash is given; you have but to take the promise stamped by God's own hand, signed and sealed, believe it to be God's, and you shall have the mercy now. This is true of a very large number of the promises. Of some others I must give a second direction. You must not simply believe them, but exercise importunate prayer about them. 'Knock and it shall be opened.' These promises are not to be had for the mere believing. Of some kind of devils it was said, 'This kind goeth not out but by prayer and fasting.' Of some sort of promises it may be said, 'This kind is not fulfilled but by prayer and importunity.' You must knock, and if the gate does not open you must knock again, and continue so to do until God shall give the favour. You are certain to have the blessing if you know how to wrestle with the angel, and declare that you will not let him go unless he shall bestow it upon you. A third kind of these promises is not even to be fulfilled by prayer or by faith alone; you must obtain them by earnest seeking after them. 'Seek and ye shall find.' Where God has appended to the promise a something that is to be done, diligently do it, and you shall obtain the blessing.

FOR MEDITATION: God's promises to us in Christ are all 'Yes' (2 Corinthians 1:20); he is not reluctant to fulfil the promises he has made. However, his promises are also both 'great and precious' (2 Peter 1:4); they are not handed to everybody on a plate, but reserved for those who value them enough to approach God for them. We are to blame if we fail to ask or ask wrongly (James 1:5–8; 4:2–3).

Loving advice for anxious seekers

'If any of you lack wisdom, let him ask of God, that giveth to all men liberally, and upbraideth not; and it shall be given him.' James 1:5
SUGGESTED FURTHER READING: Isaiah 8:16–22

When a man is really under concern of soul, he is in a condition of considerable danger. Then it is that an artful false teacher may get hold of him, and beguile him into heresy. Hence the text does not say, 'If any man lack wisdom, let him ask his priest;' that is about the worst thing he can do; for he who sets himself up for a priest, is either a deceiver or deceived. 'Let him ask of God;' that is the advice of the Scripture. We are all so ready to go to books, to go to men, to go to ceremonies, to anything except to God. Man will worship God with his eyes, and his arms, and his knees, and his mouth—with anything but his heart—and we are all of us anxious, more or less, until we are renewed by grace, to get off the heart-worship of God. Juan de Valdes says that, 'Just as an ignorant man takes a crucifix and says, "This crucifix will help me to think of Christ", so he bows before it and never does think of Christ at all, but stops short at the crucifix; so,' says he, 'the learned man takes his book and says, "This book will teach me the mysteries of the kingdom", but instead of giving his thoughts to the mysteries of godliness, he reads his book mechanically and stops at the book, instead of meditating and diving into the truth.' It is the action of the mind that God accepts; it is the thought communing with him; it is the soul coming into contact with the soul of God; it is spirit-worship which the Lord accepts. Consequently, the text does not say, 'Let him ask books,' nor 'ask priests,' but, 'let him ask of God.' Above all, do not let the seeker ask of himself and follow his own imaginings and feelings. All human guides are bad, but you yourself will be your own worst guide. 'Let him ask of God.'

FOR MEDITATION: Whom or what do you see as your go-between in your dealings with God? The only mediator he will accept between you and him is the one he has appointed himself—the second Person of the Godhead, the man Christ Jesus (1 Timothy 2:5). In his name we can 'ask of God' directly (John 14:13–14; 15:16; 16:23–24).

Man's thoughts and God's thoughts

'For my thoughts are not your thoughts, neither are your ways my ways, saith the LORD. *For as the heavens are higher than the earth, so are my ways higher than your ways, and my thoughts than your thoughts.'* Isaiah 55:8–9
SUGGESTED FURTHER READING: Hebrews 10:1–18

There is an idea in the mind of many of you that the plan of just trusting in Christ, and being pardoned on the spot, is too simple to be safe. You want a plan which involves a host of Latin and Greek and all kinds of thing; you want a long palaver of baptism, confirmation, confession, and I know not what; but the gospel is, 'Trust Jesus, and live.' 'Believe on the Lord Jesus Christ, and thou shalt be saved.' It is too simple, you think, to be safe. Now, it is a well-known fact that the simplest remedies are the most potent and safe; and certainly, the simplest rules in mechanics are just those upon which the greatest engineers erect their most wonderful constructions. The moment you get to complexity you get into a snarl, and are on the brink of weakness. Simplicity, how solid it is! See the old-fashioned plan of putting a plank across the village brook—that was the old way of making a bridge. Well, then, somebody came in and invented an arch—a grand invention, certainly, but not in all cases suitable. The Menai tubular bridge is nothing more than the old plan of a plank thrown across the brook, and more and more great engineers revert to simplicities. When man grows wisest, he comes back to where he was when he started. I suppose that a swan sailing across a lake gave to the navigator the best possible model of a vessel, to which navigation will always have to keep close if it would keep close to the true and beautiful. Now, as in nature simplicity is strength, so is it certainly in grace. Trust Christ and live!

FOR MEDITATION: Pride makes us reluctant to accept a salvation which affords us no personal credit or glory (2 Kings 5:9–14). Are you rejecting God's free gift of forgiveness in Christ and complicating your life with wasted efforts, which will never result in a satisfactory conclusion (Isaiah 55:1–2)?

Human depravity and divine mercy

'And the LORD *smelled a sweet savour; and the* LORD *said in his heart, I will not again curse the ground any more for man's sake; for the imagination of man's heart is evil from his youth; neither will I again smite any more every thing living, as I have done.'* Genesis 8:21
SUGGESTED FURTHER READING: John 3:1–15

I cannot give myself a new nature. A crab tree cannot transform itself into an apple tree; if I am a wolf I cannot make myself a sheep; water can rise to its own proper level, but it cannot go beyond it without pressure. I must have, then, something wrought in me more than I can work in myself, and this indeed is good scriptural doctrine. 'That which is born of the flesh'— what is it? When the flesh has done its very best—what is it? 'That which is born of the flesh is flesh'—it is filthy to begin with and filth comes of it. Only 'that which is born of the Spirit is spirit. Marvel not that I said unto thee, Ye must be born again.' My soul must come under the hand of the Spirit; just as a piece of clay is on the potter's wheel and is made to revolve and is touched by the fingers of the potter and moulded into what he wishes it to be, so must I lie passively in the hand of the Spirit of God, and he must work in me to will and to do of his own good pleasure, and then I shall begin to work out my own salvation with fear and trembling, but never, never till then. I must have more than nature can give me, more than my mother gave me, more than my father gave me, more than flesh and blood can produce under the most favourable circumstances. I must have the Spirit of God from heaven. Then comes this enquiry, 'Have I received him? What is the best evidence of it?' The best evidence of it is this: am I resting upon Christ Jesus alone for salvation?

FOR MEDITATION: In giving his Spirit to point us to the gift of his only-begotten Son, God has indeed given us far more than nature, parents, flesh and blood could ever give us. But have you received God's gift? God's children are only those who have received the Lord Jesus Christ by trusting in him (John 1:12–13).

SERMON NO. 615

The centurion: or, an exhortation to the virtuous

'They came to Jesus...saying, That he was worthy for whom he should do this: for he...hath built us a synagogue...; the centurion sent friends to him, saying unto him, Lord, trouble not thyself: for I am not worthy that thou shouldest enter under my roof:...but say in a word, and my servant shall be healed...When Jesus heard these things, he...said...I have not found so great faith, no, not in Israel.' Luke 7:4–9
SUGGESTED FURTHER READING: Proverbs 26:28–27:2

This centurion certainly had a high reputation. Two features of character blend in him which do not often meet in such graceful harmony. He won the high opinion of others and yet he held a low estimation of himself. There are some who think little of themselves; and they are quite correct in their feelings, as all the world would endorse the estimate of their littleness. Others there are who think great things of themselves; but the more they are known, the less they are praised. Nor is it unusual for men to think great things of themselves because the world commends or flatters them; so they robe themselves with pride and cloak themselves with vanity, because they have by some means, either rightly or wrongly, won the good opinion of others. There are very few who have the happy combination of the text. The elders say of the centurion, that he is worthy; but he says of himself, 'Lord, I am not worthy!' They commend him for building God a house; but he thinks that he is not worthy that Christ should come under the roof of his house. They plead his merit; but he pleads his demerit. Thus he appeals to the power of Christ, apart from anything that he felt in himself or thought of himself. O that you and I might have this blessed combination in ourselves; to win the high opinion of others, so far as it can be gained by integrity, by uprightness, and by decision of character, and yet at the same time to walk humbly with our God!

FOR MEDITATION: A good reputation amongst outsiders and an absence of pride are characteristics which must be true of those appointed as church leaders (1 Timothy 3:6–7). They should also be amongst the aims of every believer (Matthew 5:3,16).

Nothing but leaves

'He found nothing but leaves.' Mark 11:13
SUGGESTED FURTHER READING: Romans 14:4–13

Some you meet with have a censorious tongue. What good people they must be; they can see the faults of other people so plainly! This church is not right, and the other is not right, and yonder preacher—well some people think him a very good man, but they do not. They can see the deficiencies in the various denominations, and they observe that very few really carry out Scripture as it should be carried out. They complain of want of love, and are the very people who create that want. Now if you will watch these very censorious people, the very faults they indicate in others, they are indulging in themselves; and while they are seeking to find out the mote in their brother's eye, they have a beam in their own. These are the people who are indicated by this fig tree, for they ought, according to their own showing, taking them on their own ground, to be better than other people. If what they say be true, they are bright particular stars, and they ought to give special light to the world. They are such that even Jesus Christ himself might expect to receive fruit from them, but they are nothing but deceivers, with these high soarings and proud boastings; they are nothing after all but pretenders. Like Jezebel with her paint, which made her all the uglier, they would seem to be what they are not. As old Adam says, 'They are candles with big wicks and no tallow, and when they go out they make a foul and nauseous smell.' 'They have summer sweating on their brow, and winter freezing in their hearts.' You would think them the land of Goshen, but prove them the wilderness of sin. Let us search ourselves, lest such be the case with us.

FOR MEDITATION: How would you react to hearing a tape-recording of yourself in full flow? God takes note of evil speech and the judging of others (Exodus 20:7; Matthew 7:1–2; 12:33–37; Romans 2:1–3). Colossians 4:6 tells us what the speech of a Christian should be like.

The greatest trial on record

*'The kings of the earth set themselves, and the rulers take counsel together,
against the LORD, and against his anointed.' Psalm 2:2*
SUGGESTED FURTHER READING: Ephesians 4:17–24

This day I put before you Christ Jesus, or your sins. The reason why many
come not to Christ is because they cannot give up their lusts, their pleasures,
their profits. Sin is Barabbas; sin is a thief; it will rob your soul of its life; it
will rob God of his glory. Sin is a murderer; it stabbed our father Adam; it
slew our purity. Sin is a traitor; it rebels against the king of heaven and earth.
If you prefer sin to Christ, Christ has stood at your tribunal, and you have
given in your verdict that sin is better than Christ. Where is that man? He
comes here every Sunday; and yet he is a drunkard! Where is he? You prefer
that reeling demon Bacchus to Christ. Where is that man? He comes here.
Yes; and where are his midnight haunts? The harlot and the prostitute can
tell! You have preferred your own foul, filthy lust to Christ. I know some here
that have their consciences often pricked, and yet there is no change in them.
You prefer Sunday trading to Christ; you prefer cheating to Christ; you
prefer the theatre to Christ; you prefer the harlot to Christ; you prefer the
devil himself to Christ, for he it is that is the father and author of these
things. 'No,' says one, 'I don't.' Then I do again put this question, and I put
it very pointedly to you—'If you do not prefer your sins to Christ, how is it
that you are not a Christian?' I believe this is the main stumbling-stone, that
'Men love darkness rather than light, because their deeds are evil.' We come
not to Christ because of the viciousness of our nature, and depravity of our
heart; and this is the depravity of your heart, that you prefer darkness to
light, put bitter for sweet, and choose evil as your good.

FOR MEDITATION: We ought to fear and serve God (Joshua 24:14–24); if we
won't, the only choice left to us is to follow one false way or another and
serve sin in either its scandalous or more sophisticated forms. The intention
to serve God is not something to be professed lightly, but by God's grace it is
possible to serve him. Whom do you serve 'this day'?

SERMON NO. 495

A sermon for Spring

'My beloved spake, and said unto me, Rise up, my love, my fair one, and come away. For, lo, the winter is past, the rain is over and gone; the flowers appear on the earth; the time of the singing of birds is come, and the voice of the turtle is heard in our land; the fig tree putteth forth her green figs, and the vines with the tender grape give a good smell.' Song of Solomon *2:10–13*
SUGGESTED FURTHER READING: Psalm 74:9–17

The things which are seen are types of the things which are not seen. The works of creation are pictures to the children of God of the secret mysteries of grace. The very seasons of the year find their parallel in the little world of man within. We have our winter when the north wind of the law rushes forth against us, when every hope is nipped, when all the seeds of joy lie buried beneath the dark clods of despair, when our soul is fast fettered like a river bound with ice. Thanks be unto God, the soft south wind breathes upon our soul, and at once the waters of desire are set free, the spring of love comes on, flowers of hope appear in our hearts, the trees of faith put forth their young shoots, the time of the singing of birds comes in our hearts, and we have joy and peace in believing through the Lord Jesus Christ. That happy springtide is followed in the believer by a rich summer, when his graces, like fragrant flowers, are in full bloom, loading the air with perfume; and fruits of the Spirit like citrons and pomegranates swell into their full proportion in the genial warmth of the Sun of Righteousness. Then comes the believer's autumn, when his fruits grow ripe, and his fields are ready for the harvest; the time has come when his Lord shall gather together his 'pleasant fruits,' and store them in heaven; the feast of ingathering is at hand—the time when the year shall begin anew, an unchanging year, like the years of the right hand of the Most High in heaven.

FOR MEDITATION: Until we trust in the Lord Jesus Christ, our souls languish in an eternal winter's night. Faith in him is the gateway to a new life in which we advance through the seasons of the soul towards eternal day (Zechariah 14:7; Revelation 21:25; 22:5).

SERMON NO. 436

God—all in all

'When he giveth quietness, who then can make trouble? and when he hideth his face, who then can behold him? whether it be done against a nation, or against a man only.' Job 34:29
SUGGESTED FURTHER READING: 2 Corinthians 10:1–5

If some of us were fallen asleep, and the faithful ones buried—if the Spirit of God were gone, you would say, 'Well, we are still a large and influential congregation; we can afford to get a talented minister, money will do anything;' and you would get the man of talents, and many other pretty things which we now count it our joy to do without. Then, if such were the case, all these vain attempts at grandeur would be unsuccessful, and this church would ere long become a scorn and a hissing, or else a mere log upon the water. Then it would be said, 'We must change the management,' and there would be this change and that change; but if the Lord were gone, what could you do? By what means could you ever make this church to revive again, or any other church? Alas! for the carnal, spasmodic efforts we have seen made in some churches! Prayer meetings badly attended, no conversions, but still they have said, 'Well, it is imperative upon us to keep up a respectable appearance; we must collect the congregation by our singing, by our organ, or some other outward attraction:' and angels might have wept as they saw the folly of men who sought anything except the Lord, who alone can make a house his temple; who alone can make a ministry to be a ministration of mercy; without whose presence the most solemn congregation is but as the herding of men in the market, and the most melodious songs but as the shoutings of those who make merry at a marriage. Without the Lord, our solemn days, our new moons, and our appointed feasts, are an abomination such as his soul hates.

FOR MEDITATION: Attempts at 'fearing the Lord' with a combination of his ordinances and man-made outward attractions usually lead to the same conclusion—'they fear not the Lord' (2 Kings 17:27–34); yet someone in that position will still presume upon God's blessing (Judges 17:5–6,12–13). Is your church in danger?

SERMON NO. 737

Praise thy God, O Zion

'The whole multitude of the disciples began to rejoice and praise God with a loud voice ...' Luke 19:37
SUGGESTED FURTHER READING: Psalm 100:1–5

I hope the doctrine that Christians ought to be gloomy will soon be driven out of the universe. There are no people in the world who have such a right to be happy, nor have such cause to be joyful as the saints of the living God. All Christian duties should be done joyfully; but especially the work of praising the Lord. I have been in congregations where the tune was dolorous to the very last degree; where the time was so dreadfully slow that one wondered whether they would ever be able to sing through the 119th Psalm; whether, to use Watts's expression, eternity would not be too short for them to get through it; and altogether, the spirit of the people has seemed to be so damp, so heavy, so dead, that we might have supposed that they were met to prepare their minds for hanging rather than for blessing the ever-gracious God. Why, brethren, true praise sets the heart ringing its bells, and hanging out its streamers. Never hang your flag at half-mast when you praise God; no, run up every colour, let every banner wave in the breeze, and let all the powers and passions of your spirit exult and rejoice in God your Saviour. They 'rejoiced'. We are really most horribly afraid of being too happy. Some Christians think cheerfulness a very dangerous folly, if not a ruinous vice. That joyous 100th Psalm has been altered in all the English versions. The first verse includes the words 'him serve with fear', but the Scottish version has less thistle and more rose. Listen and catch its holy happiness—'Him serve with mirth'.

FOR MEDITATION: Praising God in song does not demand silliness and drawing attention to ourselves; nor does it mean singing 'as if' we mean it! Spiritual singing expresses true heartfelt thanksgiving to God (Ephesians 5:19–20; Colossians 3:16) in joyful unison and with a healthy volume (2 Chronicles 5:13).

SERMON NO. 678

Christ our life—soon to appear

'When Christ, who is our life, shall appear, then shall ye also appear with him in glory.' Colossians 3:4
SUGGESTED FURTHER READING: 1 John 2:28–3:3

Christ will appear. The text speaks of it as a fact to be taken for granted. 'When Christ, who is our life, shall appear.' It is not a matter of question in the Christian church whether Christ will appear or not. Has not Christ appeared once? Yes, after a certain sort. I remember reading a quaint expression of some old divine, that the book of Revelation might quite as well be called an obvelation, for it was rather a hiding than a revealing of things to come. So, when Jesus came it was hardly a revealing, it was a hiding of our Lord. It is true that he was 'manifest in the flesh,' but it is equally true that the flesh shrouded and concealed his glory. The first manifestation was very partial; it was Christ seen through a glass, Christ in the mist of grief, and the cloud of humiliation. Christ is yet to appear in the strong sense of the word 'appearing;' he is to come out and shine forth. He is to leave the robes of scorn and shame behind, and to come in the glory of the Father and all his holy angels with him. This is the constant teaching of the word of God, and the constant hope of the church, that Christ will appear. A thousand questions at once suggest themselves: How will Christ appear? When will Christ appear? Where will Christ appear? and so on. What God answers we may enquire, but some of our questions are mere impertinence. How will Christ appear? I believe Christ will appear in person. Whenever I think of the second coming, I never can tolerate the idea of a spiritual coming. That always seems to me to be the most transparent folly that can possibly be put together; Christ cannot come spiritually, because he is always here: 'Lo, I am with you alway, even unto the end of the world.'

FOR MEDITATION: Review Christ's three appearances—past (Hebrews 9:26), present (Hebrews 9:24), prospective (Hebrews 9:28). We will not require any spokesmen to inform us of his second coming (Matthew 24:23–27); every eye will see him (Revelation 1:7).

A jealous God

'For the LORD, *whose name is jealous, is a jealous God.'* Exodus 34:14
SUGGESTED FURTHER READING: 2 Kings 10:15–31

How careful should we be when we do anything for God, and God is pleased to accept of our doings, that we never congratulate ourselves. The minister of Christ should unrobe himself of every rag of praise. 'You preached well,' said a friend to John Bunyan one morning. 'You are too late,' said honest John, 'the devil told me that before I left the pulpit.' The devil often tells God's servants a great many things which they should be sorry to hear. Why, you can hardly be useful in a Sunday School but he will say to you 'How well you have done it!' You can scarcely resist a temptation, or set a good example, but he will be whispering to you 'What an excellent person you must be!' It is, perhaps, one of the hardest struggles of the Christian life to learn this sentence—'Not unto us, O LORD, not unto us, but unto thy name give glory.' Now God is so jealous on this point that, while he will forgive his own servants a thousand things, this is an offence for which he is sure to chasten us. Let a believer once say, 'I am,' and God will soon make him say 'I am not'. Let a Christian begin to boast, 'I can do all things,' without adding 'through Christ which stengtheneth me,' and before long he will have to groan, 'I can do nothing,' and bemoan himself. Many sins of true Christians, I do not doubt, have been the result of their glorifying themselves. Many a man has been permitted by God to stain a noble character and to ruin an admirable reputation, because the character and the reputation had come to be the man's own, instead of being laid, as all our crowns must be laid, at the feet of Christ. You may build the city, but if you say with Nebuchadnezzar, 'Behold this great Babylon that I have built!' you shall be smitten to the earth. The worms which ate Herod when he gave not God the glory are ready for another meal; beware of vain glory!

FOR MEDITATION: The temptation to pat ourselves on the back should be the cue for us to recall how the Lord Jesus Christ instructs us to think and speak about our good deeds (Luke 17:10). Any glory resulting from them should go to God (Matthew 5:16).

Where to find fruit

'*From me is thy fruit found.*' Hosea 14:8
SUGGESTED FURTHER READING: John 15:1–8

If I could bear fruit without my God, I would loathe the accursed thing, for it would be the fruit of pride—the fruit of an arrogant setting up of myself in independence of the Creator. No; the Lord deliver us from all faith, all hope, all love which do not spring from himself! May we have none of our own-manufactured graces about us. May we have nothing but that which is minted in heaven, and is therefore made of the pure metal. May we have no grace, pray no prayer, do no works, serve God in nothing except as we depend upon his strength and receive his Spirit. Any experience which comes short of a knowledge that we must get all from God, is a deceiving experience. But if you have been brought to find everything in him, beloved, this is a mark of a child of God. Cultivate a spirit of deep humiliation before the Most High; seek to know more your nothingness, and to prove more the omnipotence of the eternal God. There are two books I have tried to read, but I have not got through the first page yet. The first is the book of my own ignorance, and emptiness, and nothingness—what a great book is that! It will take us all our lives to read it, and I question whether Methuselah ever got to the last page. There is another book I must read, or else the first volume will drive me mad—it is the book of God's all-sufficiency. I have not got through the first word of that, much less the first page, but reading the two together, I would spend all my days. This is heaven's own literature, the wisdom which comes from above. Less than nothing I can boast, and yet 'I can do all things through Christ which strengtheneth me.' 'Having nothing yet possessing all things.'

FOR MEDITATION: Apparent fruit produced by our own efforts independently of God is no better than a mirage; it will vanish upon inspection on the Last Day (1 Corinthians 3:12–15). Fruit which is derived from Christ and acknowledged to be produced in us by him will abide in abundance to God's glory (John 15:5,8,16). Joseph did not forget the source of his fruitfulness (Genesis 41:52).

SERMON NO 557

The procession of sorrow

'And they took Jesus, and led him away.' John 19:16
SUGGESTED FURTHER READING: John 15:18–21

I will not say it is because we are unfaithful to our Master that the world is more kind to us, but I half suspect it is, and it is very possible that if we were more thoroughly Christians the world would more heartily detest us, and if we would cleave more closely to Christ we might expect to receive more slander, more abuse, less tolerance, and less favour from men. You young believers, who have lately followed Christ, should father and mother forsake you, remember you were bidden to reckon upon it; should brothers and sisters deride, you must put this down as part of the cost of being a Christian. Godly working men, should your employers or your fellow-workers frown upon you; wives, should your husbands threaten to cast you out, remember, without the camp was Jesus' place, and without the camp is yours. O you Christian men, who dream of trimming your sails to the wind, who seek to win the world's favour, I do beseech you cease from a course so perilous. We are in the world, but we must never be of it; we are not to be secluded like monks in the cloister, but we are to be separated like Jews among Gentiles; men, but not of men; helping, aiding, befriending, teaching, comforting, instructing, but not sinning. The more manifestly there shall be a great gulf between the church and the world, the better shall it be for both; the better for the world, for it shall be thereby warned; the better for the church, for it shall be thereby preserved. Go then, like the Master, expecting to be abused, to wear an ill name, and to earn reproach; go, like him, without the camp.

FOR MEDITATION: The doctrine that Christians can befriend and please both God and the world is not a biblical one (Galatians 1:10; James 4:4; 1 John 2:15). Are you trying to do the impossible?

SERMON NO. 497

A sight of self

'But we are all as an unclean thing, and all our righteousnesses are as filthy rags; and we all do fade as a leaf; and our iniquities, like the wind, have taken us away. And there is none that calleth upon thy name, that stirreth up himself to take hold of thee: for thou hast hid thy face from us, and hast consumed us, because of our iniquities.' Isaiah 64:6–7
SUGGESTED FURTHER READING: Acts 26:9–20

When you really feel your sinfulness, and mourn it, do not stop here; never give yourself any rest till you know that you are delivered from it, for it is one thing to say 'Ah, I do sin,' but it is quite another thing to say 'He has saved me from my sin.' It is one thing to have a repentance which makes you leave the sin you loved before, and another thing to talk about repentance. Ah, I have sometimes seen a child of God when he has sinned, and I have seen his broken-hearted actions, and heard his piteous confessions, and I can say that my heart goes out toward the man in whom there are tears of repentance of the right kind. It is one of the fairest sights that is seen under heaven when a believer who has gone wrong is willing to say, 'I have sinned,' and when he no more sets himself proudly up against his God, but humbles himself like a little child. Such a man as that shall be exalted. But I have seen—and it is a fearful sight to see—I have seen one who can sin and repent, and sin and repent. O that dry-eyed repentance is a damnable repentance! Take heed of it, brethren. I have known a man who professed to have been converted years and years ago, who, ever since that pretended conversion, has lived in a known sin, and yet he thinks he is a child of God because after he has fallen into the sin he has a little season of darkness arising from his conscience, but he quiets that conscience after a time, and presumptuously says, 'I will not give up my hope.' Oh, that is an awful thing. God deliver you from dry-eyed repentance, for it is no repentance.

FOR MEDITATION: Repentance is a change of mind; are you tempted to repent of your repentance? That would be an attempt to short-change God and can easily develop into a vicious circle. For God's attitude to such behaviour see Jeremiah 34:12–17.

SERMON NO. 437

Grieve not the Holy Spirit

'And grieve not the Holy Spirit of God, whereby ye are sealed unto the day of redemption.' Ephesians 4:30
SUGGESTED FURTHER READING: Isaiah 63:7–19

Grieving the Holy Spirit produces a lamentable result. In the child of God it will not lead to his utter destruction, for no heir of heaven can perish; neither will the Holy Spirit be utterly taken away from him, for the Spirit of God is given to abide with us for ever. But the ill-effects are nevertheless most terrible. You will lose, my dear friends, *all sense of the Holy Spirit's presence*: he will be as one hidden from you—no beams of comfort, no words of peace, no thoughts of love—there will be what Cowper calls, 'an aching void the world can never fill.' Grieve the Holy Spirit, and you will lose all *Christian joy*; the light shall be taken from you, and you shall stumble in darkness; those very means of grace which once were such a delight, shall have no music in your ear. Your soul shall be no longer as a watered garden, but as a howling wilderness. Grieve the Spirit of God, and you will lose all *power*; if you pray, it will be a very weak prayer—you will not prevail with God. When you read the Scriptures, you shall not be able to lift the latch and force your way into the inner mysteries of truth. When you go up to the house of God, there shall be none of that devout exhilaration, that running without weariness, that walking without fainting. You shall feel yourself like Samson when his hair was lost, weak, captive, and blinded. Let the Holy Spirit depart, and *assurance* is gone, doubts follow, questionings and suspicions are aroused. Grieve the Spirit of God, and *usefulness* will cease: the ministry shall yield no fruit; your Sunday School work shall be barren; your speaking to others and labouring for others shall be like sowing the wind.

FOR MEDITATION: If it is unprofitable for us to cause our church leaders to grieve, (Hebrews 13:17), how much worse it must be for us if we cause our God to grieve (Hebrews 3:7–18).

SERMON NO. 738

The Amen

'The Amen.' Revelation 3:14
SUGGESTED FURTHER READING: 2 Corinthians 1:18–22

Jesus Christ is yea and Amen in all *his offices*. He was a priest to pardon and cleanse once; he is Amen as priest still. He was a King to rule and reign for his people, and to defend them with his mighty arm; he is an Amen King, the same still. He was a prophet of old to foretell good things to come; his lips are most sweet, and drop with honey still—he is an Amen Prophet. He is Amen as to the merit of his blood:-

'Dear dying Lamb, thy precious blood
Shall never lose its power.'

He is Amen as to his righteousness. That sacred robe shall remain most fair and glorious when nature shall decay. He is Amen in every single title which he bears; your Husband, never seeking a divorce; your Head, the neck never being dislocated; your Friend, sticking closer than a brother; your Shepherd, with you in death's dark vale; your help and your deliverer; your castle and your high tower; the horn of your strength, your confidence, your joy, your all in all, and Amen in all. He is Amen with regard to *his person*. He is still faithful and true, immutably the same. Not less than God! No furrows on that eternal brow—no palsy in that mighty arm—no faintness in that Almighty heart—no lack of fulness in his all-sufficiency—no diminution in the keenness of his eye—no defalcation [shortcoming] in the purpose of his heart. Omnipotent, unchangeable, eternal, omnipresent still! God over all, blessed for ever. O Jesus, we adore thee, thou great Amen. He is the same, too, as to his manhood. Bone of our bone still; in all our afflictions still afflicted. Our brother in ties of blood as much today as when he wore a peasant's garb.

FOR MEDITATION: It is customary to honour other people with 'three cheers'. Our Amen God is worthy of much more; the psalmists glorify him in a manner befitting his Amen character—with three double Amens (Psalm 41:13; 72:19; 89:52).

SERMON NO. 679

The Great Physician and his patients

'They that be whole need not a physician, but they that are sick.' Matthew
9:12
SUGGESTED FURTHER READING: Ephesians 2:8–10

'Christ Jesus came into the world to save sinners.' That is the gospel—'He
that believeth and is baptized shall be saved; he that believeth not shall be
damned;' so that those who are bidden to believe are evidently those who
deserve to be damned. Need alone quickens the physician's footsteps,
bringing Jesus from the throne of glory to the cross, and in his spiritual
power, bringing him every day from the throne of his Father down to
broken-hearted heavy-laden souls. Now, this is very plain talking, but still
the most of people do not understand it. A minister, when he had done
preaching in a country village, said to a farm-labourer who had been
listening to him, 'Do you think Jesus Christ died to save good people, or bad
people?' 'Well, sir,' said the man, 'I should say he died to save good people.'
'But did he die to save bad people?' 'No sir; no, certainly not, sir.' 'Well,
then, what will become of you and me?' 'Well, sir, I do not know. I dare say
you be pretty good, sir; and I try to be as good as I can.' That is just the
common doctrine; and after all, though we think it has died out among us,
that is the religion of ninety-nine English people out of every hundred who
know nothing of divine grace—we are to be as good as we can; we are to go
to church or to chapel, and do all that we can, and then Jesus Christ died for
us, and we shall be saved. Whereas the gospel is, that he did not do anything
at all for people who think they can rely on themselves, but gave himself for
lost and ruined ones. He did not come into the world to save self-righteous
people; on their own showing, they do not want to be saved.

FOR MEDITATION: Respectability and being religious are among Satan's most
effective weapons to blind men and women to their true sinful condition and
to their need of the Lord Jesus Christ as the only one who can save them
(2 Corinthians 4:4). Is Satan successfully pulling the wool over your eyes?

A bundle of myrrh

'A bundle of myrrh is my well-beloved unto me; he shall lie all night betwixt my breasts.' Song of Solomon 1:13
SUGGESTED FURTHER READING: Psalm 21:1–7

The Christian has joy, just like other men, in the common mercies of life. For him there are charms in music, excellence in painting, and beauty in sculpture; for him the hills have sermons of majesty, the rocks hymns of sublimity, and the valleys lessons of love. He can look upon all things with an eye as clear and joyous as another man's; he can be glad both in God's gifts and God's works. He is not dead to the happiness of the household: around his hearth he finds happy associations, without which life were drear indeed. His children fill his home with glee, his wife is his solace and delight, his friends are his comfort and refreshment. He accepts the comforts which soul and body can yield him according as God sees it wise to afford them unto him; but he will tell you that in all these separately, and in all of them added together, he does not find such substantial delight as he does in the person of his Lord Jesus. Brethren, there is a wine which no vineyard on earth ever yielded; there is a bread which even the corn-fields of Egypt could never bring forth. You and I have said, when we have seen others finding their god in earthly comforts, 'You may boast in gold, and silver, and raiment, but I will rejoice in the God of my salvation.' In our esteem, the joys of earth are little better than husks for swine compared with Jesus the heavenly manna. I would rather have one mouthful of Christ's love, and a sip of his fellowship, than a whole world full of carnal delights. What is the chaff to the wheat? What is the sparkling paste to the true diamond? What is a dream to the glorious reality?

FOR MEDITATION: Material earthly joys are only temporary; even when deprived of them, Christians have still got spiritual joys which are permanent (Hebrews 10:34; John 16:22). Do you know these joys? If so, do you value them?

God's will and man's will

'So then it is not of him that willeth, nor of him that runneth, but of God that sheweth mercy.' Romans 9:16.
'Whosoever will, let him take the water of life freely.' Revelation 22:17
SUGGESTED FURTHER READING: 2 Timothy 2:8–19

Some brethren have altogether forgotten one order of truths, and then, in the next place, they have gone too far with others. We have all one blind eye, and too often we are like Nelson in the battle, we put the telescope to that blind eye, and then protest that we cannot see. I heard of one man who said he had read the Bible through thirty-four times, but could not see a word about election in it—he put the telescope to the blind eye. Many of us do that; we do not want to see a truth, and therefore we say we cannot see it. On the other hand, there are others who push a truth too far. 'This is good; this is precious!' say they, and then they think it is good for everything; as if it were the only truth in the world. You know how often things are injured by over-praise; how a good medicine, which really was a great boon for a certain disease, comes to be despised utterly by the physician, because a certain quack has praised it up as being a universal cure; so puffery [exaggeration] in doctrine leads to its dishonour. Truth has thus suffered on all sides; on the one hand brethren would not see all the truth, and on the other hand they magnified out of proportion that which they did see. You have seen those mirrors, those globes that are sometimes hung up in gardens; you walk up to them and you see your head ten times as large as your body, or you walk away and put yourself in another position, and then your feet are monstrous and the rest of your body is small; this is an ingenious toy, but I am sorry to say that many go to work with God's truth upon the model of this toy; they magnify one capital truth, till it becomes monstrous; they minimise and speak little of another truth till it becomes altogether forgotten.

FOR MEDITATION: Are any Biblical doctrines your pet favourites? Are there some you love to hate? Doctrinal balance depends on us believing 'all scripture' (2 Timothy 3:16) and accepting 'all the counsel of God' (Acts 20:27) without picking and choosing as we like.

The gladness of the Man of sorrows

'Thou lovest righteousness, and hatest wickedness: therefore God, thy God, hath anointed thee with the oil of gladness above thy fellows. All thy garments smell of myrrh, and aloes, and cassia, out of the ivory palaces, whereby they have made thee glad.' Psalm 45:7–8
SUGGESTED FURTHER READING: Zephaniah 3:11–17

As he sees us day by day more conformed to his image, he rejoices in us. Just as you see the sculptor with his chisel fetching out the statue which lies hidden in the block of marble, taking off a corner here, and a chip there, and a piece here—see how he smiles when he brings out the features of the form divine—so our Saviour, as he proceeds with his graving tool, working through the operation of the Spirit, and making us like unto himself, finds much delight in us. The painter makes rough drafts at first, and lays on the colours roughly; some do not understand what he is doing, and for three or four sittings the portrait is much unlike the man it aims at representing; but the painter can discern the features in the canvas; he sees it looming through that mist and haze of colour; he knows that beauty will yet beam forth from yonder daubs and blotches. So Jesus, though we are yet but mere outlines of his image, can discover his own perfection in us where no eye but his own, as the Mighty Artist, can perceive it. Dear friends, it is for this reason, because we are the work of his hands, that he takes delight in us. We are his brethren—and brothers should delight in brothers. We are his spouse—and where should the husband find his comfort but in his bride? We are his body—shall not the head be content with the members? We are one with him, vitally, personally, everlastingly one; and it is little marvel, therefore, if we have a mutual joy in each other, so that his garments smell of myrrh, aloes, and cassia, out of the ivory palaces of his church, wherein he has been made glad.

FOR MEDITATION: As yet we do not see The Lord Jesus Christ or what we will be as the finished product of his work for us and in us (1 John 3:2), but that fact should not lessen our joy (1 Peter 1:8). Our Saviour is totally satisfied with the fruit of his work for sinners (Isaiah 53:11).

God or self—which?

'Speak unto all the people of the land, and to the priests, saying, When ye fasted and mourned in the fifth and seventh month, even those seventy years, did ye at all fast unto me, even to me? And when ye did eat, and when ye did drink, did not ye eat for yourselves, and drink for yourselves?' Zechariah 7:5–6

SUGGESTED FURTHER READING: 1 Corinthians 11:19–22

Is it not true that some of you do not use the day of rest and the house of prayer for their real purpose, which is that man may meet with God? There was a man who professed great love to his friend, and therefore he would spend a day in his company. He rapped at the door, and the servant said the master was not at home. 'It does not matter,' said he, 'I will wait inside and take my ease; I shall do quite as well though the master be not at home if you will bring me abundance to eat and drink.' So he entered, and took a chair and made himself very comfortable, and feasted to his heart's content; and he went home boasting that he had enjoyed the visit. Then his companions asked him—'Was the master there?' 'Oh no, he was not there.' 'But I thought you went to see him?' He had pretended a great desire to have converse with his friend but evidently he was false, for if he had gone to see the master, and the master had not been at home, he would have said— 'Well, I will call another day, but I have missed my errand this time.' So there are some who go up to the house of God; they think they go there to worship the Lord; they have no enjoyment of his presence, they have no communion with his Son, they have no indwellings of his Spirit, but they enjoy the day for all that, which shows they did not go to worship God at all. When we put the question to them—'Did ye at all fast unto the Lord?' their answer must be—'No, truly, we only sought self; we did not seek the Master's presence.'

FOR MEDITATION: Everything in our lives should be a sacrifice of worship to the Lord (Romans 11:36–12:1). Do you really meet with him when you talk to him, sing to him and listen to his Word or are you simply playing a superstitious religious game? God does not accept lip-service (Isaiah 29:13; Amos 5:21–23).

SERMON NO. 438

The sin offering

'If the priest that is anointed do sin according to the sin of the people; then let him bring for his sin, which he hath sinned, a young bullock without blemish, unto the LORD for a sin offering.' Leviticus 4:3
SUGGESTED FURTHER READING: Revelation 5:1–14

Those who would preach Christ, but not Christ crucified, miss the very soul and essence of our holy faith. 'Let him come down from the cross, and we will believe in him,' is the Unitarian cry. Anything but a crucified God. But there, indeed, lies the secret of that mystery, and the very core and kernel of our confidence. A reigning Saviour I do rejoice in: the thought of the splendour yet to come makes glad our eyes; but after all, it is a bleeding Saviour that is the sinner's hope. It is to the cross, the centre of misery, that the sinner turns his eyes for comfort rather than to the stars of Bethlehem, or to the blazing sun of the millennial kingdom. I remember one joining this church, who said, 'Sir, I had faith once in Christ glorified, but it never gave me comfort: I have now come to a faith in Christ crucified, and I have peace.' At Calvary there is the comfort, and there only. That Jesus lives is delightful; but the basis of the delight is, 'He lives who once was slain.' That he will reign for ever is a most precious doctrine of our faith, but that the hand that wields the silver sceptre, once was pierced, is the great secret of the joy. O beloved, abide not in any place from which your eye cannot behold the cross of Christ. When you are thinking of the doctrines of the gospel, or the precepts of the Word, or studying the prophecies of Scripture, never let your mind relinquish the study of the cross. The cross was the place of your spiritual birth; it must ever be the spot for renewing your health, for it is the sanatorium of every sin-sick soul. The blood is the true balm of Gilead; it is the only catholicon [remedy] which heals every spiritual disease.

FOR MEDITATION: Paul's evangelistic principle was to present nothing but Jesus Christ and him crucified (1 Corinthians 1:23; 2:2). The Lord Jesus Christ instituted the Lord's Supper to keep his sacrifice on the cross in the centre of our thinking (1 Corinthians 11:23–26).

SERMON NO. 739

Have you forgotten him?

'I do remember my faults this day.' Genesis 41:9
SUGGESTED FURTHER READING: 2 Peter 1:5–15

We have a greater power for remembering evil than good. Very plain is this in your children. If you mention anything good in their hearing you need to say it many times, and very plainly, before they are likely to remember it; but if one bad word shall casually meet their ear in the street, it will not be long before you have the pain of hearing them repeat it. Our memory is like theirs, but as it is more developed, this peculiarity is more manifest. We have a most convenient warehouse for storing the merchandise of evil, but the priceless jewels of goodness are readily stolen from their casket. We have a fireproof safe for worthless matters, and enclose the rarest gems in mere pasteboard cases. Our memory, like a strainer, often suffers the good wine to pass through but retains all the dregs. It holds the bad in an iron grasp, and plays with the good till it slips through the fingers. Our memories, like ourselves, have done the things which they ought not to have done, and have left undone the things which they ought to have done, and there is no health in them.

Among other things, it is not always easy to recollect our faults. We have special and particular reasons for not wishing to be too often reminded of them. Few men care to keep their faults in the front room of the house. Underground, in the darkest cellar, and, if possible, with the door locked and the key lost; it is there we would like to conceal our faults from ourselves. If, however, the grace of God has entered into a man he will pray that he may remember his faults, and he will ask grace that if he should forget any excellencies which he once supposed he had, he may not forget his defects, his sins, his infirmities, and his transgressions, but may have them constantly before him, that he may be humbled by them and led to seek pardon for them and help to overcome them.

FOR MEDITATION: Read Proverbs 28:13—if we try to hide our sins, God will remember them; if we own up to him about them and trust in the Lord Jesus Christ for forgiveness, he will remember them no more (Jeremiah 31:34).

SERMON NO. 680

The golden key of prayer

'Call unto me, and I will answer thee, and shew thee great and mighty things, which thou knowest not.' Jeremiah 33:3
SUGGESTED FURTHER READING: Matthew 26:36–46

Remember that prayer is always to be offered in submission to God's will; that when we say, God hears prayer, we do not intend by that, that he always gives us literally what we ask for. We do mean, however, this, that he gives us what is best for us; and that if he does not give us the mercy we ask for in silver, he bestows it upon us in gold. If he does not take away the thorn in the flesh, yet he says, 'My grace is sufficient for thee,' and that comes to the same in the end. Lord Bolingbroke said to the Countess of Huntingdon, 'I cannot understand, your ladyship, how you can make out earnest prayer to be consistent with submission to the divine will.' 'My lord,' she said, 'that is a matter of no difficulty. If I were a courtier of some generous king, and he gave me permission to ask any favour I pleased of him, I should be sure to put it thus, 'Will your majesty be graciously pleased to grant me such-and-such a favour; but at the same time though I very much desire it, if it would in any way detract from your majesty's honour, or if in your majesty's judgment it should seem better that I did not have this favour, I shall be quite as content to go without it as to receive it.' So you see I might earnestly offer a petition, and yet I might submissively leave it in the king's hands.' So with God. We never offer up prayer without inserting that clause, either in spirit or in words, 'Nevertheless, not as I will, but as thou wilt; not my will but thine be done.' We can only pray without an 'if' when we are quite sure that our will must be God's will, because God's will is fully our will.

FOR MEDITATION: Prayer is not a weapon for forcing God to come into line with our demands, but a gracious means of communication by which we can seek his will and express our willingness to play our part in furthering it (1 John 5:14–15).

The arrows of the Lord's deliverance

'Thou shouldest have smitten five or six times; then hadst thou smitten Syria till thou hadst consumed it: whereas now thou shalt smite Syria but thrice.' 2 Kings 13:19

SUGGESTED FURTHER READING: Matthew 9:35–10:7

Point me to a single period in the history of the church where God has worked without instrumentality, and I will tell you that I suspect whether God has worked at all if I do not see the instruments he has employed. Take the Reformation, can you think of it without thinking of God? At the same time, can you mention it without the names of Luther, Calvin, Zwingli, and Melanchthon? Then in the later revival in England, when our slumbering churches were suddenly started from their sleep, who did it? The Holy Spirit himself: but you cannot talk of the revival without mentioning the names of Whitefield and Wesley, for God worked by means then, and he works by means still. I need to notice a remark which was made concerning the revival in the north of Ireland, that there seemed to be no prominent instrumentality. The moment I saw that, I mistrusted it. Had it been God's work more fully developed through instrumentality, I believe it would not have so speedily come to a close. We grant you that God can work without means, and even when he uses means he still takes the glory to himself, for it is all his own; yet it has been the rule, and will be the rule till the day of means shall come to an end; that just as God saved man by taking upon himself man's flesh, so everywhere in the world he calls men by speaking to them through men of their own flesh and blood. God incarnates himself— in his Spirit, incarnates himself in the chosen men, especially in his church, in which he dwells as in a temple; and then through that church he is pleased to bless the world.

FOR MEDITATION: We have Scriptural precedents for praying for revival (Psalm 85:6; Habakkuk 3:2); there is a danger of that becoming too vague and general—a 'Lord, bless us' prayer, so we have a more specific instruction from our Saviour himself—we are to pray for workers (Luke 10:2).

SERMON NO. 569

Present privilege and future favour

'The eternal God is thy refuge, and underneath are the everlasting arms: and he shall thrust out the enemy from before thee; and shall say, Destroy them.' Deuteronomy 33:27
SUGGESTED FURTHER READING: Hebrews 13:8,20–21

I wish you to notice those two words which are the pith of the text. 'The *eternal* God,' '*everlasting* arms.' The *eternal* God.' Here is *antiquity*. The God who was before all worlds is for ever my God. O how I love that word 'eternal;' but, brethren and sisters, there are some people who do not believe in an *eternal* God, at any rate they do not believe in him as being theirs eternally. They do not believe that they belonged to Christ before they were born; they have a notion that they only had God to be theirs when they believed on him for the first time. They do not believe in covenant settlements, and eternal decrees, and the ancient purposes of the Most High; but let me say that for comfort, there is no thought more full of sweetness than that of an *eternal* God engaged in Christ Jesus to his people; to love, and bless, and save them *all*. One who has made them the distinguished objects of his discriminating regard from all eternity, it is the *eternal* God. And then there are the '*everlasting arms*,' arms that will never flag, arms that will never grow weary, arms that will never lose their strength. Then put the two words 'eternal' and 'everlasting' together, and they remind us of another sweet word—*unchangeability*. An everlasting God that faints not, neither is weary, that changes not, and turns not from his promise, such is the God we delight to adore and to use as our eternal shelter, our dwelling-place, and our support.

FOR MEDITATION: Each person of the Trinity is eternal; it should be no surprise that the eternal God has secured an eternal salvation for all who believe (1 Timothy 1:16–17; Hebrews 9:12,14–15; 13:8,20). Knowing the eternal God is life eternal (John 17:3). What right have we to question this?

Ebenezer!

'Then Samuel took a stone, and set it between Mizpeh and Shen, and called the name of it Eben-ezer, saying, Hitherto hath the LORD helped us.'
1 Samuel 7:12
SUGGESTED FURTHER READING: Psalm 103:1–22

We do our Lord an injustice when we suppose he wrought all his mighty acts in days of old, and showed himself strong for those in the early time, but does not perform wonders or lay bare his arm for the saints that are now upon the earth. Let us review, I say, our own diaries. Surely in these modern pages we may discover some happy incidents, refreshing to ourselves and glorifying to our God. Have you had no *deliverances*? Have you passed through no rivers, supported by the divine presence? Have you walked through no fires unharmed? Have you not been saved in six troubles? Yea, in seven has not Jehovah helped you? Have you had no *manifestations*? The God that spoke to Abraham at Mamre, has he never spoken to you? The angel that wrestled with Jacob at Peniel, has he never wrestled with you? He that stood in the fiery furnace with the three holy children, has he never trodden the coals at your side? O beloved, he has manifested himself unto us as he does not unto the world. Forget not these manifestations; fail not to rejoice in them. Have you had no *choice favours*? The God that gave Solomon the desire of his heart, has he never listened to you and answered your requests? That God of lavish bounty, has he never satisfied you with fatness? Have you never been made to lie in green pastures? Have you never been led by the still waters? Surely, beloved, the goodness of God of old has been repeated unto us. The manifestations of his grace to those gone to glory has been renewed to us, and delivering mercies as experienced by them are not unknown even to us.

FOR MEDITATION: Spurgeon chose this text as an appropriate motto with which to praise God on the occasion of the preaching of sermon number 500 in his weekly New Park Street Pulpit and Metropolitan Tabernacle Pulpit series. What is your reaction to the benefits which God has showered upon you? Check it against Psalm 116:12–14.

SERMON NO. 500

The danger of doubting

'And David said in his heart, I shall now perish one day by the hand of Saul.' 1 Samuel 27:1
SUGGESTED FURTHER READING: Job 4:1–6

This wicked exclamation of David was contrary to what he himself had often said. Here I convict myself. I remember on one occasion, to my shame, being sad and doubtful of heart, and a kind friend took out a paper and read to me a short extract from a discourse upon faith. I very soon detected the author of the extract; my friend was reading to me from one of my own sermons. Without saying a word he just left it to my own conscience, for he had convicted me of committing the very fault against which I had so earnestly declaimed. Often might you, brethren, be found out in the same inconsistency. 'O' you have said, 'I could trust him though the fig-tree did not blossom, and though there were no flocks in the field, and no herd in the stall.' Ah you have condemned the unbelief of other people, but when it touched you, you have trembled, and when you have come to run with the horsemen they have wearied you, and in the swellings of Jordan you have been troubled. So was it with David. What strong words he had often said when he addressed others! He said of Saul, 'His time shall come to die; I will not stretch out my hand and touch the Lord's anointed.' He felt sure that Saul's doom was signed and sealed; and yet in the hour of his unbelief he says, 'I shall yet one day fall.' What a strange contradiction was that! What a mercy it is that God changes not, for we are changing two or three times a day. But our own utterances, our own convictions before, are clean contrary to the idea that he can ever leave us or forsake us.

FOR MEDITATION: We must be extremely careful and sure of what we say, if we do not want it to be used in evidence against us (Judges 9:38; Job 15:6; Ecclesiastes 5:2–6; Luke 19:22). How good it is to trust in God who never has to defend or explain away the words that come from his mouth (Isaiah 55:11).

Stephen's martyrdom

'But he, being full of the Holy Ghost, looked up stedfastly into heaven, and saw the glory of God, and Jesus standing on the right hand of God, and said, Behold, I see the heavens opened, and the Son of man standing on the right hand of God.' Acts 7:55–56
SUGGESTED FURTHER READING: Mark 13:9–13

You will be struck in reading *Foxe's Acts and Monuments,* to find how many of the humblest men and women acted as if they were of noblest blood. When the King of France told Bernard Palissy that, if he did not change his sentiments, he should be compelled to surrender him to the Inquisition, the brave potter said to the king, 'You say I shall be compelled, and yet you are a king; but I, though only a poor potter, cannot be compelled to do other than I think to be right.' Surely the potter was more royal than the king. The cases are numberless, and should be as household words among you, in which humble men, feeble women, and little children have shown a heroism which chivalry could not equal. The Spirit of God has taken the wise in their own craftiness, and answered the learned out of the mouths of babes. The answers of uneducated persons among the martyrs were frequently so pat to the point, and hit the nail so well on the head, that you might almost suppose they had been composed by an assembly of divines; they came from a better source, for they were given by the Holy Spirit. The bearing of the bleeding witnesses for our Lord has been worthy of their office, and right well have they earned the title of 'The noble army of martyrs.' Now, my brethren, if you and I desire to walk among the sons of men without pride, but yet with a bearing that is worthy of our calling and adoption as princes of the blood royal of heaven, we must be trained by the Holy Spirit.

FOR MEDITATION: All believers should be ready to answer those who would ask questions (1 Peter 3:15). The best preparation is to have been with Jesus (Acts 4:13) and to be filled with the Holy Spirit (Acts 4:8; Ephesians 5:18). That will produce the right answers (Acts 4:12).

Eyes opened

'And God opened her eyes, and she saw a well of water.' Genesis 21:19
'And their eyes were opened, and they knew him.' Luke 24:31
SUGGESTED FURTHER READING: Isaiah 43:8–13

Through the fall the spiritual *taste* of man became perverted, so that he puts bitter for sweet and sweet for bitter; he chooses the poison of hell and loathes the bread of heaven; he licks the dust of the serpent and rejects the food of angels. The spiritual *hearing* became grievously injured, for man naturally no longer hears God's word, but stops his ears at the Maker's voice. Let the gospel minister charm never so wisely, yet is the unconverted soul like the deaf adder which hears not the charmer's voice. The spiritual feeling by virtue of our depravity is fearfully deadened. Whether the thunders of Sinai or the turtle notes of Calvary claim his attention, man is resolutely deaf to both. Even the spiritual *smell* with which man should discern between that which is pure and holy and that which is unsavoury to the Most High has become defiled, and now man's spiritual nostril while unrenewed derives no enjoyment from the sweet savour which is in Christ Jesus, but seeks after the putrid joys of sin. As with other senses so is it with man's *sight*. He is so spiritually blind that things most plain and clear he cannot and will not see. The understanding, which is the soul's eye, is covered with scales of ignorance, and when these are removed by the finger of instruction, the visual orb is still so affected that it sees men as trees walking. Our condition is thus most terrible, but at the same time it affords ample room for a display of the splendours of divine grace. Dear friends, we are naturally so entirely ruined, that if saved the whole work must be of God, and the whole glory must crown the head of the Triune Jehovah.

FOR MEDITATION: Silent mouths, blind eyes, deaf ears and other non-functioning features are the Bible's description of idols and all who trust in them (Psalm 115:4–8). Before conversion we are equally as dead to God and to the things of God; we are totally dependent upon him for the gift of spiritual life (Ephesians 2:1,5).

A warning against hardness of heart

'But exhort one another daily, while it is called to-day; lest any of you be hardened through the deceitfulness of sin.' Hebrews 3:13
SUGGESTED FURTHER READING: Titus 2:1–10

This duty belongs primarily to the *pastor* and to *church officers*. We are set in the church to see after the good of the people, and it is our business both in public and in private, as far as we have opportunity, to exhort daily; and especially where we see any coldness creeping over men, where there begins to be a decline in the ways of God, it is our duty to be most earnest in exhortation. The duty belongs to you all. 'Exhort one another daily.' *Parents* should be careful concerning their children in this matter. You act not the part of a true father unless you see to your son whether he be in church membership or not, that upon the slightest inconsistency he receives a gentle word of rebuke from you. *Sunday school teachers*, this is peculiarly your work with regard to your own classes. Watch over your children, not only that they may be converted, but that after being converted they may be as watered gardens, no plants withering, but all the graces of the Spirit coming to perfection through your care. Here is work for the *elders* among us. You whose grey heads betoken years of experience, and whose years of experience ought to have given you wisdom and knowledge, you may use the superiority which age affords you to offer a word of exhortation, lovingly and tenderly to the young. You can speak as those of us who are younger cannot speak, for you can tell what you have tasted and have handled; perhaps you can even tell where you have smarted by reason of your own faults and follies. *All of you without exception*, whether you be rich or poor, see to each others' souls; say not, 'Am I my brother's keeper?' but seek your brother's good for edification.

FOR MEDITATION: The exhortations God gives us in his Word (Joshua 1:6–9; Hebrews 10:19,22) should be the pattern for our mutual exhortations (Joshua 1:18; Hebrews 10:24–25). Beloved, if God so exhorts us, we ought also to exhort one another.

SERMON NO. 620

Christ is glorious—let us make him known

'And he shall stand and feed in the strength of the LORD, *in the majesty of the name of the* LORD *his God; and they shall abide: for now shall he be great unto the ends of the earth.' Micah 5:4*
SUGGESTED FURTHER READING: Matthew 16:13–18

Why is it that we have seen the Church endure to this day? How is it that we are confident that should even worse times arrive, the church would weather the storm and abide till moons shall cease to wax and wane? Why this security? Only because Christ is in the midst of her. You do not believe, I hope, in the preservation of orthodoxy by legal instruments and trust deeds. This is what too many Dissenters have relied upon, but they are like broken reeds if we rely on them. Neither can we depend on parliament and its laws. We may draw up the most express and distinct form of doctrine, but we shall find that the next generation will depart from the truth unless God shall be pleased to give it renewed grace from on high. You cannot secure the life of the church by any particular system. History shows that churches have prospered, as well as failed, under different systems. The fact is that forms of government have very little to do with the vital principle of the church. The reason why the church of God exists is not her ecclesiastical regulations, her organisation, her formularies, her ministers, or her creeds, but the presence of the Lord in the midst of her; and while Christ lives, and Christ reigns, and stands and feeds his church, she is safe; but if he were once gone, it would be with her as it is with you and me when the Spirit of God has departed from us; we are weak as other men, and she would be quite as powerless.

FOR MEDITATION: The foundation rock on which the church is built is neither Peter and his supposed successors nor Peter's creed and its successors, but the immovable Christ, the Son of the living God (Matthew 16:16,18; 1 Corinthians 3:11).

Work

'I must work the works of him that sent me, while it is day: the night cometh, when no man can work.' John 9:4
SUGGESTED FURTHER READING: 1 Peter 4:7–11

There are ten thousand actions good in themselves, which it might not be right for me to choose as my vocation in life. I know a great many persons who think it is their business to preach, but who had much better make it their business to hear for a little while longer. We know some who think it is their business to take the headship of a class, but who might be amazingly useful by giving away some tracts, or by taking a seat in a class themselves for a little while. The fact is, that we are not to pick and choose the path of Christian service which we are to walk in, but we are to do the work of him that sent us; and our object should be, as there is so much work to be done, to find out what part of the work the Master would have us to do. Our prayer should be, 'Show me what thou wouldst have me to do'—have *me* to do in particular; not what is generally right, but what is particularly right for me to do. My servant might, perhaps, think it a very proper thing for her to arrange my papers for me in my study, but I should feel but a very slender amount of gratitude to her. If, however, she will have a cup of coffee ready for me early in the morning, when I have to go out to a distant country town to preach, I shall be much more likely to appreciate her services. So, some friends think, 'How I could get on if I were in such-and-such a position, if I were made a deacon, if I were elevated to such a post.' Go your way, and work as your Master would have you. You will do better where he puts you than you will where you put yourself. You are no servant, indeed, at all, when you pick and choose your service.

FOR MEDITATION: No Christian should try to be a square peg in a round hole. God must decide who does what and who goes where (Mark 10:37, 40). But no Christian is to be a peg without a hole. Each has received a gift and should be using it (1 Peter 4:10).

Grace abounding

'I will love them freely.' Hosea 14:4
SUGGESTED FURTHER READING: Malachi 3:6–18

This subject invites backsliders to return; indeed, the text was specially written for such—'I will heal their backsliding; I will love them freely.' Here is a son who ran away from home. He enlisted for a soldier. He behaved so badly in his regiment that he had to be drummed out of it. He has been living in a foreign country in so vicious a way that he has reduced his body by disease. His back is covered with rags; his character is that of the vagrant and felon. When he went away he did it on purpose to vex his father's heart, and he has brought his mother's grey hairs with sorrow to the grave. One day the young lad receives a letter full of love. His father writes—'Return to me, my child; I will forgive you all; I will love you freely.' Now if this letter had said—'If you will humble yourself so much, I will love you; if you will come back and make me such-and-such promises, I will love you;' if it had said, 'If you will behave yourself for the future, I will love you,'—I can suppose the young man's proud nature rising; but surely this kindness will melt him. Surely the generosity of the invitation will at once break his heart, and he will say, 'I will offend no longer, I will return at once.' Backslider, without any condition you are invited to return. 'I am married unto you,' saith the Lord. If Jesus ever did love you he has never left off loving you. You may have left off attending to the means of grace; you may have been very slack at private prayer, but if you ever were a child of God you are a child of God still, and he cries 'How can I give thee up?'

FOR MEDITATION: God's love is not a response to our initiatives, but is 'an everlasting love' (Jeremiah 31:3), predating the very existence of us all. However, it does demand a response from us to make an effective difference to us.

The elders before the throne

'I saw four and twenty elders sitting clothed in white raiment; and they had on their heads crowns of gold...The four and twenty elders fall down before him that sat on the throne, and worship him that liveth for ever and ever, and cast their crowns before the throne, saying, Thou art worthy, O Lord, to receive glory and honour and power.' Revelation 4:4,10–11
SUGGESTED FURTHER READING: Romans 5:17–6:2

They who are Christ's are kings. Take care that you wear your crown, by reigning over your lusts. Be a king in the midst of all that would lead you astray. Christ Jesus has broken the neck of your sin; put your foot upon it; keep it under; subdue it. In the world at large act a king's part. If any would tempt you to betray Christ for gain, say, 'How can I? I am a king. How shall I betray Christ?' Let the nobility of your nature come out in your actings. Forgive in a royal manner, as a king can forgive. Be ready to give to others as God has helped you, as a king gives. Let your liberality of spirit be right royal. Let your actions never be mean, sneaking, cowardly, dastardly. Do the right thing, and defy the worst. Dare all your foes in the pursuit of that which is right, and let men see while they look upon you that there is a something under your homely appearance which they cannot understand. Men make a deal of fuss about the blood of the aristocracy; I dare say it is not very different from the blood of crossing-sweepers. But there is a great deal of difference between the lifeblood of the saints and the lifeblood of the proudest prince; for they who love Christ have fed upon his flesh, and have drunk of his blood, and have been made partakers of the divine nature. These are the royal ones; these are the aristocrats; these are the nobility, and all are mean beside. Christians, perhaps some of you have not reigned as kings during the last week. You have been either murmuring, like poor whining beggars, or you have been scraping, like dunghill rakers, with your covetousness, or you have been sinning, like idle boys in the street, who roll in the mire. You have not lived up to your kingship.

FOR MEDITATION: Christians have a royal law to fulfil (James 2:8); in keeping with our position in Christ our response to temptation ought to be 'Should such a man as I?...I will not.' (Nehemiah 6:11)

Future punishment a fearful thing

'It is a fearful thing to fall into the hands of the living God.' Hebrews
10:31
SUGGESTED FURTHER READING: Romans 5:6–11

It is the highest benevolence to warn men of their danger, and to exhort them to escape from the wrath which will surely come upon them, for 'It is a fearful thing to fall into the hands of the living God.' We feel that it must be a fearful thing to be punished for sin when you remember the atonement. It is our full belief as Christians, that, in order to pardon human sin, it was necessary that God himself should become incarnate, and that the Son of God should suffer excruciating pains, to which the dignity of his person added infinite weight. Brethren, if the wrath of God be a mere trifle, there was no need of a Saviour to deliver us; it were as well to have let so small a matter take its course; or, if the Saviour came merely to save us from a pinch or two, why is so much said in his praise? What need for heaven and earth to ring with the glories of him who would save us from a small mischief? But mark the word. As the sufferings of the Saviour were intense beyond all conception, and as no less a person than God himself must endure these sufferings for us, that must have been an awful, not to say infinite evil, from which there was no other way for us to escape except by the bleeding and dying of God's dear Son. Think lightly of hell, and you will think lightly of the cross. Think little of the sufferings of lost souls, and you will soon think little of the Saviour who delivers you from them. God grant we may not live to see such a Christ-dishonouring theology dominant in our times.

FOR MEDITATION: As Spurgeon feared, vital and inseparable biblical doctrines such as the atonement and eternal damnation have come under tremendous attack in recent years in favour of more sophisticated teaching which is more acceptable to human taste. The Bible contrasts the words of the holy prophets and the apostles of our Lord, with the words of 'scoffers, walking after their own lusts' (2 Peter 3:2–3). Beware of people who twist the Scriptures to suit themselves (2 Peter 3:16–17).

The first sermon in the Metropolitan Tabernacle

'And daily in the temple, and in every house, they ceased not to teach and to preach Jesus Christ.' Acts 5:42
SUGGESTED FURTHER READING: 2 Peter 2:1–3

He has, by one sacrifice, for ever put away sin. We shall never preach Christ unless we have a real atonement. There are certain people nowadays who are making the atonement a sort of compromise, and the next step is to make the atonement *a display* of what ought to have been, instead of *the thing* which should have been. Then, next, there are some who make it to be a mere picture, an exhibition, a shadow—a shadow, the substance of which they have not seen. And the day will come, in which in some churches the atonement shall be utterly denied, and yet men shall call themselves Christians, while they have broken themselves against the corner-stone of the entire system. There is a limit to the charity of Christians, and there can be none whatever entertained to the man who is dishonest enough to occupy a Christian pulpit and to deny Christ. It is only in the Christian church that such a thing can be tolerated. I appeal to you. Was there ever known a Buddhist who denied the basic doctrine of his religion? Was there ever known a Muslim man who cried down the Prophet? It remains for Christian churches only to have in their midst men who can bear the name of Christian, while they slander the deity of him who is the Christian's God, and speak lightly of the efficacy of his blood who is the Christian's atonement.

FOR MEDITATION: Do you get taken in by half-truths? What does the death of the Lord Jesus Christ on the cross mean to you? It does, for instance, give us an example of how to suffer (1 Peter 2:21), but to major on that is to miss the point. The essence of his death was that he bore our sins and their punishment in our place and for our deliverance (1 Peter 2:24). Have you thanked and trusted him to save you?

N.B. This was Spurgeon's first sermon in the newly-built Metropolitan Tabernacle and in his Metropolitan Tabernacle Pulpit series.

SERMON NO. 369

26 MARCH (1865)

The precious blood of Christ

'The precious blood of Christ.' 1 Peter 1:19
SUGGESTED FURTHER READING: Acts 8:25–40

Two soldiers were on duty in the citadel of Gibraltar; one of them had obtained peace through the precious blood of Christ, the other was in very great distress of mind. It happened to be their turn to stand, both of them, sentinel the same night; and there are many long passages in the rock; these passages are able to convey sounds a very great distance. The soldier in distress of mind was ready to beat his breast for grief: he felt he had rebelled against God, and could not find how he could be reconciled; when, suddenly, there came through the air what seemed to him to be a mysterious voice from heaven saying these words, 'The precious blood of Christ.' In a moment he saw it all: it was that which reconciled us to God; and he rejoiced with joy unspeakable and full of glory. Now did these words come directly from God? No. They did as far as the effect was concerned—they did come from the Holy Spirit. Who was it that had spoken these words? Curiously enough, the other sentinel at the far end of the passage was standing still and meditating, when an officer came by and it was his duty of course to give the word for the night, and with soldier-like promptitude he did give it, but not accurately, for instead of giving the proper word, he was so taken up by his meditations that he said to the officer, 'The precious blood of Christ.' He corrected himself in a moment, but however, he had said it, and it had passed along the passage and reached the ear for which God meant it, and the man found peace and spent his life in the fear of God, being in after years the means of completing one of our excellent translations of the Word of God into Hindi. Who can tell, dear friends, how much peace you may give by only telling the story of our Saviour.

FOR MEDITATION: The mighty saving power of God is contained only in the straightforward gospel message of Christ crucified (Romans 1:16; 1 Corinthians 1:17–18,23–24). What a glorious message!

SERMON NO. 621

'Alas for us, if thou wert all, and nought beyond, O earth.'

'If in this life only we have hope in Christ, we are of all men most miserable.' 1 Corinthians 15:19

SUGGESTED FURTHER READING: Titus 2:11–14

The most practical thing in all the world is the hope of the world to come; and you see the text teaches this, for it is just this which keeps us from being miserable; and to keep a man from being miserable, let me say, is to do a great thing for him, for a miserable Christian—what is the use of him? Keep him in a cupboard, where nobody can see him; nurse him in the hospital, for he is of no use in the field of labour. Build a monastery, and put all miserable Christians in it, and there let them meditate on mercy till they learn to smile; for really there is no other use for them in the world. But the man who has a hope for the next world goes about his work strong, for the joy of the Lord is our strength. He goes against temptation mighty, for the hope of the next world repels the fiery darts of the adversary. He can labour without present reward, for he looks for a reward in the world to come. He can suffer rebuke, and can afford to die a slandered man, because he knows that God will avenge his own elect who cry day and night unto him. Through the Spirit of God the hope of another world is the most potent force for the product of virtue; it is a fountain of joy; it is the very channel of usefulness. It is to the Christian what food is to the vital force in the animal frame. Let it not be said of any of us that we are dreaming about the future and forgetting the present, but let the future sanctify the present to highest uses.

FOR MEDITATION: It was this hope that marked the lives of even the Old Testament heroes of faith (Hebrews 11:10,13–16,35). But what men and women of action they were in God's service! Who would dare accuse them of being dreamers and of being no earthly use?

The interest of Christ and his people in each other

'My beloved is mine, and I am his,' Song of Solomon 2:16
SUGGESTED FURTHER READING: Galatians 2:15–21

How is my beloved mine? He is mine because he gave himself to me of old. Long ere I knew it, or had a being, he covenanted to bestow himself on me—on all his chosen. When he said, 'Lo, I come: in the volume of the book it is written of me, I delight to do thy will, O my God,' he did in fact become my substitute, giving himself to do my work and bear my sorrow. Mine he is because that covenant has been fulfilled in the actual gift. For me (I speak in the first person, because I want you each to speak in the first person too), for you, my soul, he laid aside his robes of glory to become a man; for you he was swaddled in the weakness of infancy, and lay in the poverty of the manger; for you, my soul, he bore the infant body, the childish form, and the human flesh and blood; for you the poverty which made him cry, 'Foxes have holes, and birds of the air have nests; but the Son of man hath not where to lay his head.' For you, my soul, for you that shame and spitting, that agony and bloody sweat, that cross, that crown of thorns, those expiring agonies, that dying groan. 'My Beloved,' in all this, 'is mine.' No, yours the burial; yours the resurrection and its mystic meaning; yours the ascension and its triumphant shouts; yours the session at the right hand of God; yes, and by holy daring we avow it, he who sits today, 'God over all, blessed for ever,' is ours in the splendour of his majesty, in the invincibility of his might, in the omnipresence of his power, in all the glory of his future advent. Our beloved is ours, because he has given himself to us, just as he is.

FOR MEDITATION: Can you call Jesus 'My Lord and my God' (John 20:28)? Do you take time to count your possessions in Christ (1 Corinthians 1:30)? 'All things' (Romans 8:32; 1 Corinthians 3:21) would take more than eternity to exhaust!

Christ set forth as a propitiation

'Christ Jesus, whom God hath set forth to be a propitiation through faith in his blood.' Romans 3:24–25
SUGGESTED FURTHER READING: Exodus 25:17–22

God has set forth Christ as being a propitiation. The Greek word is *hilasterion* which, being translated, may mean a mercy seat or a covering. Now God has said to the sinner, 'Do you desire to meet me? Would you be no longer my enemy? Would you tell me your sorrows? Would you receive my blessing? Would you establish a commerce between your Creator and your soul? I set forth Christ to you as being the mercy seat, where I can meet with you and you can meet with me.' Or take the word as signifying a covering; as the mercy seat covered the tables of the law, and so covered that which was the cause of divine anger, because we had broken his commandment. 'Would you have anything which can cover your sin? Cover it from me your God, so that I need not be provoked to anger; cover it from you so that you need not be cowed with excessive fear, and tremble to approach me as you did when I came in thunders and lightnings upon Sinai? Would you have a shelter which shall hide altogether your sins and your iniquities? I set it forth to you in the person of my bleeding Son. Trust in his blood, and your sin is covered from my eyes; it shall be covered from your own eyes too; and being justified by faith, you shall have peace with God through Jesus Christ your Lord.' O that we may have grace to accept now what God the Father sets forth! The Romish priest sets forth this and that; our own Romish hearts set forth such-and-such-another thing; but God sets forth Christ. The preacher of doctrine sets forth a dogma; the preacher of experience sets forth a feeling; the preacher of practice often sets forth an effort; but God puts before you Christ. 'There I will meet with thee.'

FOR MEDITATION: Christ is the only propitiation that God in his mercy will accept as a covering for our sin (Romans 3:25; Hebrews 2:17; 1 John 2:2; 4:10). Have you accepted him too, or are you still trying to bodge your own cover-up job? It won't work (Genesis 3:7–9).

The old, old story

'In due time Christ died for the ungodly.' Romans 5:6
SUGGESTED FURTHER READING: John 5:39–47

Unbeliever, if God cannot and will not forgive the sins of penitent men without taking their punishment, rest assured he will surely bring you to judgment. If, when Christ, God's Son, had imputed sin laid on him, God smote him, how will he smite you who are his enemy, and who have your own sins upon your head? God seemed at Calvary, as it were, to take an oath—sinner, hear it!—he seemed, as it were, to take an oath and say, 'By the blood of my Son I swear that sin must be punished,' and if it is not punished in Christ for you, it will be punished in you for yourselves. Is Christ yours, sinner? Did he die for you? Do you trust him? If you do, he died for you. Do you say, 'No, I do not?' Then remember that if you live and die without faith in Christ, for every idle word and for every ill act that you have done, stroke for stroke, and blow for blow, vengeance must chastise you. Again, to another class of you, this word. If God has in Christ made an atonement and opened a way of salvation, what must be your guilt who try to open another way; who say, 'I will be good and virtuous; I will attend to ceremonies; I will save myself'? Fool that you are, you have insulted God in his tenderest point, for you have insulted his Son. You have said, 'I can do it without that blood;' you have, in fact, trampled on the blood of Christ, and said, 'I need it not.' Oh, if the sinner who repents not be damned, with what accumulated terrors shall he be damned, who, in addition to his impenitence, heaps affront upon the person of Christ by going about to establish his own righteousness. Leave it!

FOR MEDITATION: The readings for most of the past week have concentrated on the shed blood and atoning sacrifice of the Lord Jesus Christ. Do these truths cause you relief, satisfaction and grateful thanksgiving in response to his love (1 John 4:10,19)? If not, you either hate him or couldn't care less about him, which in God's sight boils down to the same thing. 'How shall we escape, if we neglect so great salvation?' (Hebrews 2:3).

SERMON NO. 446

Temple glories

'They... praised the LORD, saying, For he is good; for his mercy endureth for ever.' 2 Chronicles 5:13; 7:3
SUGGESTED FURTHER READING: Psalm 136:1–26 (read earlier in the service)

The more Scriptural our hymns are the better. In fact there will never be found music which can excel old David's Psalms. Let us interpret them in an evangelical spirit, let us fill them full of the gospel of Christ, of which they are, indeed, already full in prophecy, and we shall sing the very words of the Spirit, and shall surely edify each other and glorify our God. If, then, our music has been scriptural, if our praise has been hearty, if our song has been unanimous, if we have sung of that mercy which endureth for ever, we have good cause to expect that God will manifest himself to us, and faith will perceive the cloud. That is a grand old Calvinistic Psalm, 'His mercy endureth for ever.' What Arminian can sing that? Well, he will *sing* it, I dare say; but if he be a thoroughgoing Arminian he really cannot enjoy it and believe it. You can fall from grace, can you? Then how does his mercy endure for ever? Christ bought with his blood some that will be lost in hell, did he? Then how did his mercy endure for ever? There are some who resist the offers of divine grace, despite all that the Spirit of God can do for them, yet disappoint the Spirit and defeat God, are there? How then does his mercy endure for ever? No, no, this is no hymn for you, this is the Calvinist's hymn. This is the hymn which you and I will sing as long as life shall last, and going through the dark valley of the shadow of death we will make the shades resound with the joyous strain—'For his mercies shall endure ever faithful, ever sure.'

FOR MEDITATION: Genuine Christians will persevere as the result of being united with Christ in the likeness of his resurrection (Romans 6:5); Christ will die no more and over him death has no more dominion; that is the nature of the eternal life Christians live with him (Romans 6:8–9). Rejoice in the one who said 'Fear not; ... I am he that liveth, and was dead; and, behold, I am alive for evermore.' (Revelation 1:17–18)

Divine gentleness acknowledged

'Thy gentleness hath made me great.' Psalm 18:35
SUGGESTED FURTHER READING: Deuteronomy 8:11–20

There are several readings of this text. The word is capable of being translated, 'thy *goodness* hath made me great.' David saw much of benevolence in God's action towards him, and he gratefully ascribed all his greatness not to his own goodness, but to the goodness of God. 'Thy *providence*' is another reading, which is indeed nothing more than goodness in action. Goodness is providence in embryo; providence is goodness fully developed. Goodness is the bud of which providence is the flower; or goodness is the seed of which providence is the harvest. Some render it, 'thy *help*,' which is but another word for providence; providence being the firm ally of the saints, aiding them in the service of their Lord. Some learned annotators tell us that the text means, 'thy *humility* hath made me great.' 'Thy *condescension*' may, perhaps, serve as a comprehensive reading, combining the ideas which we have already mentioned, as well as that of humility. It is God's making himself little which is the cause of our being made great. We are so little that if God should manifest his greatness without condescension, we should be trampled under his feet; but God, who must stoop to view the skies and bow to see what angels do, bends his eye yet lower and looks to the lowly and contrite, and makes them great. While these are the translations which have been given to the adopted text of the original, we find that there are other readings altogether; as for instance, the Septuagint, which reads, 'thy discipline'—thy fatherly correction— 'hath made me great;' while the Chaldee paraphrase reads, 'thy word hath increased me.' Still the idea is the same. David ascribes all his own greatness to the condescending goodness and graciousness of his Father in heaven. I trust we all feel that this sentiment is echoed in our hearts.

FOR MEDITATION: We should rejoice in the Lord Jesus Christ—in his gentleness (2 Corinthians 10:1), goodness (Acts 10:38), help (Hebrews 4:14,16) and humility (Philippians 2:8). As the result of these attributes God has done great things for us (Psalm 126:2–3; Matthew 12:29; Luke 8:39; 2 Corinthians 8:9).

SERMON NO. 683

Travelling expenses on the two great roads

'So he paid the fare thereof.' Jonah 1:3
SUGGESTED FURTHER READING: Haggai 1:1–15

With all your kicking and rebelling, you will have to go where you were originally ordered to go; you might as well go at first—you will go with better grace; you will go with your master's comfortable presence; but you will have to go one way or another. Many men have found this true. They have struggled against duty, and perhaps, year after year they have drawn back from it, finding miserable excuses for their consciences; but they never prospered in business, they could not get on in the world, they had trouble on trouble, and at last it came to this, they had to go back to the very place where they were ten or twenty years ago, and there they discharged the duty which they had been so long seeking to avoid, which had proved a burdensome stone unto them until they were rid of it by yielding to its demands. Now, my dear brother, do not play the Jonah, for you will have to pay the fare of it. If you know your duty, do it. I may be speaking very pointedly to some of you. 'I should have to sever the bonds of many a fond connection.' Do it for Christ's sake. 'I should have to leave the camp and go outside of it, take up a very heavy cross, and bear Christ's reproach.' You may as well do it now as by and by, for you will have to do it. 'But,' says one, 'this business of mine—I have nothing left to live upon; I feel it is a bad business, but I do not like to give it up just yet.' You will have to do so sooner or later, you may as well do it now, before, like Jonah, you have had to pay for your wit; remember that 'The fear of the Lord is the beginning of wisdom, and a good understanding have all they that keep his commandments.'

FOR MEDITATION: Delayed obedience to God includes an initial period of disobedience. Better late than never (Matthew 21:28–32), but instant obedience is the best course of action (Psalm 119:60).

'He claims my will, that I may prove
How swift obedience answers love.'

The barley field on fire

'Absalom sent for Joab ... but he would not come to him: and when he sent again the second time, he would not come. Therefore he said unto his servants, See, Joab's field is near mine, and he hath barley there; go and set it on fire ... Then Joab arose, and came to Absalom unto his house, and said unto him, Wherefore have thy servants set my field on fire?' 2 Samuel 14:29–31*

SUGGESTED FURTHER READING: Romans 5:1–5

Under your cross you have many special comforts. There are cordials which God gives to sick saints which he never puts to the lips of those who are in health. Dark caverns keep not back the miners, if they know that diamonds are to be found there: you need not fear suffering when you remember what riches it yields to your soul. There is no hearing the nightingale without night, and there are some promises which only sing to us in trouble. It is in the cellar of affliction that the good old wine of the kingdom is stored. You shall never see Christ's face so well as when all others turn their backs upon you. When you have come into such confusion that human wisdom is at a nonplus, then shall you see God's wisdom manifest and clear. Oh! the love-visits which Christ pays to his people when they are in the prison of their trouble! Then he lays bare his very heart to them, and comforts them as a mother does her child. They sleep daintily who have Jesus to make their beds. Suffering saints are generally the most flourishing saints, and well they may be, for they are Jesus' special care. If you would find a man whose lips drop with pearls, look for one who has been in the deep waters. We seldom learn much except as it is beaten into us by the rod in Christ's school-house under Madam Trouble. God's vines owe more to the pruning knife than to any other tool in the garden; superfluous shoots are sad spoilers of the vines. But even while we carry it, the cross brings present comfort; it is a dear, dear cross, all hung with roses and dripping with sweet smelling myrrh.

FOR MEDITATION: The comforts arising from our afflictions as believers are for our own benefit (Psalm 119:50,52), but they should also overflow from us for the blessing of others (2 Corinthians 1:4; 7:5–7).

I know that my redeemer liveth

'For I know that my redeemer liveth, and that he shall stand at the latter day upon the earth: and though after my skin worms destroy this body, yet in my flesh shall I see God.' Job 19:25–26
SUGGESTED FURTHER READING: Ruth 3:1–4:10

The word 'redeemer' here used, is in the original *'goel'*—kinsman. The duty of the kinsman, or *goel,* was this: suppose an Israelite had alienated his estate, as in the case of Naomi and Ruth; suppose a patrimony which had belonged to a family, had passed away through poverty, it was the *goel's* business, the redeemer's business to pay the price as the next of kin, and to buy back the heritage. Boaz stood in that relation to Ruth. Now, the body may be looked upon as the heritage of the soul—the soul's little farm, that little plot of earth in which the soul has been wont to walk and delight, as a man walks in his garden or dwells in his house. Now, that becomes alienated. Death, like Ahab, takes away the vineyard from us who are as Naboth; we lose our patrimonial estate; death sends his troops to take our vineyard and to spoil the vines thereof and ruin it. But we turn round to death and say, 'I know that my *Goel* liveth, and he will redeem this heritage; I have lost it; thou takest it from me lawfully, O death, because my sin hath forfeited my right; I have lost my heritage through my own offence, and through that of my first parent Adam; but there lives one who will buy this back.' Brethren, Job could say this of Christ long before he had descended upon earth, 'I know that my redeemer liveth;' and now that he has ascended up on high, and led captivity captive, surely we may with double emphasis say, 'I know that my *Goel,* my Kinsman liveth, and that he hath paid the price, that I should have back my patrimony, so that in my flesh I shall see God.'

FOR MEDITATION: The Christian can correctly view redemption as something past (Galatians 3:13) and present (Ephesians 1:7); but to stop at the redemption of the soul is to ignore the last vital chapter of the story. We still await the day of redemption (Ephesians 4:30) and the actual redemption of our bodies (Romans 8:23).

Death and life in Christ

'Now if we be dead with Christ, we believe that we shall also live with him: knowing that Christ being raised from the dead dieth no more; death hath no more dominion over him. For in that he died, he did unto sin once: but in that he liveth, he liveth unto God. Likewise reckon ye also yourselves to be dead indeed unto sin, but alive unto God through Jesus Christ our Lord.' Romans 6:8–11

SUGGESTED FURTHER READING: Revelation 1:12–18

I would to God that on one of these four anchor-holds your faith might be able to get rest. *Jesus died*, poor trembler; if he died and took your griefs, will not his atonement save you? Rest here. Millions of souls have rested on nothing but Jesus' death, and this is a granite foundation; no storms of hell can shake it. Get a good hand-hold on his cross; hold it, and it will hold you. You cannot depend on his death and be deceived. Try it; taste and see, and you shall find that the Lord is good, and that none can trust a dying Saviour without being with him in paradise. But if this suffice you not, *he rose again.* Fasten upon this. He is proved to be victor over your sin and over your adversary; can you not, therefore, depend upon him? Doubtless there have been thousands of saints who have found the richest consolation from the fact that Jesus rose again from the dead. He rose again for our justification. Sinner, hang on that. Having risen, *he lives.* He is not a dead Saviour, a dead sacrifice. He must be able to hear our plea and to present his own. Depend on a living Saviour; depend on him now. *He lives for ever*, and therefore it is not too late for him to save you. If you cry to him he will hear your prayer, even though it be in life's last moment, for he lives for ever. Though the ends of the earth were come, and you were the last man, yet he ever lives to intercede before his Father's face. O gad not about to find any other hope! Here are four great stones for you; build your hope on these; you cannot want surer foundation—he dies, he rises, he lives, he lives for ever.

FOR MEDITATION: All kinds of questions, doubts and fears attack our faith (Romans 8:32–34); the very best answers are to be found in the crucified and risen Saviour who intercedes for us at the right hand of God.

SERMON NO. 503

The two draughts of fishes

'Now when he had left speaking, he said unto Simon, Launch out into the deep, and let down your nets for a draught.' Luke 5:4
'And he said unto them, Cast the net on the right side of the ship, and ye shall find. They cast therefore, and now they were not able to draw it for the multitude of fishes.' John 21:6
SUGGESTED FURTHER READING: John 6:22–35

The whole life of Christ was a sermon. He was a prophet mighty in word and deed; and by his deeds as well as his words he taught the people. It is perfectly true that the miracles of Christ attest his mission. But we ought not to overlook that probably a higher reason for the miracles is to be found in the instruction which they convey. To the world without, at the present time, the miracles of Christ are more hard to believe than the doctrine which he taught. Sceptics turn them into stones of stumbling, and when they cannot cavil at the marvellous teaching of Jesus, they attack the miracles as monstrous and incredible. I doubt not that even to minds seriously vexed with unbelief, the miracles, instead of being helps to belief, have been trials of faith. Few indeed are there in whom faith is wrought by signs and wonders; nor indeed is this the gospel way of bringing conviction to the soul: the secret force of the living word is the chosen instrumentality of Christ, and wonders are left to be the resort of that antichrist by whom the nations shall be deceived. We, who by grace have believed, view the miracles of Christ as noble attestations to his mission and divinity, but we confess that we value them even more as instructive homilies than as attesting witnesses; it is our conviction that we should lose much of the benefit which they were meant to convey to us, if we were merely to view them as seals to the roll, for they are a part of the writing of the roll itself. The marvels wrought by our blessed Lord are acted sermons full of holy doctrine, set forth to us more vividly than it could have been in words.

FOR MEDITATION: The Lord Jesus Christ taught lessons as follow-up to and spiritual application of some of his miracles (Matthew 21:21–22; Mark 2:9–11; Luke 5:9–10; John 6:26–27; 9:39–41). Are you learning them?

Perfect cleansing

'For I will cleanse their blood that I have not cleansed.' Joel 3:21
SUGGESTED FURTHER READING: 1 Corinthians 15:51–58

If it be promised to us that the old nature shall thus be removed, and we shall be purged, what then? Why, then, let us struggle against our corruption, because we shall get the victory. Nothing makes a man fight like the hope of getting the victory. When poor soldiers feel that it is of no use, then they are only too glad to hear the trumpet sound a retreat; but when they are confident of victory, how they draw their swords, how they haste to the struggle, how they weary not of the fight. Even now, today, my soul takes hold upon her sword. Sin, death, and hell I defy you, for I shall bear the palm as surely as I bear the sword. I shall wear the crown as certainly as I agonised unto death. Struggle with yourselves, strive daily to get the mastery of your passions. The victory is sure. Let no discouragement weaken you. 'Be strong in the Lord, and in the power of his might.' He is able to give you the victory through Jesus Christ your Lord. And what next? Why, today, pray against your corruptions more than ever you have done. You have got a promise to plead. Take it, salt it with your tears. Lay it upon the altar; put your hands upon the horns of the altar, and say, 'Great God, I will not rise, I will not let thee go until I know by divine assurance that this promise shall be fulfilled to me.' So shall you go forth to your daily struggle with temptation, wearing a smile upon your face, and smoothing those wrinkles on your brow. Sorrow does not become the man who has so rich a promise. Be glad. The joy of the Lord shall be your strength. You shall at last win the victory. Sinner! he that believes in Christ may claim this text for himself. Believe, and this text is yours as well as mine.

FOR MEDITATION: As a young man David knew that the battle was the Lord's (1 Samuel 17:47); as an old man he knew that the victory also was the Lord's (1 Chronicles 29:11). By faith the Christian shares in the victory over the world now (1 John 5:4) and over death in the time to come (1 Corinthians 15:57).

Hope, yet no hope. No hope, yet hope

'Thou art wearied in the greatness of thy way; yet saidst thou not, there is no hope.' Isaiah 57:10
'And they said, there is no hope: but we will walk after our own devices, and we will every one do the imagination of his evil heart.' Jeremiah 18:12
SUGGESTED FURTHER READING: Job 8:11–9:2

Most men must have a secret hope somewhere of a false kind; for, look at the way in which they are employing themselves. Surely those men must have some fictitious hope somewhere, or they would not act as they do. We see many busy about their persons, decorating themselves when their soul is in ruin; like a man painting the front door when the house is in flames. Surely they must harbour some baseless hope which makes them thus insensible. We see men who do not quail and tremble, though they profess to believe the Bible which tells them that God is angry with them every day. Surely their quietness of heart must arise from some secret hope lurking in their spirits. The rope of mercy is cast to the sinner, and he will not lay hold of it. Surely he cannot be such a fool as to love to die; he must have some hope somewhere that he can swim by his own exertions, and it is this hopefulness of the man in himself that is his ruin and destruction. Until you are completely separate from all consciousness of hope in yourself, there is no hope that the gospel will ever be any power to you; but when you shall throw up your hands like a drowning man, feeling, 'It is all over with me: I am lost, unless a stronger than I shall interpose,' then there is hope for you. If we can once get you to say, 'One thing I know, I cannot save myself. One thing I feel, I must have a stronger arm than mine to rescue me from ruin,' when you have come to this, we will begin to rejoice over you, and may God grant that our rejoicing may not be in vain.

FOR MEDITATION: Christians may sometimes imagine that God has deserted them (Psalm 10:1), but he will not disappoint them (Psalm 10:14,17). Unbelievers are the ones to be pitied; despite ignoring God, they delude themselves that all is well (Psalm 10:4,6,11,13).

SERMON NO. 684

Satan considering the saints

'And the LORD *said unto Satan, Hast thou considered my servant Job,'*
Job 1:8
SUGGESTED FURTHER READING: Luke 22:31–34

It strikes me if Satan could be absolutely certain that any one soul was chosen of God, he would scarcely waste his time in attempting to destroy it, although he might seek to worry and to dishonour it. It is however more likely that he no more knows who God's elect are than we do, for he can only judge as we do by outward actions, though he can form a more accurate judgement than we can through longer experience, and being able to see persons in private where we cannot intrude. By their fruits he knows them, and we know them in the same manner. Since, however, we are often mistaken in our judgment, he too may be so; and it seems to me that he therefore makes it his policy to endeavour to destroy them all—not knowing in which case he may succeed. He goes about seeking whom he *may* devour, and, as he knows not whom he may be permitted to swallow up, he attacks all the people of God with vehemence. Someone may say, 'How can one devil do this?' He does not do it by himself alone. I do not know that many of us have ever been tempted directly by Satan: we may not be notable enough among men to be worth *his* trouble; but he has a whole host of inferior spirits under his supremacy and control, and as the centurion said of himself, so he might have said of Satan—'he saith to this spirit, 'Do this', and he doeth it, and to his servant, 'Go', and he goeth.' Thus all the servants of God will more or less come under the direct or indirect assaults of the great enemy of souls, and that with a view of destroying them; for he would, if it were possible, deceive the very elect.

FOR MEDITATION: Judas Iscariot, described by Jesus himself as 'a devil' (John 6:70–71) was the only apostle Satan could devour (Luke 22:3); that didn't stop him trying to seize the other eleven (Luke 22:31—'you' is plural), whom the Father had entrusted to his Son's safe keeping (John 17:12) and for whose protection from Satan the Saviour prayed (John 17:15).

SERMON NO. 623

A promise for us and for our children

'I will pour water upon him that is thirsty ... I will pour my spirit upon thy seed ... and they shall spring up as among the grass, as willows by the water courses, One shall say, I am the LORD's; *and another shall call himself by the name of Jacob.'* Isaiah 44:3–5
SUGGESTED FURTHER READING: Acts 2:1–21

The thirsty land shall be springs of water. O my brethren, when the Holy Spirit visits a man, what a difference is made in him! I know a preacher, once as dull and dead a man as ever misused a pulpit; under his slumbering ministrations there were few conversions, and the congregation grew thinner and thinner, good men sighed in secret, and the enemy said, 'Aha! so would we have it.' The revival came, the Holy Spirit worked gloriously, the preacher felt the divine fire and suddenly woke up to energy and zeal. The man appeared to be transformed; his tongue seemed touched with fire; elaborate and written discourses were laid aside, and he began to talk out of his own glowing heart to the hearts of others. He preached as he had never done before; the place filled; the dry bones were stirred, and quickening began. Those who knew him once so elegant, correct, passionless, dignified, cold, lifeless, and unprofitable, asked in amazement, 'Is Saul also among the prophets?' The Spirit of God is a great wonder-worker. You will notice certain church members; they have never been good for much; we have had their names on the roll, and that is all: suddenly the Spirit of God has come upon them, and they have been honoured among us for their zeal and usefulness. We have seen them here and there and everywhere diligent in the service of God, and foremost in all sorts of Christian labour, though before you could hardly get them to stir an inch. I would then that the quickening Spirit would come down upon me, and upon you, upon every one of us in abundance, to create men valiant for truth and mighty for the Lord. O for some of the ancient valour of apostolic times.

FOR MEDITATION: This abundant watering is carried out by the Holy Spirit in the heart of the believer (John 7:37–39; Romans 5:5; Titus 3:5–6). Are you overflowing or not really thirsty enough?

SERMON NO. 564

Exposition of the doctrines of grace (1. Opening of proceedings)

SUGGESTED READING: 1 Corinthians 1:17–2:5

It is a fact that the system of doctrines called Calvinism is so *exceedingly simple* and so readily learned, that as a system of divinity it is more easily taught and more easily grasped by unlettered minds than any other. The poor have the gospel preached to them in a style which assists their memories and commends itself to their judgments. It is a system which was practically acknowledged on high philosophic grounds by such men as Bacon and Newton, and yet it can charm the soul of a child. And then it has another virtue. I take it that the last is no mean one, but it has another—that when it is preached, there is a something in it which *excites thought*. A man may hear sermons upon the other theory which shall glance over him as the swallow's wing gently sweeps the brook, but these old doctrines either make a man so angry that he goes home and cannot sleep for very hatred, or else they bring him down into lowliness of thought, feeling the immensity of the things which he has heard. Either way it excites and stirs him up not temporarily, but in a most lasting manner. These doctrines haunt him, he kicks against the goads, and full often the word forces a way into his soul. And I think this is no small thing for any doctrine to do, in an age given to slumber, and with human hearts so indifferent to the truth of God. I know that many men have gained much good by being made angry under a sermon than by being pleased by it, for being angry they have turned the truth over and over again, and at last the truth has burned its way right into their hearts.

FOR MEDITATION: Gospel truths have always provoked joyful acceptance or bitter opposition (Acts 8:1–8;39; 9:1–2; 13:45,48); but the most zealous opponents of the Gospel can be saved (Acts 9:21–22). The most fearful cases are those who can hear the Word of God comfortably and remain unmoved one way or the other (Ezekiel 33:30–33); among them are people who sit through sermons about hell and the judgement of God and then tell the preacher how much they 'enjoyed the nice message.' What effect do these daily readings have upon you?

The root of the matter

'The root of the matter is found in me.' Job 19:28
SUGGESTED FURTHER READING: Ezekiel 34:1–24

There are many young Christians who have been made to suffer for years through the roughness of some more advanced believers. Christian! you that are strong, be very tender towards the weak, for the day may come when you will be weaker than he. Never did bullock push with side and shoulder the lean cattle of the herd when they came to drink, but what the Lord took away the glory from the fat bull of Bashan, and made him willing to associate with the very least of the herd. You cannot hector a child of God without making his Father angry; and though you be a child of God yourself, yet if you deal harshly with one of your brethren you shall smart for it, for the Master's rod is always ready even for his own beloved children when they are not tender with the sons and daughters of Zion, who are kept as the apple of God's eye. Remember, too, brethren, that the day may come when you will want consolation from the very friend whom you have treated so roughly. I have known some great people—some very great people, that have at last been made to sit at the feet of those whom before they called all sorts of ill names. God has his ways of taking the wind out of men's sails. While their sails were full, and the wind blew, they said, 'No, no; we do not care about that little port over yonder; we do not care to put in there; it is only a miserable little fishing-village.' But when the wind came howling on, and the deep rolled heavily, and it seemed as if the dread artillery of God were all mustering for the battle; ah! how with the reef-sail they have tried to fly, as best they could, into the little harbour!' Do not speak ill of the little harbour. Do not be ashamed of little Christians. Stand up for the weaklings of the flock.

FOR MEDITATION: Maturity in the faith is expressed by a humble and gentle attitude towards believers who have even further to grow (Galatians 6:1; 1 Thessalonians 2:6–7; 1 Peter 5:2–3). In the kingdom of God 'the great' serve the rest, not vice versa (Matthew 20:25–28). The words 'minister' and 'deacon' both mean 'servant'.

The portion of the ungodly

'Behold, they shall be as stubble; the fire shall burn them; they shall not deliver themselves from the power of the flame: there shall not be a coal to warm at, nor fire to sit before it.' Isaiah 47:14
SUGGESTED FURTHER READING: Luke 16:19–31

In Scripture this wrath to come is sometimes spoken of as the second death. Imagine a man dying, dying in pangs, and then rising again to die again, and so continually dying and yet living; expiring and yet breathing; perishing and yet existing; being dissolved, but yet being still in the body. You have now before you, then, the Biblical view of punishment—'the second death.' O soul, there are no words that human eloquence can ever find, however dreadful, that can reach the thousandth part of this great argument! No language that was ever uttered by the sternest prophet, could ever attain to the tremendous terror of the wrath to come. I know men say of God's preachers that at times they speak too harshly: we cannot speak half harshly enough. We tell you again, even weeping, that our poor feeble words cannot portray your danger; that we cannot ourselves even feel the danger as we would wish; but if our lips had language, if we could but speak as sometimes we feel, we would move you till you should neither eat, nor drink, nor sleep, until you had sought and found a refuge in the wounds of Christ. But we are so dull, or else your hearts are so hard, that when we speak we are like men who throw stones against a wall, and the stones come back upon us. O that instead thereof we might be like the man who drew the bow at a venture, that the arrow may find a place in the joints of your harness, where your heart may be wounded with the arrows of the King!

FOR MEDITATION: Human nature understandably likes to imagine that everybody goes to heaven or at least that those who are excluded are simply wiped out of existence. But our sin is far more serious than that; it is out of love, not spite, that the Bible warns us of an everlasting existence which makes physical death look like child's play (Mark 9:43–48; Revelation 14:11). Do you weep for yourself or for those who are heading for it (Philippians 3:18–19)?

SERMON NO. 444

The last census

'The LORD *shall count, when he writeth up the people, that this man was born there.'* Psalm 87:6
SUGGESTED FURTHER READING: Revelation 20:11–15

The matters with which the census shall have to do will be decisive. Perhaps, my hearer, your name could not be written today among the regenerate, but there is hope yet, and we trust by God's grace before you leave here you may have a portion among the sanctified. If we could take today the number of God's people, at present converted, I thank God that before another hour it would be imperfect, for there would have been others added to the visibly called of God. But the last census shall be decisive. To its number none shall be added; from its multitude none subtracted. Once let that be taken, and the angel shall cry in heaven, 'He that is holy, let him be holy still;' and his voice shall reverberate to hell, but other words shall he sound there, 'He which is filthy, let him be filthy still.' That shall be decisive, the last polling of the people, the last counting of the jewels and casting away of the counterfeits, the last bringing in of the sheep and banishment of the goats. This makes it all-important that you and I should know today whether, when the Lord 'writeth up the people,' it shall be said 'that this man was born there.' Oh that we were wise to look into futurities! We are so short sighted we see so small a distance. We only see time and its trickeries, its paint, its gilt. Oh that we were wise that we understood this, that we would remember our latter end! So, come the census day when it may, we may each have our name written beneath our Lord the Lamb in some humble place among the chosen of the Lord our God.

FOR MEDITATION: While voting at an election may be voluntary, registration before a certain date at a census is compulsory and failure to do so is a punishable offence. God has commanded all people everywhere to repent (Acts 17:30) and trust in the Saviour. Failure to register and be found in Christ (Philippians 3:9) will spell disaster (Revelation 20:15).

N.B. This sermon followed the taking of the 1861 census during the previous week.

Heedlessness in religion

'But Jehu took no heed to walk in the law of the LORD *God of Israel with all his heart: for he departed not from the sins of Jeroboam, which made Israel to sin.'* 2 Kings 10:31
SUGGESTED FURTHER READING: Luke 6:37–42

Jehu was very angry at other people's sins, and we may be without being delivered from our own. It is a very fine sight to see a man work himself up into a furore against drunkenness; he himself has never been guilty of it. It is true that all the indignation which he pours upon it, it well deserves; for is it not the great net of the devil, in which he catches multitudes? I may be very furious against adultery, or theft, or immorality of some other kind, which I do not happen to practise myself, yet my own sins may cry out against me; and it will not be possible to compound for my own sins by denouncing those of others. That is a very cheap sort of virtue; bullying other people's vices. The easiest thing in all the world is to be constantly denouncing popular faults; but to wring the neck of one of my own bosom sins is a harder work by far, and a much better sign of conversion. To be earnest against the sin of others may be praiseworthy, but it is no sign of grace in the heart; for natural men have been some of the greatest leaders in this matter. To loathe my own sin, to humble myself on account of my own personal faults, and to endeavour in the sight of God to renounce every false way, is a work of something more than human nature. Will you also notice Jehu was very bitter against one sin. The very mention of the name of Baal brought the blood into his face, and there are persons in the world who cannot bear some one sin to which they have aversion; they love to hammer away against that; their whole soul takes fire at the mention of it. This is all very well; but, unless you hate all sin, unless you hate especially the besetting sin which is most congenial to your own nature, you need to be converted.

FOR MEDITATION: The Lord Jesus Christ could rightly be described as 'the friend of sinners' (Luke 7:34; 15:2), but never as 'the friend of fault-finders' (Matthew 12:2,7; Mark 7:5–9; Luke 5:30–32; 7:39,44–47; 11:38–40,42; John 8:3–7). What fault do you habitually find in others?

Jesus appearing to Mary Magdalene

'Now when Jesus was risen early the first day of the week, he appeared first to Mary Magdalene, out of whom he had cast seven devils.' Mark *16:9*
SUGGESTED FURTHER READING: John 20:11–18

He said, 'Go tell my brethren;' and away she went to tell others that she had found the Saviour. If you have the privilege of seeing Christ, do not eat the morsel behind the door. Have you found honey? Taste it yourself, but go and tell others. You cannot have seen much of the Saviour, unless you desire to let others see him. Your piety is a mere sham if it does not lead to practical service. Are there not some Mary Magdalenes here who have had seven devils cast out of them? You have felt the power of divine grace in your heart; you love the Saviour; you long for communion with him. My dear sister, as soon as you have fellowship, do not be afraid to speak to others what the Lord shall say in private to you. We do not want women to enter the pulpit; that is a violation both of grace and nature, and as much an offence to good manners as it is to God's own law; but you have your own sphere, you have your own place of work, you can gather your own sex about you, also your children; you have many opportunities; tell others that Jesus has risen, that there is a risen life; that you know it, and that you pant and long that others too should rise from the grave of sin to the new life in Jesus.

As for you, men and brethren, to whom it pertains more particularly to be teachers and pastors, I charge you, whatsoever you have found within the circle of fire where the closest communion is, whatsoever Christ has revealed to you in hours of retirement when you have come nearest to him, tell it to his family, feed his flock with it.

FOR MEDITATION: Women are not to exercise spiritual authority over men (1 Corinthians 14:33–35; 1 Timothy 2:11–14), but men should value and encourage their numerous God-given ministries both at home (Acts 16:15; 1 Corinthians 7:13,16; 1 Timothy 5:14; 2 Timothy 1:5; 3:15; Titus 2:4–5; 1 Peter 3:1–2,5) and in the wider church family (Luke 8:2; Acts 9:36,39; 18:26; Romans 16:1–6; Philippians 4:2–3; 1 Timothy 5:10; Titus 2:3–4).

The great liberator

'If the Son therefore shall make you free, ye shall be free indeed.' John 8:36
SUGGESTED FURTHER READING: Romans 8:12–17

If you are free, then remember that *you have changed your lodging-place*, for the slave and the son sleep not in the same room of the house. The things which satisfied you when a slave will not satisfy you now. You wear a garment which a slave may never wear, and you feel an instinct within you which the slave can never feel. There is an Abba, Father cry in you, which was not there once. Is it so? If you are free *you live not as you used to do.* You go not to the slave's work, you have not now to toil and sweat to earn the wages of sin which is death, but now as a son serves his father, you do a son's work and you expect to receive a son's reward, for the gift of God is eternal life through Jesus Christ our Lord. One thing I know, if you are free, then *you are thinking about setting others free*; and if you have no zeal for the emancipation of other men, you are a slave yourself. If you are free *you hate all sorts of chains*, all sorts of sin, and you will never willingly put on the fetters any more. You live each day, crying unto him who made you free at first, to hold you up that you fall not into the snare. If you are free, this is not the world for you; this is the land of slaves; this is the world of bondage. If you are free, your heart has gone to heaven, the land of the free. If you are free today, your spirit is longing for the time when you shall see the great liberator face to face. If you are free, you will bide your time until he calls you; but when he says, 'Friend, come up hither,' you will fearlessly mount to the upper spheres, and sin shall be no hindrance to your advent to his glory.

FOR MEDITATION: Men can promise freedom and deliver the opposite (2 Peter 2:19); Christ can actually free us from sin and from sinning (Romans 6:18,22; 8:2). The Christian should not return to slavery (Galatians 5:1), but say with the Psalmist 'I walk at liberty' (Psalm 119:45).

N.B. Spurgeon began this sermon by referring to the visit of Garibaldi, the Italian patriot and liberator, to England (3–27 April 1864).

SERMON NO. 565

Exposition of the doctrines of grace (2. Introduction to evening session)

SUGGESTED READING: Ezekiel 37:1–14

There are some who say, 'To what purpose after all, is your inviting any to come, when the Spirit of God alone constrains them to come; and why, especially, preach to those whom you believe to be so depraved that they cannot and will not come?' Just so, this is a serious difficulty to everything except faith. Do you see Ezekiel yonder; he is about to preach a sermon. By his leave, we will stop him. 'Ezekiel, where are you about to preach?' 'I am about,' says he, 'to preach to a strange congregation—dead, dry bones, lying in a mass in a valley.' 'But, Ezekiel, they have no power to live.' 'I know that,' says he. 'To what purpose, then, is your preaching to them? If they have no power, and if the breath must come from the four winds, and they have no life in themselves, to what purpose do you preach?' 'I am ordered to preach,' says he, 'commanded;' and he does so. He prophesies, and afterwards mounting to a yet higher stage of faith, he cries, 'Come from the four winds, O breath, and breathe upon these slain, that they may live.' And the wind comes, and the effect of his ministry is seen in their life. So we preach to dead sinners; so we pray for the living Spirit. So, by faith, do we expect his divine influence, and it comes, not from man, nor of man, nor by blood, nor by the will of the flesh, but from the sovereign will of God. But notwithstanding it comes instrumentally through the faith of the preacher while he pleads with man—'as though God did beseech you by us: we pray you in Christ's stead, be ye reconciled to God.'

FOR MEDITATION: The necessary ingredients for a work of salvation are a dead sinner, a loving Father, a crucified and risen Saviour, a life-giving Spirit, and last, but by no means least, the faithful communication of the Gospel. Without it how shall people hear, believe in the Lord and call on him (Romans 10:14)? Remember the God-ordained route to saving faith (Romans 10:17).

Strong meat

'But strong meat belongeth to them that are of full age, even those who by reason of use have their senses exercised to discern both good and evil.'
Hebrews 5:14
SUGGESTED FURTHER READING: 1 Corinthians 10:1–11

Holy Scripture is to be received, not only as a literal description of facts which really did occur, but as a picture in which grace-taught souls, illuminated by the Holy Spirit, may see portrayed in express characters the great gospel of the living God. Those of you who are well instructed will have found out by this time that Genesis is the *History of Dispensations*; that in all its types it sets forth, from Adam to Joseph the various dispensations of primeval innocence, man without law, under law, in covenant and many other things. You will have discovered that Exodus is the *Book of Redemptions*. Here is redemption by blood when the paschal lamb was slain; redemption by power when God broke the armies of Egypt, smiting Pharaoh in the midst of the Red Sea. Leviticus is the *Handbook of communion*, the *Guide to Access*, opening to us the way in which God can come to man, and man can go to God. And I am sure the least observant of you must have discovered that Numbers is the *Record of Experience*, for all those journeyings of the children of Israel to and fro when they lived in the wilderness, sometimes by bitter fountain, and at other times by spreading palms, all describe the constant forward march of the sacred army of God to the Promised Land; while the Books of Joshua and Judges typify the history of the people who have entered into the land of Canaan, who are saved, but who have to fight with their corruptions, who have to fight with the Canaanites that are still in the land, and to drive them out despite their chariots of iron. I believe that every book of Scripture has some special lesson beyond its historical import.

FOR MEDITATION: Is much of the Old Testament a closed book to you? The Lord Jesus Christ said to His enemies 'Did ye never read in the scriptures?' (Matthew 21:42) and 'Ye do err, not knowing the scriptures' (Matthew 22:29). It is very sad if the same things can be said to his friends.

Resurrection—Christ the firstfruits

'But now is Christ risen from the dead, and become the firstfruits of them that slept.' 1 Corinthians 15:20

SUGGESTED FURTHER READING: Romans 6:5–11

Why is it that the resurrection of Christ is of so much importance? Upon it we have said that the whole system of Christianity rests; for 'if Christ be not risen, then is our preaching vain, and your faith is also vain... ye are yet in your sins' (1 Corinthians 15:14,17). The *divinity* of Christ finds its surest proof in his resurrection, since the apostle tells us that Christ was 'declared to be the Son of God with power, according to the spirit of holiness, by the resurrection from the dead' (Romans 1:4). It would not be unreasonable to doubt his deity if he had not risen. Moreover, Christ's *sovereignty* also depends upon his resurrection, for Scripture affirms: 'to this end Christ both died, and rose, and revived, that he might be Lord both of the dead and living' (Romans 14:9). Again, our *justification*, that choice blessing of the covenant, hangs upon Christ's resurrection. He 'was delivered for our offences, and was raised again for our justification' (Romans 4:25). Our very *regeneration* depends upon his resurrection, for Peter, speaking by the Holy Spirit, exclaims, 'Blessed be the God and Father of our Lord Jesus Christ, which according to his abundant mercy hath begotten us again unto a lively hope by the resurrection of Jesus Christ from the dead' (1 Peter 1:3). And most certainly our *ultimate resurrection* rests here; for 'if the Spirit of him that raised up Jesus from the dead dwell in you, he that raised up Christ from the dead shall also quicken your mortal bodies by his Spirit that dwelleth in you' (Romans 8:11). If Christ be not risen, then we shall not rise; but if he be risen, then they who are asleep in Christ have not perished, but in their flesh shall surely behold their God.

FOR MEDITATION: A great emphasis was placed by the preachers of the early church upon the resurrection of the Lord Jesus Christ as well as upon his death (Acts 2:24,31–32; 3:15,26; 4:10,33; 5:30; 10:40–41; 13:30,33–34,37; 17:3,18,31; 26:23). Is it important to you?

The missionaries' charge and authority

'And Jesus came and spake unto them, saying, All power is given unto me in heaven and in earth; go ye, therefore, and teach all nations, baptizing them in the name of the Father, and of the Son, and of the Holy Ghost.'
Matthew 28:18–19
SUGGESTED FURTHER READING: Acts 13:1–13

There are some young men who get the idea into their minds that they would like to go into foreign lands; but these are frequently the most unfit men, and have not the power and ability. I pray that the divine call would come to some gifted men. You who have, perhaps, some wealth of your own, what could be a better object in life than to devote yourself and your substance to the Redeemer's cause? You young men, who have brilliant prospects before you, but who as yet have not the anxieties of a family to maintain, why, would it not be a noble thing to surrender your brilliant prospects, that you may become a humble preacher of Christ? I have questioned my own conscience, and I do not think I could be in the path of duty if I should go abroad to preach the Word, leaving this field of labour; but I think many of my brethren now labouring at home might with the greatest advantage surrender their charges, and go where their presence would be as valuable as the presence of a thousand such as they are here. And I long that we may see young men out of the universities, and students in our grammar schools— that we may see our physicians, advocates, tradesmen and educated mechanics, when God has touched their hearts, giving all they have, that they may teach and preach Christ. We want Judsons and Brainerds over again. It will never do to send out to the heathen men who are of no use at home; we must send the highest, and best.

FOR MEDITATION: Missionary work depends not upon the call of adventure but upon the call of God. Christ's apostles were properly prepared and stood the test of time (Mark 3:14; Luke 22:28; John 14:9; Acts 11:25–26; Galatians 1:15–18). John Mark became very useful in later years (2 Timothy 4:11) but appears to have gone out originally before he was called and ready (Acts 13:13; 15:38).

SERMON NO. 383

Messengers wanted

'Also I heard the voice of the LORD, saying, Whom shall I send, and who will go for us? Then said I, Here am I; send me.' Isaiah 6:8
SUGGESTED FURTHER READING: Romans 15:14–21

Ask any man whether he is a Christian against his will, and he will tell you certainly not, for he loves the Lord, and delights in his law after the inward man. Thy people are not led unwillingly to thee in chains, O Jesus, but 'Thy people shall be willing in the day of thy power.' We willingly choose Christ, because he has from of old chosen us. In the matter of holy work, every man who becomes a worker for Jesus is so because he was chosen to work for him; but he would be a very poor worker if he himself had not chosen to work for Jesus. I can say that I believe God ordained me to preach the gospel, and that I preach it by his will, but I am sure I preach it with my own; for it is to me the most delightful work in all the world, and if I could exchange with an emperor, I would not consent to be so lowered. To preach the gospel of Jesus Christ is one of the sweetest and noblest employments, and even an angel might desire to be engaged in it. The true worker for God must be impelled by divine election, but yet he must make and will make, by divine grace, his own election of his work. Here are the persons wanted. Are there not many such persons here who feel 'God has chosen me to do something for him; woe is unto me if I preach not the gospel'? but who, on the other hand, can testify, 'I choose the work too. For Christ's sake, whether it be teaching in the Sunday school, or tract distributing, or talking to ones or twos, or whatever it may be, my God, I choose the vocation; help me to follow it heartily, for it is my delight to do thy will, O my God.' Here is the divine side then, the man is chosen; but there is also the human side, the man is led to choose the engagement for himself.

FOR MEDITATION: We tend to assume that God's will must be diametrically opposed to our wills and that we can only do it grudgingly. But God can so transform our thinking that his will becomes 'good, and acceptable, and perfect' (Romans 12:2), our delight (Psalm 40:8) and joy (Romans 15:32).

SERMON NO. 687

The waterer watered

'He that watereth shall be watered also himself.' Proverbs 11:25
SUGGESTED FURTHER READING: Job 29:11–25

You would often find that in trying to water others you *gained instruction.*
Go talk to some poor saint to comfort her, and she will tell you what will
comfort you. Oh what gracious lessons some of us have learned at sick beds!
We went to teach the Scriptures; we came away blushing that we knew so
little of them. We went to talk experimental truth, and we found we were
only up to the ankles while here were God's poor saints breast-deep in the
river of divine love. We learn by teaching, and our pupils often teach us. You
will also *get comfort in your work.* Rest assured that working for others is
very happy exercise. Comfort God's people and the comfort will return into
your own soul. Watering others will make you *humble.* You will find better
people in the world than yourself. You will be astonished to find how much
grace there is where you thought there was none, and how much knowledge
some have gained, while you, as yet, have made little progress with far
greater opportunities. You will also *win many prayers.* Those who work for
others, get prayed for, and that is a swift way of growing rich in grace. Let me
have your prayers, and I can do anything! Let me be without my people's
prayers, and I can do nothing. You Sunday-school teachers, if you are
blessed to the conversion of the children, will get your children's prayers.
You that conduct the larger classes, in the conversion of your young people,
will be sure to have a wealth of love come back into your own hearts,
swimming upon the stream of supplication. You will thus be a blessing to
yourselves. In watering others you will *get honour to yourselves,* and that
will help to water you by stimulating your future exertions.

FOR MEDITATION: Nobody worked harder for others in the early church than
the apostle Paul (2 Corinthians 11:23,28); he received much refreshment
from those he served (Acts 27:3; Romans 15:32; 1 Corinthians 16:18;
2 Corinthians 7:4,13; 2 Timothy 1:16; Philemon 7,20). Do you lack
refreshment? Do you serve anybody?

General and yet particular

'Thou hast given him power over all flesh, that he should give eternal life to as many as thou hast given him.' John 17:2
SUGGESTED FURTHER READING: Ephesians 5:21–33

You know that passage: 'Husbands love your wives, even as Christ also loved the church and gave himself for it.' How did he love the church? He loved the church with a special love, far above that which he gives to others, or else according to that metaphor a husband ought to love his wife and love every other woman just as much. That is the natural inference of that text; but you clearly see there must have been a special love intended in the husband towards the wife, and so there must be a special love in Christ. He loved the church and gave himself for it. Now do you not think, brethren, as there are two sets of texts in the Bible, the one of which very clearly speaks about the infinite value of the atonement (e.g. 1 Timothy 2:6; 1 John 2:2), and another which very evidently speaks about the intention of that atonement being for the chosen and for the chosen only (e.g. John 10:11; Ephesians 5:25; Revelation 14:4), that the best way is to believe them both, and to say, 'Yes, I see it—as the result of Christ's death all men are put under the system of mediatorial grace so that Christ has power over them; but the object of his doing this is not that he may save all of them, but that he may save out of these all which he now has in his own hand—those whom the Father has given him.' The farmer trusts me with all his sheep in order that I may sever from them twenty which he has marked. A father tells me to go into the midst of his family, his whole family, in order that I may take out of it one of his sons to be educated. So God gives to Christ all flesh, says the text, but still always with this definite and distinct purpose that he may give eternal life to those whom he has given to him.

FOR MEDITATION: As 'the Saviour of all men, specially of those that believe' (1 Timothy 4:10), God displays common grace to all people and special grace to his chosen people. Christians should likewise 'do good unto all men, especially unto them who are of the household of faith' (Galatians 6:10).

SERMON NO. 566

Exposition of the doctrines of grace (3. Introduction of closing speaker)

SUGGESTED READING: Romans 11:25–36

Has it never struck you that the scheme of doctrine which is called Calvinism has much to say concerning God? It commences and ends with the Divine One. It dwells with God; he begins, he carries on, he perfects; it is for his glory and for his honour. Father, Son, and Spirit co-working, the whole gospel scheme is carried out. Perhaps there may be a defect in our theology; we may perhaps too much forget man. I think that is a very small fault, compared with the fault of the opposite system, which begins with man, and all but ends with him. Man is a creature; how ought God to deal with him? That is the question some theologians seem to answer. The way we put it is—God is the Creator, he has a right to do as he wills; he is Sovereign, there is no law above him, he has a right to make and to unmake, and when man has sinned, he has a right to save or to destroy. If he can save, and yet not impair his justice, heaven shall ring with songs; if he destroy, and yet his goodness be not marred, then hell itself with its deep bass of misery, shall swell the mighty rollings of his glorious praise. We hold that God should be most prominent in all our teaching; and we hold this to be a gauge by which to test the soundness of ministers. If they exalt God and sink the sinner to the very dust, it is all well; but if they lower the prerogatives of deity, if he be less sovereign, less just, or less loving than the Scripture reveals him to be, and if man be puffed up with that fond notion that he is anything better than an unclean thing, then such theology is utterly unsound. Salvation is of the Lord, and let the Lord alone be glorified.

FOR MEDITATION: We are to boast in the Lord and exalt his name (Psalm 34:2–3). Does your theology in every way exalt him and humble yourself or in any way do the opposite? We should always glory in him, never in ourselves (1 Corinthians 1:29,31; 2 Corinthians 10:17).

God's estimate of time

'But, beloved, be not ignorant of this one thing, that one day is with the Lord as a thousand years, and a thousand years as one day.' 2 Peter 3:8
SUGGESTED FURTHER READING: Exodus 3:1–15

With God there is neither past, present, nor future. He takes for his name the 'I AM.' He does not call himself the 'I WAS,' for then we should conceive that he used to be something which he is not now, that some part of his character had changed, or some attribute ceased from existence; for there is an ominous sound of annihilation in the sound of the word, 'HE WAS.' Is it not rather a knell for the dead, than a name for the living? Nor does our Lord God speak of himself as the 'I SHALL BE,' for that might lead us to imagine that he is not now something which he is to be in the ages to come: whereas we know that his being is perfect, his essence infinite, his dominion absolute, his power unlimited, and his glory transcendent. Development is out of the question; he is all today that he will be in the future. Of the Lord Jesus we read that he is the everlasting Father, and yet he has the dew of his youth. Childhood, manhood and old age belong to creatures, but at the right hand of the Most High they have no abode. Growth, progress, advancement, all these are virtues in finite beings, but to the Infinite the thought of such change would be an insult. Yesterday, today, and tomorrow belong to dying mortals; the Immortal King lives in an eternal today. He is the I AM; I AM in the present; I AM in the past; and I AM in the future. Just as we say of God that he is everywhere, so we may say of him that he is always; he is everywhere in space; he is everywhere in time. God is today in the past; he is today already in the future; he is today in that present in which we are.

FOR MEDITATION: The fact that God never changes is absolutely fundamental and essential to the wellbeing and survival of his people (Malachi 3:6; Mark 12:26–27; Hebrews 13:5,8; James 1:17).

27 APRIL (1862)

The Lord's care of His people

'He that toucheth you, toucheth the apple of mine eye.' Zechariah 2:8
SUGGESTED FURTHER READING: Ecclesiastes 8:10–14

I am not one of those who look upon everything that happens in this world as being a judgment from God. If a boat goes down to the bottom of the sea on a Sunday, I do not look upon that as a judgment on those who are in it, any more than if it had gone to the bottom on a Monday; and though many good people get frightened when they hear one affirm this doctrine, yet I cannot help their frights, but like my Master I must tell them that they who perish so are not sinners above all the sinners that be in Jerusalem. I looked the other day at *Foxe's Book of Martyrs,* and I saw there an illustration of that deeply-rooted mistake of Christian people, concerning God's always punishing men's sins in this life. Foxe draws a picture of a Popish priest who is insulting the faith, speaking lightly of the blood of Jesus, and exalting Mary, and he drops down dead in the pulpit; and Foxe holds him up as a picture of a great sinner who dropped down dead for speaking lightly of Jesus, and the good man affirms the wicked priest's death to be a judgment from heaven. Well, perhaps Foxe is correct, but still I do not see the connection between his dropping down dead and the language he employed, for many a preacher who has been exalting Christ has fallen down dead in the pulpit; and happy was it for such a man that he was engaged in minding his charge at the time. The fact is, providence smites good men and bad men too; and when the storm rages, and the hurricane howls through the forest, not only are the brambles and briars shaken and uprooted, but goodly oaks crack and break too. We are not to look for God's judgments, except in special cases, in this life. This judgment is in the world to come.

FOR MEDITATION: Beware of jumping to false conclusions. The apostle Paul was the frequent victim not only of persecution (2 Corinthians 11:23–25), but also of natural accidents (2 Corinthians 11:25–27). The latter were not inconsistent with him being in the centre of God's will (Acts 27:21–26).

Full assurance

'Say unto my soul, I am thy salvation.' Psalm 35:3
SUGGESTED FURTHER READING: Micah 7:1–10

Let us hear the text. 'Say unto my soul, I am thy salvation.' The first thing the text seems to say is, *David had his doubts, then*; for why would he pray, 'Say unto my soul, I am thy salvation,' if he were not sometimes exercised with doubts and fears? Cheer up, Christian brother! If David doubted, you must not say, 'I am no Christian, because I have doubts.' The best of believers sometimes are troubled with fears and anxieties. Abraham had the greatest faith, but he had some unbelief. I envy the brother who can say that his faith never wavered. He can say more than David did, for David had cause to cry, 'Say unto my soul, I am thy salvation.'

But, next, the text says that *David was not content while he had doubts and fears*, but he repaired at once to the mercy seat to pray for assurance; for he valued it as much fine gold. 'O Lord!' David seems to say, 'I have lost my confidence; my foot slips; my feet are almost gone; my doubts and fears prevail; but I cannot bear it. I am wretched, I am unhappy.' 'Say—say unto my soul, I am thy salvation.''

And then the text tells you yet a third thing—that *David knew where to obtain full assurance*. He goes at once to God in prayer. He knows that knee-work is that by which faith is increased; and there, in his closet, he cries out to the Most High, 'Say unto my soul, I am thy salvation.' O my brethren, we must be much alone with God, if we would have a clear sense of his love! Let your cries cease, and your eyes will grow dim. Much in prayer, much in heaven; slow in prayer, slow in progress.

FOR MEDITATION: What is your recipe for dealing with doubts, fears and cares? The biblical way is not to pretend that they don't exist, but to face up to them before the Lord (Luke 12:29–31; Philippians 4:6; 1 Peter 5:7; 1 John 3:19–20).

Sweet savour

'I will accept you with your sweet savour.' Ezekiel 20:41
SUGGESTED FURTHER READING: Matthew 11:20–30

The Saviour's character has all goodness in all perfection; he is full of grace and truth. Some men, nowadays, talk of him as if he were simply incarnate benevolence. It is not so. No lips ever spoke with such thundering indignation against sin as the lips of the Messiah. 'He is like a refiner's fire, and like fullers' soap;' his 'fan is in his hand, and he will throughly purge his floor.' While in tenderness he prays for his tempted disciple, that his faith may not fail, yet with awful sternness he winnows the heap, and drives away the chaff into unquenchable fire. We speak of Christ as being meek and lowly in spirit, and so he was, but his meekness was balanced by his courage, and by the boldness with which he denounced hypocrisy. 'Woe unto you, scribes and Pharisees, hypocrites! ...Ye fools and blind; ...ye serpents, ye generation of vipers, how can ye escape the damnation of hell?' These are not the words of the milksop some authors represent Christ to have been. He is a man—a real man throughout—a God-like man—gentle as a woman, but yet stern as a warrior in the midst of the day of battle. The character is balanced; as much of one virtue as of another. As in Deity every attribute is full orbed; justice never eclipses mercy, nor mercy justice, nor justice faithfulness; so in the character of Christ you have all the excellent things, 'whatsoever things are true, whatsoever things are honest, whatsoever things are just, whatsoever things are pure, whatsoever things are lovely, whatsoever things are of good report;' you have them all; but not one of them casts a shadow on another; they shine each and all with undimmed splendour.

FOR MEDITATION: Is this the Jesus you love and worship, or do you only believe in a 'Gentle Jesus, meek and mild'? Failure to accept fully the Lord Jesus Christ of the New Testament, is to follow a 'false Christ' (Matthew 24:24) or 'another Jesus' (2 Corinthians 11:4), an idol of your own or somebody else's imagination. That is no better than following Baal or some other false god!

Justification and glory

'Whom he justified, them he also glorified.' Romans 8:30
SUGGESTED FURTHER READING: Revelation 21:22–22:5

If I might very hastily divide this glory into its constituent elements, I think I should say it means perfect rest. 'There remaineth therefore a rest to the people of God;' life in its fullest sense; life with emphasis; eternal life; nearness to God; closeness to the divine heart; a sense of his love shed abroad in all its fulness; likeness to Christ; fulness of communion with him; abundance of the Spirit of God, being filled with all the fulness of God; an excess of joy; a perpetual influx of delight; perfection of holiness; no stain nor thought of sin; perfect submission to the divine will; a delight and acquiescence in, and conformity to that will; absorption as it were into God, the creature still the creature, but filled with the Creator to the brim; serenity caused by a sense of safety; continuance of heavenly service; an intense satisfaction in serving God day and night; bliss in the society of perfect spirits and glorified angels; delight in the retrospect of the past, delight in the enjoyment of the present, and in the prospect of the future; something ever new and evermore the same; a delightful variety of satisfaction, and a heavenly sameness of delight; clear knowledge; absence of all clouds; ripeness of understanding; excellence of judgment; and, above all, an intense vigour of heart, and the whole of the heart set upon him whom our eye shall see to be altogether lovely! I have looked at the crests of a few of the waves as I see them breaking over the sea of immortality. I have tried to give you the names of a few of the peaks of the long alpine range of glory. But where are my words, and where are my thoughts? 'Eye hath not seen, nor ear heard, neither have entered into the heart of man, the things which God hath prepared for them that love him.'

FOR MEDITATION: We cannot comprehend the glory of our Christian inheritance (1 Corinthians 13:12; 1 John 3:2), which is the opposite of what we deserve as those who 'have sinned, and come short of the glory of God' (Romans 3:23). Are you 'justified by faith' in the Lord Jesus Christ and able to 'rejoice in hope of the glory of God' (Romans 5:1–2)?

SERMON NO. 627

Labour in vain

'Jonah said unto them, Take me up, and cast me forth into the sea; so shall the sea be calm unto you: for I know that for my sake this great tempest is upon you. Nevertheless the men rowed hard to bring it to the land; but they could not.' Jonah 1:12–13
SUGGESTED FURTHER READING: Matthew 12:38–42

Jesus came down into this ship of our common humanity to deliver it from tempest. The vessel had been tossed about on all sides by the waves of divine wrath. Men had been tugging and toiling at the oar; year after year philosopher and teacher had been seeking to establish peace with God; victims had been offered and rivers of blood had flowed, and even the first-born of man's body had been offered up; but the deep was still tempestuous. But Jesus came, and they took him and cast him overboard. Out of the city they dragged him; 'Away with him, away with him, it is not fit that he should live.' As he, Jesus dies, there is a calm. Deep was the peace which fell upon the earth that dreadful day; and joyous is that calm which yet shall come as the result of the casting out of that representative man who 'suffered for sins, the just for the unjust, that he might bring us to God.' Brethren I wish I had suitable words with which I could fitly describe the peace which comes to a human heart when we learn to see Jesus cast into the sea of divine wrath on our account. Conscience accuses no longer. Judgment now decides for the sinner instead of against him. Memory can look back upon past sins, with sorrow for the sin it is true, but yet with no dread of any penalty to come. It is a blessed thing for a man to know that he cannot be punished, that heaven and earth may shake, but he cannot be punished for his sin.

FOR MEDITATION: Jonah was a type of Christ. He was sent by God (Jonah 1:1–2; 1 John 4:10); sacrificed as God's gift to save the perishing (Jonah 1:6,11–15; John 3:16); swallowed and buried (Jonah 1:17; 1 Corinthians 15:4a); surfacing again (Jonah 2:10; 1 Corinthians 15:4b); successful (Jonah 3:5,10; Luke 24:46–47). At every point 'a greater than Jonas is here' (Matthew 12:41).

SERMON NO. 567

The great arbitration case

'Neither is there any daysman betwixt us, that might lay his hand upon us both.' Job 9:33
SUGGESTED FURTHER READING: 1 Timothy 2:1–6

We have all been thinking lately about the Atlantic cable. It is a very interesting attempt to join two worlds together. That cable has had to be sunk into the depths of the sea, in the hope of establishing a union between the two worlds, and now we are disappointed again. But what an infinitely greater wonder has been accomplished. Christ Jesus sank down deep into the woes of man till all God's waves and billows had gone over him, that he might become the great telegraphic communication between God and poor sinners. Let me say to you, sinner, that there was no failure in the laying down of that blessed cable. It went down deep; the end was well secured, and it went into the depths of our sin and woe; and on the other side it has gone right up to the eternal throne, and is fastened there by God himself. You may work that telegraph today, and you may easily understand the art of working it too. A sigh or a tear will work it. Say, 'God be merciful to me a sinner,' and along the wire the message will flash, and will reach God before it comes from you. It is swifter far than earthly telegraphs; and there will come an answer back much sooner than you ever dream of, for it is promised—'Before they call I will answer; and while they are yet speaking, I will hear.' Who ever heard of such a communication as this between man and man? But it really does exist between sinners and God, since Christ has opened up a way from the depths of our sin to the heights of his glory.

FOR MEDITATION: Unlike the Atlantic cable, the way between God and man has needed establishing once only (Romans 6:10; Hebrews 7:25,27; 9:12,26,28; 10:10; 1 Peter 3:18); he has worked perfectly well ever since for all who come to God by him and will never need repairing.

N.B. A telegraph cable across the Atlantic was first established, after three failures, in 1866. This undated sermon appeared in November 1865.

The power of prayer and the pleasure of praise

'Ye also helping together by prayer for us, that for the gift bestowed upon us by the means of many persons thanks may be given by many on our behalf.' 2 Corinthians 1:11

SUGGESTED FURTHER READING: Acts 1:12–15

We cannot all preach; we cannot all rule; we cannot all give gold and silver, but we can all contribute our prayers. There is no convert, though he be only two or three days old in grace, who cannot pray. There is no bedridden sister in Jesus who cannot pray; there is no sick, aged, illiterate or penniless believer, who cannot add his supplications to the general stock. This is the church's riches. We put boxes at the door that we may receive your offerings to God's cause—remember there is a spiritual chest within the church, into which we should all drop our loving intercessions, as into the treasury of the Lord. Even the widow, without her two mites, can give her offering to this treasury. See, then, dear friends, what union and communion there are among the people of God, since there are certain mercies which are only bestowed when the saints unitedly pray. How we ought to feel this bond of union! How we ought to pray for one another! How, as often as the church meets together for supplication, should we all make it our bounden duty to be there! I would that some of you who are absent from the prayer meeting upon any little excuse would reflect how much you rob us all. The prayer meeting is an invaluable institution, ministering strength to all other meetings and agencies. Are there not many of you who might come among us a little oftener? And what if you lose a customer now and then, do you not think that this loss could be well made up to you by your gains on other days? Or if not so, would not the spiritual profit much more than counterbalance any little temporal loss? 'Not forgetting the assembling of yourselves together, as the manner of some is.'

FOR MEDITATION: United congregational and group prayer is of vital importance (2 Chronicles 7:14; Ezra 8:21–23; Daniel 2:17–19; Matthew 18:19–20; Acts 1:14,24; 2:1,42; 4:24,31; 12:5,12; 1 Timothy 2:1,8). How much of a contribution do you make to the prayer meeting?

SERMON NO. 507

Another and a nobler exhibition

'To the intent that now unto the principalities and powers in heavenly places might be known by the church the manifold wisdom of God.'
Ephesians 3:10
SUGGESTED FURTHER READING: Revelation 7:9–12

Let the angel speak awhile for himself. 'Here,' says he, 'I see men of all nations, and kindreds, and tongues, from Britain to Japan, from the frozen north to the burning zone beneath the equator; here I see souls of all ages, babes hither snatched from the womb and breast, and spirits that once knew palsied age to whom the grasshopper was a burden. Here I see men from all periods, from Adam and Abel down to the men who were alive and remained at the coming of the Son of God from heaven. Here I see them of all classes. There is one who was a king, and another that tugged the oar as a galley-slave. There I see a merchant prince who counted not his riches dear unto him, and by his side a poor man who was rich in faith and heir of the kingdom. Here I see Magdalene and Saul of Tarsus, repenting sinners of all shades and saints of all varieties, those who showed their patience on a lingering sick bed, those who triumphed with holy boldness amid the red flames, those who wandered about in sheepskins and goatskins, destitute, afflicted, tormented, of whom the world was not worthy; the monk who shook the world, and he who cast salt into the stream of doctrine and made it wholesome and pure; the man who preached to his millions, and brought tens of thousands of souls to Christ, and the humble cottager who knew but this Bible true—here they all are.'

FOR MEDITATION: God alone knows how many Christ has redeemed from every kindred, tongue, people and nation (Revelation 5:9; 7:9–10). Do you want to be in that number? Have you responded to the gospel proclaimed worldwide (Revelation 14:6–7)?

N.B. This sermon followed the opening in London of the 2nd Great International Exhibition on 1 May 1862.

SERMON NO. 448

The first resurrection

'Blessed and holy is he that hath part in the first resurrection; on such the second death hath no power, but they shall be priests of God and of Christ, and shall reign with him a thousand years.' Revelation 20:6
SUGGESTED FURTHER READING: John 5:19–29

Damnation, the second death, shall have no power on those who rise at the first resurrection. How can damnation fall on any but those who are sinners and are guilty of sin? But the saints are not guilty of sin. They have sinned like others, and they were by nature the children of wrath even as others. Their sin has been lifted from them: it was laid upon the scapegoat's head of old. He, the eternal substitute, even our Lord Jesus, carried all their guilt and their iniquity into the wilderness of forgetfulness, where it shall never be found against them for ever. They wear the Saviour's righteousness, even as they have been washed in his blood; and what wrath can lie on the man who is not only guiltless through the blood, but is meritorious through imputed righteousness? O arm of justice, you are nerveless to smite the blood-washed! O flames of hell, how could even so much as the breath of your heat pass upon the man who is safe covered in the Saviour's wounds? How is it possible for you, O deaths, destructions, horrors, glooms, plagues, and terrors, so much as to flit like a cloud over the serene sky of the spirit which has found peace with God through the blood of Christ? No, brethren, 'Bold shall I stand in that great day …' There shall be a second death; but over us it shall have no power. Do you understand the beauty of the picture? As if we might walk through the flames of hell and they should have no power to devour us any more than when the holy children paced with ease over the hot coals of Nebuchadnezzar's seven times heated furnace.

FOR MEDITATION: Only God's saving power can free us from the power of the second death (Jude 25). How terrifying must be the fate of the unbeliever, cut off from God's saving power (2 Thessalonians 1:9), but still under his condemning power (Luke 12:5).

SERMON NO. 391

Temptations on the pinnacle

'Then the devil taketh him up into the holy city, and setteth him on a pinnacle of the temple, and saith unto him, If thou be the Son of God, cast thyself down: for it is written, He shall give his angels charge concerning thee: and in their hands they shall bear thee up, lest at any time thou dash thy foot against a stone. Jesus said unto him, It is written again, Thou shalt not tempt the Lord thy God.' Matthew 4:5–7

SUGGESTED FURTHER READING: 2 Peter 2:9–22

It is a precious doctrine that the saints are safe, but it is a damnable inference from it, that therefore they may live as they please. It is a glorious truth that God will keep his people, but it is an abominable falsehood that sin will do them no harm. Remember that God gives us liberty, not licence, and while he gives us protection, he will not allow us presumption. I did know a person once when I was a child; I remember seeing him go into a country wake in a little village where I lived, though he was a professed Christian, going to spend the evening in a dancing booth with others, drinking as other men did, and when I in my warm zeal said to him, 'What doest thou here, Elijah?' his reply was, 'I am a child of God, and I can go where I like and yet be safe,' and though for the moment I knew not what text to quote to answer him, yet my soul revolted from the man ever afterwards, for I felt that no child of God would ever be so wicked as to take poison in the faith that his Father would give him the antidote, or thrust himself into the fire, in the hope that he should not be burned. If God sends me trouble he will yield me deliverance from it, but if I make trouble myself I must bear it. If providence permits the devil to set me upon a pinnacle, even then God will help me, but if I throw myself down, and go in the very teeth of providence, then woe unto me, for I give proof by my presumption that the grace of God is not in me at all. Yet the temptation is not uncommon.

FOR MEDITATION: How would you have answered this man 'Elijah' who had no regard for his own soul or for the young Spurgeon's? Christian liberty does not provide a loophole for the flesh (Romans 13:13–14; Galatians 5:13) or for being a stumbling block to others (Romans 14:13).

A glorious church

'Husbands, love your wives, even as Christ also loved the church, and gave himself for it; that he might sanctify and cleanse it with the washing of water by the word, that he might present it to himself a glorious church, not having spot, or wrinkle, or any such thing.' Ephesians 5:25–27
SUGGESTED FURTHER READING: Jeremiah 31:1–3; 31–34

A husband loves his wife with a *constant* love, and so does Christ his church. He will not cast her away tomorrow having loved her today. He does not vary in his affection. He may change in his display of affection, but the affection itself is still the same. A husband loves his wife with an *enduring* love; it never will die out: he says, 'Till death us do part will I cherish thee;' but Christ will not even let death part his love to his people. Nothing 'shall be able to separate us from the love of God, which is in Christ Jesus our Lord.' A husband loves his wife with a *hearty* love, with a love that is true and intense. It is not mere lip-service. He does not merely speak, but he acts; he is ready to provide for her wants; he will defend her character; he will vindicate her honour, because his heart is set upon her. It is not merely with the eye that he delights now and then to glance upon her, but his soul has her continually in his remembrance: she has a mansion in his heart from whence she can never be cast away. She has become a portion of himself; she is a member of his body, she is part of his flesh and of his bones; and so is the church to Christ for ever, an eternal spouse. He says, 'Forget thee, I will not, I cannot ...' This church is only a church of Christ, because he has made her so. She had no right or title to his affection; he loved her because he chose to do so, and having once loved her, he never will divorce her: she shall be his, world without end.

FOR MEDITATION: The institution of marriage has been marred by divorce and human hardness of heart (Matthew 19:3–9); but it was designed both to depict the relationship between Christ and the church (Ephesians 5:31–32) and to follow the example of that relationship (Ephesians 5:23–25).

SERMON NO. 628

What God cannot do!

'God, that cannot lie.' Titus 1:2
SUGGESTED FURTHER READING: John 17:6–19

Walking through our museums nowadays, we smile at those who think that Scripture is not true. Every block of stone from Nineveh, every relic which has been brought from the Holy Land, speaks with a tongue which must be heard even by the deaf adder of secularism, and which says, 'Yes, the Bible is true, and the Word of God is no fiction.' Beloved, we may rest assured that we have not a word in the Book of God which is untrue. There may be an interpolation or two of man's which ought to be revised and taken away, but the Book as it comes from God is truth, and nothing but truth; not only containing God's Word, but being God's Word; being not like a lump of gold inside a mass of quartz, but all gold, and nothing but gold; and being inspired to the highest degree. I will not say verbally inspired but more than that, having a fulness more than that which the letter can convey, having in it a profundity of meaning such as words never had when used by any other being, God having the power to speak a multitude of truths at once. And when he means to teach us one thing according to our capability of receiving it, he often teaches us twenty other things, which for the time we do not comprehend, but which by and by, as our senses are exercised, reveal themselves by the Holy Spirit. Every time I open my Bible I will read it as the Word of 'God, that cannot lie;' and when I get a promise or a threatening, I will either rejoice or tremble because I know that these stand fast.

FOR MEDITATION: Because God cannot lie (Hebrews 6:18), he does not lie (Numbers 23:19). Every word of his is pure truth (Proverbs 30:5; John 17:17). Do you love that as good news or hate it as bad news?

SERMON NO. 568

Quiet musing!

'While I was musing the fire burned.' Psalm 39:3
SUGGESTED FURTHER READING: Psalm 119:97–104

The world has put a little letter before the word 'musing,' and these are the days, not for musing, but for a-musing. People will go anywhere for amusement; but to muse is a strange thing to them, and they think it dull and wearisome. Our fathers loved the quiet hour, and loved it so well, that they cherished those times which they could spend in musing as the most happy, because the most peaceful seasons of their life. We drag such time off to execution in a moment, and only ask men to tell us how we may kill it. Now there is much virtue in musing, especially if we muse upon the best, the highest, and the noblest of subjects. If we muse upon the things of which we hear and read in sacred Scripture, we shall do wisely. It is well to muse upon the things of God, because we thus get the real nutriment out of them. A man who hears many sermons, is not necessarily well-instructed in the faith. We may read so many religious books, that we overload our brains, and they may be unable to work under the weight of the great mass of paper and printer's ink. The man who reads but one book, and that book his Bible, and then muses much upon it, will be a better scholar in Christ's school than he who merely reads hundreds of books, and muses not at all. And he, too, who gets but one sermon in a day, though it is an ill habit to stay away from half our Sabbath engagements, and only go out once, yet, he who hears but one sermon in a day, if he meditates much upon it, will get far more out of it than he who hears two or three but meditates not. Truth is something like the cluster of the vine: if you would have wine from it, you must bruise it; you must press and squeeze it many times.

FOR MEDITATION: The world sometimes describes Christians as killjoys. If meditation upon God's Word is the believer's joy and delight (Psalm 1:2; 104:34; 119:48,97) and if we fail to engage in it, perhaps the accusation is more accurate than we realise!

Comfort to seekers from what the Lord has not said

'I have not spoken in secret, in a dark place of the earth: I said not unto the seed of Jacob, Seek ye me in vain.' Isaiah 45:19
SUGGESTED FURTHER READING: Psalm 65:1–5

For the Lord to hear prayer is consistent with his nature. Whatever is consistent with God's nature, we believe is true. Now, we cannot perceive any attribute of God which would stand in the way of his hearing prayer. It might be supposed that his *justice* would; but that has been so satisfied by the atonement of Christ, that it rather pleads the other way. Since Christ has 'put away sin,' since he has purchased the blessing, it seems but just that God should accept those for whom Jesus died, and give the blessing which Christ has bought. All the attributes of God say to a sinner, 'Come, come; come to the throne of grace, and you shall have what you want.' *Power* puts out his strong arm and cries, 'I will help thee; fear not.' *Love* smiles through her bright eyes, and cries, 'I have loved thee with an everlasting love: therefore with lovingkindness have I drawn thee.' *Truth* speaks in her clear, plain language, saying, 'He that seeketh findeth; and to him that knocketh it shall be opened.' *Immutability* says, 'I am the Lord, I change not; therefore ye sons of Jacob are not consumed.' Every single attribute of the divine character—but you can think of these as well as I can—pleads for the man who prays; and I do not know—I never dreamed of a single attribute of Deity which could enter an objection. Therefore, I think, if the thing really will glorify God, and not dishonour him, he will certainly do it. 'But,' you say, 'I am such a great sinner.' That gives me another argument. Would it not greatly extol the love and the grace of God for him to give his grace to those that deserve it least?

FOR MEDITATION: The God whom we have all offended is not further offended, but pleased, when we admit that we deserve to be punished for our sin but ask him to save us for Jesus' sake (Luke 18:13–14; 2 Peter 3:9). The people who continue to offend him are those who by their refusal to seek him say 'Pay me that thou owest' (Matthew 18:28); that is extremely foolish, 'for the wages of sin is death' (Romans 6:23).

Joseph and his brethren

'*Joseph said ..., I am Joseph; ... And his brethren ... were troubled at his presence. And Joseph said ..., Come near to me ... And they came near. And he said, I am Joseph your brother, whom ye sold into Egypt. Now therefore be not grieved ... that ye sold me hither: for God did send me before you to preserve life.*' Genesis 45:3–5
SUGGESTED FURTHER READING: James 4:1–10

Every time you prefer the pleasures of this world to the joys of heaven, you spit in the face of Christ; every time when to gain in your business, you do an unrighteous thing, you are like Judas selling him for thirty pieces of silver; every time you make a false profession of religion, you give him a traitor's kiss; every word you have spoken against him, every hard thought you have had of him, has helped to complete your complicity with the great crowd which gathered around the cross of Calvary, to mock and jeer the Lord of life and glory. Now, if there be any sin which will make a man deeply penitent, I think that this sin when it is really brought home to the conscience will affect us. To slay him who did me no hurt, the holy and the harmless One! To assist in hounding to the tree the man who scattered blessings with both his hands, and who had no thought, nor care, nor love, save for those who hated him. To pierce the hands that touched the leper, and that broke the bread, and multiplied the fishes! To fasten to the accursed wood the feet which had often carried his weary body upon painful journeys of mercy! This is base indeed, but when I think he loved *me*, and gave himself for *me*, that he chose *me*, before the stars were made, and that I, when he came to me in the gospel, should have rejected and despised, and even mocked at him, this is intensely, infinitely cruel. Jesus, thou dost forgive me, but I can never forgive myself for such a sin as this.

FOR MEDITATION: Consider the effect of Christ's crucifixion upon those who mourn their guilt in it (Zechariah 12:10; 13:1; Acts 2:36–37). Are you washed from your sin by his blood (Revelation 1:5) or does your guilt wash off you like water off a duck's back (Acts 4:10,18; 5:30,40)? Many will regret it when it is too late (Revelation 1:7).

SERMON NO. 449

Trust in God—true wisdom

'He that handleth a matter wisely shall find good: and whoso trusteth in the LORD, happy is he.' Proverbs 16:20
SUGGESTED FURTHER READING: Proverbs 3:1–7

I am persuaded that faith is as much the rule of temporal as of spiritual life, and that we ought to have faith in God for our shops as well as for our souls. Worldly men may sneer at this, but it is none the less true; at any rate, I pray that it may be my course as long as I live. My dear friends, let me commend to you a life of trust in God in temporal things, by these few advantages among a great many others. First, trusting in God, you will not have to mourn because you have used sinful means to grow rich. Should you become poor through it, better to be poor with a clear conscience, than to be rich and guilty. You will have always this comfort should you come to the lowest position of human nature, that you have come there through no fault of your own. You have served God with integrity, and even if some should say you have missed your mark, and achieved no success, at least there is no sin upon your conscience. And then again, trusting God, you will not be guilty of self-contradiction. He who trusts in craft, sails this way today, and that way the next, like a vessel propelled by the fickle wind; but he that trusts in the Lord is like a vessel propelled by steam; she cuts through the waves, defies the wind, and makes one bright silvery track to her destined haven. Let men see that the world has changed, not you—that man's opinions and man's maxims have veered round to another quarter, but that you are still invincibly strong in the strength which trusting in God alone can confer.

FOR MEDITATION: It would be a sad situation if we had only the affairs of this life for which to trust God (1 Corinthians 15:19); but if we cannot trust him in material matters that we can see, how can we be sure that we are trusting him in spiritual matters that we cannot see? Great men of God did both (Psalm 23:6; 2 Timothy 4:18).

A lesson from the great panic

'The removing of those things that are shaken, as of things that are made, that those things which cannot be shaken may remain.' Hebrews 12:27
SUGGESTED FURTHER READING: 2 Peter 3:1—13

It is a most popular error that the world stands still, and is fixed and immovable. This has been scouted as an astronomical theory, but as a matter of practical principle it still reigns in men's minds. Galileo said, 'No, the world is not a fixed body, it moves;' Peter had long before declared that all these things should be dissolved; at last men believed the astronomer, but they still doubt the apostle, or at least forget his doctrine. Though it is clear as noonday in Scripture and in experience that stability is not to be found beneath the moon, yet men are for ever building upon earth's quicksand as if it were substantial rock, and heaping up its dust, as though it would not all be blown away. 'This is the substance,' cries the miser, as he clutches his bags of gold; 'heaven and hell are myths to me.' 'This is the main chance,' whispers the merchant, as he pushes vigorously his commercial speculations; 'as for spiritual things they are for mere dreamers and sentimentalists. Cash is the true treasure.' Ah, sirs, you base your statements upon a foundation of falsehood. This world is as certainly a mere revolving ball as to human life as it is astronomically; and hopes founded thereon will as surely come to nought as will card houses in a storm. Here we have no abiding city, and it is in vain to attempt to build one. This world is not the rock beneath our feet which it seems to be; it is no better than those green, but treacherous, soft, and bottomless bogs, which swallow up unwary travellers. We talk of *terra firma* as if there could be such a thing as solid earth; never was adjective more thoroughly misused, for 'the world passeth away' and the fashion thereof.

FOR MEDITATION: Spurgeon's sermons on 13 May 1866 (see also tomorrow's reading) were occasioned by an unexpected commercial panic over the previous two days. We should not rest our hopes on earthly possessions for this life (Haggai 1:5—6; Matthew 6:19; 1 Timothy 6:17), let alone for the life to come (Luke 12:15—21; 16:19—23; James 5:1—3).

SERMON NO. 690

An immovable foundation

'If the foundations be destroyed, what can the righteous do?' Psalm 11:3
SUGGESTED FURTHER READING: Psalm 46:1–11

There is something which the righteous man can do, if the foundations are removed, and that is, he can trust in God that it will be well in the end. The worldling says, 'It will be all the same a hundred years hence.' The Christian says, 'I do not want to look so far ahead as that; it is all right now.' But the wind blows! 'It is all right.' But the waves dash! 'It is all right.' But all the sails are reefed! 'It is all right!' But the ship flies before the wind! 'It is all right.' But there are rocks ahead! 'It is all right.' Why? 'Because he who is at the helm knows all about it; he created both wind and wave, and he knows how to cope with the storm. I cannot see that it is right, but I know that it is, and I walk by faith, and not by sight.' Christian, this is what you can do. If the foundations be removed, you can bring faith into heavenly exercise, and you can sail against the wind. The night may be dark and dreary but it will usher in the brighter morn, and merrily will the celestial music and songs greet his ears as the fresh dawning light triumphs over the fleeing darkness, and spreads itself till it bathes with its splendour all things which even in the darkness were working together for the good of God's people. Yes, the rough March winds and the dreary April showers were all fulfilling their task then, and now we can see it and rejoice in it as well as in their result. We will sing in our dungeon with Paul and Silas, for all is well now as it will be hereafter in heaven. It is only in degree and realisation that earth's joys differ from heaven's to the true believer in Christ.

FOR MEDITATION: Even in his darkest hours the Christian is already an heir of a hidden treasure kept safe for him in heaven (Matthew 6:20; Ephesians 1:18; 1 Timothy 6:19; 1 Peter 1:4). Are you going to inherit it?

The first five disciples

'The two disciples ... followed Jesus; ... One of the two ... was Andrew, Simon Peter's brother. He ... first findeth his own brother Simon; ... And he brought him to Jesus; ... The day following Jesus ... findeth Philip; ... Philip findeth Nathanael.' John 1:37,40–43,45
SUGGESTED FURTHER READING: 1 Corinthians 9:16–23

In the work of grace, there is ever the same kind of operation, and yet ever a difference in the manner of operation. There is always the same worker in the conversion of the soul, and yet different methods for breaking the heart and binding it up again are continually employed. Every sinner must be quickened by the same life, made obedient to the same gospel, washed in the same blood, clothed in the same righteousness, filled with the same divine energy, and eventually taken up to the same heaven, and yet in the conversion of no two sinners will you find matters precisely the same; but from the first dawn of the divine life to the day when it is consummated in the noontide of perfect sanctification in heaven, you shall find that God works this way in that one, and that way in the other, and by another method in the third; for God still will be the God of variety. Let his order stand fast as it may, still will he ever be manifesting the variety, the many-sidedness of his own thoughts and mind. If then you look at this narrative (John 1:37–51)— somewhat long, but I think very full of instruction—you may notice four different methods of conversion; and these occur in the conversion of the first five who formed the nucleus of the college of apostles—the first five who came to Christ, and were numbered among his disciples. It is very remarkable that there should be among five individuals four different ways of conversion. Pick out five Christians indiscriminately and begin to question how they were brought to know the Lord, and you would find methods other than those you have here.

FOR MEDITATION: The Lord Jesus Christ is the one and only way to God (John 14:6), but there are no end of ways of being led to faith in him. God may vary his methods, but he never changes his principles (1 Corinthians 12:4–6).

Turning back in the day of battle

'The children of Ephraim, being armed, and carrying bows, turned back in the day of battle.' Psalm 78:9
SUGGESTED FURTHER READING: Luke 9:51–62

They turned back in the day of battle. They turned back, it seems then, just when they were to be tried. How much there is we do that will not stand trial! How much there is of godliness which is useful for anything excepting that which it is meant for! It is all in vain for me to say, if I have bought a waterproof coat, that it is good for everything except keeping the water out. Why, then it is good for nothing, and so there are some Christians who have got a religion that is good for every day except the day when it has to be tested, and then it is good for nothing. An anchor may be very pretty on shore, and it may be very showy as an ornament when it lies on the ship's deck or hangs from the side, but what is the good of it if it will not hold when the wind blows and the vessel needs to be held fast? So, alas! there is much of religion and of godliness, so called, that is no good when it comes to the day of trial. The soldier is truly proved to be a soldier when the war-trumpet sounds and the regiment must go up to the cannon's mouth. Then shall you know, when the bayonets begin to cross, who has the true soldier's blood in him; but how many turn back when it really comes to the conflict, for then the day of trial is too much for them! They turned back at the only time when they were of any sort of use. A man who has to fight is not of any particular use to his country, that I know of, except when there is fighting to be done. Like a man in any other trade, there is a season when he is wanted. Now, if the Christian soldier never fights, of what good is he at all?

FOR MEDITATION: Some things tempt us to turn back—affliction, persecution, cares, riches, greed (Mark 4:17,19), pleasures (Luke 8:14), cowardice (2 Timothy 1:15), worldliness (2 Timothy 4:10). On the day of battle the Lord Jesus Christ headed straight for the front line on our behalf (Luke 9:51); are you prepared to 'fight the good fight of faith' (1 Timothy 6:12) on his behalf?

SERMON NO. 696

Lead us not into temptation

'Lead us not into temptation, but deliver us from evil.' Matthew 6:13
SUGGESTED FURTHER READING: Matthew 4:1–11

The text does not say, 'Tempt us not;' if it did, then there would be a difficulty; it does not say, 'Lord, tempt us not,' but it says, 'Lead us not into temptation;' and I think I shall very rapidly be able to show you that there is a vast difference between leading into temptation and actually tempting. God tempts no man. For God to tempt in the sense of enticing to sin would be inconsistent with his nature, and altogether contrary to his known character; but for God to lead us into those conflicts with evil which we call temptations, is not only possible, but usual. Full often the great Captain of salvation leads us by his providence to battle fields where we must face the full array of evil, and conquer through the blood of the Lamb; and this leading into temptation is by divine grace overruled for our good, since by being tempted we grow strong in grace and patience. Our God and Father may, for wise ends, which shall ultimately subserve his own glory and our profit, lead us into positions where Satan, the world and the flesh may tempt us; and the prayer is to be understood in that sense of a humble self-distrust which shrinks from the conflict. There is courage here, for the suppliant calmly looks the temptation in the face, and dreads only the evil which it may work in him, but there is also a holy fear, a sacred self-suspicion, a dread of contact with sin in any degree. The sentiment is not inconsistent with 'all joy' when the divers temptations do come; it is akin to the Saviour's 'If it be possible, let this cup pass from me,' which did not for a moment prevent his drinking the cup even to its dregs.

FOR MEDITATION: Temptations to sin are bound to come (Luke 17:1), but never from God (James 1:13). It was the Holy Spirit who led the Lord Jesus Christ into the wilderness to be tempted, Satan who did the tempting (Matthew 4:1) and God who provided the means of escape (Matthew 4:4,7,10; 1 Corinthians 10:13).

An exhortation

'But David tarried still at Jerusalem.' 2 Samuel 11:1
SUGGESTED FURTHER READING: 1 Timothy 5:9–15

Let us watch unto prayer, and be diligent in our Master's business, 'fervent in spirit, serving the Lord.' My dear friends, we do not exhort you to serve Christ, to be saved by it. David *was* saved. I only speak to you who are saved, and I beg and beseech of you to take notice of David's fall, and of the sloth that was at the beginning of it, as a warning to yourselves. Some temptations come to the industrious, but all temptations attack the idle. Notice the invention used by country people to catch wasps. They will put a little sweet liquor into a long and narrow-necked phial. The do-nothing wasp comes by, smells the sweet liquor, plunges in, and is drowned. But the bee comes by, and if she does stop for a moment to smell, yet she enters not, because she has honey of her own to make; she is too busy in the work of the commonwealth to indulge herself with the tempting sweets. Master Greenham, a Puritan divine, was once waited upon by a woman who was greatly tempted. Upon making enquiries into her way of life, he found she had little to do, and Greenham said, 'That is the secret of your being so much tempted. Sister, if you are very busy, Satan may tempt you, but he will not easily prevail, and he will soon give up the attempt.' Idle Christians are not so much tempted of the devil as they are tempting the devil to tempt them. Idleness sets the door of the heart ajar, and asks Satan to come in; but if we are occupied from morning till night, if Satan shall get in, he must break through the door. Under sovereign grace, and next to faith, there is no better shield against temptation than being 'Not slothful in business; fervent in spirit, serving the Lord.'

FOR MEDITATION: 'Satan finds some mischief still for idle hands to do' (Isaac Watts). The more we are occupied with the Lord's business, the less time we will have for Satan's business. When busy for the Lord, Nehemiah was tempted to meet his enemies in the plain Ono. His reply? A plain 'O, no' (Nehemiah 6:2–4)! Could you do the same?

SERMON NO. 450

The church—conservative and aggressive

'The church of the living God, the pillar and ground of the truth.'
1 Timothy 3:15
SUGGESTED FURTHER READING: 1 Corinthians 5:9–6:11

I remember a somewhat ludicrous incident which occurred to a church in which there were great quarrellings and bickerings. The minister and the deacons, and the people, were all at arm's length, and daggers drawn. It was determined at last that the matter should come to a settlement, and it was by mutual consent given up to the judgment of a good Christian farmer, who lived in the neighbourhood. He was to hear the case, and write an answer to be read at the next church meeting. Our friend, the farmer, sat down to write his letter; at the same time he had a letter from a steward or tenant asking advice about his farm, and by a mistake, or rather by a blessed providence as God would have it, he put the wrong letters into the envelopes, so that the letter which was intended for the church went to the steward, and that which was intended for the steward went to the church. At the church meeting, when they were all assembled, this letter was read to the church; it ran thus: 'Dear friend, mind you see to the hedges well. Keep them up as best you can, and take special care of the old black bull.' Now that was a most extraordinary letter to write to a church. It had been sent by mistake, but the minister, thinking it was a bona fide piece of advice, said he could not comprehend it. Some brother got up and said it was plain enough; it was meant that they must be very watchful as to whom they should receive into the church. They must keep their hedges up and see there were no gaps. 'And,' said he, 'by 'the old black bull' I have no doubt he means that spirit of Satan that would get in and trouble and divide us.' So understanding it in that sense they made up their difference, repaired their hedges, and were careful of 'the old black bull.' Every church must do the same.

FOR MEDITATION: A church that is badly divided (1 Corinthians 1:10–12; 3:3–4; 6:1,6–8; 11:18–19) is a church that is ignorant of the ways of Satan and badly in need of appropriate instruction about him and his followers (1 Corinthians 7:5; 10:20–21; 2 Corinthians 2:11; 11:3–4,14–15).

Joy and peace in believing

'Joy and peace in believing.' Romans 15:13
SUGGESTED FURTHER READING: Ezekiel 13:1–16

You must take care, while valuing joy and peace, that you do not overestimate them; for, remember that joy and peace are, though eminently desirable, not infallible evidences of safety. There are many persons who have great joy and much peace who are not saved, for their joy springs from a mistake, and their peace is the false peace which does not rest upon the rock of divine truth but upon the sand of their own imaginations. It is certainly a good sign that the spring is come, that you find the weather to be so warm, but there are very mild days in winter. I must not therefore infer because the heat of the sun is at such and such a degree, that therefore it is necessarily spring. And, on the other hand, we have had very cold days this week—cold days which, if we had to judge by such evidences, might have indicated to us that we were rather in November than in May. And so, joy and peace are like fine sunny days. They come to those that have no faith, that are in the winter of their unbelief, and they may not visit you who have believed; or, if they come, they may not abide, for there may be cold weather in May, and there may be some sorrow and some distress even to a truly believing soul. Understand, that you must not look upon the possession of joy and peace as being the absolutely necessary consequence of your being saved. A man may be in the lifeboat, but that lifeboat may be so tossed about that he may still feel himself exceedingly ill, and think himself to be still in peril. It is not his sense of safety that makes him safe; he is safe because he is in the lifeboat, whether he is sensible of this or not.

FOR MEDITATION: Luke 16:25; the Christian may have a tough time in this life, but the best is yet to come (Romans 8:18; 2 Corinthians 4:17; Hebrews 12:11; 1 Peter 5:10). The unbeliever may have a good time in this life, but the worst is yet to come (Psalm 73:3–5,17–20).

The believer sinking in the mire

'Deliver me out of the mire, and let me not sink.' Psalm 69:14
SUGGESTED FURTHER READING: Matthew 14:22–31; 15:21–28

Luther was a man of the strongest faith, and yet at times of the faintest hope. He was, and he was not, a firm believer. His faith never wavered as to the truth of the cause which he advocated; but his faith as to his own interest in Christ, seldom, if ever, amounted to full assurance. The force of his faith spent itself in carrying on with fearful vigour the war against antichrist and error of all shapes. He believed the truth, and held right manfully to justification by faith; but he was at times very doubtful as to whether he himself was justified in Christ Jesus. He believed in salvation by the precious blood of Christ; but, especially at the last, it became a very serious matter with him as to whether he had ever been washed in that precious blood. Roman Catholic biographers, who, of course, if they can, will slander him, say that he had doubts as to everything which he preached, and that at the last, he found his faith was not in accordance with truth. Not so; no man stuck to his testimony with more tenacity than the great reformer; but yet I marvel not that they should say so. He never doubted the truth of the things which he preached; but he did doubt his own interest in them frequently; and when he came to die, his testimony, though amply sufficient, was nothing like so brilliant as that of many a poor old woman who has died in a humble cottage, resting upon Jesus. The poor peasant who knew no more than her Bible true, was utterly unknown to the Vatican, and fame's trumpet will never resound her name, but yet she entered into eternal peace with far louder shoutings of joy than Martin Luther, who shook the world with his thundering valour.

FOR MEDITATION: You don't have to be great to be rich in faith (James 2:5). The Lord's apostles often displayed a weak faith (Matthew 8:26; 14:31; 16:8; 17:20; Mark 4:40; John 20:25) which was overshadowed by the faith of anonymous believers (Matthew 15:28; Luke 7:9).

Unbelievers stumbling; believers rejoicing

'As it is written, Behold I lay in Sion a stumblingstone and rock of offence: and whosoever believeth on him shall not be ashamed.' Romans 9:33
SUGGESTED FURTHER READING: 1 Peter 2:4–8

Who are they who shall never be ashamed? The answer is general and special. The text says, '*Whosoever* believeth'—that is, any man who ever lived, or ever shall live, who believes in Christ, shall never be ashamed. Whether he has been a gross sinner or a moralist; whether he is learned or illiterate; whether he is a prince or a beggar, it matters not—'Whosoever believeth on him shall not be ashamed.' Though you may very seldom come to the house of God, yet if you believe in Christ today you shall never be ashamed of him. You who have sat in God's house for years, and feel yourselves guilty of having rejected Christ, yet if now you trust him you shall not be ashamed. But there is a speciality; it is 'Whosoever *believeth.*' Others shall be ashamed. There must be a real and hearty believing; there must be a simple confidence in the person and work of Jesus: wherever this is, there shall be no shame. One says, 'But I have such a little faith; I am afraid I shall be confounded.' No; you come in under the 'Whosoever'—'Whosoever believeth,' though his faith be never so little, 'shall never be ashamed.' Another says, 'But I have so many doubts.' Still, dear heart, since you believe you shall not be ashamed; all your doubtings and your fearings shall never damn you, for your faith will prevail. 'But,' says another, 'my corruption is so strong; I have come today lamenting because of my imperfections; they have obtained the mastery of my faith, and I have fallen during the week.' Yes, soul, all fallen as you are, yet if you believe you shall never be ashamed.

FOR MEDITATION: Whosoever trusts in the Lord Jesus Christ shall not perish, but have everlasting life (John 3:15–16), shall not abide in darkness (John 12:46), shall receive forgiveness of sins (Acts 10:43) and shall not be ashamed (Romans 10:11). The opposite will be true of whosoever does not trust in him. Which 'whosoever' are you?

SERMON NO. 571

The Holy Spirit compared with the wind

*'The wind bloweth where it listeth, and thou hearest the sound thereof,
but canst not tell whence it cometh, and whither it goeth: so is every one
that is born of the Spirit.' John 3:8*
SUGGESTED FURTHER READING: Song of Solomon 4:12–16

I have known ministers who had some peculiar idiosyncrasy of experience
which was not important; but their people all began to think and talk in the
same way, and to have the same doubts and fears. Now that will not do. It is
not the way in which the Most High acts with regard to the wind, and if he
chooses to take all the points of the compass, and make use of them all, let
us bless and glorify his name. Are not the different winds various in their
qualities? Few of us like an east wind. Most of us are very glad when the
wind blows from the south. Vegetation seems to love the south-west. A stiff
north-easter is enough to make us perish; and long continuance of the north
wind may well freeze the whole earth; while from the west, the wind seems
to come laden with health from the sea; and though sometimes too strong
for the sick, yet it is never a bad time when the west wind blows. The ancients
all had their different opinions about wind; some were dry, some were rainy,
some affected this disease, some touched this part of men, some the other.
Certain it is that God's Holy Spirit has different qualities. In the Canticles he
blows softly with the sweet breath of love: turn on farther, and you get the
same Spirit blowing fiercely with threatening and denunciation; sometimes
you find him convincing the world 'of sin, and of righteousness, and of
judgment;' that is the north wind: at other times opening up Christ to the
sinner, and giving him joy and comfort; that is the south wind, that blows
softly, and gives a balminess in which poor troubled hearts rejoice; and yet
'all these worketh that one and the selfsame Spirit.'

FOR MEDITATION: When the Holy Spirit blows like a wind, healthy effects
follow, for example, causing the Scriptures to be written (2 Peter 1:21),
stimulating the early church into evangelism (Acts 2:1–2) and bringing
sinners to new birth (John 3:8). Beware of other winds and their unhealthy
spiritual effects (Ephesians 4:14).

Pentecost

'And when the day of Pentecost was fully come, they were all with one accord in one place. And suddenly there came a sound from heaven as of a rushing mighty wind, and it filled all the house where they were sitting. And there appeared unto them cloven tongues like as of fire, and it sat upon each of them. And they were all filled with the Holy Ghost, and began to speak with other tongues, as the Spirit gave them utterance.' Acts 2:1–4
SUGGESTED FURTHER READING: 2 Corinthians 3:1–6

How absolutely necessary is the presence and power of the Holy Spirit! It is not possible for us to promote the glory of God or to bless the souls of men, unless the Holy Spirit shall be in us and with us. Those who were assembled on that memorable day of Pentecost, were all men of prayer and faith; but even these precious gifts are only available when the celestial fire sets them on a blaze. They were all men of experience; most of them had been preachers of the Word and workers of miracles; they had endured trials and troubles in company with their Lord, and had been with him in his temptation. Among them were the apostles and the seventy evangelists, and with them were those honoured women in whose houses the Lord had often been entertained, and who had ministered to him of their substance; yet even these favoured and honoured saints can do nothing without the breath of God the Holy Spirit. Apostles and evangelists dare not even attempt anything alone; they must tarry at Jerusalem till power be given them from on high. It was not a want of education; they had been for three years in the college of Christ, with perfect wisdom as their tutor, matchless eloquence as their instructor, and immaculate perfection as their example; yet they must not venture to open their mouths to testify of the mystery of Jesus, until the anointing Spirit has come with blessed unction from above. Surely if so it was with them, much more must it be the case with us.

FOR MEDITATION: Unbelievers are unspiritual by nature (1 Corinthians 2:14); believers can be unspiritual by practice (1 Corinthians 3:1). Anything in our lives not derived from the gifts (1 Corinthians 12:4,7) or fruit (Galatians 5:22–23) of the Holy Spirit is by definition unspiritual.

25 MAY (1862)

Choice portions

'For the LORD*'s portion is his people.'* Deuteronomy 32:9
'The LORD *is my portion, saith my soul.'* Lamentations 3:24
SUGGESTED FURTHER READING: 1 John 4:7–19

The love of God changes us into its own image, so that what the Lord says concerning us, we can also declare concerning him. God is love essentially, and when this essential love shines forth freely upon us, we reflect it back upon him. He is like the sun, the great father of lights, and we are as the moon and the planets, we shine in rays borrowed from his brightness. He is the golden seal, and we, his people, are the wax receiving the impression. Our heaven is to be likeness to Christ, and our preparation for heaven consists in a growing imitation of him in all things. See, brethren, how the Lord gives the word, and our heart, like an echo, repeats every syllable. The Lord loves his people, and we love him because he first loved us; he has chosen his saints, and they have also made him their chosen heritage. The saints are precious to Jesus, and unto us who believe he is precious; Christ lived for us, and for us to live is Christ; we gain all things by his death, and for us to die is gain. The church is the looking-glass in which Christ sees himself reflected; she is like a fair songstress taking up the refrain of Jesus' canticles of love; while he sings, 'My sister, my spouse,' she answers, 'My beloved is mine, and I am his.' It is most delightful to perceive how, through divine grace, believers come to have the same feeling towards their God which their gracious Lord has towards them. Our two texts present us with an interesting instance: the church is God's portion, he delights in her, he finds in her his solace and his joy; but God is also, as the result of this, the church's portion, her full delight and bliss. Beloved, the love is mutual.

FOR MEDITATION: God has loved us (Malachi 1:2); how are you responding to him? With unbelief, self-justification and self-defence (Malachi 1:2,6–7; 2:17; 3:8,13)? Or with love displayed in thankful trust and obedience (Psalm 56:10–13; 116:1–2,12–14)? Are you being changed into his image (2 Corinthians 3:18)?

SERMON NO. 451

Even so, Father!

'At that time Jesus answered and said, I thank thee, O Father, Lord of heaven and earth, because thou hast hid these things from the wise and prudent, and hast revealed them unto babes.' Matthew 11:25
SUGGESTED FURTHER READING: 1 Samuel 3:1–18

'At that time Jesus answered.' If you will look at the context you will not perceive that anybody had asked him a question, or that he was indeed in conversation with any human being. Yet it says, 'Jesus answered and said, I thank thee, O Father.' Now when a man answers, he answers a person who has been speaking to him. Who, then, had been speaking to him? Why, his Father. Yet there is no record of it; which should just teach us that Christ had constant fellowship with his Father, and often did his Father silently speak into his ear. As we are in this world even as Christ was, let us catch this lesson. May we likewise have silent fellowship with the Father; so that often we may answer him. And when the world knows not to whom we speak, may we speak to God and respond to that secret voice which no other ear has heard, while our own ear, opened by the Spirit of God, has attended to it with joy. I like the Christian sometimes to find himself obliged to speak out or, if not to speak out, to feel an almost irrepressible desire to say something though no one be near, because a thought has been brought to him by the Holy Spirit, a suggestion has just been cast into the midst of his soul by the Holy Spirit, and he answers to it. God has spoken to him and he longs to speak to God—either to set to his seal that God is true in some matter of revelation, or to confess some sin of which the Spirit of God has convinced him, or to acknowledge some mercy which God's providence has given, or to express assent to some great truth which God the Holy Spirit has then opened to his understanding. Keep your hearts, my brethren, in such a state, that when God speaks to you, you may be ready to answer.

FOR MEDITATION: Where the specific promptings of the Holy Spirit are recorded in Scripture, the hearers were in a prepared and receptive state of mind (Acts 10:9,19,20; 13:2). Like Martha (Luke 10:39–40), Christians are sometimes too busy or distracted to be aware that God is speaking.

SERMON NO. 394

The stony heart removed

'I will take away the stony heart out of your flesh, and I will give you an heart of flesh.' Ezekiel 36:26
SUGGESTED FURTHER READING: Proverbs 30:7–9

Men who have lost their stony hearts are afraid of sin, even *before sin* they are afraid of it. The very shadow of evil across their path frightens them. The temptation is enough for them, they flee from it as from a serpent; they would not dally and toil with it, lest they should be betrayed. Their conscience is alarmed even at the approach of evil, and away they fly; and *in sin*, for even tender hearts do sin, they are uneasy. As well might a man seek to obtain quiet rest on a pillow stuffed with thorns, as the tender conscience get any peace while a man is sinning. And then, *after sin*—here comes the pinch—the heart of flesh bleeds as though it were wounded to its very core. It hates and loathes and detests itself that ever it should have gone astray. Ah, stony heart, you can think of sin with pleasure, you can live in sin and not care about it; and after sin you can roll the sweet morsel under your tongue and say, 'Who is my master? I care for none; my conscience does not accuse me.' But not so the tender broken heart. Before sin, and in sin, and after sin, it smarts and cries out to God. So also in duty as well as in sin, the new heart is tender. Hard hearts care nothing for God's commandment; hearts of flesh wish to be obedient to every statute. 'Only let me know my Master's will and I will do it.' The hearts of flesh when they feel that the commandment has been omitted, or that the command has been broken, mourn and lament before God. Oh! there are some hearts of flesh that cannot forgive themselves, if they have been lax in prayer, if they have not enjoyed the Sabbath day, if they feel that they have not given their hearts to God's praise as they should.

FOR MEDITATION: The tender heart before sin (Genesis 39:7–12), in sin (Romans 7:14–25) and after sin (Psalm 51:1–5). God will not despise a broken and contrite heart (Psalm 51:17). Spurgeon asks, 'Have you, dear friends, such a heart of flesh as this?'

A troubled prayer

'Look upon mine affliction and my pain; and forgive all my sins.' Psalm
25:18
SUGGESTED FURTHER READING: Hebrews 11:23–28

A Christian counts sorrow lighter in the scale than sin; he can bear that his
troubles should continue, but he cannot endure the burden of his guilt, or
the weight of his transgressions. Here are two guests come to my door; both
of them ask to have a lodging with me. The one is called *Affliction*; he has a
very grave voice, and a very heavy hand, and he looks at me with fierce eyes.
The other is called *Sin*, and he is very soft-spoken, and very fair, and his
words are softer than butter. Let me scan their faces, let me examine them as
to their character; I must not be deceived by appearances. I will ask my two
friends who would lodge with me, to open their hands. When my friend
Affliction, with some little difficulty, opens his hand, I find that, rough as it
is, he carries a jewel inside it, and that he meant to leave that jewel at my
house. But as for my soft-spoken friend Sin, when I force him to show me
what it is that is hidden in his sleeve, I find that it is a dagger with which he
would have stabbed me. What shall I do, then, if I am wise? Why, I should be
very glad if they would both be good enough to go and stop somewhere else,
but if I must entertain one of the two, I would shut my door in the face of
smooth-spoken Sin, and say to the rougher and uglier visitor, Affliction,
'Come and stop with me, for maybe God has sent you as a messenger of
mercy to my soul.' *'Look upon* mine affliction and my pain, and *forgive* all
my sin.' We must be more express and explicit about sin than we are about
trouble.

FOR MEDITATION: Anything has got to be better than sin; the Christian is not
short of alternatives to prefer (Psalm 84:10; Matthew 18:8–9; Ephesians
4:28; 5:4,11; Hebrews 11:25). Are these your sentiments or would you rather
hold on to your sin (John 3:19), regardless of what it has done to you
(Romans 7:11) and what it will do to you (Romans 6:23)?

Laus Deo (Glory to God)

'For of him, and through him, and to him, are all things: to whom be glory for ever. Amen.' Romans 11:36
SUGGESTED FURTHER READING: 1 Corinthians 10:31–11:1

The apostle puts his pen back into the ink bottle and falls on his knees—he cannot help it—he must have a doxology. 'To whom be glory for ever. Amen.' Beloved, let us imitate this devotion. I think that this sentence should be the prayer, the motto for every one of us—'To whom be glory for ever. Amen.' This should be the single desire of the Christian. I take it that he should not have twenty wishes but only one. He may desire to see his family well brought up, but only that 'To God may be glory for ever.' He may wish for prosperity in his business, but only so far as it may help him to promote this—'To whom be glory for ever.' He may desire to attain more gifts and more graces, but it should only be that 'To him may be glory for ever.' This one thing I know, Christian, you are not acting as you ought to do when you are moved by any other motive than the one motive of your Lord's glory. As a Christian, you are 'of him, and through him;' I pray you be 'to him.' Let nothing ever set your heart beating but love to him. Let this ambition fire your soul; be this the foundation of every enterprise upon which you enter, and this your sustaining motive whenever your zeal would grow cold—only make God your object. Depend upon it, where self begins, sorrow begins; but if God be my supreme delight and only object,

'To me 'tis equal whether love ordain
My life or death—appoint me ease or pain.'

To me there shall be no choice, when my eye singly looks to God's glory.

FOR MEDITATION: If some of us were given one wish, it would not be a patch on the single-minded desires expressed by God's people in the Bible, such as David (Psalm 27:4), Asaph (Psalm 73:25) and Paul (Philippians 3:8–10, 13–15). What would your wish be? Could you pray for it with a clear conscience?

SERMON NO. 572

The church's love to her loving Lord

'Tell me, O thou whom my soul loveth, where thou feedest, where thou makest thy flock to rest at noon: for why should I be as one that turneth aside by the flocks of thy companions?' Song of Solomon 1:7
SUGGESTED FURTHER READING: Mark 9:2–9

When Tigranes and his wife were both taken prisoners by Cyrus, turning to Tigranes, he said, 'What will you give for the liberation of your wife?' The king answered, 'I love my wife so that I would cheerfully give up my life if she might be delivered from servitude;' whereupon Cyrus said that if there was such love as that between them, they might both go free. So when they were away and many were talking about the beauty and generosity of Cyrus, and especially about the beauty of his person, Tigranes, turning to his wife, asked her what she thought of Cyrus, and she answered that she saw nothing anywhere but in the face of the man who had said that he would die if she might only be released from servitude. 'The beauty of that man,' she said, 'makes me forget all others.' And verily we would say the same of Jesus. We would not decry the angels, nor think ill of the saints, but the beauties of that man who gave his life for us are so great that they have eclipsed all others, and our soul only wishes to see him and not another; for, as the stars hide their heads in the presence of the sun, so may you all be gone, delights and excellencies, when Christ Jesus, the chief delight, the chief excellency, makes his appearance. Seeing him, you must love him. It was said of Henry VIII, that if all portraits of tyrants, and murderers, and thieves were out of existence, they might all be painted from the one face of Henry VIII; and turning that round another way, we will say, that if all the excellencies, beauties, and perfections of the human race were blotted out, they might all be painted again from the face of the Lord Jesus.

FOR MEDITATION: The Lord Jesus Christ really did give up his life to deliver his bride, the church (Ephesians 5:25), from the dominion of darkness and sin (Colossians 1:13–14). Do you express appropriate wonder, love and gratitude (Galatians 2:20; 1 Peter 1:8)?

A precious drop of honey

'Behold, I have graven thee upon the palms of my hands.' Isaiah 49:16
SUGGESTED FURTHER READING: Deuteronomy 33:1–5

We have heard of one, an eastern queen, who so loved her husband that she thought even to build a mausoleum to his memory was not enough. She had a strange way of proving her affection, for when her husband's bones were burned she took the ashes and drank them day by day, that, as she said, her body might be her husband's living sepulchre. It was a strange way of showing love. But what shall I say of this divine, celestial, unobjectionable, sympathetic mode of showing remembrance, by cutting it into the palms? Words fail to express our intense content with this most admirable sign of tenderness and fond affection. It appears to me as though the King had said, 'Shall I carve my people upon precious stones? Shall I choose the ruby, the emerald, the topaz? No; for these all must melt in the last general conflagration. What then? Shall I write on tables of gold or silver? No, for all these may canker and corrupt, and thieves may break through and steal. Shall I cut the memorial deep on brass? No, for time would wear it, and the letters would not long be legible. I will write on myself, on my own hand, and then my people will know how tender I am, that I would sooner cut into my own flesh than forget them; I will have my Son branded in the hand with the names of his people, that they may be sure he cannot forsake them; hard by the memorial of his wounds shall be the memorial of his love to them, for indeed his wounds are an everlasting remembrance.' How loving, then, how full of superlative, super-excellent affection is God toward you and toward me in so recording our names.

FOR MEDITATION: When he appeared before God on behalf of the people, the Old Testament high priest carried on his clothing the names of the twelve tribes of Israel (Exodus 28:9–12,29) and the guilt of the people (Exodus 28:36–38). Our great High Priest has carried in his own body the sins of his people (Isaiah 53:4–6; 1 Peter 2:24), knows every believer by name (John 10:3) and appears before God on their behalf (Hebrews 7:25; 9:24). Are you represented by him?

SERMON NO. 512

Compassion for the multitude

'And they say unto him, We have here but five loaves, and two fishes. He said, Bring them hither to me.' Matthew 14:17–18
SUGGESTED FURTHER READING: Romans 12:1–8

The Church's first duty is, when she looks to her resources and feels them to be utterly insufficient for her work, still to bring all that she has to Christ. But how shall she bring them? Why, in many ways. She must bring them to Christ in consecration. There is a brother yonder who says, 'Well, I have but little money to spare!' 'Never mind,' says Christ, 'let what you have be brought to me.' 'Ah,' says another, 'I have very short time that I can spare in labouring to do good.' 'Bring it to me.' 'Ah,' says another, 'but I have small ability; my stock of knowledge is very slender; my speech is contemptible.' 'Bring it to me.' 'Oh,' says one, 'I could only teach in the Sunday School.' 'Bring it to me.' 'Ah,' says another, 'and I do not know that I could do that; I could but distribute a tract.' 'Bring it to me.' Every talent that the Church has is to be brought to Christ, and consecrated. And mark you this—I speak a strong thing which some will not be able to receive—anything which you have in this world, which you do not consecrate to Christ's cause, you do rob the Lord of. Every true Christian, when he gave himself to Christ, gave everything he had. Neither calls he anything that he has his own, but it is all the Master's. We are not true to the Master's cause unless it be so. 'What! not provide for our families?' Yes, but that is given to God. 'Not provide for ourselves?' Yes, so long as you are not covetous. Remember, it is your Master's business to provide for you. If he provides for you through your own exertions, you are doing your Master's work and receiving of his bounty, for it is his work to provide for you. But there still must always be a thorough consecration of everything you have to Christ. Where your consecration ends, your honesty with God ends.

FOR MEDITATION: Six things you should commit to God—your cause (Job 5:8), your self (Psalm 10:14), your spirit (Psalm 31:5), your ways (Psalm 37:5), your works (Proverbs 16:3), your soul (1 Peter 4:19). Does he have them all? He is able to look after all that we commit to him (2 Timothy 1:12).

Jehovah-tsidkenu—the Lord our Righteousness

'This is his name whereby he shall be called, THE LORD OUR RIGHTEOUSNESS.' Jeremiah 23:6
SUGGESTED FURTHER READING: Isaiah 61:1–11

In Scripture, Christ's righteousness is compared with fair white linen; then I am, if I wear it, without spot. It is compared with wrought gold; then I am, if I wear it, dignified and beautiful, and worthy to sit at the wedding feast of the King of kings. It is compared, in the parable of the prodigal son, with the best robe; then I wear a better robe than angels have, for they have not the best; but I, poor prodigal, once clothed in rags, companion to the nobility of the pigsty—I, fresh from the husks that swine do eat, am nevertheless clothed in the best robe, and am so accepted in the Beloved. Moreover, it is also everlasting righteousness. This is, perhaps, the fairest point of it—that the robe shall never be worn out; no thread of it shall ever give way. It shall never hang in tatters upon the sinner's back. He shall live, and even though it were a Methuselah's life, the robe shall be as if it were woven yesterday. He shall pass through the stream of death, and the black stream shall not foul it. He shall climb the hills of heaven, and the angels shall wonder what this whiteness is which the sinner wears, and think that some new star is coming up from earth to shine in heaven. He shall wear it among principalities and powers, and find himself no whit inferior to them all. Cherubic garments and seraphic mantles shall not be so lordly, so priestly, so divine, as this robe of righteousness, this everlasting perfection which Christ has wrought out, and brought in and given to all his people. Glory unto thee, O Jesus, glory unto thee! Unto thee be hallels for ever; Hallelu-Jah! Thou art Jah— 'Jehovah, the Lord our Righteousness.'

FOR MEDITATION: The robe of Christ's righteousness which the Christian has received (Isaiah 61:10) is not only for show; it also serves as a vital piece of the Christian's spiritual armour (Ephesians 6:14). To rely on our own righteousness is no better than fighting a battle armed in nothing but filthy rags (Isaiah 64:6).

SERMON NO. 395

Expiation

'Thou shalt make his soul an offering for sin.' Isaiah 53:10
SUGGESTED FURTHER READING: Luke 15:11–24

The great arms of the eternal Father are ready to save you as you are, because the great work of Christ has effected all that is wanted before God for the acceptance of the vilest sinner. How is it that the Father can embrace the prodigal? He is fresh from the swine-trough: look at him; look at his rags; how foul they are! We would not touch them with a pair of tongs! Take him to the fire and burn the filth! Take him to the bath and wash him! That lip is not fit to kiss; those filthy lips cannot be permitted to touch that holy cheek of the glorious Father. But it is not so. While he was yet a great way off, his father saw him—rags, and poverty, and sin, and filth, and all—and he did not wait till he was clean, but ran and fell upon his neck and kissed him, just as he was. How could he do that? Why, the parable does not tell us; for it did not run on with the subject to introduce the atonement; but this explains it: when God accepts a sinner, he is in fact only accepting Christ. He looks into the sinner's eyes, and he sees his own dear Son's image there, and he takes him in. As we have heard of a good woman, who, whenever a poor sailor came to her door, whoever he might be, would always make him welcome, because she said, 'I think I see my own dear son who has been these many years away, and I have never heard of him; but whenever I see a sailor, I think of him, and treat the stranger kindly for my son's sake.' So, my God, when he sees a sinner long for pardon and desirous of being accepted, thinks he sees his Son in him, and accepts him for his Son's sake.

FOR MEDITATION: It is possible to be accepted by God in his beloved Son (Ephesians 1:6), but the acceptable time to be accepted is now (2 Corinthians 6:2). After death comes judgment (Hebrews 9:27), not a further opportunity to be washed from our sins.

SERMON NO. 561

In whom art thou trusting?

'Now on whom dost thou trust?' Isaiah 36:5
SUGGESTED FURTHER READING: 2 Chronicles 14:1–15

I rest with my whole soul upon the finished work of Christ, and I have not found anything yet that leads me to suspect I am resting where I shall meet with a failure. No, the older one grows, the more one gets convinced that he who leans by faith on Christ, rests where he never needs to be afraid. He may go and return in peace and confidence, for the mountains may depart, and the hills be removed, but God shall not change, and his purpose shall not cease to stand. Yes, God is worthy of our confidence. And I think we can say, by way of commending our God to others, that we feel we can rest upon him for the future. We have been in strange places, and in very peculiar conditions in the past, but we were never thrown where we could not find in God all we needed; and we are therefore encouraged to believe that when death's dark night shall come, with all its gathering of terror, we shall fear no evil, for the same God will be with us to be our succour and our stay. The Isle of Man has for its coat of arms three legs, and turn them which way you will, you know they always stand; and such is the believer—throw him which way you will, he finds something to stand on; throw him into death, or into life, into the lion's den, or into the whale's belly, cast him into fire, or into water, the Christian still trusts in his God, and finds him a very present help in time of trouble. 'On whom dost thou trust?' We can answer boldly, 'We trust in him whose power will never be exhausted, whose love will never cease, whose kindness will never change, whose faithfulness will never be sullied, whose wisdom will never be nonplussed, and whose perfect goodness never can know a diminution.'

FOR MEDITATION: Study the testimonies of some who have trusted in the Lord—(Psalm 28:7; 56:3–4,9–11; 73:28; 2 Corinthians 1:9–10). People or material things can betray our trust (Psalm 41:9; 52:7; 146:3; Proverbs 11:28). On whom are you trusting?

Baptismal regeneration

'He that believeth and is baptized shall be saved; but he that believeth not shall be damned.' Mark 16:15–16
SUGGESTED FURTHER READING: Romans 6:3–4

What connection has baptism with faith? I think it has just this, *baptism is the avowal of faith*; the man was Christ's soldier, but now in baptism he puts on his regimentals. The man believed in Christ, but his faith remained between God and his own soul. In baptism he says to the baptizer, 'I believe in Jesus Christ;' he says to the church, 'I unite with you as a believer in the common truths of Christianity;' he says to the onlooker, 'Whatever you may do, as for me, I will serve the Lord.' It is the avowal of his faith.

Next, we think baptism is also to the believer a *testimony of his faith*; he does in baptism tell the world what he believes. 'I am about,' says he, 'to be buried in water. I believe that the Son of God was metaphorically baptized in suffering: I believe he was literally dead and buried.' To rise again out of the water sets forth to all men that he believes in the resurrection of Christ. There is a showing forth in the Lord's Supper of Christ's death, and there is a showing forth in baptism of Christ's burial and resurrection. It is a type, a sign, a symbol, a mirror to the world: a looking-glass in which religion is as it were reflected. We say to the onlooker, when he asks what is the meaning of this ordinance, 'we mean to set forth our faith that Christ was buried, and that he rose again from the dead, and we avow this death and resurrection to be the ground of our trust.'

Again, baptism is also *faith taking her proper place*. It is, or should be, one of her first acts of obedience.

FOR MEDITATION: This sermon, preached against the doctrine of baptismal regeneration, provoked a fierce backlash against Spurgeon. Baptism comes second to repentance (Acts 2:38), receiving the word (Acts 2:41) and believing the gospel (Acts 8:12,37; 18:8), things which a baby cannot consciously do.

Obedience better than sacrifice

'Behold, to obey is better than sacrifice, and to hearken than the fat of rams.' 1 Samuel 15:22

SUGGESTED FURTHER READING: James 4:11–17

If you are failing to keep the least of one of Christ's commands to his disciples, I pray you, brethren, be disobedient no longer. I know, for instance, that some of you can see it to be your duty, as believers, to be baptized. If you did not think it to be your duty, I would not bring this text to bear upon you; but if you feel it to be right, and you do it not, let me say to you that all the pretensions you make of attachment to your Master, and all the other actions which you may perform, are as nothing compared with the neglect of this. 'To obey,' even in the slightest and smallest thing, 'is better than sacrifice,' and to hearken diligently to the Lord's commands is better than the fat of rams. It may be that some of you, though you are professed Christians, are living in the prosecution of some evil trade, and your conscience has often said, 'Get out of it.' You are not in the position that a Christian ought to be in; but then you hope that you will be able to make a little money, and you will retire and do a world of good with it. God cares nothing for this rams' fat of yours; he asks not for these sacrifices which you intend to make. 'To obey is better than sacrifice, and to hearken than the fat of rams.' Perhaps you are in connection with a Christian church in which you may see much that is wrong, and you know that you ought not to tolerate it, but still you do so. You say, 'I have a position of usefulness, and if I come out I shall not be so useful as I am now.' My brother, your usefulness is but as the fat of rams, and 'to obey is better than' it all.

FOR MEDITATION: To argue that the end justifies the means is to claim to know better than God. Saul knew God's will (1 Samuel 15:3), failed to do it (1 Samuel 15:11), claimed to have done so (1 Samuel 15:13,20) and paraded the best of motives (1 Samuel 15:15,21). Ignorance of God's will and failure to do it is a lesser evil than knowledge of God's will and failure to do it (Luke 12:47–48).

The young man's prayer

'O satisfy us early with thy mercy; that we may rejoice and be glad all our days.' Psalm 90:14

SUGGESTED FURTHER READING: Ecclesiastes 11:6–12:7

They who love Jesus Christ early, have the best hope of enjoying the happiest days as Christians. *They will have the most service*, and the service of God is pure delight. Their youthful vigour will enable them to do more than those who enlist when they are old and decrepit. The joy of the Lord is our strength; and on the other hand, to use our strength for God is a fountain of joy. Young man, if you give fifty years of service unto God, surely you shall rejoice all your days. The earlier we are converted, having the longer time to study in Christ's college, *the more profound shall be our knowledge of him*. We shall have more time for communion, more years for fellowship. We shall have more seasons to prove the power of prayer, and more opportunities to test the fidelity of God than we should if we came late. Those who come late are blessed by being helped to learn so much, but those that come in early shall surely outstrip them. Let me be young, like John, that I may have years of loving service, and like him may have much of intimate acquaintance with my Lord. Surely those who are converted early may reckon upon more joy, because *they never will have to contend with and to mourn over what later converts must know*. Your bones are not broken, you can run without weariness, you have not fallen as some have done, you can walk without fainting. Often the grey-headed man who is converted at sixty or seventy, finds the remembrance of his youthful sins clinging to him; when he would praise, an old lascivious song revives upon his memory; when he would mount up to heaven, he suddenly remembers some scene in a haunt of vice which he would be glad to forget. But you, saved by divine grace before you thus fall into the jaw of the lion, or under the paw of the bear, will certainly have cause for rejoicing all your life.

FOR MEDITATION: Consider some young believers who bore much fruit for God—Joseph (Genesis 41:12), Joshua (Exodus 33:11), Samuel (1 Samuel 2:18), David (1 Samuel 17:33), Solomon (1 Chronicles 22:5), Josiah (2 Chronicles 34:3), Jeremiah (Jeremiah 1:6), Timothy (1 Timothy 4:12). Tomorrow's church leaders will come from today's young believers.

SERMON NO. 513

The child Samuel's prayer

'Speak, LORD; for thy servant heareth.' 1 Samuel 3:9
SUGGESTED FURTHER READING: Matthew 21:6–16

Children who are taught a form of prayer may perhaps by divine grace be enabled to use the form in all sincerity of heart: I hope they may; but I think they are more likely to understand the things of God, if instead of teaching them the form, you explain to them the meaning and the value of prayer. I take this to be the best plan. Let the Christian parent explain to the child what prayer is; tell him that God answers prayer; direct him to the Saviour, and then urge him to express his desires in his own language, both when he rises, and when he goes to rest. Gather the little ones around your knee and listen to their words, suggesting to them their needs, and reminding them of God's gracious promise. You will be amazed and, I may add, somewhat amused too; but you will be frequently surprised at the expressions they will use, the confessions they will make, the desires they will utter; and I am certain that any Christian person standing within earshot, and listening to the simple prayer of a little child earnestly asking God for what it thinks it wants, would never afterwards wish to teach a child a form, but would say, that as a matter of education to the heart, the extemporaneous utterance was infinitely superior to the best form, and that the form should be given up for ever. However, do not let me speak too sweepingly. If you must teach your child to say a form of prayer, at least take care that you do not teach him to say anything which is not true. If you teach your children a catechism, mind that it is thoroughly scriptural, or you may train them up to tell falsehoods.

FOR MEDITATION: When secondhand man-made devotions begin in the mouth rather than in the heart, they are not acceptable to God (Isaiah 29:13). The Lord Jesus Christ loved children to come to him as children (Mark 10:13–16); God can teach them heartfelt praise (Matthew 21:15–16).

SERMON NO. 586

Peace by believing

'Therefore being justified by faith, we have peace with God through our Lord Jesus Christ.' Romans 5:1
SUGGESTED FURTHER READING: Exodus 12:1–13

Write this for your motto—'None but Jesus.' Men and brethren, if those Israelites of old, who were inside their houses that night, had gone outside to the lintel of their door-post, and said, 'Now here is this lintel made of very common wood; we will paint and grain it;' and if they had then gone inside, and trusted to the painting and graining of the lintel, the destroying angel would have found them out and destroyed them. If, again, they had said, 'We will write up our name over the door—it is a respectable name; we will record the list of our charities and good works over the door,' the plague-angel would have smitten through the whole, and there would have been a wailing through the house as through the houses of the Egyptians. But what did they do? They took the blood; they marked the lintel and the two side posts, and smeared them with a crimson stain. Then in they went, and ate the passover with joy; and while the shrieks of Egypt went up in the cold midnight air, the sons of Israel went up also into heaven, for the angel of death had seen the blood, and by that mark he knew that he must pass by that habitation, and smite none that were there. The word of the Lord was not 'When I see your faith,' but 'when I see the blood, I will pass over you.' O soul, if you trust Christ, the blood is on your brow today; before the eye of God there is no condemnation. Why, then, do you need to fear? You are safe, for the blood secures every soul that once is sheltered thereby. Believe in the Lord Jesus Christ, and you shall be saved, but if you believe not, trust where you may, you shall be damned.

FOR MEDITATION: A lamb within the house, dead or alive, was not enough for the Israelites. It had to be sacrificed and its blood applied (Exodus 12:6–7). Likewise it is not enough for us to admire the life of Christ, our Passover Lamb (1 Corinthians 5:7), or to assume that his death automatically saves us. His blood had to be shed and must be 'sprinkled' upon us individually by faith (Hebrews 9:22; 12:24; 1 Peter 1:2).

SERMON NO. 510

Sin laid on Jesus

'All we like sheep have gone astray; we have turned every one to his own way; and the LORD *hath laid on him the iniquity of us all.'* Isaiah 53:6
SUGGESTED FURTHER READING: 1 Peter 2:22–25

There was a relationship between our Lord and his people, which is too often forgotten, but which rendered it natural that he should bear the sin of his people. Why does the text speak of our sinning like sheep? I think it is because it would call to our recollection that Christ is our Shepherd. It is not, my brethren, that Christ took upon himself the sins of strangers. Remember that there always was a union of a most mysterious and intimate kind between those who sinned and the Christ who suffered. What if I say that it is not unjust but according to law that when a woman gets into debt her husband should bear it? And with the church of God sinning, it was but right that her Husband, who had espoused her unto himself, should become the debtor on her behalf. The Lord Jesus stood in the relationship of a married husband unto his church, and it was not, therefore, a strange thing that he should bear her burdens. It was natural for the next of kin to redeem the inheritance, it was most seemly that Immanuel, the next of kin, should redeem his lost church by his own blood. Recollect that there was a union closer even than the marriage bond, for we are members of his body. You shall not punish this hand of mine without making the sentient nature which dwells in the brain to suffer therewith; and does it seem strange to you that when the inferior members of the body have transgressed, the Head should be made to suffer? It seems to me, my brethren, that while substitution is full of grace, it is not unnatural, but according to the laws of everlasting love.

FOR MEDITATION: The identification of the Lord Jesus Christ with sinners whom he would call his brothers was entirely appropriate (Matthew 3:13–15; Hebrews 2:10–14,17). For God to forgive repentant sinners is not a matter of justice abandoned but of justice applied (1 John 1:9).

SERMON NO. 694

A word in season

'When men are cast down, then thou shalt say, There is lifting up; and he shall save the humble person.' Job 22:29
SUGGESTED FURTHER READING: Lamentations 3:17–29

There is hope! He who said there is no hope is a liar and a murderer from the beginning, and the father of lies: there is hope because Jesus died; there is hope anywhere except in the infernal lake. There is hope in the hospital, where a man has sickened, and is within the last hour of his departure. There is hope, though men have sinned themselves beyond the pale of society; hope for the convict, though he has had to smart under the lash; hope for the man who has cast himself away. Able to save is Jesus still. 'No hope' is not to be said by any of the crew of the lifeboat while he sights the crew of the sinking vessel. 'No hope' is not to be said by any one of the fire brigade while he knows there are living men in the burning pile. 'No hope' is not to be said by any one of the valiant brigade of the Christian church while the soul is still within reach of the sound of mercy. 'No hope' is a cry which no human tongue should utter, which no human heart should heed. May God grant us grace whenever we get an opportunity to go and tell all we meet with that are bowed down, 'There is lifting up.' And tell them where it is likewise. Tell them it is only at the cross. Tell them it is through the precious blood. Tell them it is to be had for nothing, through simply trusting Christ. Tell them it is of free grace, that no merits of theirs are wanted, that no good things are they to bring, but that they may come just as they are, and find lifting up in Christ.

FOR MEDITATION: It is a fact that those in the world who are without Christ are currently also without hope (Ephesians 2:12); but while they are still in the land of the living there is still hope (Ecclesiastes 9:4) that the whole situation can be reversed.

The superlative excellence of the Holy Spirit

'Nevertheless I tell you the truth; it is expedient for you that I go away: for if I go not away, the Comforter will not come unto you; but if I depart, I will send him unto you.' John 16:7
SUGGESTED FURTHER READING: 1 Corinthians 2:9–16

Without the Holy Spirit no good thing ever did or ever can come into any of your hearts—no sigh of penitence, no cry of faith, no glance of love, no tear of hallowed sorrow. Your heart can never beat with life divine, except through the Spirit; you are not capable of the smallest degree of spiritual emotion, much less spiritual action, apart from the Holy Spirit. Dead you lie, living only for evil, but absolutely dead for God until the Holy Spirit comes and raises you. The flowers of Christ are all exotics—'In me (that is, in my flesh,) dwelleth no good thing.' 'Who can bring a clean thing out of an unclean? not one.' Everything must come from Christ, and Christ gives nothing to men except through the Spirit of all grace. Prize, then, the Spirit as the channel of all good which comes into you. And further, no good thing can come out of you apart from the Spirit. Let it be in you, yet it lies dormant unless God works in you to will and to do of his own good pleasure. Do you desire to preach? How can you unless the Holy Spirit touches your tongue? Do you desire to pray? Alas, what dull work it is unless the Spirit makes intercession for you. Do you desire to subdue sin? Would you be holy? Would you imitate your Master? Do you desire to rise to superlative heights of spirituality? Are you wanting to be made like the angels of God, full of zeal and ardour for the Master's cause? You cannot without the Spirit— 'Without me ye can do nothing.' O branch of the vine, you can have no fruit without the sap. O child of God, you have no life within you apart from the life which God gives you through his Spirit.

FOR MEDITATION: Christians are what they are as the result of receiving the Holy Spirit, his teaching and his gifts (1 Corinthians 2:12–14). As recipients of everything we have, we should neither boast of our gifts as if they originated with us (1 Corinthians 4:7), nor should we monopolise them (1 Peter 4:10).

SERMON NO. 574

The restoration and conversion of the Jews

'Thus saith the Lord GOD *unto these bones: Behold, I will cause breath to enter into you, and ye shall live: and I will lay sinews upon you, and will bring up flesh upon you, and cover you with skin, and put breath in you, and ye shall live; and ye shall know that I am the* LORD.' Ezekiel 37:5–6
SUGGESTED FURTHER READING: Romans 11:1–12

Israel is to have a spiritual restoration or a conversion. Both the text and the context teach this. The promise is that they shall renounce their idols, and, behold, they have already done so. 'Neither shall they defile themselves any more with their idols' (Ezekiel 37:23). Whatever faults the Jew may have besides, he certainly has no idolatry. 'The LORD thy God is one God,' is a truth far better conceived by the Jew than by any other man on earth except the Christian. Weaned for ever from the worship of all images, of whatever sort, the Jewish nation has now become infatuated with traditions or duped by philosophy. She is to have, however, instead of these delusions, a spiritual religion: she is to love her God. 'They shall be my people, and I will be their God' (verse 23). The unseen but omnipotent Jehovah is to be worshipped in spirit and in truth by his ancient people; they are to come before him in his own appointed way, accepting the Mediator whom their sires rejected; coming into covenant relation with God, for so the context tells us—'I will make a covenant of peace with them' (verse 26), and Jesus is our peace, therefore we gather that Jehovah shall enter into the covenant of grace with them, that covenant of which Christ is the federal head, the substance, and the surety. They are to walk in God's ordinances and statutes, and so exhibit the practical effects of being united to Christ who has given them peace. All these promises certainly imply that the people of Israel are to be converted to God, and that this conversion is to be permanent.

FOR MEDITATION: Do you find time in your theology and prayers for the Jews? Join the apostle Paul and pray (Romans 10:1) that more and more Jewish people will accept the new covenant which God has made, that he will be their God and that they will be his people (Hebrews 8:8,10).

Tell it all

'But the woman fearing and trembling, knowing what was done in her,
came and fell down before him, and told him all the truth.' Mark 5:33
SUGGESTED FURTHER READING: 1 Thessalonians 1:1–10

You do not know, dear friends, of how much service your open confession of
Christ might be to some trembling soul. One reason why we have churches,
and are joined in fellowship, is that we may help the weak; that by our daring
to say 'Christ has saved me,' others may take heart, and may come to him
and find the same mercy. 'Oh,' but you say, 'the church does not want me.'
Then, I might say the same, and all Christians might say the same. Where
would there be a visible church on earth at all? What is right for one
Christian to do is right for all to do; and if it is right for you to neglect
professing Christ, then it is right for all believers to do so. And then, where is
the church? Where is the ministry? Where is Christ's truth? How are sinners
to be saved at all? Suppose, my brother, that John Calvin and Martin Luther
had said, 'Well now we know the truth; but we had better be quiet, for we
can go to heaven much more comfortably. If we begin preaching we shall set
all the world by the ears, and there will be a deal of mischief done; hundreds
of persons will have to be martyrs for their faith, and we shall be subject to
many hardships.' They had quite as much right to hide their religion as you
have. They had quite as much reason for the concealment of their godliness
as you have. But alas! for the world, where would have been the
Reformation, if these had been as cowardly as you are, and like you had
skulked to the rear in the day of battle. I ask again, what would be the
wretched lot of England, what calamities would happen to our island, if all
who know Christ as you know him were to act as you do?

FOR MEDITATION: Do you have to plead guilty? Many of us are more ready
with our excuses than we are with our testimonies (1 Peter 3:15). The only
excuses the early church made use of were excuses for spreading the Gospel
(Acts 2:14–15; 3:12–13; 4:9–10,19–20,29; 5:29,41–42).

SERMON NO. 514

Sunshine in the heart

'Delight thyself also in the LORD, *and he shall give thee the desires of thine heart.'* Psalm 37:4

SUGGESTED FURTHER READING: Psalm 84:1–12

'I can't understand,' once said a bird to a fish, 'how it is that you always live in the cold element; I could not live there. It must be a great self-denial to you not to fly up to the trees. See how I can mount aloft.' 'Ah,' said the fish, 'it is no self-denial to me to live here, it is my element; I never aspire to fly, for it would not suit me. If I were taken out of my element I should die unless I was restored to it very soon, and the sooner the better.' So the believer feels that God is his native element. He does not escape from his God, or from his Master's will and service; and if for a time he were taken out of it, the sooner he could get back to it the better. If he is thrown into bad company he is miserable and wretched until he gets out of it again. Does the dove deny itself when it does not eat carrion? No, verily the dove could not delight in blood, it would not feed thereon if it could. When a man sees a company of swine under the oak delighting themselves in their acorns, and grunting out their satisfaction, does he deny himself when he passes them by without sharing their feast? No, verily. he has better bread at home whereof he can eat, and swines' meat is no dainty to him. So it is with the believer; his religion is a matter of delight, a matter of satisfaction; and that which he avoids and turns from is very little self-denial to him. His tastes are changed, his wishes are altered. He delights himself in his God, and joyously receives the desire of his heart.

FOR MEDITATION: If you are a Christian, unbelievers should have problems trying to understand your lifestyle (1 Peter 4:3–4). If that isn't the case, are you enjoying something you shouldn't be, or not enjoying something you should be? Is your delight in the Lord's word (Psalm 1:2), the Lord's will (Psalm 40:8), the Lord's day (Isaiah 58:13) and in the Lord himself (Isaiah 58:14)?

Climbing the mountain

'Who shall ascend into the hill of the LORD?*' Psalm 24:3*
SUGGESTED FURTHER READING: Hebrews 12:18–24

From lofty mountains you can look on that side and see the lakes and the rivers; and on this side the green and laughing valleys, and far away, the wild black forest. The view is wide, but what a view is that which we shall have in heaven! There 'shall I know even as also I am known.' Here 'we see through a glass, darkly;' but there 'face to face.' And chief and foremost, best of all, my eyes shall see the King in his beauty. We shall behold his face; we shall look into his eyes; we shall drink love from the fountain of his heart, and hear the music of his love from the sweet organ of his lips; we shall be entranced in his society, emparadised on his bosom. Up, Christian, up, Christ waits for thee! Come, man, tread the thorny way and climb, for Christ stands on the summit stretching out his hands, and saying, 'Come up hither;' 'to him that overcometh will I grant to sit with me in my throne, even as I also overcame, and am set down with my Father in his throne.' And there is this sweet reflection—all that we shall see upon the top of the hill of God shall be ours. We look from earthly mountains and we see, but we do not possess. That mansion yonder is not ours; that crystal stream belongs not to us; those widespread lawns are beautiful, but they are not in our possession. But on the hill-tops of heaven, all that we see we shall possess. We shall possess the streets of gold, the harps of harmony, the palms of victory, the shouts of angels, the songs of cherubim, the joy of the divine Trinity, and the song of God as he rests in his love, and rejoices over us with singing, and God the Eternal One himself shall be ours, and ours for ever and for ever.

FOR MEDITATION: Since the Lord Jesus Christ has ascended into heaven (Acts 1:9–11), the Christian should set his affection on things above where Christ sits (Colossians 3:1–2). The best thing about ascending to heaven is that the Lord is there (Psalm 139:8) in all his love and beauty (Revelation 21:22–23; 22:3); the worst thing about descending to hell is that the Lord is there (Psalm 139:8) in his just wrath and judgment.

SERMON NO. 396

The axe at the root—a testimony against idolatry

'But the hour cometh, and now is, when the true worshippers shall worship the Father in spirit and in truth, for the Father seeketh such to worship him. God is a Spirit: and they that worship him must worship him in spirit and in truth.' John 4:23–24

SUGGESTED FURTHER READING: Philippians 3:1–8

Let me give a sketch of this worship as it actually exhibits itself. A man may have been to a place of worship from his youth up, and he may have fallen into a habit of repeating a sacred form every morning and every evening; he may even have been a tolerably diligent reader of the Word of God, and yet though this may have continued for sixty years and more, he may never once have worshipped God after the fashion prescribed in the text. But see him! The Father seeks him, truth comes home to his soul, and in the light of that truth he feels himself a sinner, and feeling himself so, he cries, 'Father, I have sinned.' That is his first true worship. See, brethren, his spirit feels it, he means what he says. All that he said before was as nothing, but that first cry 'I have sinned' has in it the vitality of worship. He hears the story of the cross, the full atonement made by God's appointed sacrifice, and he prays, 'Lord, I believe in Jesus, and I trust him;' here is another specimen of true worship; here is the spirit resting upon God's appointed sacrifice, and reverencing God's way of salvation by accepting it. Being saved by the precious blood of Jesus, he cries, 'Father, I bless thee that I am saved, I thank thee that my sins are washed away.' This is true worship. The whole of the Christian's life, consisting as it must do of dealings with the invisible God through Jesus Christ by his heart, is a life of worship, and when at last he comes to die, you perceive that his worship will not cease with death, because it has always been spiritual, and did not depend upon the body.

FOR MEDITATION: Worship consists of trusting Christ and living for him (Romans 12:1), not merely of singing hymns and saying prayers. Paul's first act of true worship was to replace his faith in religious ceremonies and his religious upbringing (Philippians 3:3–6) by faith in Christ (Philippians 3:7–9). Are you a so-called 'worshipper' who needs to do the same?

SERMON NO. 695

'The love of Jesus, what it is—none but his loved ones know.'

'And to know the love of Christ which passeth knowledge.' Ephesians 3:19
SUGGESTED FURTHER READING: 2 Thessalonians 2:16–3:5

An increase of love, a more perfect apprehension of Christ's love is one of the best and most infallible gauges whereby we may test ourselves whether we have grown in grace or not. If we have grown in grace, it is absolutely certain that we shall have advanced in our knowledge and reciprocation of the love of Christ. Many here present have believed in Jesus, and they do know the love of Jesus. But they know it not as some others here do, who have gone into the inner chamber, and have been made to drink of the spiced wine of Christ's pomegranate. Some of you have begun to climb the mountain, and the view which lies at your feet is lovely and passing fair, but the landscape is not such as would greet your eyes if you could but stand where advanced saints are standing now, and could look to the east and to the west, to the north and to the south, and see all the lengths and breadths, and depths and heights, of 'the love of Christ which passeth knowledge.' To change the figure: the love of Christ is comparable with Jacob's ladder; some of us are standing on the lower rungs, and there are others who are ascending and who rest half way; others still are getting up so high that we can scarce see them by reason of the dimness of our sight; and there are some, perhaps, at this hour, who have just reached the topmost rung of this knowledge, and are now stepping as it were into the arms of Christ who awaits them at the top; they have attained unto their perfection. Here they shall find repose. They shall rest in his love, and with the eternal songs of heaven they shall rejoice for ever and for ever.

FOR MEDITATION: A realisation of Christ's love towards us should affect us inwardly (Romans 5:5; 2 Corinthians 5:14) and outwardly (John 13:34; 15:12; Ephesians 5:2; 1 John 4:11). Is this increasingly the case with you?

The pierced One pierces the heart

'And I will pour upon the house of David, and upon the inhabitants of Jerusalem, the spirit of grace and of supplications: and they shall look upon me whom they have pierced, and they shall mourn for him, as one mourneth for his only son, and shall be in bitterness for him, as one that is in bitterness for his firstborn.' Zechariah 12:10
SUGGESTED FURTHER READING: John 4:27–42

A personal faith it must be, and what if I urge you to let it be immediate faith? It will be no easier to flee tomorrow, than it is today. It is the same thing that you will have to believe tomorrow as it is today—that Jesus Christ gave himself for your sins. This is God's testimony, that Christ is able to save. O that you would trust him. My soul, you have regretted a thousand things, but you have never regretted trusting Christ in your youth. Many have wept that they did not come to Christ before, but none ever lamented that they came too early. Why not this very day? O Holy Spirit, make it so! Behold the fields are showing the green ears ready for the harvest; the season advances, and the fields are prophesying the harvest. O that we might see some green ears today, some green ears prophetic of a blessed harvest of souls. As to myself, I cross this day into another year of my own life and history, and I bear witness that my Master is worth trusting. O it is a blessed thing to be a Christian; it is a sweet thing to be a believer in Christ, and though I, of all men, perhaps, am the subject of the deepest depression of spirits at times, yet there lives not a soul who can say more truthfully than I, 'My soul doth magnify the Lord, and my spirit hath rejoiced in God my Saviour.' He who is mighty has looked upon me with eyes of love and made me his child, and I trust him this day as I have trusted him aforetime. But now I would to God that this day some of you would begin to trust in him.

FOR MEDITATION: This was Spurgeon's 30th birthday. Just as it is impossible to live on earth without having been born, it will be impossible to enter heaven without having been born again (John 3:3,5,7). If you haven't yet got a spiritual birthday, the best date to be born again is today's date (2 Corinthians 6:2).

The minister's stock-taking

'And some believed the things which were spoken, and some believed not.'
Acts 28:24
SUGGESTED FURTHER READING: John 3:16–18

There has never been a cross-breed between a believer and an unbeliever. A man must be either dead or alive. There is no neutral ground. You must either be on one side with those who are alive, or on the other side with those who are dead and need to be quickened. Think not to halt between two opinions. For the most part those who are said to be halting between two opinions are really of one opinion; they do not intend to serve the Lord, and they say in their hearts, 'Who is the Lord that I should serve him?' Now will you do me this favour? I asked it once, and it was blessed to the conversion of several. Will you take a little time alone, perhaps this evening; take a paper and pencil, and after you have honestly and fairly thought on your own state, and weighed your own condition before the Lord, will you write down one of two words: if you feel that you are not a believer write down this word—'*Condemned*,' and if you are a believer in Jesus, and put your trust in him alone, write down the word '*Forgiven*.' Do it, even though you have to write down the word 'Condemned.' We lately received into church-fellowship a young man, who said, 'Sir, I wrote down the word 'Condemned', and I looked at it; there it was; I had written it myself— 'Condemned'.' As he looked the tears began to flow, and the heart began to break; and before long he fled to Christ, put the paper in the fire, and wrote down 'Forgiven.' This young man was about the sixth who had been brought to the Lord in the same way. So I pray you try it, and God may bless it to you.

FOR MEDITATION: What is suggested is not a little game, but a matter of spiritual life and death. Are you prepared to examine yourself in this way (2 Corinthians 13:5) and to let God examine you and show you your real spiritual position (Psalm 26:2)?

SERMON NO. 516

The sinner's advocate

'My little children, these things write I unto you, that ye sin not. And if any man sin, we have an advocate with the Father, Jesus Christ the righteous.' 1 John 2:1
SUGGESTED FURTHER READING: 1 John 1:5–10

This truth, so evangelical and so divine, should be practically remembered. It should be practically remembered, dear friends, at all times. Every day I find it most healthy to my own soul to try and walk as a saint, but in order to do so I must continually come to Christ as a sinner. I would seek to be perfect; I would strain after every virtue, and forsake every false way; but still, as to my standing before God, I find it happiest to sit where I sat when I first looked to Jesus, on the rock of his works, having nothing to do with my own righteousness, but only with his. Depend on it, dear friends, the happiest way of living is to live as a poor sinner and as nothing at all, having Jesus Christ as your all in all. You may have all your growths in sanctification, all your progress in graces, all the development of your virtues that you will; but still I do earnestly pray you never to put any of these where Christ should be. If you have begun in Christ then finish in Christ. If you have begun in the flesh and then go on in the flesh, we know what the sure result will be. But if you have begun with Jesus Christ as your Alpha, let him be your Omega. I pray you never think you are rising when you get above this, for it is not rising, but slipping downwards to your ruin. Stand still to this—

'Nothing in my hand I bring,
Simply to thy cross I cling.'

Still a sinner, but still having an advocate with the Father, Jesus Christ the righteous—let this be the spirit of your everyday life.

FOR MEDITATION: Three things about the Christian life which the Christian needs to remember at all times:- the fact of sin (1 John 1:8,10), the forgiveness of sin (1 John 1:7,9; 2:1–2) and the fight with sin (1 John 2:1). The first should protect us from pride, the second from despair and the third from licence. Forget any one of these and you are at risk.

Religion—a reality

'For it is not a vain thing for you, because it is your life.' Deuteronomy
32:47
SUGGESTED FURTHER READING: 1 Corinthians 3:18–23

Where is the folly of true religion? Is it a folly to be providing for the world to
come? 'Oh, no.' Is it a folly to make the Author of your being its first end?
'No, no.' Is it altogether a folly to believe that there is such a thing as justice?
I think not. And that, if there be such a thing as justice, it involves
punishment? There is no great folly there. Well, then, is it any folly to
perceive that there is no way of escaping from the effects of our offences
except justice be satisfied? Is that folly? And if it be the fact that Christ has
satisfied justice for all who trust in him, is it folly to trust him? If it be a folly
to escape from the flames of hell, then let us be fools. If it be folly to lay hold
of him who gives us eternal life—oh, blessed folly! Let us be more foolish
still. Let us take deep dives into the depths of this foolishness. God forbid
that we should do anything else but glory in being such fools as this for
Christ's sake! What, sirs, is your wisdom? Your wisdom dwells in denying
what your eyes can see—a God; in denying what your consciences tell you—
that you are guilty; in denying what should be your best hope, what your
spirit really craves after—redemption in Christ Jesus. Your folly lies in
following a perverted nature, instead of obeying the dictates of one who
points you to the right path. You are wise and you drink poison; we are fools
and we take the antidote. You are wise and you hunt the shadow; we are
fools and we grasp the substance. You are wise, and you labour and put your
money into a bag which is full of holes, and spend it for that which is not
bread, and which never gives you satisfaction; and we are fools enough to be
satisfied, to be happy, to be perfectly content with heaven and God.

FOR MEDITATION: Better to become a fool in the world's eyes for Christ's sake
(1 Corinthians 3:18; 4:10) than to remain a fool in God's eyes for the world's
sake (Luke 12:19–20; 1 Corinthians 3:19). Which kind of fool are you?

Fire! Fire! Fire!

'When thou walkest through the fire, thou shalt not be burned; neither shall the flame kindle upon thee.' Isaiah 43:2
SUGGESTED FURTHER READING: 1 Peter 4:12–19

Through much tribulation we must inherit the kingdom. Think it no strange thing when the fiery trial shall happen to you. If you have the common afflictions of the world do not wonder. You must have them. The same thing happens both to the evil and to the good. You lose in business, you have reverses and disappointments; do not stagger at these on the way to heaven. You must have these; they are necessary to your spiritual health. Worse than that, you have strange temptations, you are placed in a position where you are constantly exposed to sin. It must be so. This too is the pathway of God's people; you must have these fiery temptations, that you, being tried in the fire, may come forth as gold seven times purified. You have mental anxieties. Neither let these seem a wonder to you. They fall to the lot of all the saints of the Most High. Moreover, you will have to endure the attacks of Satan, you must go through the valley of the shadow of death, and fight with Apollyon as Christian did; you are not to be exempted from the hardness of Christian warfare. If you will mount the hill, you must climb; if you are to win the crown, you must win it by sheer might. Think not this a strange thing. And if in doing good you meet with difficulties, let that not stagger you. It is but right and natural. I tell you again, if there be any pathway in which there be not fire, tremble; but if your lot be hard, thank God for it. If your sufferings be great, bless the Lord for them; and if the difficulties in your pathway be many, surmount them by faith, but let them not cast you down. Be of good courage, and wait on the Lord, setting this constantly in your minds that he has not promised to keep you from trouble, but to preserve you in it.

FOR MEDITATION: The early Christians were properly taught to expect problems in the Christian life (John 16:33; Acts 14:22; 1 Thessalonians 3:4). Are you forewarned and forearmed for trouble (1 Peter 4:12) or does it take you by surprise and throw you into doubt and confusion?

SERMON NO. 397

God's cure for man's weakness

'Out of weakness were made strong.' Hebrews 11:34
SUGGESTED FURTHER READING: Hebrews 11:1–7

Faith makes the crown of eternal life glitter before the believer's eye; it waves before him the palm branch. Sense pictures the grave, loss, suffering, defeat, death, forgetfulness: but faith points to the resurrection, the glorious appearance of the Son of Man, the calling of the saints from every corner of the earth, the clothing of them all in their triumphant array, and the entrance of the blood-washed conquerors into the presence of God with eternal joy. Thus faith makes us out of weakness to become strong. Let me remind you that the essential ingredients of faith's comfort are just these: faith sees the invisible and beholds the substance of that which is afar off: faith believes in God, a present, powerful God, full of love and wisdom, effecting his decree, accomplishing his purpose, fulfilling his promise, glorifying his Son. Faith believes in the blood of Jesus, in the effectual redemption on the cross, it believes in the power of the Holy Spirit, his might to soften the stone and to put life into the very ribs of death. Faith grasps the reality of the Bible; she does not look upon it as a sepulchre with a stone laid thereon, but as a temple in which Christ reigns, as an ivory palace out of which he comes riding in his chariot, conquering and to conquer. Faith does not believe the gospel to be a worn-out scroll, to be rolled up and put away; she believes that the gospel instead of being in its dotage is in its youth; she anticipates for it a manhood of mighty strugglings, and a grand maturity of blessedness and triumph. Faith does not shirk the fight; she longs for it, because she foresees the victory.

FOR MEDITATION: In the world's estimation those who trust in the living God are the underdogs (2 Kings 18:22,35; 19:10). It may seem that way to us also, but the reality is that by faith in Christ we become more than conquerors over the world (2 Chronicles 32:7–8; Romans 8:37; 1 John 5:4–5). 'When I am weak, then am I strong' (2 Corinthians 12:10).

Jericho captured

'And the LORD *said unto Joshua, See, I have given into thine hand Jericho, and the king thereof, and the mighty men of valour. And ye shall compass the city, all ye men of war, and go round the city once. Thus shalt thou do six days.'* Joshua 6:2–3
SUGGESTED FURTHER READING: Hebrews 11:29–38

'Go round about her: tell the towers thereof. Mark ye well her bulwarks.' These men were practical surveyors of Jericho; they could well understand the strength of the battlements, how many feet long the huge stones were at the corners, and how near the stars the loftiest towers were raised. They had the difficulty, I say, always before them, yet they kept on in simple faith, going round the city. Sometimes we get into the habit of shutting our eyes to difficulty; that will not do: faith is not a fool, faith does not shut her eyes to difficulty, and then run head-foremost against a brick wall—never. Faith sees the difficulty, surveys it all, and then she says, 'By my God will I leap over a wall;' and over the wall she goes. She never brings out the flaming accounts of 'Signs of the Times,' in her favour; she does not sit down, and say that evidently public sentiment is changing; she does not reckon upon any undercurrents that may be at work, which she is told by Mistress Gossip really are doing great things, but she just looks at it, and does not mind how bad the thing is reported to be; if anyone can exaggerate the difficulty, faith is of the same noble mind as that famous warrior, who when told there were so many thousand soldiers against him, replied, 'There are so many more to be killed.' So faith reckons: 'So many more difficulties, so many more things to be overcome;' and even impossibilities she puts down as only so much burden to be cast upon him, with whom nothing is impossible. She keeps Jericho's walls before her.

FOR MEDITATION: Walking by faith and not by sight (2 Corinthians 5:7) does not mean having blind faith. The Christian is not to close his eyes to the difficulties (Romans 8:35,38–39), but to open them to see the hand of the invisible God at work (Hebrews 11:27). Hezekiah had the right approach (2 Kings 19:14–19).

Let us go forth

'Let us go forth therefore unto him without the camp, bearing his reproach.' Hebrews 13:13
SUGGESTED FURTHER READING: 2 Corinthians 6:14–18

The Christian is to be separate from the world as to his company. He must buy, and sell, and trade like other men in the world, but yet he is not to find his intimate friends in it. He is not to go out of society and shut himself up in a monastery; he is to be in the world but not of it; and his choice company is not to be among the loose, the immoral, the profane, no, not even among the merely moral—his choice company is to be the saints of God. He is to select for his associates those who shall be his companions in the world to come. As idle boys were accustomed to mock at foreigners in the streets, so do worldlings jeer at Christians; therefore the believer flies away to his own company when he wants good fellowship. The Christian must come out of the world as to his company. I know this rule will break many a fond connection; but 'be ye not unequally yoked together with unbelievers.' I know it will snap ties which are almost as dear as life, but it must be done. We must not be overruled even by our own brother when the things of God and conscience are concerned. You must follow Christ, whatever may be the enmity you may excite, remembering that unless you love Christ better than husband, or father, or mother, yes, and your own life also, you cannot be his disciple. If these be hard terms, turn your backs, and perish in your sins! Count the cost; and if you cannot bear such a cost as this, do not undertake to be a follower of Christ.

FOR MEDITATION: Godly King Jehoshaphat of Judah seemed incapable of learning this lesson. Note the contrast with wicked King Ahab of Israel (2 Chronicles 17:3–6; 1 Kings 16:30–33), his compromise with him (2 Chronicles 18:1–3), the chastisement it caused (2 Chronicles 19:1–3) and the correction this brought (2 Chronicles 20:1–4). But the continuation of the account is salutary—Jehoshaphat fell for the same trick again (2 Chronicles 20:35–37) and again (2 Kings 3:6–7)! 'I am as thou art' is a false and foolish attitude for a Christian to adopt towards a non-Christian.

The garden of the soul

'A *place called Gethsemane.'* *Matthew 26:36*
SUGGESTED FURTHER READING: Matthew 27:35–56

Watch inward. Look at Christ. 'Consider him that endured such contradiction of sinners against himself.' Watch the Saviour, and watch with the Saviour. Brethren and sisters, I should like to say this to you so emphatically that you would never forget it. Be familiar with the passion of your Lord. Get right up to the cross. Do not be satisfied with that, but get the cross on your shoulders; get yourself bound to the cross in the spirit of the apostle when he said, 'I am crucified with Christ: nevertheless I live.' I do not know that I have had sweeter work to do for a long time than when a few weeks ago I was looking over all the hymn-writers and all the poets I knew of for hymns upon the passion of the Lord. I tried to enjoy them as I selected them, and to get into the vein in which the poets were when they sung them. Believe me, there is no fount that yields such sweet water as the fount that springs from Calvary just at the foot of the cross. Here it is that there is a sight to be seen more astounding and more ravishing than ever from the top of Pisgah. Get into the side of Christ; it is a cleft of the rock in which you may hide until the tempest is overpassed. Live in Christ; live near to Christ; and then, let the conflict come, and you will overcome even as he overcame, and rising up from your sweat and from your agony you will go forth to meet even death itself with a calm expression on your brow, saying, 'My Father, not as I will, but as thou wilt.'

FOR MEDITATION: The recent research connected with hymns to which Spurgeon refers was probably in preparation for *Our Own Hymnbook* which he was compiling and which was published in September 1866 (this undated sermon appeared in June 1866). Do the hymns and spiritual songs you like to sing have an important and meaningful place for the Lord Jesus Christ, his death and the salvation of sinners (Revelation 5:9,12) or are they more taken up with yourself and your own experiences?

The rainbow

'And the bow shall be in the cloud; and I will look upon it, that I may remember the everlasting covenant between God and every living creature of all flesh that is upon the earth.' Genesis 9:16
SUGGESTED FURTHER READING: 2 Timothy 2:8–13

Whenever we think of Christ let us *be little children*, and look, and look, and look again; and let us long to get at him, for unlike the rainbow, we can get at him. Pliny, who by the way talks a deal of nonsense, declares that wherever the rainbow's foot rests the flowers are made much sweeter; and Aristotle says, the rainbow is a great breeder of honey-dew. I do not know how that is, but I know that wherever Jesus Christ is he makes the perfume of his people very sweet. His 'name is as ointment poured forth,' and I know he is 'a great breeder of honey-dew.' There is sure to be much more loving-kindness in that man's heart who has seen much of Jesus. I recommend to you to follow that divine rainbow till you reach the foot of it, and till you embrace it, and say with Simeon, 'Now lettest thou thy servant depart in peace ... for mine eyes have seen thy salvation.' Play the child then. While we gaze, ought we not to *praise and admire*? One or two of the nations of antiquity had it as a part of their religion always to sing hymns when they saw the rainbow. Should not we whenever we see Christ? Should it not be a red-letter day marked in our diary? 'This day let us praise his name.' And as we ought always to see him, I may improve upon this, and bid you say—'I will praise thee every day.' And again, when we see Christ, we ought to *confess our sin with humiliation*. An old writer says that the Jews confess their sins when they see the rainbow. I am sure, whenever we see Christ, we ought to remember the deluge of wrath from which he has delivered us, the flames of hell from which he has saved us; and so, humbly bowing ourselves in the dust, let us love, and praise, and bless his name.

FOR MEDITATION: Consider God's promises to remember when he looked upon the bow (Genesis 9:16) and to pass over when he saw the blood (Exodus 12:13). The Christian can rejoice in God's faithfulness.

SERMON NO. 517

The friend of sinners

'He was numbered with the transgressors; and he bare the sin of many, and made intercession for the transgressors.' Isaiah 53:12
SUGGESTED FURTHER READING: John 7:37–52

Trust Christ and you are saved. Outside in the street there is a drinking-fountain. When you get there, if you are thirsty go to it; you will find no policeman there to send you away. No one will cry, 'You must not drink because you do not wear a satin dress.' 'You must not drink because you wear a corduroy jacket.' No, go and drink; and when you have hold of the ladle and are putting it to your lips, if there should come a doubt—'I do not feel my thirst enough,' still take a drink whether you do or not. So I say to you, Jesus Christ stands like a great flowing fountain in the corners of the street, and he invites every thirsty soul to come and drink. You need not stop and say, 'Am I thirsty enough? Am I dirty enough?' You do need it whether you think you do or not. Come as you are. Every fitness is legality; every preparation is a lie; every getting ready for Christ is coming the wrong way. You are only making yourselves worse while you think you are making yourselves better. You are like a boy at school who has made a little blot, and he gets out his knife to scratch it out, and makes it ten times worse than before. Leave the blots alone. Come as you are. If you are the dirtiest soul out of hell, trust Christ, and that act of trust shall make you clean. This seems a simple thing, and yet it is the hardest thing in the world to bring you to it; so hard a thing that all the preachers that ever preached cannot make a man believe in Christ.

FOR MEDITATION: Those who take their spiritual thirst to the living God (Isaiah 55:1; John 7:37; Revelation 22:17) know where to drink in the future (Psalm 42:2; 63:1; 143:6) and never need to try to satisfy that thirst anywhere else (John 4:14–15; 6:35).

The new nature

'Love one another .... being born again, not of corruptible seed, but of incorruptible, by the word of God, which liveth and abideth for ever.'
1 Peter 2:22–23
SUGGESTED FURTHER READING: Colossians 1:9–14

Looking upon God's people, as being heirs of glory, princes of the royal blood, descendants of the King of kings, earth's true and only royal aristocracy, Peter says to them, 'See that you love one another, because of your noble birth, being born of incorruptible seed; because of your pedigree, being descended from God, the Creator of all things; and because of your immortal destiny, for you shall never pass away, though the glory of flesh shall fade, and even its very existence shall cease.' I think it would be well, my brethren, if in a spirit of humility, you and I recognised the true dignity of our regenerated nature, and lived up to it. Oh! what is a Christian? If you compare him with a king, he adds priestly sanctity to royal dignity. The king's royalty often lies only in his crown, but with a Christian it is infused into his very nature. Compare him with a senator, with a mighty warrior, or a master of wisdom, and he far excels them all. He is of another race than those who are only born of woman. He is as much above his fellows through his new birth, as man is above the beast that perishes. As humanity towers in dignity high above the grovelling brute, so does the regenerate man o'ertop the best of human once-born mortals. Surely he ought to bear himself, and act as one who is not of the multitude, one who has been chosen out of the world, distinguished by sovereign grace, written among 'the peculiar people,' and who therefore cannot grovel as others grovel, nor even think as others think. Let the dignity of your nature, and the brightness of your prospects, O believers in Christ, make you cleave to holiness, and hate the very appearance of evil.

FOR MEDITATION: The apostle Paul, though a prisoner in chains, would never have changed places with an earthly king in royal robes (Acts 26:28–29). Do you value and seek to live up to your high calling in Christ (Ephesians 4:1; 1 Thessalonians 2:12; 1 Peter 2:9)?

Seeing is not believing, but believing is seeing

'Whom having not seen, ye love; in whom, though now ye see him not, yet believing, ye rejoice with joy unspeakable and full of glory.' 1 Peter 1:8
SUGGESTED FURTHER READING: John 20:19–31

Carnal people will imagine that if there could be something to touch or smell they should get on, but mere believing and loving are too hard for them. Yet such thought is not reasonable, and I can show you so. Occasionally one meets with an illiterate working man who will say to those whose occupation is mental, 'I work hard for my living,' insinuating that the mind-worker does not work at all. Yet I ask any man who is engaged in a mental pursuit, whether he does not know that mental work is quite as real work—and some of us think more so—as working with the hand or the arm. The thing is mental, but is none the less real. Just transfer that thought. Coming into contact with Christ by touch looks to most people to be most real; that is because their animal nature is uppermost; coming into contact with Jesus by the spirit seems to them to be unreal, only because they know nothing of spiritual things. Mere animal men will often say, 'I can understand the headache, I can understand the pain of having a leg cut off;' but the pain of injured affection, or of receiving ingratitude from a trusted friend, this is by the rough mind thought to be no pain at all. 'Oh,' says he, 'I could put up with that.' But I ask you who have minds, is there any pain more real than mental pain? Is it not the sharpest when the iron enters into the soul? Just so the mental operation—for it is a mental operation—of coming into contact with Christ by loving him and trusting him is the most real thing in all the world, and no one will think it unreal who has once exercised it.

FOR MEDITATION: Unlike Thomas we cannot touch the Lord to bolster our faith (John 20:27–29). Claiming that unscriptural religious acts are not articles of faith but visual aids to faith is carnal, not spiritual, in both origin and outcome (John 3:6). Finding it 'helpful' to confess sins to a human 'priest' ignores the existence of the Great High Priest in heaven who makes such a go-between surplus to requirements (Hebrews 4:14,16; 8:1).

The dove's return to the ark

'But the dove found no rest for the sole of her foot.' Genesis 8:9
SUGGESTED FURTHER READING: Mark 12:28–34

We must love something, or some one. Man was not made to live alone, and therefore no man lives unto himself. Our heart must flow like a river, or it corrupts like a stagnant pool. Some have great hearts, and they require a great object on which to spend their love. They love fondly and firmly, too fondly and too firmly for earthly love. These are they who suffer from broken hearts. They have so much love that when they set it upon an unworthy object they reap a proportionate degree of misery and disappointment. Now let me say solemnly that no heart of a child of God will ever be satisfied with any object or person short of the Lord Jesus Christ. There is room for wife and children, there is room for friend and acquaintance, and all the more room in one's heart because Christ is there, but neither wife, nor children, nor friends, nor kinsfolk can ever fill the believers's heart. He must have Christ Jesus; there is no rest for him elsewhere. Do I address any believer who has been making an idol? Have you set up any god in your heart? Have you loved any creature so as to forget your Saviour? Be it child, or husband, or friend, take heed of the sin of idolatry. You cannot, you shall not find rest for the sole of your foot in the creature, however fair that creature may seem. God will break your idol before your eyes, or if he suffer that idol to stand, it shall remain to plague and curse you, for 'thus saith the Lord; Cursed be the man that trusteth in man, and maketh flesh his arm.' 'Cease ye from man, whose breath is in his nostrils: for wherein is he to be accounted of?' Give your hearts to the Lord Jesus and he will never disappoint you. Lean on him with all your weight of affection, for he will never fail you.

FOR MEDITATION: The Lord Jesus Christ has told us that we must love both God and man, but he has also specified who should come first (Mark 12:28–30), who should come second (Mark 12:31) and where we should place the emphasis (Matthew 10:37).

SERMON NO. 637

A bad excuse is worse than none

'And they all with one consent began to make excuse.' Luke 14:18
SUGGESTED FURTHER READING: Jonah 3:1–4:2

The doctrine of election is a great and precious truth, but it never can be a valid reason for a man's not believing in Christ. You are ill today, and the doctor comes; 'There,' says he, 'there is the medicine, I will guarantee if you take it, it will heal you.' You say, 'Sir, I would take it at once, but I do not know whether I am predestined to get over this fever. If I am predestined to live, why then, sir, I will take the medicine, but I must know first.' 'Ah!' says the doctor, 'I tell you what, if you do not take it, you are predestined to die.' And I will tell you this, if you will not believe in Jesus Christ, you will be damned, be you who you may, but you will not be able to lay it at predestination's door; it will lie at your own. A man has fallen overboard; a rope is thrown to him, but he says, 'I should like to grasp that rope, only I do not know whether I am predestined to be drowned.' Fool! he will go down to the bottom with a lie in his mouth. We do not say, 'I would sit down to dinner today, but I will not eat, because I do not know whether I am predestined to have any dinner today.' We do not talk so foolishly in common things, why then do we so in religion? When men are hard-up for an excuse, they are glad to run to the mysteries of God to use them as a veil to cover their faces. O my dear friends, you must know that though God has a chosen people, yet when he commands you to believe in Christ, his having a chosen people, or not having a chosen people cannot excuse you from obedience to the divine command: 'Believe on the Lord Jesus Christ, and thou shalt be saved.'

FOR MEDITATION: The people of Nineveh used God's threat of judgment as a reason to repent and hope against hope for his forgiveness (Jonah 3:5,9). It is not surprising that on the Day of Judgment they will condemn those who have rejected Christ's forgiveness (Matthew 12:41) by disobeying the gospel command to repent and trust in him (Mark 1:15). Will the people of Nineveh have to condemn you?

SERMON NO. 578

The great privation: or, the great salvation

'O that thou hadst hearkened to my commandments! then had thy peace been as a river, and thy righteousness as the waves of the sea.' Isaiah 48:18
SUGGESTED FURTHER READING: Ezekiel 47:1–5

A river increases in breadth, and its waters augment their volume. You can leap across the Thames, say at Cricklade, or Kemble; it is so tiny a little brook, you may almost take it up in a cup. There is a narrow plank across which laughing village girls go tripping over; but who thinks of laying down a plank across the Thames at Southend, or at Grays? Who would imagine that at Gravesend it might be crossed by the tripping girls, or by the skipping lambs? No, the river has grown—how deep! At the mouth of it, I suppose, comparable to the sea—how broad! It is a sort of ocean in miniature. There go the ships, and that leviathan might play therein. Not behemoth himself, I think, would have the presumption to suppose that he could sniff up this Jordan at a draught, for it has grown too great for him. Such is the Christian's peace. Pure and perfect though it is at the first, little temptations seem to mar it; oftentimes the troubles of this life threaten to choke it. Not that they ever do. True, it seems little at the point of its rise. Be not deceived. Wait. When the Christian is ten years older, and has meandered a few more miles along the tortuous course of a gracious experience, his peace will be like a broad river. Wait twenty or thirty years, till he has traversed these rich lowlands of fellowship with Christ in his sufferings, and conformity to his death, then his peace will be like a deep river, for he shall know 'the peace of God which passeth all understanding;' and he will have cast all his care upon God, who cares for him. Thus that peace will go on increasing till it melts into the infinite peace of the beatific vision.

FOR MEDITATION: Rivers in Scripture are often pictures of God's blessings to his people—bringing to them fruitfulness (Psalm 1:3), pleasure (Psalm 36:8), gladness (Psalm 46:4) and peace (Isaiah 66:12). Think on these things.

The bridgeless gulf

'Beside all this, between us and you there is a great gulf fixed: so that they which would pass from hence to you cannot; neither can they pass to us, that would come from thence.' Luke 16:26
SUGGESTED FURTHER READING: 2 Thessalonians 1:5–12

Heaven is *rest*, perfect rest—but there is no rest in hell; it is labour in the fire, but no ease, no peace, no sleep, no calm, no quiet; everlasting storm; eternal hurricane; unceasing tempest. In the worst disease, there are some respites: spasms of agony, but then pauses of repose. There is no pause in hell's torments. The dreadful music of the eternal miserere has not so much as a single stop in it. It is on, on, on, with crash of battle, and dust and blood, and fire and vapour of smoke. Heaven, too, is a place of *joy*; there happy fingers sweep celestial chords; there joyous spirits sing hosannahs day without night; but there is no joy in hell; for music there is the groan; for joy there is the pang; for sweet fellowship there is the binding up in bundles; for everything that is blissful there is everything that is dolorous. No, I could not exaggerate, that were impossible; I cannot come up to the doleful facts, therefore there I leave them. Nothing of the joy of heaven can ever come to hell. Heaven is the place of *sweet communion* with God—

'There they behold his face,
And never, never sin;
There from the rivers of his grace,
Drink endless pleasures in.'

There is no communion with God in hell. There are prayers, but they are unheard; there are tears, but they are unaccepted; there are cries for pity, but they are all an abomination unto the Lord. God wills not the death of any; he had rather that he should turn unto him and live, but if that grace be refused, then eternal vengeance is his portion.

FOR MEDITATION: 'There's a way back to God from the dark paths of sin'— but the only route is from earth to heaven; there never has been and there never will be a route from hell to heaven (Luke 13:24–28).

SERMON NO. 518

A sermon for men of taste

'Wherefore laying aside all malice, and all guile, and hypocrisies, and envies, and all evil speakings, as newborn babes, desire the sincere milk of the word, that ye may grow thereby: If so be ye have tasted that the Lord is gracious.' 1 Peter 2:1–3
SUGGESTED FURTHER READING: Psalm 34:8–14 (this Psalm was read earlier)

Evils to be avoided—*malice*. 'Revenge is sweet,' is the proverb of the Italians, and many an Englishman has half learned it, if not wholly. 'Revenge is sweet;' but not to the man who has tasted Christ, for he says, 'How can I have vengeance upon my fellow, when Christ has put away my sin?' Now, forgiveness is sweet, and he loathes malice, and turns aside from it as from venom itself. *Guile*: that is craftiness whereby men rob their fellow-creatures. Some men think guile a very fine thing. See that trader; you must keep both your eyes open or he will take you in; he does not exactly tell lies, but, well, he shaves very closely to the truth. It is guile; low craftiness and cunning. A man of God hates that thing. 'What! Am I, the servant of the God of truth, to crouch, bend, fawn, do anything but what is upright, to gain wealth?' As surely as the Lord says concerning the Laodicean church, 'I will spue thee out of my mouth,' so the believer says concerning anything that is not true and straightforward, 'I am sick of it; I loathe it; I abhor it; I turn from it.' The next thing is *hypocrisy*, whereby men are not so much robbed and injured as deceived. A Christian can be no hypocrite. Hypocrisy, like all other sins, lurks in man till the very last; but a believer hates to pretend to be what he is not. A man who has once tasted that the Lord is gracious, is a true and transparent man in his profession. If any suppose him to be better than he is, he does not wish to wear feathers that are not his own; he would not be glorified by another man's labours, nor build upon another man's foundation; hypocrisy he utterly detests.

FOR MEDITATION: The best way of avoiding these sins is to seek their opposites with the Lord's help—kindness for malice (Ephesians 4:31–32), openness for guile (2 Corinthians 4:2) and genuineness for hypocrisy (Matthew 6:2–6; Romans 12:9).

SERMON NO. 459

A peal of bells

'*In that day shall there be upon the bells of the horses, HOLINESS UNTO THE LORD.*' *Zechariah 14:20*
SUGGESTED FURTHER READING: Psalm 8:1–9

Even pleasure and recreation shall become Holiness to the Lord. When you are travelling in Alpine regions, you will be amused by the ringing of the little bells upon the horses. You are there for rest, to recruit the body, but let that rest be taken in the spirit of holiness. I fear that many leave their religion behind them when they go away. It ought not to be so; in our pleasures as well as in everything else, on the very bells of the horses there should be, Holiness unto the Lord. A Christian man needs recreation as well as another man. There must be times for breathing the fresh country air, and looking upon the meadows and the fields. I wish such days came oftener to the poor toiling population of this huge labyrinth of brick. But mark this; let us as Christians see to it that we carry the spirit of this text with us wherever we go; that the bells of the horses be, Holiness to the Lord, and our very recreations be done as sacredly and as much in the sight of God as our sacraments and our solemn feast days. Does recreation mean sin? Then, indeed, you have nothing to do with it. Does pleasure mean iniquity? Deny yourselves. But there are pleasures which mean no such thing. As you traverse Alpine regions, let your thoughts stand on the mountain tops and talk with God, or if you walk the fair lanes of England, let the cool retreat become a private place of worship for your soul. Why, everything that your eye looks upon, from the kingcup in the meadow to the cedar upon the mountain may make you praise God.

FOR MEDITATION: God is not opposed to holidays. He rested on the seventh day of creation (Genesis 2:2) and on that basis established a weekly day of rest for his people to enjoy with him, not apart from him (Exodus 20:8–11; 31:15–17). When his disciples returned from a preaching tour, Jesus invited them to have a rest in his presence away from the crowds (Mark 6:30–32). Is he a welcome companion on your holidays or would you prefer to leave him at home?

SERMON NO. 399

Sin condemned and executed by Christ Jesus

'For what the law could not do, in that it was weak through the flesh, God sending his own Son in the likeness of sinful flesh, and for sin, condemned sin in the flesh.' Romans 8:3
SUGGESTED FURTHER READING: Luke 7:34–50

The Friend of sinners was emphatically beyond all other public teachers the Enemy of sin. His hatred towards sin was not a mere passion, it was a principle; it did not flash forth now and then, it was a constant flame. He hated sin, if I may so say, implacably, never making a moment's truce with it; he pursued it by day in his ministry, and by night in his prayers; he lived to smite it, and he died to destroy it; and now in his risen glory it is upon sin as well as upon Satan that he sets his heel. He was manifested that he might destroy the works of the devil, and he has erected a battering engine which will not leave of Satan's strongholds so much as one stone upon another which shall not be thrown down. In the life of our Lord his tenderness for sinners was but the natural form in which his hatred for sin displayed itself; just as a physician, from the very fact that he is the antagonist of disease displays a deep interest in those afflicted thereby. Our Lord's keeping company with sinners by no means proved that he was the friend of sin any more than the physician's attendance at the hospital would at all lead to the suspicion that he was the friend of disease. The skilful physician is the friend of the diseased, but to the disease itself what enemy shall be found more determined and inveterate? Because the whole have no need of a physician, Jesus seeks them not; but since the sick need him he seeks them, not out of love to their sin, but out of love to them, that they may be delivered from the cruel bondage under which their sin has held them.

FOR MEDITATION: God hates all sins (Proverbs 6:16–19; Zechariah 8:17; Malachi 2:16; Revelation 2:6). Amazingly he takes no pleasure in our destruction, but wants us to turn away from sin and back to him (Ezekiel 33:11). The Lord Jesus Christ is neither prepared to condone your sin nor eager and impatient to condemn you for it (John 8:11; 2 Peter 3:9). Are you making the most of your present opportunity to trust in him?

SERMON NO. 699

Who are elected?

'And the LORD *said, Arise, anoint him, for this is he.'* 1 Samuel 16:12
SUGGESTED FURTHER READING: Psalm 23:1–6

I have laboured in your presence to preach up the privilege of strong faith; I have urged you to strive after full assurance of faith; but never let these lips say a word or a syllable against that holy carefulness which makes a broad distinction between presumption and assurance. Depend upon it, privilege preached always without precept will breed a surfeit and lethargy in God's people: what we want at certain seasons is, not a promise, but a telling, burning word of self-examination, the flavour of which we may not like, but which shall work in our souls spiritual good of a more lasting sort than sweet comforts would bring to us. Examine yourselves, dear friends, then, by this. I do not ask you whether your hearts are perfect—they are not; I do not ask you whether your hearts never go astray, for they are prone to wander; but I do ask you: Is your heart resting upon Jesus Christ? Is it a believing heart? Does your heart meditate upon divine things? Does it find its best solace there? Is your heart a humble heart? Are you constrained to ascribe all to sovereign grace? Is your heart a holy heart? Do you desire holiness? Do you find your pleasure in it? Is your heart bold for God? Does your heart ascribe praises to God? Is it a grateful heart? And is it a heart that is wholly fixed upon God, desiring never to go astray? If it be, then you have marks of election. Search for these, and add to all your searching this prayer, 'Search me, O God, and know my heart: try me, and know my thoughts: and see if there be any wicked way in me, and lead me in the way everlasting.'

FOR MEDITATION: Earlier in this sermon, Spurgeon illustrated the marks of election from Psalm 23: a heart that is believing (v 1), meditative (v 2), humble (vv 2–3a), holy (v 3b), brave (v 4), contented and grateful (v 5), constant (v 6). Can you see these marks in yourself?

SERMON NO. 638

God pleading for saints, and saints pleading for God

'O Lord, thou has pleaded the causes of my soul; thou hast redeemed my life.' Lamentations 3:58

SUGGESTED FURTHER READING: Psalm 126:1–6

A man went to preach for seven summers on the village green, and good was done. Joseph sometimes listened to the preacher, but he remained as hard as ever. A certain John who had felt the power of truth, worked with him in the barn, and one day, between the strokes of the flail, John spoke a word for truth and for God, but Joseph laughed at him. Now, John was very sensitive, and his whole soul was filled with grief at Joseph's banter; so after he had spoken, he turned to the corner of the barn and hid his face, while a flood of tears came streaming from his eyes. He wiped them away with the corner of his smock-frock, and came back to his flail; but Joseph had noticed the tears though the other tried to hide them; and what argument could not do, those tears through God the Holy Spirit did effectually, for Joseph thought, 'What! does John care for my soul, and weep for my soul? then it is time I should care and weep for it too.' Beloved, witness thus for Christ! Be it mine to weep for the sins of the times, and prophesy against them. Be it yours in your own private walk and conversation to rebuke private sin; and by your loving earnestness to make Jesus Christ dear to many souls! Tell them that Jesus Christ came to save sinners; that he is able to save to the uttermost all who come to him, and that 'whosoever believeth on him should not perish, but have everlasting life;' and in this way you shall plead the cause of God, who has pleaded the causes of your soul.

FOR MEDITATION: Apparently insignificant people often have a disproportionately significant role to play in God's work. The curing of Naaman's leprosy resulted from his obedience to the word of the famous prophet Elisha (2 Kings 5:10,14); but this would not have happened without him being invited by a little maid (2 Kings 5:2–4) and being followed up by his servants (2 Kings 5:13) after he had initially poured scorn upon Elisha's message (2 Kings 5:11–12).

The cripple at Lystra

'The same heard Paul speak: who stedfastly beholding him, and perceiving that he had faith to be healed, said with a loud voice, Stand upright on thy feet. And he leaped and walked.' Acts 14:9–10

SUGGESTED FURTHER READING: Acts 10:34–43

God, looking upon the race of men, beheld them lost and ruined. Out of love to them he sent his only-begotten Son, the Lord Jesus Christ, who was born of the virgin Mary, lived some thirty-two or thirty-three years a life of spotless innocence and perfect obedience to God. He was God: he was man. In due time he was delivered up by the traitor Judas. He was crucified, and actually put to death. Though he was the Lord of life and glory, 'who only hath immortality,' yet he bowed his head and gave up the ghost. After three days he rose again, and showed himself to many of his disciples, so that they were well assured he was the same person who had been put into the grave; and when the forty days were finished he ascended up to heaven in the sight of them all, where he sits at the right hand of God, and shall also come before long a second time to judge both the living and the dead. These were the facts which Paul would state. God was made flesh and dwelt amongst us, and we beheld his glory, the glory as of the only-begotten of the Father, full of grace and truth. 'This is a faithful saying, and worthy of all acceptation, that Christ Jesus came into the world to save sinners, of whom I am chief.' Briefly, these were the facts which Paul would preach, and if any of these facts be preached doubtfully, or be left out of any ministry, then the gospel is not preached; for the foundations upon which the gospel rests have been removed, and then what can the righteous do?

FOR MEDITATION: Paul's summary of the central facts of the gospel he preached (1 Corinthians 15:1–4). He was not ashamed of the gospel (Romans 1:16) but preached it fully (Romans 15:19). Do you want to avoid or hush up any of the facts of the gospel? Alternative versions of the gospel are actually perversions (Galatians 1:6–7).

SERMON NO. 559

Believing with the heart

'For with the heart man believeth unto righteousness; and with the mouth confession is made unto salvation.' Romans 10:10
SUGGESTED FURTHER READING: 2 Timothy 4:9–18

What, my dear brethren, is your testimony today to the truth as it is in Jesus? Does your heart believe it? I think I see some grey-headed man rise up, and leaning upon his staff, he says, 'In my young days I gave my heart to Christ, and I had a peace and joy such as I had never known before, though I had tried the pleasures and allurements of sin. My heart can bear its witness to the peace which I found in religion's ways. Since that time, this brow has been furrowed with many cares, and as you see, this head has become bleached with many winter's snows, but the Lord has been my heart's stay and confidence. I have rested on Christ, and he has never failed me. When trouble has come in upon me, I have never been bowed down under it; I have been able to sustain it. I have had bereavements;' and he points to the many graves he has left behind him in the wilderness; 'but I have been helped to bury wife and children, and faith has enabled me to say with bursting heart, 'the Lord gave, and the Lord hath taken away; blessed be the name of the Lord'. I have had many conflicts, but I have always overcome through the blood of the Lamb. I have been slandered, as all men must be, but I have taken that with all my other crosses upon my shoulder, and I have found it light when I have carried it by faith. I can say that such is the hallowed serenity and calm which the religion of Jesus gives to my heart at all times and all seasons, that I do believe it, not as a matter of head, but as a matter of heart. My heart is itself experimentally convinced that this cannot but be the religion of God, seeing that it works such wonders for me.'

FOR MEDITATION: Is your testimony warmly personal or coldly clinical? Does it concentrate on you to the virtual exclusion of Christ or does it give him the glory and credit for the story you can tell about your conversion and Christian life? Would it help others towards faith in your Saviour? See how the apostle Paul summarised his testimony (1 Timothy 1:15–16; 2 Timothy 4:7–8,16–18).

SERMON NO. 519

Faith and repentance inseparable

'Repent ye, and believe the gospel.' Mark 1:15
SUGGESTED FURTHER READING: Hebrews 12:1–4

'Repent ye, and believe the gospel,' is advice to the young beginner, and it is advice to the old grey-headed Christian, for this is our life all the way through—'Repent ye, and believe the gospel.' St Anselm, who *was* a saint— and that is more than many of them who were called so—St Anselm once cried out 'Oh! sinner that I have been, I will spend all the rest of my life in repenting of my whole life!' And Rowland Hill, whom I think I might call St Rowland, when he was near death, said he had one regret, and that was that a dear friend who had lived with him for sixty years would have to leave him at the gate of heaven. 'That dear friend,' said he, 'is repentance; repentance has been with me all my life, and I think I shall drop a tear,' said the good man, 'as I go through the gates, to think that I can repent no more.' Repentance is the daily and hourly duty of a man who believes in Christ; and as we walk by faith from the wicket gate to the celestial city, so our right-hand companion all the journey through must be repentance. Why, dear friends, the Christian man, after he is saved, repents more than ever he did before, for now he repents, not merely of overt deeds, but even of imaginations. He will take himself to task at night, and chide himself because he has tolerated one foul thought; because he has looked on vanity, though perhaps the heart has gone no further than the look of lust; because the thought of evil has flitted through his mind—for all this he will vex himself before God; and were it not that he still continues to believe the gospel, one foul imagination would be such a plague and sting to him, that he would have no peace and no rest.

FOR MEDITATION: We tend to regard repentance as a step to be taken to begin the Christian life and become a member of Christ's church, but repentance is a command which he himself has issued to established Christian churches and individuals in them (Revelation 2:5,16,21–22; 3:3,19). Repentance is started, not finished, at conversion.

SERMON NO. 460

Our miseries, messengers of mercy

'Come, and let us return unto the LORD: for he hath torn, and he will heal us; he hath smitten, and he will bind us up. After two days he will revive us: in the third day he will raise us up, and we shall live in his sight.' Hosea 6:1–2

SUGGESTED FURTHER READING: Psalm 116:12–19

A missionary was preaching to a Maori tribe in New Zealand. He had been telling them of the suffering love of Christ, how he had poured forth his soul unto death for them; and as he concluded, the hills rung to the thrilling question 'Is it nothing to you, all ye that pass by? Behold, and see if there be any sorrow like unto my sorrow.' Then stood forth a plumed and painted chief, the scarred warrior of a thousand fights, and as his lips quivered with suppressed emotion, he spoke. 'And did the Son of the Highest suffer all this for us men? Then the chief would like to offer him some poor return for his great love. Would the Son of God deign to accept the chief's hunting dog? Swift of foot and keen of scent, the tribe has not such another, and he has been to the chief as a friend.' But the missionary told him that the Son of God had need of no such gifts as these. For a moment the chief paused; then as a new thought struck him, suddenly despoiling himself of his striped blanket he cried with childlike earnestness, 'Perhaps he who had not where to lay his head will yet accept the chieftain's blanket. The poor chief will be cold without it, yet it is offered joyfully.' Touched by love's persistency, the missionary tried to explain to him the real nature of the Son of God; that it was not men's gifts but men's hearts that he yearned for. For a moment a cloud of grief darkened the granite features of the old chief; then as the true nature of the Son of God slowly dawned upon him, casting aside his blanket he clasped his hands, and looking right up into the blue sky, his face beaming with joy, he exclaimed 'Perhaps the Son of the Blessed One will deign to accept the poor chief himself!'

FOR MEDITATION: Christ chiefly gave us himself (Galatians 2:20); blessings come with him (Romans 8:32; Ephesians 1:3). From you God chiefly wants yourself, not your material possessions, but your repentance and faith in him, the Saviour of the world.

SERMON NO. 400

Order and argument in prayer

*'Oh that I knew where I might find him! that I might come even to his seat!
I would order my cause before him, and fill my mouth with arguments.'*
Job 23:3–4
SUGGESTED FURTHER READING: Daniel 9:1–19

The true spiritual order of prayer seems to me to consist of something more
than mere arrangement. It is most fitting for us first to feel that we are now
doing something that is real; that we are about to address ourselves to God,
whom we cannot see, but who is really present; whom we can neither touch
nor hear, nor by our own senses can apprehend, but who, nevertheless, is as
truly with us as though we are speaking to a friend of flesh and blood like
ourselves. Feeling the reality of God's presence, our mind will be led by
divine grace into a humble state; we shall feel like Abraham, when he said, 'I
have taken upon me to speak unto the Lord, which am but dust and ashes.'
Consequently we shall not deliver ourselves of our prayer as boys repeating
their lessons, as a mere matter of rote, much less shall we speak as if we were
rabbis instructing our pupils, or as I have heard some do, with the
coarseness of a highwayman stopping a person on the road and demanding
his purse of him; but we shall be humble yet bold petitioners, humbly
importuning mercy through the Saviour's blood. We shall not have the
reserve of a slave but the loving reverence of a child, yet not an impudent,
impertinent child, but a teachable obedient child, honouring his Father, and
therefore asking earnestly, but with deferential submission to his Father's
will. When I feel that I am in the presence of God, and take my rightful
position in that presence, the next thing I shall want to recognise will be that
I have no right to what I am seeking, and cannot expect to obtain it except as
a gift of grace, and I must recollect that God limits the channel through
which he will give me mercy—he will give it to me through his dear Son. Let
me put myself then under the patronage of the great Redeemer.

FOR MEDITATION: In emergencies believers can pray to God on the spur of
the moment (Nehemiah 2:4). At other times it is only right and proper to
take both care and time (Nehemiah 1:4; Matthew 6:5–7).

Zealots

'Simon called Zelotes.' Luke 6:15
SUGGESTED FURTHER READING: 2 Corinthians 7:5–11

Christian zeal feeds itself upon *a sense of gratitude.*

'Loved of my God, for him again, with love intense I'd burn,
Chosen of thee ere time began, I choose thee in return.'

Look 'to the hole of the pit whence ye are digged,' and you will see abundant reason why you should spend and be spent for God. Zeal for God feeds itself upon *the thought of the eternal future.* It looks with tearful eyes down to the flames of hell and it cannot slumber: it looks up with anxious gaze to the glories of heaven, and it cannot but bestir itself. Zeal for God thinks of death, and hears the hoofs of the white horse with the skeleton rider close behind. Zeal for God feels that all it can do is little compared with what is wanting, and that time is short compared with the work to be done, and therefore it devotes all that it has to the cause of its Lord. Next, zeal for God feeds itself on *love to Christ.* Lady Powerscourt says somewhere, 'If we want to be thoroughly hot with zeal, we must go near to the furnace of the Saviour's love.' Get to know how Christ loved you, and you cannot but love him. Do but know how he was spat upon and despised, and how he bled and died for us, and we cannot but feel that we can do and bear all things for his name's sake. Above all, Christian zeal must be sustained by *a vigorous inner life.* If we let our inner life dwindle, if it begins to be dwarfish, if our heart beats slowly before God, we shall not know zeal; but if all be strong and vigorous within, then we cannot but feel a loving anxiety to see the kingdom of Christ come, and his will done on earth, even as it is in heaven.

FOR MEDITATION: While misplaced zeal is a worthless and dangerous thing (Romans 10:2; Philippians 3:6), the Lord is zealous (Isaiah 9:7; 37:32; John 2:17) and he expects his people to be zealous too (Titus 2:14; Revelation 3:19).

God is with us

'If God be for us, who can be against us?' Romans 8:31
SUGGESTED FURTHER READING: Psalm 118:1–14

God is for us. But, O my brethren, though this brings in the context, it is impossible for any human speech to bring out the depth of the meaning of how God is for us. He was for us before the worlds were made: he was for us, or else he never would have given his Son; he was for us even when he smote the only-begotten, and laid the full weight of his wrath upon him—he was for us, though he was against him; he was for us when we were ruined in the fall—he loved us notwithstanding all; he was for us when we were against him, and with a high hand were bidding him defiance: he was for us, or else he never would have brought us humbly to seek his face. He has been for us in many struggles; we have had to fight through multitudes of difficulties; we have had temptations from without and within—how could we have held on until now if he had not been with us? He is for us, let me say, with all the infinity of his heart, with all the omnipotence of his love; for us with all his boundless wisdom; arrayed in all the attributes which make him God he is for us—eternally and immutably for us; for us when the blue skies shall be rolled up like a worn out vesture; for us throughout eternity. Here, child of God, is matter enough for thought, even though you had ages to meditate upon it: God is for you; and if God be for you, who can be against you?

FOR MEDITATION: If we are believers and God is for us, we will actually have no end of enemies trying to oppose us, but we will be able to withstand them (Ephesians 6:10–13). However, it is a big 'IF'; the opposite is true for unbelievers—if this same almighty God is against us (Romans 1:18; 1 Peter 3:12), whoever or whatever may be for us will be of absolutely no assistance whatsoever to us.

The power of Aaron's rod

'But Aaron's rod swallowed up their rods.' Exodus 7:12
SUGGESTED FURTHER READING: Revelation 12:7–17

What multitudes of foes has our faith had to meet with; but how it has swallowed them all up. There were our old sins. The devil threw them down before us, and they turned to serpents. What multitudes! How they hiss in the air! How horrible are their deadly poison-fangs, the gaping jaws, their forked tongues! But the cross of Jesus, like Aaron's rod, destroys them all. Faith in Christ makes short work of all our sins, for it is written, 'The blood of Jesus Christ his Son cleanseth us from all sin.' Then the devil stirs up another generation of vipers, and shows us our inbred corruptions, our neglects of duty, our slackness in prayer, our unbeliefs, our backslidings, our wanderings of heart; and sometimes you and I get so tormented by these reptiles, that we grow alarmed, and are half inclined to flee. Do not run, brother, but throw down Aaron's rod, and it will swallow up all these serpents, even though they were poisonous as the cobra, or fierce as the rattlesnake. You shall overcome through the blood of the Lamb. Jesus is able 'to save them to the uttermost that come unto God by him.' The battle is the Lord's, and he will deliver them into your hands. The old enemy will throw down another host of serpents in the form of worldly trials, diabolical suggestions, temptations to blasphemy, ill thoughts of God, hard thoughts of his providence, rash thoughts of his promises, and such like, till you will be almost distracted. You will wonder how you can meet such a host as this. Remember to stand fast, and throw down Aaron's rod—your simple trust and faith in Jesus Christ—and it must and shall swallow up all these rods.

FOR MEDITATION: Pharoah's magicians could to some extent mimic the work of God (Exodus 7:11,22; 8:7), but they were really no match for him (Exodus 7:12) and their power had strict limitations (Exodus 8:18–19; 2 Timothy 3:8–9). Satan and his servants can also do some amazing things (2 Thessalonians 2:9–10; Revelation 13:13–15), but the Christian trusts in and is indwelt by One who is greater (1 John 4:4).

Confession with the mouth

'With the heart man believeth unto righteousness: and with the mouth confession is made unto salvation.' Romans 10:10
SUGGESTED FURTHER READING: Proverbs 1:7–15

Young Joseph has his garment seized by his wanton mistress: his answer is, 'How can I do this great wickedness, and sin against God?' The woman might have answered, 'God? What do I know of him? Jehovah—who is he?' There was a bold, distinct confession of his allegiance to Jehovah, as a reason why he could not sin. The case of Nehemiah is equally to the point. When they invite him to a secret conference in the temple, he says, 'Should such a man as I flee?' He avows his confidence in his God as a reason why he cannot for a moment act dishonourably. Now, Christian, here it is that you are to make confession with the mouth. Some dirty trick in business, which has become so common that nobody thinks any harm of it, comes in your way. Now, play the man, and say, 'I would rather starve than do it; I cannot and I will not live by robbery, even though it should be half legalised by society.' Now is your opportunity, young man. When the Sabbath morning comes round, and you are pulled by the sleeve to go with others to waste its holy hours, you can say, 'No,' and give the reason, 'I cannot do it; I am a Christian.' Or, it may be you have come up from the country, and your friend—your *friend* proposes to take you to a den of infamy, just to show you life. Tell him he does not understand how to cater to your appetite, for you are a Christian. For some ends I would prefer the affirmation of one's faith in Jesus in the time of temptation to any other form of confession, since there surely can be no hypocrisy in it. Take care, brethren, that you never fail to acknowledge your Lord in the time of temptation.

FOR MEDITATION: A word of testimony is a means of conquering the devil (Revelation 12:11). Our Saviour demonstrated to Satan that he was the Son of God by resistance, not by the requested submission (Matthew 4:3–7). Being a Christian is not only a good reason for taking a stand for God in times of temptation, but also a powerful excuse to use for our own protection at such moments.

Am I clear of his blood?

'The voice of thy brother's blood crieth unto me from the ground.' Genesis
4:10
SUGGESTED FURTHER READING: Ephesians 5:15–20

The servants of Satan shame me; they shame me! There comes at night a
message to some of you who are the servants of Satan—'The master is
come, and calleth for thee.' You leave your wife and your children without a
tear, you go to your master's house, and there are foul cups passing round,
and you will drink, and drink still on; never denying your master; confessing
him with many an oath; saying to your comrades many things which injure
your poor souls; and yet you do it so bravely. You hardly know how you get
home at night, but when the morning comes, and you wake, there is the
redness of the eyes, the headache, and the sickness; but the next night when
your master wants you, you go again; and so you will do year after year, even
though delirium tears you like a whirlwind. But here am I, a servant of God,
and when my Master calls for me and bids me go and confess him, I am
tempted to be still, and when he tells me to speak to yonder man I would
wickedly avoid the task; and whereas you confess your master and
imprecate a curse upon your head, how often do some of us confess our
master as timidly as if we feared a curse, when instead thereof it is by
confession that the curse is turned away! It is enough to make us Christians
ashamed to think how sinners will confess their god! Hear them at night, as
they reel home through the streets; they are not ashamed of their lord and
master. Hear how they swear, and defy heaven! They are ashamed of
nothing for their lord; and yet we, who have heaven for our reward, and such
a Christ to serve, and one so good and gracious to us—look at us! What
poor lovers of our Saviour are we! What poor lovers of the souls of men!

FOR MEDITATION: Do you find yourself being ashamed firstly of Christ and
then, as a result, of yourself (Mark 14:66–72)? Failure to speak for him is a
common temptation and sin of omission, but with God's help it is possible
to get the victory over it (Psalm 119:46; Romans 1:16; 2 Timothy 1:8).

SERMON NO. 461

Jacob's waking exclamation

'And Jacob awaked out of his sleep, and he said, Surely the LORD *is in this place; and I knew it not.'* Genesis 28:16
SUGGESTED FURTHER READING: Ephesians 4:25–5:4

Cheerfulness is a virtue, levity a vice. How much foolish talking and jesting would at once end if we said, 'Surely the LORD is in this place.' The next time you have been indulging in mirth—I mean not innocent mirth, but that which is connected with uncleanness, or with any sort of ill, imagine you see a finger lifted up, and that you hear a voice saying, 'Surely the LORD is in this place.' Let your recreation be free from sin; let your amusements be such that you can enjoy them while God looks on. If, too, we felt that God was in this place, how much oftener should we talk of him and of Christ. This afternoon what will many of you talk of? Sunday afternoon talk is generally a great difficulty to some professors. They do not like to go right down into what they think worldly conversation, so they generally talk about ministers. They consider that to be a spiritual subject; and generally, this talk about ministers is more wicked than talk about the devil himself, for I had rather you should speak religiously concerning Satan, than irreligiously concerning even the angels of the churches. There is one tale retailed about this minister, and another tale about the other, and the conversation gives no edification. If they heard an angel say, 'The LORD is in this place,' the afternoon of the day of rest would be spent in much more profitable conversation. But suppose that I have some here today who have been lately exposed to personal danger and peril; brethren, do you not think if in the midst of the storm you had heard a voice saying, 'Surely the LORD is in this place,' you would have been perfectly at rest?

FOR MEDITATION: 'I am with you alway' (Matthew 28:20) is a great encouragement to Christians both when alone (Acts 18:9–10) and when together (Matthew 18:20). It should also be a check on our behaviour. In everything you should be able to thank God and ask for his blessing (Romans 14:6). Don't do anything which your conscience prevents you from committing to him (Romans 14:23).

SERMON NO. 401

Seeing and not seeing, or men as trees walking

'He took the blind man by the hand ...; when he had spit on his eyes, and put his hands upon him, he asked him if he saw ought. And he looked up, and said, I see men as trees, walking. After that he put his hands again upon his eyes, ... and he ... saw every man clearly.' Mark 8:23–25
SUGGESTED FURTHER READING: Hebrews 5:11–14

Be not satisfied, my dear friends, with being saved; desire to know *how* you are saved, *why* you are saved, *the method* by which you are saved. It is a rock on which you stand, I know, but think upon the questions—how you were put upon that rock, by whose love you came there, and why that love was set on you. I would to God that all the members of this church were not only *in* Christ Jesus, but *understood* him, and knew by the assurance of the understanding whereunto they have attained. Recollect there are many grave distinctions in Scripture which will save you a world of trouble if you will know and remember them. Try to understand the difference between the old nature and the new. Never expect the old nature to improve into the new, for it never will. The old nature can never do anything but sin, and the new nature never can sin. These are two distinct principles; never confound them. Do not see men as trees walking. Do not confuse sanctification and justification. Recollect that the moment you trust in Christ you are justified as completely as you will be in heaven, but sanctification is a gradual work, which is carried on from day to day by God the Holy Spirit. Distinguish between the great truth that salvation is all of God, and the great lie that men are not to be blamed if they are lost. Be well assured that salvation is of the Lord, but do not lay damnation at God's door. Be not ashamed if men call you a Calvinist, but hate with all your heart Antinomianism. On the other hand, while you believe human responsibility, never run into the error that man ever turns to God of his own free will. There is a narrow line between the two errors; ask for grace to see it.

FOR MEDITATION: Recently born again believers cannot be expected to be experts in doctrine, but long-standing converts ought to know better (1 Corinthians 3:1–2; 13:11; 14:20; Ephesians 4:14–15).

Confession of sin illustrated by two murder trials

'I acknowledged my sin unto thee, and mine iniquity have I not hid. I said, I will confess my transgressions unto the LORD; *and thou forgavest the iniquity of my sin.'* Psalm 32:5
SUGGESTED FURTHER READING: Psalm 51:1–19

David's grief for sin was long and terrible. Its effects were visible upon his outward frame; his 'bones waxed old;' his moisture was 'turned into the drought of summer.' He tells us, that for a time he kept silence, and then his heart became more and more filled with grief: like some mountain tarn whose outlet is blocked up, his soul was swollen with torments of sorrow. He dreaded to confront his sin. He fashioned excuses; he endeavoured to divert his thoughts, but it was all to no purpose; the arrow of conviction made the wound bleed anew, and made the gash more wide and deep every day. Like a festering sore his anguish gathered and increased, and as he would not use the lancet of confession, his spirits became more and more full of torment, and there was no rest in his bones because of sin. At last it came to this, that he must return unto his God in humble penitence, or he must die outright; so he hastened to the mercy-seat, and there unrolled the volume of his iniquities before the eye of the all-seeing One, acknowledging all the evil of his ways. Having done this, a work so simple and yet so difficult to pride, he received at once the token of divine forgiveness; the bones which had been broken were made to rejoice, and he came forth from his closet to sing the blessedness of the man whose transgression is forgiven, and whose sin is covered.

FOR MEDITATION: David was painfully aware of the spiritual and physical effects of his sin (Psalm 32:3–4; 51:8–10). Confessing sin to God always heals the Christian's inward spiritual disease (1 John 1:9) and may relieve outward physical symptoms (James 5:16).

N.B. This sermon was illustrated by the contrasting cases of two murderers tried during the previous week. One tried to cover up his crime; the other voluntarily confessed her guilt.

SERMON NO. 641

Children brought to Christ, not to the font

'Suffer the little children to come unto me, and forbid them not: for of such is the kingdom of God.' Mark 10:14

SUGGESTED FURTHER READING: Deuteronomy 6:4–7

We can say with the apostle John, 'I have no greater joy than to hear that my children walk in truth.' We continue, therefore, to bring them to Christ by daily, constant, earnest prayer on their behalf. As soon as they become of years capable of understanding the things of God, we endeavour to bring them to Christ by teaching them the truth. Hence our Sabbath schools, hence the use of the Bible and family prayer, and catechizing at home. Any person who shall say, 'Do not teach your children; they will be converted in God's own time if it be his purpose; therefore leave them to run wild in the streets,' will certainly both 'sin against the child' and the Lord Jesus. We might as well say, 'If that piece of ground is to grow a harvest, it will do so if it be God's good pleasure; therefore leave it, and let the weeds spring up and cover it; do not endeavour for a moment to kill the weeds, or to sow the good seed.' Why, such reasoning as this would be not only cruel to our children, but grievously displeasing to Christ. Parents! I do hope you are all endeavouring to bring your children to Christ by teaching them the things of God. Let them not be strangers to the plan of salvation. Never let it be said that a child of yours reached years in which his conscience could act, and he could judge between good and evil, without knowing the doctrine of the atonement, without understanding the great substitutionary work of Christ. Set before your child life and death, hell and heaven, judgment and mercy, his own sin, and Christ's most precious blood; and as you set these before him, labour with him, persuade him, as the apostle did his congregation, with tears and weeping, to turn unto the Lord.

FOR MEDITATION: Christian parents should bring their children up 'in the nurture and admonition of the Lord' (Ephesians 6:4). This may be harder in non-Christian marriages when only one of the partners becomes a Christian, but it is not hopeless (1 Corinthians 7:14); Timothy was proof (Acts 16:1; 2 Timothy 1:5; 3:15).

SERMON NO. 581

Salvation altogether by grace

'Who hath saved us, and called us with an holy calling, not according to our works, but according to his own purpose and grace, which was given us in Christ Jesus before the world began.' 2 Timothy 1:9
SUGGESTED FURTHER READING: Ephesians 2:11–22

To say that we save ourselves is to utter a manifest absurdity. We are called in Scripture 'a temple'—a holy temple in the Lord. But shall any one assert that the stones of the edifice were their own architect? Shall it be said that the stones of the building in which we are now assembled cut themselves into their present shape, and then spontaneously came together, and piled this spacious edifice? Should anyone assert such a foolish thing, we should be disposed to doubt his sanity; much more may we suspect the spiritual sanity of any man who should venture to affirm that the great temple of the church of God designed and erected itself. No: we believe that God the Father was the architect, sketched the plan, supplies the materials, and will complete the work. Shall it be also said that those who are redeemed have redeemed themselves? That slaves of Satan break their own fetters? Then why was a Redeemer needed at all? How should there be any need for Jesus to descend into the world to redeem those who could redeem themselves? Do you believe that the sheep of God, whom he has taken from between the jaws of the lion, could have rescued themselves? It were a strange thing if such were the case. We cannot believe that Christ came to do what the sinners might have done themselves. No. 'I have trodden the winepress alone; and of the people there was none with me;' and the redemption of his people shall give glory unto himself only. Shall it be asserted that those who were once dead have spiritually quickened themselves? Can the dead make themselves alive?

FOR MEDITATION: The Greek usually translated 'save yourselves' in Acts 2:40 should be translated 'be saved' as found in other places in the New Testament (cf. Acts 2:21,47; 4:12; 16:30–31; Ephesians 2:8). Have you been redeemed by the precious blood of Christ (1 Peter 1:18–19) and built into God's church (Ephesians 2:22; 1 Peter 2:5)?

From death to life

'The LORD *killeth, and maketh alive: he bringeth down to the grave, and bringeth up.'* 1 Samuel 2:6
SUGGESTED FURTHER READING: John 14:4–11

I heard the other day a trembling woman—I hope she will yet be rejoicing in the Lord—I heard her saying she was afraid she never should be saved, and I told her I was afraid so too, for she *would not* believe in Christ, but was always raising questions, and doubts, and peradventures. Well, she said, she did not know whether the Lord had begun a good work in her. I told her I did not know that either, and that I did not enquire about it; I knew what the gospel said, and that was, 'Believe on the Lord Jesus Christ, and thou shalt be saved.' But she said, perhaps it was not God's time. I said, 'Now is the accepted time; behold, now is the day of salvation.' Ah! she said, but she could not believe. I asked her why she could not believe. Could she not believe what Christ said? Was he a liar? Could she dare to say that she could not believe her God? Well, she did not exactly mean that, but then there were her sins. But, said I, 'The blood of Jesus Christ his Son cleanseth us from all sin.' Well, she said, she hoped she should have the strivings of the Spirit, and that one day she should get right. 'My sister,' said I, 'I charge you before God, do not get any hope out of that; your business is to come to Christ and to come to Christ *now*; but if you stop anywhere short of that, in any sort of feelings or experience, then you will never get to your journey's end.' A believing sinner's business is with Jesus and not with the Spirit's operations. The Spirit works salvation in him, but he is nowhere bidden to look to the Spirit for salvation. No man can come to the Father but by Christ.

FOR MEDITATION: The fact that we cannot 'save ourselves' but have to 'be saved' is no excuse for anyone to sit back and hope for the best. God has revealed to us the way to be saved—by trusting in the Lord Jesus Christ (Mark 16:16; John 3:16–17; Romans 10:9; Ephesians 2:8) —and that step of faith is commanded, not suggested (Acts 16:30–31).

SERMON NO. 523

Creation—an argument for faith

'Ah Lord GOD, behold, thou hast made the heaven and the earth by thy great power and stretched out arm, and there is nothing too hard for thee.'
Jeremiah 32:17
SUGGESTED FURTHER READING: Psalm 107:23–32

My brother in Christ, you are greatly troubled are you? It is a common lot with us all. And so, you have nothing on earth to trust to now, and are going to be cast on your God alone? Your vessel is on her beam-ends, and now there is nothing for you but just to be rolled on the providence and care of God. What a blessed place to be rolled on! Happy storm that wrecks a man on such a rock as this! O blessed hurricane that drives the soul to God and God alone! On some few occasions I have had troubles which I could not tell to any but my God, and I thank God that I have, for I learned more of my Lord then than at any other time. There is no getting at our God sometimes because of the multitude of our friends. But when a man is so poor, so friendless, so helpless that he has nothing, he flies into his Father's arms, and how blessedly he is clasped there! So that, I say again, happy trouble that drives you to your Father! Blessed storm that wrecks you on the rock of ages! Glorious billow that washes you upon this heavenly shore! And now you have nothing but your God to trust to, what are you going to do? To fret? To whine? O, I pray you, do not thus dishonour your Lord and Master! Now, play the man, play the man of God. Show the world that your God is worth ten thousand worlds to you. Show rich men how rich you are in your poverty when the Lord God is your helper. Show the strong man how strong you are in your weakness when underneath you are the everlasting arms. Now man, now is your time to glorify God.

FOR MEDITATION: Do you take refuge in the Lord (Psalm 73:25–26; Proverbs 18:10)? When God gets his hands upon them, even bad experiences eventually turn out for the believer's good (Psalm 119:71; Lamentations 3:27; Romans 8:28) and the blessing overflows to others (Genesis 50:20). That is the story of Good Friday (Isaiah 53:10–11; 1 Peter 2:23–24).

The joint heirs and their divine portion

'Joint heirs with Christ.' Romans 8:17
SUGGESTED FURTHER READING: Galatians 3:23–4:7

The apostle has proceeded through a simple but exceedingly forcible train of reasoning till he gains this glorious point—'Joint heirs with Christ.' He begins thus—'Ye have not received the spirit of bondage again to fear; but ye have received the Spirit of adoption, whereby we cry, Abba, Father.' This is a fact which he takes for granted because he has perceived it in the hearts of believers. We do cry, 'Abba, Father.' From this he infers that if God has given us the Spirit whereby we call him 'Father,' then we are his children, which is plain, fair, and clear reasoning. Then he adds—'If children, then heirs'— though this does not hold true in all families, because all children are not heirs; frequently the first-born may take all the estate; but with God so long as they are children they have equal rights—'If children then heirs.' He goes on to say, 'Heirs of God;' for if they are heirs they inherit their Father's property. God is their Father; they are therefore God's heirs! Well, but God has another Son, one who is the first-born of every creature. Exactly so, therefore if we be heirs, as Christ Jesus is the heir of all things, we are 'joint heirs with Christ.' I think you will see that, like links in a chain, these different truths draw each other on—the spirit of adoption proves the fact of adoption; by the act of adoption we are children; if children then heirs; if heirs, heirs of God; but since there is another heir, we must therefore be joint heirs with Christ Jesus. Blessed is the man to whom this reasoning is not abstract, but experimental. Happy is he who can follow the apostle step by step.

FOR MEDITATION: Christ has been appointed 'heir of all things' (Hebrews 1:2). His joint-heirs inherit, among other things, the earth (Matthew 5:5), everlasting life (Matthew 19:29), the kingdom (Matthew 25:34; James 2:5), salvation (Hebrews 1:14), the promises (Hebrews 6:12), righteousness by faith (Hebrews 11:7), and the grace of life (1 Peter 3:7). Are all things yours in Christ (1 Corinthians 3:21–23)?

Fields white for harvest

*'Say not ye, There are yet four months, and then cometh harvest? behold,
I say unto you, Lift up your eyes, and look on the fields; for they are white
already to harvest.' John 4:35*
SUGGESTED FURTHER READING: 3 John 5–12

Grind your *sickles*; you must go to work with such cutting truths as
justification by faith, as the total ruin of mankind, as the hope that is laid up
in the cross, as the energy of the Holy Spirit; and when you know these
truths, and know how to use them, you shall then be made great reapers in
the Master's harvest. It is idle to say, 'I will go,' and then go with no tool in
your hand. Get the truth; get a hold of it well, get it sharp and in good order,
and who knows, under the blessing of God the Holy Spirit, what you may
do! The next want of harvest is *some close binders*. When the wheat is cut
down you must tie it up with sheaves. We want some of you who cannot
preach, who cannot use the sickle, to go and gather up the wheat which falls
under the sickle when it is used by others. Invite them to come into church
fellowship; talk to them, get them into union with the people of God. And if
you happen to be in the church yourselves, try to keep the church knit
together in love. Bind the sheaves together. We cannot have good harvest
work without loving hands to bind the people of God in one. Then we want
beside these *some to take the sheaves home*. The church of God is the barn;
it is the Master's garner here; he has another garner yonder on the hill-top in
heaven, but here we want you to assist in bringing them into the church of
Christ. When God has saved them, try if you can get them to practise the
ordinances of God, and to be joined with his people. And we want some of
you, if you cannot do anything yourselves either in reaping, or binding, or
bringing the sheaves home, at least by kind words and loving speeches to
bring refreshments to the reapers.

FOR MEDITATION: There is a great mission-field to be harvested. What part
do you play?—praying, labouring (Luke 10:2); sowing, reaping (John
4:36–38) or just sleeping (Proverbs 10:5)?

Withholding corn

'He that withholdeth corn, the people shall curse him: but blessing shall be upon the head of him that selleth it.' Proverbs 11:26
SUGGESTED FURTHER READING: 2 Kings 7:3–9

Commend me to the Christian who says, 'I bless God I am saved; now what can I do for others?' The first thing in the morning he prays, 'God help me to say a word to some soul this day.' During the day, wherever he may be, he is watching his opportunity, and will do good if he can. He is concerned about his children: it sometimes breaks his heart to think that they are not saved. If he happens to have an ungodly wife, it is his daily burden, 'O God, save my wife!' When he goes to a place of worship he does not expect the minister to make sermons always on purpose for him, but he says, 'I shall sit here and pray God to bless the word,' and if he looks round the chapel and sees one that he loves, he prays for him, 'God send the word home to him.' When service is over, a man of this kind will waylay the unconverted, and try to get a personal word with them, and see if he cannot discover some beginnings of grace in their souls. This is how earnest Christians live; and let me tell you, as a rule, though they have the griefs of other men's souls to carry, they do not have much grief about their own; they are watering others and they are watered themselves also. May this be your work and mine! But some of you say nothing for Christ at all. You are too timid you say, and others of you are too indifferent, too thoughtless about others. O the opportunities many of you have lost! O the many who have died to whom you might have spoken but you did not! O the people that are now in the darkness of ignorance who get no light from you! You have light, but you keep it. They are dying, and you have the healing medicine, but you will not tell them of it. May God deliver you from the curse of those who thus withhold the corn.

FOR MEDITATION: The unconverted people who know you are spiritually hungry, thirsty, estranged, naked, sick and imprisoned. What would they have to say about your attitude to them? That you help them (Matthew 25:35–36) or that you ignore them (Matthew 25:42–43)?

SERMON NO. 642

The Lamb—the light

'And the city had no need of the sun, neither of the moon, to shine in it: for the glory of God did lighten it, and the Lamb is the light thereof.'
Revelation 21:23
SUGGESTED FURTHER READING: Luke 20:27–38

They need no social ties in heaven. We need here the associations of friendship and of family love, but they are neither married nor are given in marriage there: their God is enough. They shall need no teachers there; they shall doubtless commune with one another concerning the things of God, and tell to one another the strange things which the Lord has wrought for them, but they shall not need this by way of instruction; they shall all be taught of the Lord, for in heaven 'the glory of God did lighten it, and the Lamb is the light thereof.' There is an utter independence in heaven, then, of all the creatures. No sun and no moon are wanted—no creatures whatever. Here we lean upon the friendly arm, but there they lean upon their beloved and upon him alone. Here we must have the help of our companions, but there they find all they want in Christ alone. Here we look to the meat which perishes, and to the raiment which decays before the moth, but there they find everything in God. We have to use the bucket to get water from the well, but there they drink from the well-head, and put their lips down to the living water. Here the angels bring us blessings, but we shall want no messengers from heaven then. O what a blessed time that shall be, when we shall have mounted above every second cause and shall hang upon the bare arm of God! What a glorious hour when God, and not his creatures, God, and not his works, but God himself, Christ himself shall be our eternal joy.

FOR MEDITATION: God's people, having his perfect presence in heaven, will no longer need the pleasant things they enjoyed on earth and will no longer face the unpleasant things they suffered on earth, such as hunger, thirst, excessive heat, tears (Revelation 7:15–17), death, sorrow, crying and pain (Revelation 21:3–4). The lost in hell will suffer all of these and miss all that they enjoyed in their earthly lives (Luke 16:23–25).

SERMON NO. 583

A hearer in disguise

'And it was so, when Ahijah heard the sound of her feet, as she came in at the door, that he said, Come in, thou wife of Jeroboam; why feignest thou thyself to be another? for I am sent to thee with heavy tidings.' 1 Kings 14:6
SUGGESTED FURTHER READING: Isaiah 56:1–7

Here was an occasional hearer; and we make the observation that this occasional hearer was totally destitute of all true piety. Most occasional hearers are. Those who have true religion are not occasional hearers. You will find that truly gracious persons are diligent in the use of the means. Instead of thinking it a toil to come up to the place of worship, I know there are some of you who wish there were two Sundays in the week; and the happiest times you ever have are when you are sitting in these seats and joining in our sacred songs. There are no words which give you a better idea of heaven as a place than:

'Where congregations ne'er break up, And Sabbaths have no end.'

Gracious souls love the place where God's honour dwells, and the assembling of themselves together is always a blessed thing to them; but occasional hearers are generally graceless persons—I know how you spend your Sunday. There is the morning: you are not up very early; it takes a long time to dress on a Sunday morning; then follows the Sunday paper, with the news of the week; that must be gone through. The wife has been toiling hard all the morning with the dinner; what do you care? Then there is the afternoon, when there is a little more lolling about. Then in the evening, there is the walk. But the day, after all, is not very happy and comfortable: and sometimes you have wished there were no Sundays except that they give your body a little rest. You do not fear God, nor do you care for his service.

FOR MEDITATION: For many today business, shopping and sport would have to be added to Spurgeon's description of the occasional hearer's Sunday. The Christian Sunday has been attacked in exactly the same way as the Jewish Sabbath (Nehemiah 13:15–17). Is the Lord's Day important enough for you to keep Sunday special?

SERMON NO. 584

Mealtime in the cornfields

'And Boaz said unto her, At mealtime come thou hither, and eat of the bread, and dip thy morsel in the vinegar. And she sat beside the reapers: and he reached her parched corn, and she did eat, and was sufficed, and left.' Ruth 2:14
SUGGESTED FURTHER READING: 1 Peter 1:22–2:3

God has ordained certain mealtimes for his reapers; and he has appointed that one of these shall be when they come together to listen to the Word preached. We, of ourselves, cannot feed one soul, much less thousands; but when the Lord is with us, we can keep as good a table as Solomon himself, with all his fine flour, and fat oxen, and roebucks, and fallow deer. When the Lord blesses the provisions of his house, no matter how many thousands there may be, all his poor shall be filled with bread. I hope, beloved, you know what it is to sit under the shadow of the Word with great delight, and find the fruit thereof sweet unto your taste. Where the doctrines of grace are boldly and plainly delivered to you in connection with the other truths of revelation, where Jesus Christ upon his cross is ever lifted up, where the work of the Spirit is not forgotten, where the glorious purpose of the Father is never despised, there is sure to be food for the children of God. We have learned not to feed upon oratorical flourishes, or philosophical refinings; we leave these fine things, these twelfth-cake ornaments, to be eaten by those little children who can find delight in such unhealthy dainties: we prefer to hear truth, even when roughly spoken, to the fine garnishings of eloquence without the truth. We care little about how the table is served, or of what ware the dishes are made, so long as the covenant bread and water, and the promised oil and wine, are given us.

FOR MEDITATION: Those who reject truth and sound doctrine will listen to unsound preachers who say what they want to hear, end up believing in fables (2 Timothy 4:3–4) and get carried away by new-fangled winds of doctrine (Ephesians 4:14). 'Labour not for the meat which perisheth, but for that meat which endureth unto everlasting life' (John 6:27).

N.B. 'Twelfth-cake'—a cake traditionally prepared for Twelfth Day (epiphany). Festivities were held seeking good crops in the coming year.

SERMON NO. 522

Christ's servant—his duty, and reward

'If any man serve me, let him follow me; and where I am, there shall also my servant be: if any man serve me, him will my Father honour.' John 12:26

SUGGESTED FURTHER READING: John 13:12–17

This is just what Jesus Christ says to us. We are his deacons, his servants. We engaged, in the day when we gave ourselves to Him, that we would take up our cross and follow him; and he points today to some high mountain, saying, 'If you would serve me, follow me.' He asks you not to lead; he himself has gone before; he calls you to no labour which he has not himself already accomplished. Oh! can you say in your heart today -

'Through floods and flames if Jesus leads, I'll follow where he goes;
'Hinder me not,' shall be my cry, Though earth and hell oppose.'

This is true service, the best that can be rendered, to follow where he leads the way, let the way be never so rough or arduous, to persevere to the end, even though the end be a martyr's death. Come, brethren, and especially those who are beginners, and have but lately enlisted in Christ's cause, let me mark you out Christ's way, and then, if you would serve him, follow him. I know the proud flesh wants to serve Christ, by striking out new paths. Proud man has a desire to preach new doctrine, to set up a new Church, to be an original thinker, to judge, and consider, and do anything but obey. This is no service to Christ. He that would serve Christ must follow him; he must be content to tread only in the old footsteps, and go only where Christ has led the way. There must be nothing about our religion of our own inventing; it is for us to lay thought, and judgment, and opinion at the feet of Christ, and do what he bids us, simply because he gives the command. Look then disciples at your Lord.

FOR MEDITATION: Don't be like those who rejected God's command to walk in the good old paths (Jeremiah 6:16). His paths are the only safe places for our footsteps (Psalm 17:5).

SERMON NO. 463

The broken column

'And another also said, Lord, I will follow thee: but—.' Luke 9:61
SUGGESTED FURTHER READING: Matthew 19:16–30

'Lord, I will follow thee: but -.' How remarkably does Scripture prove to us that the mental characteristics of mankind are the same now as in the Saviour's day! We occasionally hear stories of old skeletons being dug up which are greater in stature than men of these times. Some credit the story, some do not, for there are many who maintain that the physical conformation of man is at this day just what it always was. Certainly, however, there can be no dispute whatever among observant men as to the identity of the inner nature of man. The gospel of Christ may well be an unchanging gospel, for it is a remedy which has to deal with an unaltering disease. The very same objections which were made to Christ in the days of his flesh are made to his gospel now. The same effects are produced under the ministry of Christ's servants in these modern times as were produced by his own ministry. Still are the promised hopes which made glad the preacher's heart, blasted and withered by the same blights and the same mildews which of old withered and blasted the prospects of the ministry during our Lord's own personal sojourn in the world. O what hundreds, what myriads of persons have we whose consciences are aroused, whose judgments are a little enlightened, and yet they vacillate—they live and die unchanged. Like Reuben, 'unstable as water' they do 'not excel.' They would follow Christ, *but* something lies in the way: they would join with him in this generation, *but* some difficulty suggests itself: they would enter the kingdom of heaven, *but* there is a lion in the street. They lie in the bed of the sluggard, instead of rising up with vigour and striving to enter in at the strait gate.

FOR MEDITATION: 'But' is a wonderful word when it expresses God's gracious attitude towards sinful man (Romans 5:8; Ephesians 2:4), but a terrible word when it expresses sinful man's disgraceful attitude towards him (Jeremiah 6:16–17).

SERMON NO. 403

Hezekiah and the ambassadors, or vainglory rebuked

'At that time Berodach-baladan ... king of Babylon, sent letters and a present unto Hezekiah ... And Hezekiah hearkened unto them, and shewed them all the house of his precious things ... and all the house of his armour, and all that was found in his treasures: there was nothing in his house, nor in all his dominion, that Hezekiah shewed them not.'
2 Kings 20:12–13
SUGGESTED FURTHER READING: Colossians 2:16–23

Should we not be taught by this narrative to cry out every day against vainglory? It is not those standing in prominent spheres who are alone in danger of it, but all others. I recollect firing a shot once with much greater success than I knew of. A certain person had frequently said to me that I had been the subject of her earnest prayers lest I should be exalted above measure, for she could see my danger, and after having heard this so many times that I really knew it by heart, I just made the remark, that I thought it would be my duty to pray for her too, lest she should be exalted above measure. I was greatly amused when this answer came, 'I have no temptation to be proud; my experience is such that I am in no danger whatever of being puffed up;' not knowing that her little speech was about the proudest statement that could have been made, and that everybody else thought her to be the most officious and haughty person within ten miles. Why, do you not believe there may be as much pride in rags as in an alderman's gown? Is it not just as possible for a man to be proud in a dust cart, as if he rode in her Majesty's chariot? A man may be just as proud with half a yard of ground as Alexander with all his kingdoms, and may be just as lifted up with a few pence as Croesus with all his treasure. Pray against pride, dear friends, wherever you may be. Pride will grow on a dunghill, as well as in the king's garden. Pray against pride and vainglory, and God give you grace to keep it under!

FOR MEDITATION: Pride can lead every one of us astray (Proverbs 11:2; 13:10; 16:18; 29:23). See where the pride of godly king Hezekiah eventually led (2 Chronicles 32:25–26,31).

No tears in heaven

'And God shall wipe away all tears from their eyes.' Revelation 7:17
SUGGESTED FURTHER READING: Matthew 6:25–7:5

How numerous are the tears of *unbelief!* We manufacture troubles for ourselves by anticipating future ills which may never come, or which, if they do come, may be like the clouds, all 'big with mercy,' and 'break with blessings on our head.' We get supposing what we should do if such-and-such a thing occurred, which thing God has determined never shall occur. We imagine ourselves in positions where providence never intends to place us, and so we feel a thousand trials in fearing one. That bottle, I say, ought never to carry within it a tear from a believer's eyes, and yet it has had whole floods poured into it. O the wickedness of mistrust of God, and the bitterness with which that distrust is made to curse itself. Unbelief makes a rod for its own back; distrust of God is its own punishment; it brings such want of rest, such care, such tribulation of spirit into the mind, that he who loves himself and loves pleasure, had better seek to walk by faith and not by sight. Nor must I forget the scalding drops of *anger against our fellow-men*, and of petulance and irritation, because we cannot have our way with them; these are black and horrid damps, as noxious as the vaults of Tophet. May we ever be saved from such unholy tears. Sometimes, too, there are streams which arise from *depressed spirits*, spirits desponding because we have neglected the means of grace and the God of grace. The consolations of God are small with us because we have been seldom in secret prayer; we have lived at a distance from the Most High, and we have fallen into a melancholy state of mind. I thank God that there shall never come another tear from our eyes into that bottle when eternal love shall take us up with Jesus in his kingdom.

FOR MEDITATION: There is a time to weep (Ecclesiastes 3:4); Jesus wept (Luke 19:41; John 11:35). But there are other times when it is inappropriate (Numbers 11:4,10,13,18–20; Nehemiah 8:9–10; Mark 5:38–39; John 20:15–16; Acts 21:13; Revelation 5:4–5).

SERMON NO. 643

A mystery! Saints sorrowing and Jesus glad!

'Then said Jesus unto them plainly, Lazarus is dead. And I am glad for your sakes that I was not there, to the intent ye may believe; nevertheless let us go unto him.' John 11:14–15
SUGGESTED FURTHER READING: 2 Thessalonians 1:1–4

Jesus is talking of the death of his friend; let us listen to his words; perhaps we may find the key to his actions in the words of his lips. How surprising! He does not say, 'I regret that I have tarried so long.' He does not say, 'I ought to have hastened, but even now it is not too late.' Hear and marvel! Wonder of wonders, he says, 'I am *glad* that I was not there.' *Glad?* The word is out of place. Lazarus, by this time, is stinking in his tomb, and here is the Saviour glad! Martha and Mary are weeping their eyes out for sorrow, and yet their friend Jesus is glad. It is strange, it is passing strange. However, we may rest assured that Jesus knows better than we do, and our faith may therefore sit still and try to spell out his meaning, where our reason cannot find it at the first glance. 'I am glad,' says he, '*for your sakes* that I was not there, to the intent ye may believe.' We see it now: Christ is not glad because of sorrow, but only on account of the result of it. He knew that this temporary trial would help his disciples to a greater faith, and he so prizes their growth in faith that he is even glad of the sorrow which occasions it. He does as good as say, 'I am glad for your sakes that I was not there to prevent the trouble, for now that it is come, it will teach you to believe in me, and this shall be much better for you than to have been spared the affliction.' We have thus plainly before us the principle, that our Lord in his infinite wisdom and superabundant love, sets so high a value upon his people's faith, that he will not screen them from those trials by which faith is strengthened.

FOR MEDITATION: While we may find the individual ingredients which test our faith distasteful, we also should learn to rejoice in the hope of tasting the finished product (Romans 5:2–5; Hebrews 12:11; James 1:2–4; 1 Peter 1:5–7).

SERMON NO. 585

Faith versus sight

'*For we walk by faith, not by sight.*' 2 *Corinthians* 5:7
SUGGESTED FURTHER READING: Proverbs 31:10–31

In Scripture we often read of men who, by faith, did great exploits. 'By thee I have run through a troop: by my God have I leaped over a wall.' Now, this is a very great thing to do; and some Christians are always fixing their eyes upon exploits of faith. The apostle Paul did cut through troops and leap over walls, but in this place he speaks of the common actions of life. It is as if he said, 'I not only leap walls by faith, but I walk by faith; I not only break through troops by faith, but I go and do my business by faith.' That man has not yet learned the true spirit of Christianity who is always saying, 'I can preach a sermon by faith.' Yes, sir, but can you make a coat by faith? 'I can distribute tracts, and visit the district by faith.' Can you cook a dinner by faith? I mean, can you perform the common actions of the household, and the daily duties which fall to your lot, in the spirit of faith? This is what the apostle means. He does not speak about running, or jumping, or fighting, but about walking; and he means to tell you that the ordinary life of a Christian is different from the life of another man; that he has learned to introduce faith into everything he does. It was not a bad saying of one who said that he 'did eat and drink, and sleep eternal life.' We want not a home-spun religion, but a religion that was spun in heaven, and that will do to wear at home and about the house. 'We *walk* by faith.' The Muslim worships at the 'holy hour;' the true Christian calls all hours 'holy' and worships God always.

FOR MEDITATION: Do you regard your Christian faith and worship as being just a matter of Sunday services and church activities? True faith should extend to what we eat, drink and wear (Matthew 6:25,30–31) and true worship should include the manner in which we eat, drink and do anything else (1 Corinthians 10:31).

Intercessory prayer

'And the Lord turned the captivity of Job, when he prayed for his friends.'
Job 42:10
SUGGESTED FURTHER READING: 1 Samuel 12:19–25

How are you to prove your love to Christ or to his church if you refuse to pray for men? 'We know that we have passed from death unto life, because we love the brethren.' If we do not love the brethren, we are still dead. I will assert that no man loves the brethren who does not pray for them. It is the very least thing you can do, and if you do not perform the least, you certainly will fail in the greater. You do not love the brethren unless you pray for them, and then it follows you are dead in trespasses and sins. Let me ask you again how it is that you hope to get your own prayers answered if you never plead for others? Will not the Lord say, 'Selfish wretch, you are always knocking at my door, but it is always to cry for your own welfare and never for another's; inasmuch as you have never asked for a blessing for one of the least of these my brethren, neither will I give a blessing to you. You do not love the saints, you do not love your fellow men, how can you love me whom you have not seen, and how shall I love you and give you the blessing which you ask at my hands?' Brethren, again I say I would earnestly exhort you to intercede for others, for how can you be Christians if you do not? Christians are priests, but how priests if they offer no sacrifice? Christians are lights, but how are they lights unless they shine for others? Christians are sent into the world, even as Christ was sent into the world, but how are they sent unless they are sent to pray? Christians are meant not only to be blessed themselves, but in them shall all the nations of the earth be blessed, but how if you refuse to pray?

FOR MEDITATION: The Christian should pray for other Christians (Ephesians 6:18) including those who are suffering (Acts 12:5), speaking (Ephesians 6:19–20) and sick (James 5:16); our prayers should also have a place for enemies (Matthew 5:44), for the lost (Romans 10:1) and for political leaders (1 Timothy 2:1–2). How healthy is your prayer life?

A sermon for gleaners

'*Boaz commanded his young men, saying, Let her glean even among the sheaves, and reproach her not: and let fall also some of the handfuls of purpose for her, and leave them, that she may glean them, and rebuke her not.*' Ruth 2:15–16

SUGGESTED FURTHER READING: Psalm 104:10–15

We are too apt to think that we are independent of the operations of the country, that our trade, our commerce, our manufactures, are sufficient to support us; forgetting all the while that in vain is yonder forest of masts unless the earth shall yield her fruit; in vain the emporium, the exchange, and the place of merchandise, unless the land be ploughed and harrowed, and at last yield to the husbandman his reward. I would that I could recall to your memories, you dwellers in the city, how much you depend upon the Lord God of the earth for your daily bread. Does your food fall like manna from the skies? Do you create it at the forge, or fashion it in the loom or on the wheel? Does it not come from the earth, and is it not the Lord who gives to the fertile womb of earth the power to yield its harvests? Does not the dew come from heaven, and the sunshine from above, and do these not bring to *us* our bread as well as to those who abide in the midst of the fields? Let us not forget this time of the harvest, nor be unthankful for the bounty of the wheatsheaf; let us not forget to plead with God that he would be pleased to give us suitable weather for the ingathering of the precious grain, and when it shall be ingathered, let us not sullenly keep silence, but with the toiling labourers who, well-pleased, behold the waving yellow crop, let us lift up the shout of harvest home, and thank the God who covers the valleys with corn, and crowns the year with his goodness.

FOR MEDITATION: Today there is a tendency for churches to regard Harvest Thanksgiving as an out-of-date tradition. When the children of Israel were about to enter the promised land, Moses told them all the material blessings that God had in store for them (Deuteronomy 8:7–10) and warned them to beware of taking God's provision for granted once they had settled down (Deuteronomy 8:11–18). Do you need to think again?

SERMON NO. 464

To die or not to die

'Willing rather to be absent from the body and to be present with the Lord.' 2 Corinthians 5:8

SUGGESTED FURTHER READING: Hebrews 11:8–16

You are a child: he is not a loving child that does not wish to see his father's face. How some of us used to long for the holidays! We used to make a little almanac, and put down the days, and mark them off one by one. Six weeks before the time we would begin to count how many days there were, and every morning we would say there was one day the less before we went home. Either he is a bad child, or he has got a bad father, that does not want to go home. Now, we have got a good and blessed Father, and I hope he has made us his true children, and we want to see his face; we long for the time when we shall no longer be under tutors and governors, but shall come home to enjoy the inheritance. Brethren, we are also labourers. It would be a strange thing if the labourer did not wish to achieve the end of his toils. It would indeed be a strange thing if, industrious though he be, he did not prefer the end of his toils to the beginning. It would be contrary to nature, and I think contrary to grace, if the husbandman did not long for the harvest, and if he that toils did not desire to receive the reward. We are not only labourers, brethren, but mariners—mariners that are often tempest-tossed; the sails are rent to ribbons; the timbers are creaking; the ship drives along before the blast—who does not want to get into port? Which man among you does not desire to say, 'See, the harbour is near; lo, the red lights'? Who among you would not wish to cast anchor now, and say, 'I have passed the floods, and now I am come to my desired haven'? Brethren, we are not only mariners but pilgrims—pilgrims of the weary foot, having here no continuing city. Who does not want to get to his home?

FOR MEDITATION: As God's children Christians can look forward to heaven as the place to enjoy their Father's perfect company (John 17:24; 1 John 3:1–2); as God's servants, they can anticipate their Master's rewards for their labours (Ephesians 6:5–9; Revelation 14:13).

SERMON NO. 413

The voice of the cholera epidemic

'Will a lion roar in the forest, when he hath no prey? will a young lion cry
out of his den, if he have taken nothing? ... Shall there be evil in a city,
and the LORD hath not done it?' Amos 3:4,6
SUGGESTED FURTHER READING: Romans 2:17–24

What have you had to do, professing Christians, with the drunkenness of
this city? Are you sure that you are quite clear of it? Have you both by your
teaching and by your example shown to men that the religion of Jesus is not
consistent with drunkenness? Have you tried to put down this vice, or are
you in some degree a fellow-criminal, an accomplice before or after the fact?
You cannot wipe out all the national iniquity, but if each man reformed
himself of this vice, by God's grace, this great evil would cease. Let each
Christian look at home. You professors of religion, how far are you clear in
the matter of sins of the flesh? Has there never been any lightness of speech
about these sins? And what about your course of conversation? Have you
always been free? Have you heard ringing in your ears the precept, 'Be ye
holy, for I am holy'? Has the Holy Spirit by his mighty grace kept you from
indulging in unclean words and thoughts? Have you in any way fallen into
lightness of talk and thought, and so helped to increase the flood of this
evil? O my brethren, who among us must not confess to some guilt, when we
remember the Saviour's words, 'That whosoever looketh on a woman to lust
after her hath committed adultery with her already in his heart.' Let us bow
our heads in penitence, and seek the God of all grace.

FOR MEDITATION: The doctrine of total depravity teaches us that sin has
affected every aspect of our being (Romans 3:9–18). The believer must still
guard mouth and heart (Psalm 141:3–4; Ephesians 5:3–4), as well as eyes
and thoughts (Job 31:1; Matthew 5:28). Are your actions good or bad
examples to others (3 John 11)?

N.B. Spurgeon saw the cholera epidemic in London as a national
chastisement, teaching that nations, unlike individuals, exist only in this
world and can only be judged here.

SERMON NO. 705

God's witnesses

'Ye are my witnesses, saith the LORD, *and my servant, whom I have chosen.'* Isaiah 43:10
SUGGESTED FURTHER READING: 1 John 5:1–5

Some of you have not much to spare when the rent is paid and food is bought, yet with all that, you want no man's pity, for you are rich to all the intents of bliss. When Mr Hone, who wrote the 'Every-day Book,' was travelling through Wales—he was an infidel—he stopped at a cottage to ask for a drink of water, when a little girl said, 'Oh yes, sir, I have no doubt mother will give you some milk. Come in.' He went in and sat down. The little girl was reading her Bible. Mr Hone said, 'Well, my little girl, are you getting your task?' 'No, sir, I am not,' she replied, 'I am reading the Bible.' 'Yes,' said he, 'you are getting your task out of the Bible?' 'Oh, no,' she replied, 'It is no task to read the Bible; I love the Bible.' 'And why do you love the Bible?' said he. Her simple, childlike answer was, 'I thought everybody loved the Bible.' She thought full sure it was the greatest treat in all the world, and fancied that everybody else was delighted to read God's Word. Mr Hone was so touched with the sincerity of that expression, that he read the Bible himself, and instead of being an opponent to the things of God, came to be a friend of divine truth. Let us in the same way show to the people of the world who think our religion to be slavery, that it is a delight and a joy; that it is no more a burden to us to pray than it is for the fish to swim; that it is no more bondage for us to serve God than for a bird to fly. True godliness is our natural element now that we have a new nature given us by the Spirit of God. On that matter be witnesses for God.

FOR MEDITATION: Do you obey God because you feel you have to or because you really want to? The motive and spirit of our acts of obedience are important to God (2 Corinthians 9:7). Church leaders have the responsibility of fostering the right attitude (1 Peter 5:2–3).

SERMON NO. 644

The great white throne

'And I saw a great white throne, and him that sat on it, from whose face the earth and the heaven fled away; and there was found no place for them.' Revelation 20:11

SUGGESTED FURTHER READING: Romans 2:1–11

The thoughts of many hearts were revealed by Christ on earth, and that same Christ shall make an open exhibition of men at the last great day. He shall judge them, he shall discern their spirits, he shall find out the joints and the marrow of their being; the thoughts and intents of the heart he shall lay bare. Even you, believer, will pass the test before him; let no man deceive you with the delusion that you will not be judged: the sheep appeared before the great dividing Shepherd as well as the goats; those who used their talents were called to account as well as he who buried his pound, and the disciples themselves were warned that their idle words would bring them into judgment. Nor need you fear a public trial. Innocence courts the light. You are not saved by being allowed to be smuggled into heaven untested and unproved, but you will in the righteousness of Jesus pass the solemn test with joy. It may not be at the same moment as the wicked that the righteous shall be judged (I shall not contend for particulars), but I am clear that they will be judged, and that the blood and righteousness of Jesus are provided for this very cause, that they may find mercy of the Lord in that day. O sinner, it is far otherwise with you, for your ruin is sure when the testing time comes. There will be no witnesses needed to convict you, for the Judge knows all. The Christ whom you despised will judge you; the Saviour whose mercy you trampled on, in the fountain of whose blood you would not wash, the despised and rejected of men—it is he who shall judge righteous judgment to you.

FOR MEDITATION: All will stand before the judgment seat of God and of Christ (Romans 14:10; 2 Corinthians 5:10). What will be the verdict in your case? Will you be cleared for heaven as one who has been justified and acquitted from condemnation by faith in Christ (Romans 5:1; 8:1) or only fit, as an unbelieving sinner, for eternal judgment in hell (Romans 2:5,8–9)?

An awful premonition

'Verily I say unto you, there be some standing here, which shall not taste of death, till they see the Son of man coming in his kingdom.' Matthew 16:28

SUGGESTED FURTHER READING: Hebrews 2:6–15

This tasting of death here may be explained, and I believe it is to be explained, by a reference to the second death, which men will not taste of till the Lord comes. And what a dreadful sentence that was, when the Saviour said, perhaps singling out Judas as he spoke; 'Verily I say unto you, there be some standing here, who shall never know what that dreadful word 'death' means, till the Lord shall come.' You think that if you save your lives, you escape from death. The demise of the body is but a prelude to the perdition of the soul. The grave is but the porch of death; you will never understand the meaning of that terrible word till the Lord comes. This can have no reference to the saints, because in John 8:51–52 you find this passage:— 'Verily, verily, I say unto you, If a man keep my saying, he shall never see death. Then said the Jews unto him, Now we know that thou hast a devil. Abraham is dead, and the prophets; and thou sayest, If a man keep my saying, he shall never taste of death.' No righteous man, therefore, can ever 'taste of death.' He will fall into that deep oblivious sleep in which the body sees corruption; but that is another and a very different thing from the bitter cup referred to as tasting of death. When the Holy Spirit wanted an expression to set forth that which was the equivalent for the divine wrath, what expression was used (in Hebrews 2:9)? Christ 'by the grace of God should taste death for every man.' The expression 'to taste of death,' means the reception of that true and essential death, which kills both the body and the soul in hell for ever.

FOR MEDITATION: This terrible tasting of everlasting death will be the only course available for those who have refused in this life to taste and see that the Lord is the good and gracious giver of salvation and blessings to all who trust in him (Psalm 34:8; 1 Peter 2:3).

SERMON NO 594

The saint's horror at the sinner's hell

'Gather not my soul with sinners.' Psalm 26:9
SUGGESTED FURTHER READING: Revelation 16:1–21

When impenitent sinners are gathered at the last *their characters* will be the same. They were filthy here, they will be filthy still. Here on earth their sin was in the bud; in hell it will be full-blown. If they were bad here, they will be worse there. Here they were restrained by providence, by company, by custom—there, there will be no restraints, and hell will be a world of sinners at large, a land of outlaws, a place where every man shall fol|ow out his own heart's most horrible inclinations. Who would wish to be with them? Then again, the *place* where they will be gathered alarms us—the pit of hell, the abode of misery and wrath for ever—who would be gathered there? Then, their *occupation*. They spend their time in cursing God, in inventing and venting fresh blasphemies. They go from bad to worse; climbing down the awful ladder of detestable depravity. Who would wish to be with them? Remember too their *sufferings*; the pain of body and of soul they know, when God has cast both body and soul into hell. Who would wish to be with them? Recollect too that they are *banished for ever from God*, and God is our sun, therefore they are in darkness; God is our life, therefore they are worse than dead; God is our joy, therefore they are wretched in the extreme. Why, this would be hell, if there were no other hell to a Christian, to be banished from his God. Moreover, they are *denied the joys of Christ's society*. No Saviour's love for them, no blissful communion at his right hand, no living fountains of water to which the Lamb shall lead them. O my God, when I think of what the sinner is, and where he is, and how he must be there for ever, shut out from thee, my soul may well pray with anguish that prayer, 'Gather not my soul with sinners.'

FOR MEDITATION: At the final gathering (Matthew 3:12; 13:30) there will be a world of difference between the gathering of the saved (Matthew 13:43,47–48) and the gathering of the unsaved (Matthew 13:40–42,49–50) After this teaching Jesus asked 'Have ye understood all these things?' (Matthew 13:51). Have you? In which gathering will you be found?

The Holy Spirit glorifying Christ

'He shall glorify me: for he shall receive of mine, and shall shew it unto you.' John 16:14
SUGGESTED FURTHER READING: John 14:15–26

This is a most important principle to be held fast by all godly people, for the day may come when false prophets shall arise, and delude the people, and by this shall we be able to discover them; if they claim anything beyond what Christ has revealed, put them aside, for they are false prophets, wolves in sheep's clothing. The Spirit only teaches us that which Christ has taught beforehand either by himself or by the inspired apostles. 'He shall receive of mine, and shall shew it unto you.' Just now we are in little danger from the excesses of fevered brains, for, as a rule, our sin is in being far too cold and dead to spiritual influences. I fear we are liable to another evil, and are apt to forget the person and work of the Comforter altogether. From many modern sermons would you know that there was a Holy Spirit? If it were not for the benediction or the doxology you might go in and out of many churches and meeting-houses by the year together, and scarcely know that there was such a person as that blessed, blessed giver of all good, the Holy Spirit. Sometimes we hear a little about his influences, as if the Holy Spirit were not as truly a person as even Jesus Christ himself, who in flesh and blood trod this earth. Oh, dear friends, I fear the first danger, that of running wild with whimsies and fancies about inner lights and new revelations; but I equally dread this last, this going forth to work with the sword, forgetting that it is the sword of the Spirit, and only mighty as the Holy Spirit makes it mighty 'to the pulling down of strongholds.'

FOR MEDITATION: The Holy Spirit is grieved when we do what we shouldn't (Ephesians 4:25–30). How grieved he must be when attributed with things which are nothing to do with him. The Holy Spirit is quenched when we fail to do what we should (1 Thessalonians 5:16–19). How quenched he must be when the truth of his real work is suppressed. Are you tempted to go to one extreme or the other?

SERMON NO. 465

The triumphal entry into Jerusalem

'Tell ye the daughter of Sion, Behold, thy King cometh unto thee, meek, and sitting upon an ass, and a colt the foal of an ass.' Matthew 21:5
SUGGESTED FURTHER READING: Exodus 23:4–12

Christ would not have any pain in his kingdom; he would not have even an ass suffer by him, and if the foal had been taken away from its mother, there would have been the poor mother in the stable at home, thinking of its foal, like those oxen that the Philistines used when they took back the ark, and which went lowing as they went, because their calves were at home. Wondrous kingdom of Christ, in which the very beast shall have its share! 'For the creature was made subject to vanity' by our sin. It was the beast that suffered because we sinned, and Christ intends that his kingdom should bring back the beast to its own pristine happiness. 'The lion shall eat straw like the ox. And the sucking child shall play on the hole of the asp, and the weaned child shall put his hand on the cockatrice' den.' Old Eden's peacefulness, and the familiarity between man and the lower creatures, shall come back once more. And even now, wherever the gospel is fully known in man's heart, man begins to recognise that he has no right wantonly to kill a sparrow or a worm, because it is in Christ's dominion; and he who would not ride a foal without having its mother by its side, that it might be at peace and happy, would not have any of his disciples think lightly of the meanest creature that his hands have made. Blessed kingdom this which considers even the beasts! Does God care for oxen? Yes, he does; and for the very ass itself, that heir of toil, he cares.

FOR MEDITATION: God spent two days of creation on animals and told Noah to build an ark as big as a liner rather than a lifeboat. Why? Because He cares for animals (Genesis 8:1). Animals have their own 'fear not' (Joel 2:22). The way you treat them says something about you (Proverbs 12:10). However, while showing love to animals, we must have more love for people and most love for God. The Israelites were commanded to treat animals properly (Deuteronomy 22:1–4; 25:4), but often had to sacrifice them in their greater love for God.

SERMON NO. 405

Heavenly geometry

'That Christ may dwell in your hearts by faith; that ye, being rooted and grounded in love, may be able to comprehend with all saints what is the breadth, and length, and depth, and height; and to know the love of Christ, which passeth knowledge, that ye might be filled with all the fulness of God.' Ephesians 3:17–19
SUGGESTED FURTHER READING: 1 Corinthians 13:4–13

If we shall reach the point indicated in the text, we shall then begin to imitate the love of God in its four aspects. I am sure, if we shall ever learn the breadth of Christ's love, our love will grow broad: we shall no longer confine our love to our own church, but shall care for all the churches of God; we shall feel an affection not only for Christians of our own name, but to Christians of all names. Then our love will gain length also. We shall love Christ so that we cannot leave off loving him. We shall persevere in love, we shall abide in his love as he abides in it. We shall constantly have the flame of our love going up to heaven. And then our love will acquire depth. We shall be humbled on account of our own sinfulness, we shall sink lower and lower in our own esteem, and our love will become deeper and more grounded as it descends more fully into the core of our nature. And then love will climb the heights. We shall forget the world and the cares thereof; we shall become Christians who lie no longer among the pots, but who have received the wings of a dove covered with silver, and her feathers with yellow gold. We shall attain to such a height in our love, that we shall scale the mountain tops of the promises, and with our foreheads bathed in the sunlight shall look down upon the world that still lies in darkness, and rejoice that we are made heirs of light; till our love mounting to heaven shall there be in its height as we appear before the great white throne, and cast our crowns with many a song before him who loved us, with a breadth, and length, and depth, and height of love that even in heaven shall surpass all measurement.

FOR MEDITATION: God's love to us is not only to amaze us, but to be our example of how to love him by loving one another (John 13:34; 15:12; Ephesians 5:2; 1 John 4:11,19–21).

20 AUGUST (1865)

The blind man's earnest cries

'And when he heard that it was Jesus of Nazareth, he began to cry out, and say, Jesus, thou Son of David, have mercy upon me. And many charged him that he should hold his peace: but he cried the more a great deal, Thou Son of David, have mercy on me.' Mark 10:47–48
SUGGESTED FURTHER READING: Luke 8:4–15

The world will try to make a crying sinner hold his peace. The world will tell him that he is crying out about something that does not matter, for the book is not true, there is no God, no heaven, no hell, no hereafter. But if God has set you crying, sinner, I know you will not be stopped with that; you will cry yet the more exceedingly, 'Thou Son of David, have mercy on me.' Then the world will try pleasure; you will be invited to the theatre, you will be attracted from one ballroom to another; but if the Lord put the cry in your mouth, the intense anguish of your spirit will not be satisfied by the sound of music nor by the shouts of them that make merry. Perhaps the world will call you a fool to be vexed about such things; you are melancholy and have got the mopes. They will tell you that you will soon go where many others have gone—to Bedlam; but if once God has made you cry, you will not be stopped by a fool's laughter; the agonizing prayer will go up in secret, 'Have mercy on me.' Perhaps the world will try its cares. You will be called into more business; you will get a prosperity which will not make your soul prosper; and so it will be hoped by Satan that you will forget Christ, in accumulated wealth and growing cares. But if this be such a cry as I hope it is, poor anxious sinner, you will not be stopped by that. Then the world will affect to look down upon you with pity. Poor creature, you are being misled, when you are being led to Christ and to heaven. They will say you have become the dupe of some fanatic, when, in truth, you are now coming to your senses, and estimating eternal things at their proper value.

FOR MEDITATION: When one of his subjects starts looking for a new master, Satan can be expected to throw a spanner in the works (Matthew 23:13; Luke 11:52). Sadly, as the parable of the sower illustrates, he sometimes succeeds, but we can praise God that Satan often fails (Acts 13:6–12,43–48).

Preparatory grace

'When it pleased God, who separated me from my mother's womb, and called me by his grace, to reveal his Son in me.' Galatians 1:15–16
SUGGESTED FURTHER READING: 2 Timothy 2:23–26

Dr Gifford once went to see a woman in prison who had been a very gross offender. She was such a hardened reprobate, that the doctor began by discoursing with her about the judgments of God, and the punishments of hell, but she only laughed him to scorn, and called him opprobrious names. The doctor burst into tears, and said, 'And yet, poor soul, there is mercy for you, even for such as you are, though you have laughed in the face of him who would do you good. Christ is able to forgive you, bad though you are; and I hope that he will yet take you to dwell with him at his right hand.' In a moment the woman stopped her laughing, sat down quietly, burst into tears, and said, 'Don't talk to me in that way: I have always been told that I should be damned, and I made up my mind to be; I knew there was no chance, and so I have gone on from one sin to another: but if there is a hope of mercy for me, that is another thing: if there is a possibility of my being forgiven, that is another thing.' The doctor at once opened his Bible, and began to read to her these words, 'The blood of Jesus Christ his Son cleanseth us from all sin.' The greatest brokenness of heart followed. In subsequent visits the doctor was gratified to find that she was brought to Christ; and though she had to undergo a sentence of transportation for many years at that time, yet in after days the godly man saw her walking honestly and uprightly as a believer in Jesus Christ. Sinner, I wish that thought would bring you to Christ!

FOR MEDITATION: Those who win souls are wise (Proverbs 11:30) and must speak wisely to win souls. A soft answer is more likely to have the desired effect than harsh words (Proverbs 15:1). Jesus said 'Come unto me … and I will give you rest …; I am meek and lowly in heart' (Matthew 11:28–29). He died to enable sinners to come to God through him. Can you still harden your heart against him?

SERMON NO. 656

Peter's three calls

'The two disciples ... followed Jesus ... One ... was Andrew, Simon Peter's brother ... He brought him to Jesus.' John 1:37,40,42
'Jesus ... saw two brethren, Simon called Peter, and Andrew his brother ... And he saith ... Follow me, and I will make you fishers of men.' Matthew 4:18–19
'He called unto him his twelve disciples...the first, Simon, who is called Peter.' Matthew 10:1–2
SUGGESTED FURTHER READING: 1 Timothy 3:1–13

I will venture here to trace an analogy between this and the calling of the Christian minister. You will observe that this call comes last. The call to the apostleship does not come first. Peter is first the disciple, secondly the evangelist, and thirdly the apostle. So, no man is called to be specially set apart to the ministry of Christ, or to have a share in the apostleship until he has first of all himself known Christ, and until, secondly, as an ordinary Christian he has fully exercised himself in all the duties which are proper to Christian service. Now, some people turn this topsy-turvy. Young men who have never preached, who have never visited the sick, never instructed the ignorant, and are totally devoid of any knowledge of gospel experience except the little of their own, are dedicated to the Christian ministry. I believe this to be a radical and a fatal error. Brethren, we have no right to thrust a brother into the ministry until he has first given evidence of his own conversion, and has also given proof not only of being a good average worker but something more. If he cannot labour in the church before he pretends to be a minister, he is good for nothing. If he cannot perform all the duties of membership with zeal and energy, and if he is not evidently a consecrated man whilst he is a private Christian, certainly you do not feel the guidance of God's Holy Spirit to bid him enter the ministry. No man has a right to aspire to come into that office until he has shown that he is really devoted to Christ by having served him as others have done.

FOR MEDITATION: The ministry is a calling, not a career. Paul had no doubts (Romans 1:1; 1 Corinthians 1:1; Galatians 1:15). His calling had also come in stages (Acts 9:4–6; 11:25–26; 13:1–2).

Am I sought out?

'Thou shalt be called, Sought out.' Isaiah 62:12
SUGGESTED FURTHER READING: Matthew 4:17–25

You that have ability, and have talents, devote yourselves to God's cause. Give yourselves up to his ministry. I would to God there were more of those who are successful in professions, men who either in medicine or law would attain eminence, who would consecrate their talents to the ministry; they need not fear that in giving themselves to God he will not take care of them, and as to honour, if it be found anywhere, it is the sure heritage of the faithful ambassador of Christ. If you have been sought out, my brother, I do not blush to recommend you to give up the most lucrative employment to seek out others. If you have the power to stir others' hearts, if God has given you the tongue of the eloquent, devote it to the plucking of brands from the burning; become a herald of the cross, and let the whole world, as far as possible, hear from you the tidings of salvation. The preaching of the gospel is not the only means; it is a way of seeking out most commonly used, but there are other methods. We are not to preach merely to those who come to listen. We must carry the gospel to where men do not desire it. We should consider it our business to be generously impertinent; thrusting the gospel into men's way, whether they will hear or whether they will forbear. Let us hunt for souls by visitation. There are thousands in London who never will be converted by the preaching of the gospel, for they never attend places of worship. We may shudder when we say it; it is believed there are thousands in London who do not even know the name of Christ, living in what we call a Christian land, and yet they have not heard the name of Jesus.

FOR MEDITATION: What lasting good would have been done by the New Testament writers Matthew, Luke, Paul and Peter if they had ignored God's definite call to the ministry and remained a tax-collector, doctor, tentmaker and fisherman respectively? Even without a call to a specific office, every believer is called into the work of ministry (Ephesians 4:12) as an unofficial 'deacon' with gifts to minister to others (1 Peter 4:10). How are you advancing Christ's kingdom?

The loaded wagon

'Behold, I am pressed under you, as a cart is pressed that is full of sheaves.' Amos 2:13
SUGGESTED FURTHER READING: Isaiah 53:1–12

See him; like a cart pressed down with sheaves he goes through the streets of Jerusalem. Well may you weep, daughters of Jerusalem, though he bids you dry your tears; they hoot him as he walks along bowed beneath the load of his own cross which was the emblem of your sin and mine. They have brought him to Golgotha. They throw him on his back, they stretch out his hands and his feet. The accursed iron penetrates the tenderest part of his body, where most the nerves do congregate. They lift up the cross. O bleeding Saviour, thy time of woe has come! They dash it into the socket with rough hands; the nails are tearing through his hands and feet. He hangs in extremity, for God has forsaken him; his enemies persecute and take him, for there is none to deliver him. They mock his nakedness; they point at his agonies. They look and stare upon him with ribald jests; they insult his griefs, and make puns upon his prayers. He is now indeed a worm and no man, crushed till you can think scarcely that there is divinity within. The fever gets hold upon him. His tongue is dried up like a potsherd, and he cries, 'I thirst!' Vinegar is all they yield him; the sun refuses to shine, and the thick midnight darkness of that awful mid-day is a fitting emblem of the tenfold midnight of his soul. Out of that thick horror he cries 'My God, my God, why hast thou forsaken me?' Then, indeed, was he pressed down! O there was never sorrow like unto his sorrow. All human griefs found a reservoir in his heart, and all the punishment of human guilt spent itself upon his body and his soul. O shall sin ever be a trifle to us? Shall I ever laugh at that which made him groan?

FOR MEDITATION: Believers still have problems with sin as a weight impeding progress in the Christian life (Hebrews 12:1), but our struggle with sin on earth has its limits (Hebrews 12:4); the Lord Jesus Christ went beyond those limits and was crushed by our sin to save all who trust in him from being crushed by it eternally (Hebrews 12:2–3; 1 Peter 2:24).

SERMON NO. 466

The infallibility of God's purpose

*'But he is in one mind, and who can turn him? and what his soul desireth,
even that he doeth.' Job 23:13*
SUGGESTED FURTHER READING: Acts 4:23–31

It is a wonderful thing how God effects his purpose while still the creature is
free. They who think that predestination and the fulfilment of the divine
purpose is contrary to the free-agency of man, know not what they say, nor
whereof they affirm. It would be no miracle for God to effect his own
purpose, if he were dealing with stocks and stones, with granite and with
trees; but this is the miracle of miracles, that the creatures are free,
absolutely free, and yet the divine purpose stands. Herein is wisdom. This is
a deep unsearchable. Man walks without a fetter, yet treads in the very steps
which God ordained him to tread in, as certainly as though manacles had
bound him to the spot. Man chooses his own seat, selects his own position,
guided by his will he chooses sin, or guided by divine grace he chooses the
right, and yet in his choice, God sits as sovereign on the throne; not
disturbing, but still over-ruling, and proving himself to be able to deal as
well with free creatures as with creatures without freedom, as well able to
effect his purpose when he has endowed men with thought, and reason, and
judgment, as when he had only to deal with the solid rocks and the
imbedded sea. O Christians, you shall never be able to fathom this, but you
may wonder at it. I know there is an easy way of getting out of this great
deep, either by denying predestination altogether or by denying free-agency
altogether; but you can hold the two, if you can say, 'Yes, my consciousness
teaches me that man does as he wills, but my faith teaches me that God does
as he wills, and these two are not contrary to each other; and yet I cannot tell
how it is; I cannot tell how God effects his end; I can only wonder and
admire.'

FOR MEDITATION: Consider Romans 11:33. God searches into all our ways
and knows all the answers (Psalm 139:1–5); his ways are higher than our
ways (Isaiah 55:9)—too high for us to search out and understand. But we
can still view them with wonder and praise (Psalm 139:6,14).

Simeon

'And, behold, there was a man in Jerusalem, whose name was Simeon; and the same man was just and devout, waiting for the consolation of Israel: and the Holy Ghost was upon him.' Luke 2:25
SUGGESTED FURTHER READING: Hebrews 6:9–20

How consolatory the doctrine of *election* to the Israel of God! To some men it is repulsive. But show me the gracious soul that has come to put his trust under the wings of the Lord God of Israel. 'Chosen in Christ,' will be a sweet stanza in his song of praise. To think that before the hills were formed, or the channels of the sea were scooped out, God loved me; that from everlasting to everlasting his mercy is upon his people. Is not that a consolation? You who do not believe in election, go and fish in other waters; but in this great sea there are mighty fishes. If you could come here, you would find rich consolation. Or come again to the sweet doctrine of *redemption*. What consolation is there, beloved, to know that you are redeemed with the precious blood of Christ. Not the mock redemption taught by some people, which pretends that the ransom is paid, but the souls that are ransomed may notwithstanding be lost. No, no; a positive redemption which is effectual for all those for whom it is made. O to think that Christ has so purchased you with his blood, that you cannot be lost. Is there not consolation in that doctrine, the doctrine of redemption? Think, again, of the doctrine of *atonement*—that Christ Jesus has borne all your sins in his own body on the tree; that he has put away your sins by the sacrifice of himself. There is nothing like believing in full atonement; that all our sins are washed away and carried into the depths of the sea. Is there not consolation there? What say you, worldling, if you could know yourself elect of God the Father, if you could believe yourself redeemed by his only begotten Son, if you knew that for your sins there was a complete ransom paid, would not that be a consolation to you?

FOR MEDITATION: The Christian is not supposed to be an inactive academic, but those who consider doctrine boring rob themselves of the comfort of the Scriptures (Romans 15:4; 1 Thessalonians 4:18).

Heart's-ease

'He shall not be afraid of evil tidings: his heart is fixed, trusting in the
LORD.*' Psalm 112:7*
SUGGESTED FURTHER READING: Psalm 42:1–11

If you give way to fright and fear when you hear of evil tidings, how can you glorify God? Saints can sing God's high praises in the fires and bless his name on beds of sickness, but you cannot if you fall into distractions. Why, man, can your murmuring praise God? Your doubting and fearing, as if you had none to help you, will these magnify the Most High? Come, I pray you, if you would honour God, be brave. A certain good man was much troubled under a loss in business; his wife tried to comfort him but failed, and being a very wise woman she gave it up till the morning. In the morning when she came downstairs her face looked so sad that her husband said, 'What is the matter with you?' She, still preserving a mournful countenance, said that a dream had troubled her. 'What was it, my dear,' he said, 'you ought not to be troubled with dreams.' 'O,' she said, 'I dreamed that God was dead, and it was such reason for trouble, that all the angels were weeping in heaven, and all the saints on earth were ready to break their hearts.' Her husband said, 'You must not be foolish, you know it was only a dream.' 'O but,' she said, 'to think of God's being dead!' He replied, 'You must not even think of such a thing, for God cannot die, he ever lives to comfort his people.' Instantly her face brightened up, and she said, 'I thought I would bring you thus to rebuke yourself, for you have been dreaming that God had forsaken you, and now you see how groundless is your sorrow. While God lives his people are safe.'

FOR MEDITATION: Do you ever act as if God is dead? If God the Son had never risen from the dead, it would be right for Christians to be utterly miserable (Luke 24:17; John 20:11; 1 Corinthians 15:17–19). Christ was dead, but Christ is risen; he cannot die again (Romans 6:9), but he lives for ever (Hebrews 7:25; Revelation 1:18). So 'Why weepest thou?' (John 20:13,15); our rejoicing in these great facts should help us face all circumstances.

God's strange choice

'For ye see your calling, brethren, how that not many wise men after the flesh, not many mighty, not many noble, are called.' 1 Corinthians 1:26
SUGGESTED FURTHER READING: Ephesians 1:1–14

The church is called a *building*. With whom does the architecture of the building rest? With the building? With the stones? Do the stones select themselves? Did that stone just yonder in the corner choose its place? or that which is buried there in the foundation, did it select its proper position? No; the architect alone disposes of his chosen materials according to his own will; and thus, in building the church which is the great house of God, the great master Builder reserves to himself the choice of the stones, and the places which shall occupy. Take a yet more apparent case. The church is called *Christ's bride*. Would any man here agree to have any person forced upon him as his bride? There is not a man among us who would for a single moment so demean himself as to give up his rights to choose his own spouse; and shall Christ leave to haphazard, and to human will, who his bride shall be? No; but my Lord Jesus, the husband of the church, exercises the sovereignty which his position permits him, and selects his own bride. Again, we are said to be *members of Christ's body*. We are told by David, that in God's book all our 'members were written, which in continuance were fashioned, when as yet there was none of them;' thus every man's body had its members written in God's book. Is Christ's body to be an exception to this rule? Is that great body of divine manhood, Christ Jesus, the mystical Saviour, to be fashioned according to the whims and wishes of free will, while other bodies, vastly inferior, have their members written in the book of God? Let us not dream thus (it would be to talk idly) and not know the meaning of the metaphors of Scripture.

FOR MEDITATION: The Lord Jesus Christ does the choosing; we get chosen (John 15:16). He is the head of his own body (Ephesians 1:22–23), the builder of his own church (Matthew 16:18; Ephesians 2:20–22) and the husband of his own chosen bride (Ephesians 5:23–27).

SERMON NO. 587

The sinner's friend

A friend of publicans and sinners.' Matthew 11:19
SUGGESTED FURTHER READING: Isaiah 55:1–7

We know of a place (near Winchester) in England still existing, where there is a portion of bread served to every passer-by who chooses to ask for it. Whoever he may be he has but to knock at the door of St Cross Hospital, and there is the portion of bread for him. Jesus Christ so loves sinners that he has built a St Cross Hospital, so that, whenever a sinner is hungry, he has but to knock and have his wants supplied. No, he has done better; he has attached to this hospital of the cross a bath; and whenever a soul is black and filthy it has but to go there and be washed. The fountain is always full, always efficacious. There is no sinner who ever went into it and found it could not wash away his stains. Sins which were scarlet and crimson have all disappeared, and the sinner has been whiter than snow. As if this were not enough, there is attached to this hospital of the cross a wardrobe, and a sinner, making application simply as a sinner, with nothing in his hand, but being just empty and naked, may come and be clothed from head to foot. And if he wishes to be a soldier, he may not merely have an undergarment, but he may have armour which shall cover him from the sole of his foot to the crown of his head. If he wants a sword he shall have that given him, and a shield too. There is nothing that his heart can desire that is good for him which he shall not receive. He shall have spending money so long as he lives, and he shall have an eternal heritage of glorious treasure when he enters into the joy of his Lord.

FOR MEDITATION: Christ crucified draws sinners to himself (John 12:32–33). When they come to him, he is the perfect host, not turning anyone away (John 6:37), but offering them all the very best hospitality (John 6:35). He can be fully recommended by all who come to him in truth (John 6:68–69).

The red heifer

'... the LORD hath commanded, saying, Speak unto the children of Israel, that they bring thee a red heifer without spot, wherein is no blemish ... and ye shall give her unto Eleazer the priest ... and one shall slay her before his face.' Numbers 19:2–3
SUGGESTED FURTHER READING: John 13:1–11

What is there opened for the house of David, for sin, and for uncleanness? A cistern? A cistern that might be emptied? No, there is a fountain open. We wash, the fountain flows; we wash again, the fountain flows still. From the great depths of the deity of Christ, the eternal merit of his passion comes everlastingly welling up. Is it not said in Scripture, 'If any man sin, we have an advocate'? Why is Christ an advocate today? Only because we want an advocate every day. Does he not constantly intercede yonder before the eternal throne? Why does he do that? Because we want daily intercession. And it is because we are constantly sinning that he is constantly an advocate, constantly an intercessor. He himself has beautifully set this forth in the case of Peter: after supper the Lord took a towel and girded himself, and then, taking his basin and his water-jug, he went to Peter, and Peter said, 'Thou shalt never wash my feet.' But Jesus told him, 'If I wash thee not, thou hast no part with me.' He had been washed once; Peter was free from sin in the high sense of justification, but he needs the washing of purification. When Peter said, 'Lord, not my feet only, but also my hands and my head,' then Jesus replied, 'He that is washed'—that is, he who is pardoned—'needeth not save to wash his feet, but is clean every whit.' The feet want constant washing. The daily defilement of our daily walk through an ungodly world brings upon us the daily necessity of being cleansed from fresh sin, and that the mighty Master supplies to us.

FOR MEDITATION: In the Old Testament fresh sins required regular fresh sacrifices (Hebrews 7:27) which never removed sin (Hebrews 10:1–4). Christ's shed blood gives every believer forgiveness plus ongoing cleansing from all sin (1 John 1:7); fresh sins require fresh confession to God (1 John 1:9), never a fresh sacrifice.

SERMON NO. 527

Flesh and spirit—a riddle

'So foolish was I, and ignorant: I was as a beast before thee. Nevertheless I am continually with thee: thou hast holden me by my right hand. Thou shalt guide me with thy counsel, and afterward receive me to glory.' Psalm 73:22–24

SUGGESTED FURTHER READING: Psalm 40:1–5

I thought I saw just now before my eyes a dark and horrible pit, and down deep below, where the eye could not reach, lay a being broken in pieces, whose groans and howlings pierced the awful darkness and amazed my ears. I thought I saw a bright one fly from the highest heaven, and in an instant dive into that black darkness till he was lost and buried in it. I waited for a moment, and to my mind's eye I saw two spirits rising from the horrid deep; with arms entwined, as though one was bearing up the other, I saw them emerge from the gloom. I heard the fairest of them say, as he mounted into light, 'I have loved thee, and given myself for thee.' And I heard the other say, who was that poor broken one just now, 'So foolish was I, and ignorant: I was as a beast before thee.' Before I could write the words both spirits had risen into mid air, and I heard one of them say 'Thou shalt be with me in paradise,' and the other whispered 'Nevertheless I am continually with thee.' As they mounted higher, I heard one say, 'None shall pluck thee out of my hand,' and I heard the other say 'Thou hast holden me by my right hand.' As still they rose they continued the loving dialogue. 'I will guide thee with mine eye,' said the bright one; the other answered 'Thou shalt guide me with thy counsel.' They reached the bright clouds that separate earth from heaven, and as they parted to make way for the glorious One, he said, 'I will give thee to sit upon my throne, even as I have overcome, and sit upon my Father's throne,' and the other answered, 'And thou shalt afterward receive me to glory.'

FOR MEDITATION: When God raises us up with Christ, he seats us with him in the heavenly places (Ephesians 2:6) during our journey to heaven. If you have entered this spiritual dimension by faith in him, you have received every spiritual blessing in Christ (Ephesians 1:3).

SERMON NO. 467

Natural or spiritual?

'*But the natural man receiveth not the things of the Spirit of God, neither can he know them, because they are spiritually discerned.*' 1 Corinthians 2:14
SUGGESTED FURTHER READING: Ephesians 1:15–2:6

The same power which raised Christ Jesus from the dead must be exerted in raising us from the dead; the very same omnipotence, without which angels or worms could not have had a being, must again step forth out of its privy-chamber, and do as great a work as it did at the first creation in making us anew in Christ Jesus our Lord. There have been attempts at all times to get rid of this unpleasant necessity. Constantly the Christian church itself tries to forget it, but as often as ever this old doctrine of regeneration is brought forward pointedly, God is pleased to favour his church with a revival. The doctrine which looks at first as though it would hush every exertion with indolence, and make men sit down with listlessness and despair, is really like the trump of God to awake the dead; and where it is fully and faithfully preached, though it grate upon the carnal ear, though it excite enmity in many against the man who dares to proclaim it, yet it is owned of God. Because it honours God, God will honour it. This was the staple preaching of Whitefield. He was always great upon that which he called the great R— Regeneration. Whenever you heard him, the three Rs came out clearly— Ruin, Regeneration, and Redemption! Man ruined, wholly ruined, hopelessly, helplessly, eternally ruined! Man regenerated by the Spirit of God, and by the Spirit of God alone wholly made a new creature in Christ! Man redeemed by precious blood from all his sins, not by works of righteousness, not by deeds of the law, not by ceremonies, prayers, or resolutions, but by the precious blood of Christ! We must be very pointed, and very plain about regeneration, for this is the very pith and marrow of the matter—'Except a man be born again, he cannot see the kingdom of God.'

FOR MEDITATION: Man ruined (Titus 3:3), man regenerated (Titus 3:5), man redeemed (Titus 2:14). Have you experienced all three points or just the first?

SERMON NO. 407

The blood of Abel and the blood of Jesus

'And he said, What hast thou done? the voice of thy brother's blood crieth unto me from the ground.' Genesis 4:10
'And to Jesus the mediator of the new covenant, and to the blood of sprinkling, that speaketh better things than that of Abel.' Hebrews 12:24
SUGGESTED FURTHER READING: Hebrews 9:11–22

In the second text this blood is called 'the blood of *sprinkling.*' Whether Abel's blood sprinkled Cain or not I cannot say, but if it did it must have added to his horror to have had the blood actually upon him. But this adds to the joy in our case, for the blood of Jesus is of little value to us until it is sprinkled upon us. Faith dips the hyssop in the atoning blood and sprinkles it upon the soul, and the soul is clean. The application of the blood of Jesus is the true ground of joy, and the sure source of Christian comfort; the application of the blood of Abel must have been horror, but the application of the blood of Jesus is the root and ground of all delight. There is another matter in the text. The apostle says 'Ye are *come* ... to the blood of sprinkling.' He mentions that among other things to which we are come. Now, from the blood of Abel every reasonable man would flee away. He that has murdered his fellow desires to put a wide distance between himself and the accusing corpse. But we come to the blood of Jesus. It is a topic in which we delight as our contemplations bring us nearer and nearer to it. I ask you, dear Christian friends, to come nearer to it this morning than ever you have been. Think over the great truth of substitution. Portray to yourself the sufferings of the Saviour. Dwell in his sight, sit at the foot of Calvary, abide in the presence of his cross, and never turn away from that great spectacle of mercy and of misery. Come to it; be not afraid. You sinners, who have never trusted Jesus, look here and live! May you come to him now.

FOR MEDITATION: What adjective would you use to describe the Bible's teaching about the blood of Christ? 'Repulsive', 'disgusting', 'messy', 'immoral'? Even some churchgoers would use these terms! But the true believer has a very different description of the redeeming blood of Christ—'precious' (1 Peter 1:19).

Degrees of power attending the gospel

'For our gospel came not unto you in word only, but also in power, and in the Holy Ghost, and in much assurance; as ye know what manner of men we were among you for your sake.' 1 Thessalonians 1:5
SUGGESTED FURTHER READING: Hebrews 10:19–25

The highest point in the text is 'much assurance.' If I understand the passage, it means this: first that they were fully persuaded of its truthfulness, and had no staggering or blinding doubts about it; and secondly, that they had the fullest possible conviction of their interest in the truth delivered to them. They were saved, but better still they knew that they were so! They were clean, but better still they rejoiced in their purity! They were in Christ, but what is more joyous still, they knew that they were in Christ. They had no doubts as some of you have, no dark suspicions; the Word had come with such blessed demonstration that it had swept away every Canaanitish doubt clean out of their hearts. According to Poole, the Greek word here used has in it the idea of a ship at full sail, undisturbed by the waves which ripple in its way. A ship, when the wind is thoroughly favourable, and its sails are bearing it directly into harbour, is not held back by the surging billows. True, the vessel may rock, but it neither turns to the right hand, nor to the left. Let the billows be as they may, the wind is sufficiently powerful to overcome their contrary motion, and the vessel goes straight ahead. Some Christians get the gospel in that way. They have not a shadow of a doubt about its being true. They have not even the beginning of a doubt about their interest in it, and therefore they have nothing to do, but with God's strong hand upon the tiller, and the heavenly wind blowing right into the sail, to go straight on, doing the will of God, glorifying his name. May the Word come to you, dear friends, as it does to so very few! May it come in 'much assurance.'

FOR MEDITATION: Paul's prayer for believers was that they would enjoy 'all riches of the full assurance of understanding' (Colossians 2:2). How is your assurance? It doesn't necessarily come so easily to every believer; the maintenance of assurance requires some effort on our part (Hebrews 6:11–12).

SERMON NO. 648

The prodigal's reception

'And he arose, and came to his father. But when he was yet a great way off his father saw him, and had compassion, and ran, and fell on his neck, and kissed him.' Luke 15:20
SUGGESTED FURTHER READING: Mark 10:17–22

You have a desire towards God, and you would if you could, lay hold upon eternal life. But you feel too far off for anything like comfortable hope; now I must confess I feel many fears about you who are in this state; I am afraid lest you should come so far and yet go back; for there are many whom we thought had come as far as this, and yet they have gone back after all. Remember that desires after God will not change you so as to save you. You must find Christ. Remember that to say, 'I will arise' is not enough, nor even to arise; you must never rest till your Father has given you the kiss, till he has put on you the best robe. I am afraid lest you should rest satisfied and say, 'I am in a bad state; the minister tells me that many are brought to such a state before they are saved. I will stop here.' My dear friend, it is a good state *to pass through*, but it is a bad state *to rest in*. I pray you never be content with a sense of sin, never be satisfied with merely knowing that you are not what you ought to be. It never cures the fever for a man to know he has it; his knowledge is in some degree a good sign, for it proves that the fever has not yet driven him to delirium; but it never gives a man perfect health to know that he is sick. It is a good thing for him to know it, for he will not otherwise send for the physician; but unless it leads to that, he will die whether he feels himself to be sick or not.

FOR MEDITATION: Do you use the excuse that you feel too far away from God? It won't wash, because God is only a cry of faith away from you (Romans 10:6–9). The tax collector in the parable felt far from God, but he didn't let that prevent him from crying for God's mercy and receiving it (Luke 18:13–14).

The messenger of the covenant

'*The messenger of the covenant, whom ye delight in.*' Malachi 3:1
SUGGESTED FURTHER READING: Hebrews 8:1–13

The Lord's people delight in the covenant itself. It is an unfailing source of consolation to them so often as the Holy Spirit leads them to its green pastures, and makes them to lie down beside its still waters. They can sweetly sing of it from youth even to hoar hairs, from childhood even to the tomb, for this theme is inexhaustible.

They delight to contemplate *the antiquity* of that covenant, remembering that before the day star knew its place, or planets ran their round, the interests of the saints were made secure in Christ Jesus. It is peculiarly pleasing to them to remember *the sureness* of the covenant. They love to meditate upon 'the sure mercies of David.' They delight to celebrate the covenant in their songs of praise, as 'signed and sealed, and ratified, in all things ordered well.' It often makes their hearts dilate with joy to think of its *immutability*, as a covenant which neither time nor eternity, life nor death, things present, nor things to come, nor angels, nor principalities, nor powers, shall ever be able to violate—a covenant as old as eternity and as everlasting as the Rock of ages. They rejoice also to feast upon *the fulness* of this covenant, for they see it in all things provided for them; God is their portion, Christ their companion, the Spirit their comforter, earth their lodge and heaven their home. They see in it not only some things, but all things; not only a help to obtain some desirable possessions, but an inheritance reserved and entailed to [bestowed on] every soul that has an interest in this ancient and eternal deed of gift.

FOR MEDITATION: God's covenant with his people in Christ is described as new (1 Corinthians 11:25; Hebrews 8:8; 9:15; 12:24), better (Hebrews 7:22; 8:6) and everlasting (Hebrews 13:20). Does this agreement afford you delight? Is your future covered by it?

Chastisement—now and afterwards

'Now no chastening for the present seemeth to be joyous, but grievous:
nevertheless afterward it yieldeth the peaceable fruit of righteousness
unto them which are exercised thereby.' Hebrews 12:11
SUGGESTED FURTHER READING: Deuteronomy 8:1–10

Blessed is that chastening which being fruitful in us makes us also fruitful. It brings forth the 'fruit of righteousness'; not natural, and therefore impure fruit, but fruit such as God himself may accept—holiness, purity, patience, joy, faith, love, and every Christian grace. It does not make the Christian more righteous in the sense of justification, for he is completely so in Christ; but it makes him more apparently so in the eyes of onlookers, while he, through his experience, exhibits more of the character of his Lord. Note again, that this righteous fruit is 'peaceable.' None so happy as tried Christians—afterwards. No calm is more deep than that which follows a storm. Who has not seen clear shinings after rain? God gives sweet banquets to his children after the battle. It is after the rod that he gives the honeycomb; after climbing the Hill Difficulty, we sit down in the arbour to rest; after passing the wilderness we come to the House Beautiful; after we have gone down the Valley of Humiliation, after we have fought with Apollyon, the shining one appears to us and gives us the branch which heals us. It is always 'afterwards' with the Christian. He has his best things last, and he must be expecting, therefore, to have his worst things first. It is always 'afterwards.' Still, when it does come, it is peace, sweet, deep peace. What a delightful sensation it is, after long illness, once more to walk abroad; though perhaps, you are still pale to look upon, and feeble in body, you walk out of doors and breathe the air again; you can feel your blood leap in your veins, and every bone seems to sing out because of the mercy of God. Such is the peace which follows long and sharp affliction.

FOR MEDITATION: If you are Christ's servant, the word 'afterwards' should be in your vocabulary (Psalm 73:24; Luke 17:7–8). Every Christian needs patience (Hebrews 10:36) and patience needs time to do its work in us (James 1:3–4).

Ezekiel's deserted infant

'None eye pitied thee, to do any of these unto thee, to have compassion upon thee; but thou wast cast out in the open field, to the lothing of thy person, in the day that thou wast born. And when I passed by thee, and saw thee polluted in thine own blood, I said unto thee when thou wast in thy blood, Live.' Ezekiel 16:5–6
SUGGESTED FURTHER READING: Romans 5:12–16

A ruin so terrible and so early has fallen upon each of us. Let proud man kick against the doctrine as he may, Scripture tells us assuredly that we are born in sin and 'shapen in iniquity.' We came not into this world as Adam came into the garden, without flaw, without condemnation, without evil propensities; but by one man's offence we are all made sinners, and through his desperate fall our blood is tainted and our nature is corrupt. From the very birth we go astray, speaking lies, and in the very birth we lie under the condemnation of the law of God. It is not mine to defend this doctrine, to answer objections to it, or to bring arguments for it; I simply announce what God has himself revealed by the mouth of his servant David, and also more fully by the tongue of the apostle Paul. Man, unless God has mercy on you, you are lost, and lost from your very beginning! You did not come into this world as one who might stand or fall; you were fallen already; an original and birth-sin had seized upon you in the womb, and you were even then as an infant cast out to perish and to die. There is hardly any doctrine more humbling than that of natural depravity or original sin; it has been the main point of attack for all those who hate the gospel, and it must be maintained and valiantly vindicated by those who would exalt Christ, since the greatness and glory of his salvation lies mainly in the desperateness of the ruin from which he has redeemed us. Man, think not to save yourself by your works; boast not of the excellence of your character and of your nature.

FOR MEDITATION: We are born with the fatal disease of sin inherited from our earthly parents (Psalm 51:5). When we trust in the Lord Jesus Christ, we are born again with the perfect cure of eternal salvation received from God our new spiritual Father (1 Peter 1:23; 2:2–3).

Accidents, not punishments

'Some...told him of the Galileans, whose blood Pilate had mingled with their sacrifices. And Jesus answering said unto them, Suppose ye that these Galileans were sinners above all the Galileans?...Or those eighteen, upon whom the tower in Siloam fell, and slew them, think ye that they were sinners above all men that dwelt in Jerusalem?' Luke 13:1–4
SUGGESTED FURTHER READING: Job 1:1–22

If railways had never been constructed, there would still have been sudden deaths and terrible accidents. In taking up the old records in which our ancestors wrote down their accidents and calamities, we find that the old stage coach yielded quite as heavy a booty to death as does the swiftly-rushing train; there were gates to Hades then as many as there are now, and roads to death quite as steep and precipitous, travelled by quite as vast a multitude as in our present time. Do you doubt that? Permit me to refer you to the passage before you. Remember those eighteen upon whom the tower in Siloam fell. No collision crushed them; yet some badly-built tower, or some wall beaten by the tempest could fall upon eighteen at a time, and they could perish. Or worse than that, a despotic ruler, having the lives of men in his hand, might suddenly fall upon worshippers, and mix their blood with the blood of the bullocks which they were sacrificing. Do not think, then, that this is an age in which God is dealing more hardly with us than of old. Do not think that God's providence has become more lax than it was; there always were sudden deaths, and there always will be. Be not, therefore, cast down with any sudden fear, neither be troubled by these calamities.

FOR MEDITATION: We can also draw wrong conclusions from recent catastrophes. Foretelling disasters before his second coming, Jesus added 'but the end is not yet' (Matthew 24:6–8). Some in Spurgeon's day had the second coming pencilled in for 1866 (see 12 October).

N.B. There had been several serious accidents in 1861 including two train crashes in which 39 people had died during the previous fortnight.

Kicking against the pricks

'It is hard for thee to kick against the pricks.' Acts 9:5
SUGGESTED FURTHER READING: Luke 13:31–35

Observe the tenderness of the rebuke. It is not, 'O Saul, it is wicked, ungenerous, and mischievous of thee to resist me.' There is no rebuke of that kind; unless it be implied in the expression, 'Why persecutest thou me?' But the Saviour leaves Saul's conscience to say that, and does not utter it himself. Nor did Jesus say, 'Saul, Saul, it is very hard for my people to bear thy cruelties;' nor does he add, 'It is very provoking to me, and I shall ere long smite thee in my wrath.' No, it is not, 'It is hard for *me*,' but 'It is hard for *thee*;' as if the thoughts of the Saviour were so set upon his poor, erring, but ignorant child that he felt, 'As to what thou doest to my cause, I will say nothing; but see what thou art doing to thyself; thou art losing joy and comfort; thou art injuring thine own soul; thou art sowing for thyself the seeds of future sorrow. It is hard for *thee*.' Who but the Saviour could have spoken after this fashion? I do not believe that the most tender-hearted of the Saviour's ministers have been accustomed to look upon persecutors in that light. If we hear of tyrants breathing out threatening and slaughter against God's people, we may readily say, 'What a wicked thing! What a cruel and unrighteous thing!' but how seldom do we exclaim, 'What a sad thing it is for the persecutor!' We add, perhaps, with a little sober vindictiveness, 'What a terrible fate will be that man's!' but we feel but little deep pity for one whose terrible case it is to be an enemy to the sinner's friend. What a bitter portion the poor, ignorant, offending persecutor has chosen; may we be Christlike enough to have pity upon him! The Saviour looks at sin through the glass of compassion; we often look upon it through the lens of Pharisaic pride.

FOR MEDITATION: Christ's apostles also had problems with their attitude towards those who would not receive him (Luke 9:52–55); but, in the presence of Saul of Tarsus, Stephen displayed a Christlike attitude to his own persecutors (Acts 7:60; 8:1). Without doubt that left an impression upon Saul (Acts 22:20) and probably contributed to his conversion.

Songs for desolate hearts

'Sing, O barren, thou that didst not bear; break forth into singing, and cry aloud, thou that didst not travail with child: for more are the children of the desolate than the children of the married wife, saith the LORD.' Isaiah 54:1

SUGGESTED FURTHER READING: Revelation 3:1–6

I question if hell can find a more fitting instrument within its infernal lake than the church of Rome is for the cause of mischief. And your church will in its measure be the same if bereft of the Spirit. I do not care if it be Wesleyan, Baptist, Independent, or what it is; when the life is gone it becomes henceforth good for nothing; it is not even fit to manure the ground, as the contents of the dunghill are, but men cast it out and tread it under foot. Get conscious of that, and then let those of you who are humbled in the sight of God meet together and spread the case before the Lord. We ought to have great faith in the power of the twos and threes, 'For where two or three are gathered together in my name, there am I in the midst of them,' says the Lord. The long thin red line, which has often won the battle, will yet win it in England—I mean the thin line of the few that sigh and cry for the desolations of the church. If you, my brother, an earnest man, be the only member of the church that does really sigh and cry before God, God intends to bless that church yet, for he has already blessed it in sending you to it. Look out for others of a kindred sort, and without murmuring, without raising divisions, without seeking to expel the minister or make any changes in the discipline, just you set to work, and pray down, as Elijah did, the fire from heaven upon the sacrifice. This is the one thing which is wanted. The wrong in organisation, the mistakes in government, the unfitness of the church officers—all this will come right enough if you once get the divine life; but without this, though you should rectify everything else, you would have done but little to any real purpose.

FOR MEDITATION: Believers should be 'the salt of the earth' and 'the light of the world' (Matthew 5:13–14), but a church can lose its way and need some members to be the salt and light of the church (Mark 9:50). Are you having to do that? God knows (Revelation 3:4).

SERMON NO. 649

11 SEPTEMBER (1864)

Jesus meeting his warriors

'And Melchizedek king of Salem brought forth bread and wine: and he was the priest of the most high God. And he blessed him, and said, Blessed be Abram of the most high God, possessor of heaven and earth: and blessed be the most high God, which hath delivered thine enemies into thy hand. And he gave him tithes of all.' Genesis 14:18–20
SUGGESTED FURTHER READING: 2 Corinthians 9:6–15

Truly our holy faith deserves of us that we should give all to Christ. I would that some Christians, however, practised the rule of giving a tenth of their substance to the Lord's cause. The Lord's church need never lack if you had a bag in which you stored up for Christ: when you gave anything, you would not feel it was giving of your own; your left hand would not know what your right hand did, for you would be taking out of the Lord's stock which you had already consecrated to the Lord's cause. Not less than one-tenth should be the Lord's portion, especially with those who have a competence; and more than this, I think, should be expected of those who have wealth. But there is no *rule* binding with iron force upon you, for we are not under *law* in Christ's church, but under *grace*, and grace will prompt you to do more than law might suggest; but certainly the Christian should reckon himself to be not his own, and that he has nothing to retain for his own private account. I pray God if I have a drop of blood in my body which is not his, to let it bleed away; and if there be one hair in my head which is not consecrated to him, I would have it plucked out, for it must be the devil's drop of blood and the devil's hair. It belongs to either one or the other: if not to God, then to Satan. No, we must, brethren, have no division of ourselves, no living unto this world and unto God too.

FOR MEDITATION: It is good if our giving to the Lord's cause is systematic (1 Corinthians 16:1–2), but it will be even better if both giver and gift are consecrated to him first (2 Corinthians 8:3–5).

SERMON NO. 589

The clean and the unclean

'Speak unto the children of Israel, saying, These are the beasts which ye shall eat among all the beasts that are on the earth. Whatsoever parteth the hoof, and is cloven footed, and cheweth the cud, among the beasts, that shall ye eat.' Leviticus 11:2–3
SUGGESTED FURTHER READING: Ephesians 3:14–4:3

There are two tests, but they must both be united. The beast that was clean was to chew the cud: here is the inner-life; every true-hearted man must know how to read, mark, learn, and inwardly digest the sacred Word. The man who does not feed upon gospel truth is no heir of heaven. You must know a Christian by his inwards, by that which supports his life and sustains his frame. But then the clean creatures were also known by their walk. The Jew at once discovered the unclean animal by its having an undivided hoof; but if the hoof was thoroughly divided, then it was clean, provided that it also chewed the cud. So there must be in the true Christian a peculiar walk such as God requires. You cannot tell a man by either of these tests alone; you must have them both. But while you use them upon others, apply them to yourselves. What do you feed on? What is your habit of life? Do you chew the cud by meditation? When your soul feeds on the flesh and blood of Christ have you learned that his flesh is meat indeed, and that his blood is drink indeed? If so 'tis well. What about your life? Are your conversation and your daily walk according to the description of believers in Christ which is given in the Word? If not, the first test will not stand alone. You may profess the faith within, but if you do not walk aright without, you belong to the unclean. On the other hand, you may walk aright without, but unless there is the chewing of the cud within, unless there is a real feeding upon precious truth in the heart, all the right walking in the world will not prove you to be a Christian.

FOR MEDITATION: Claiming the inward without displaying the outward is hypocrisy (James 2:26); displaying the outward without desiring the inward is self-righteousness (Luke 18:9–14). Saving faith both admits the need of the inward and displays the outward (Philippians 2:12–13; James 2:22).

SERMON NO. 499

The cedars of Lebanon

'The trees of the LORD *are full of sap; the cedars of Lebanon, which he hath planted.'* Psalm 104:16

SUGGESTED FURTHER READING: 2 Corinthians 8:1–7

A traveller tells us that in the wood, bark, and even the cones of the cedar there is an abundance of resin. They are saturated with it so that he says he can scarcely touch one of the cedars of Lebanon without having the turpentine or resin of them upon his hands. That is always the way with a truly healthy Christian; his grace is externally manifested. There is the inner life within, it is active, and by and by when it is in a right state, it saturates everything. You talk with the gracious man, he cannot help talking about Christ; you go into his house, you will soon see that a Christian lives there; you notice his actions and you will soon see he has been with Jesus. He is so full of sap that the sap must come out. He has so much of the divine life within, that the holy oil and divine balsam must flow from him. I am afraid this cannot be said of all of us; it is because we get to be dependent upon man, and not on God, and therefore have little of this sap; but if we are independent of man, and live wholly upon God, we shall be so full of sap that every part of us will betray our piety. And then let me say that this sap is abundantly to be desired. Oh, when I think what glory a full-grown Christian brings to God, what honour the faith of a believer puts upon Jesus, when I think what a knowledge of God and divine things an advanced believer possesses, when I contemplate his own joy and peace of mind, I could wish that every one of you, (though it is well to be hyssops on God's wall), could be cedars upon God's Lebanon. Oh that we would grow in grace and in the knowledge of our Lord and Saviour Jesus Christ.

FOR MEDITATION: Inner spiritual life must be seen in outward deeds. What a joy it is when truth in the soul overflows to such an extent that it fills a Christian's life (Romans 15:14; 2 John 4; 3 John 2–4). Our perfect example is the Lord Jesus Christ who was full of grace as well as truth (John 1:14).

What meanest thou, O sleeper?

'But Jonah was gone down into the sides of the ship; and he lay, and was fast asleep. So the shipmaster came to him, and said unto him, What meanest thou, O sleeper? arise, call upon thy God, if so be that God will think upon us, that we perish not.' Jonah 1:5–6
SUGGESTED FURTHER READING: Ezekiel 33:1–11

Men can be so careless about the ruin of men's souls. Let us hear the cry of 'Fire! fire!' in the streets, and our heart is all in trepidation lest some poor creature should be burned alive; but we read of hell, and of the wrath to come, and seldom do our hearts palpitate with any compassionate trembling and fear. If we are on board a vessel, and the shrill cry is heard, 'Man overboard!' whoever hears of a passenger wrapping his overcoat around him, and lying down upon a seat to contemplate the exertions of others? But in the church, when we hear of thousands of sinners sinking in the floods of ruin, we behold professed Christians wrapping themselves up in their own security, and calmly looking upon the labours of others, but not even lifting a finger to do any part of the work themselves. If we heard tomorrow in our streets the awful cry, more terrible than fire, the cry of 'Bread! bread! bread!' and saw starving women lifting up their perishing children, would we not empty out our stores? Who among us would not spend our substance to let the poor ravenous creatures satisfy the pangs of hunger? And yet, here is the world perishing for lack of knowledge. Here we have them at our doors crying for the bread of heaven, and how many there are that hoard their substance for avarice, give their time to vanity, devote their talents to self-aggrandisement, and centre their thoughts only on the world or the flesh! Oh! could you once see with your eyes a soul sinking into hell, it would be such a spectacle that you would work night and day, and count your life too short and your hours too few for the plucking of brands from the burning.

FOR MEDITATION: What a terrible thing it is to leave someone to die in their sin. What a tremendous thing it is to help them find the Saviour (James 5:20; Jude 23).

Fellowship with God

'That which we have seen and heard declare we unto you, that ye also may have fellowship with us: and truly our fellowship is with the Father, and with his Son Jesus Christ.' 1 John 1:3
SUGGESTED FURTHER READING: 2 Corinthians 5:11–6:1

That which is the Father's employment is our employment. I speak not of you all; he knows whom he has chosen. We cannot join with the Father in upholding all worlds, we cannot send forth floods of light at the rising of the sun, we cannot feed the cattle on a thousand hills, nor can we give food and life to all creatures that have breath. But there is something which we can do which he does. He does good to all his creatures, and we can do good also. He bears witness to his Son Jesus, and we can bear witness too. The 'Father worketh hitherto' that his Son may be glorified, and we work too. O Eternal Worker! it is his to save souls, and we are co-workers with him. You are his husbandry, you are his building; he scatters the seed of truth, we scatter it too; his words speak comfort, and our words comfort the weary too, when God the Spirit is with us. We hope we can say, 'For me to live is Christ;' and is this not what God lives for too? We desire nothing so much as to glorify him, and this is the Father's will, as well as Jesus Christ's prayer, 'Glorify thy Son, that thy Son also may glorify thee.' Do you not see, brethren, that we stand on the same platform with the eternal God? When we lift our hand, he lifts up his eternal arm; when we speak, he speaks too, and speaks the same thing; when we purpose Christ's glory, he purposes that glory too; when we long to bring home the wandering sheep, and to recall the prodigal sons, he longs to do the same. So that in that respect we can say, 'Truly our fellowship is with the Father, and with his Son Jesus Christ.'

FOR MEDITATION: The essential first step in doing the work of God is to trust in the Lord Jesus Christ (John 6:28–29). Faith in him is not only the route to salvation, but also an appointment as God's fellow-worker (John 14:12; 2 Corinthians 6:1). Jesus is the light of the world (John 8:12), and so are his followers (Matthew 5:14).

A feast for faith

'This also cometh forth from the LORD *of hosts, which is wonderful in counsel, and excellent in working.'* Isaiah 28:29
SUGGESTED FURTHER READING: Exodus 35:30–36:2

We are to ascribe the thoughtful, inventive mind, and the dexterous, clever hand, to him who is the great Instructor of man. We trace directly to God the marvellous philosophy of Newton, and the skill of Watt and Stephenson, because the very slightest consideration shows us that there was originally a peculiarity in the constitution and formation of such minds as theirs. The most of us could have done nothing of the kind if we had tried all our days. There may be men of inventive genius here, but I suppose that nine out of ten of us can make no pretence to the possession of anything of the sort, and therefore we are led to ask, where did the faculty come from? Surely the fertile brain of invention must be the Creator's gift. An after providence has also a hand in the business, for many men whose minds would naturally have gone in the direction of invention, are turned into quite another course by the force of circumstances. It was surely God's providence which in other cases found a channel for the natural passion, and allowed the soul to flow as it willed. And how often, too, some of the greatest inventions have been due to the simplest accidents! The puffing of steam from a kettle, or the falling of an apple from a tree have led thoughtful minds to discover great and important truths, and who shall attribute these circumstances to any but to 'him who worketh all things after the counsel of his own will,' and who gives wisdom to the wisest of the sons of men? Let us adore the mighty God, not only as we read our Bibles, but as we traverse the halls of art and science, and visit the exhibitions which in these days of ours are being reared on every side. Let us make man's skill speak to us of God's glory.

FOR MEDITATION: 1 Corinthians 4:7. Our 'natural' abilities are God-given, whether they are practical (Exodus 36:1–2) or academic (Daniel 1:17). It is our responsibility to use our gifts for their proper purpose and we are the only ones to blame if they are misused.

Judgment threatening but mercy sparing

'Cut it down; why cumbereth it the ground? And he answering said unto him, Lord, let it alone this year also.' Luke 13:7–8
SUGGESTED FURTHER READING: Hebrews 10:26–31

Jesus Christ has pleaded for you, the crucified Saviour has interfered for you. And you ask me 'Why?' I answer, because Jesus Christ has an interest in you all. We do not believe in general redemption, but we believe in every word of this precious Bible, and there are many passages in the Scripture which seem to show that Christ's death had a universal bearing upon the sons of men. We are told that he tasted death for every man. What does that mean? Does it mean that Jesus Christ died to save every man? I do not believe it does, for it seems to me that everything which Christ intended to accomplish by the act of his death he must accomplish, or else he will be disappointed, which is not supposable. But did he in any other sense die for the rest of mankind? He did. Nothing can be much more plain in Scripture, it seems to me, than that all sinners are spared as the result of Jesus Christ's death, and this is the sense in which men are said to trample on the blood of Jesus Christ. We read of some who denied the Lord that bought them. No one who is bought with blood for eternal salvation ever tramples on that blood; but Jesus Christ has shed his blood for the reprieve of men that they may be spared, and those who turn God's sparing mercy into an occasion for fresh sin, do trample on the blood of Jesus Christ. You can hold that doctrine without holding universal redemption, or without at all contradicting that undoubted truth, that Jesus laid down his life for his sheep, and that where he suffered he suffered not in vain. Now, sinner, whether you know it or not, you are indebted to him that did hang upon the tree, for the breath that is now in you.

FOR MEDITATION: Christ suffered and died on the cross to save all who would repent and trust in Him; God's delays are to give us the opportunity to do that (2 Peter 3:9). To abuse His kindness and patience by continuing to reject Christ instead of repenting is to add insult to injury and to store up trouble for eternity (Romans 2:4–5; Hebrews 10:29).

SERMON NO. 650

The backslider's way hedged up

'*She said, I will go after my lovers ... Therefore, behold, I will hedge up thy way with thorns ... that she shall not find her paths. And she shall follow after her lovers ... but shall not find them: then shall she say, I will go and return to my first husband; for then was it better with me than now.*'
Hosea 2:5–7
SUGGESTED FURTHER READING: Jeremiah 3:1–25

By the mouth of Jeremiah God speaks these words—'Turn ... for I am married unto you.' I do not know anything which should make the backslider's heart break like the doctrine of God's immutable love to his people. Some say that if we preach that 'whom once he loves he never leaves, but loves them to the end,' it will be an inducement to man to sin. Well, I know man is very vile, and he can turn even love itself into a reason for sinning, but where there is as much as even one spark of grace, a man cannot do that. A child does not say, 'I will offend my father because he loves me;' it is not even in fallen nature generally, unless inspired by the devil to find motives for sin in God's love, and certainly no backsliding child of God can say 'I will continue in sin that grace may abound.' They who do so show that they are reprobates, and their damnation is just. But the backslider, who is a child of God at the bottom, will, I think, feel no cord so strong to hold him back from sin as this. Backslider, I hope it will also be a golden chain to draw you to Christ. Jesus meets you, meets you this morning. You were excommunicated. You were driven out from among God's people with shame, but Jesus meets you, and pointing to the wounds which he received in the house of his friends at your hands, he nevertheless says, 'Turn ... for I am married unto you.' It is a relationship which you have broken, and it might legally be broken for ever if he willed it; but he does not will it, for he hates to put away. You are married to Jesus. Come back to your first husband, for he is your husband still!

FOR MEDITATION: Backsliding is a real problem amongst God's people (Hosea 11:7), but not incurable (Hosea 14:4). The remedy is to state the obvious—'return unto the Lord' (Hosea 6:1; 14:1).

SERMON NO. 590

Two loving invitations

'Come and see.' John 1:39
'Come and dine.' John 21:12
SUGGESTED FURTHER READING: Revelation 3:14–22

We must live by faith on the Son of God, and listen to his voice as he says, 'Eat, O friends; drink, yea, drink abundantly, O beloved.' If you want to be as Mr Feeblemind, I can give you the recipe. Take only a small modicum of spiritual food morning and night in your closets; neglect family prayer; never attend a prayer-meeting; on no account speak about religious matters during the week, go late to the house of God, and fall asleep when you get there; as soon as you leave the place of worship talk about the weather. Confine yourself to these rules for a few weeks, and you will very soon be reduced low enough to allow Satan to attack you with every chance of giving you a severe and dangerous fall. Doctors tell us that nowadays the classes of disease most prevalent are those which indicate a low condition of the vital forces; and I think that we are suffering in the church from the same sort of maladies. There was a time when the church had to censure her young converts because they courted persecution and invited martyrdom; now we need to stir up the church and to urge on our people to more self-sacrifice for the cause of Christ. You need never fear that anyone will kill himself with overwork; we must rather lament that there seems so little exuberance of spirit and vital force amongst Christians. None of us need to put ourselves on low diet; on the contrary, we ought to accumulate strength and urge every power to its full tension in the Master's service. For this purpose, 'Come and dine.' All your strength depends upon union with Christ. Away from him you must wither as a branch severed from the vine. Feeding on him, you will be like the branch which is drinking up the sap from the parent stem.

FOR MEDITATION: The Christian's need of daily spiritual bread is Asked in a Prayer (Luke 11:3), Applied in a Parable (Luke 11:5–13) and Answered in a Person (John 6:34–35). Since Jesus is 'the bread of life', inadequate feeding upon him by faith is the route towards spiritual malnutrition and weakness.

SERMON NO. 633

The warrant of faith

'And this is his commandment, That we should believe on the name of his Son Jesus Christ.' 1 John 3:23
SUGGESTED FURTHER READING: Acts 16:16–34

If we heartily trust our soul with Christ, our sins, through his blood, are forgiven, and his righteousness is imputed to us. The mere knowledge of these facts will not, however, save us, unless we really and truly trust our souls in the Redeemer's hands. Faith must act in this wise: 'I believe that Jesus came to save sinners, and therefore, sinner though I be, I rest myself on him; I know that his righteousness justifies the ungodly; I, therefore, though ungodly, trust in him to be my righteousness; I know that his precious blood in heaven prevails with God on the behalf of them that come unto him; and since I come unto him, I know by faith that I have an interest in his perpetual intercession.' Now, I have enlarged the one thought of believing on God's Son Jesus Christ. 'Believing' is most clearly explained by that simple word 'trust.' Believing is partly the intellectual operation of receiving divine truths, but the essence of it lies in relying upon those truths. I believe that, although I cannot swim, yonder friendly plank will support me in the flood; I grasp it, and am saved: the grasp is faith. I am promised by a generous friend that if I draw upon his banker, he will supply all my needs; I joyously confide in him, and as often as I am in want I go to the bank, and am enriched: my going to the bank is faith. Thus faith is accepting God's great promise, contained in the person of his Son. It is taking God at his word, and trusting in Jesus Christ as being my salvation, although I am utterly unworthy of his regard. Sinner, if you take Christ to be your Saviour this day, you are justified.

FOR MEDITATION: Abraham is our example of saving faith (Romans 4:11–12). In his head he was convinced that God could do what he had promised (Romans 4:21); in his heart he trusted God (Romans 4:20); God accepted his trust and attributed righteousness to him (Romans 4:22). This is how we are to trust in the death and resurrection of the Lord Jesus Christ (Romans 4:23–25). But is this what you mean by 'faith'?

SERMON NO. 531

Accepted in the Beloved

'He hath made us accepted in the beloved.' Ephesians 1:6
SUGGESTED FURTHER READING: Romans 3:21–4:8

The Arminians say our being accepted before God, if I understand it aright, is also an acceptance in our graces. This is the English of their doctrine of falling away. When a man walks worthily, God accepts him; if he walks sinfully, then God accepts him no more. Those of you who like this way of being accepted, may choose it; for my part, I feel there is nothing can ever satisfy the craving of my spirit but an acceptance which lies utterly and wholly out of me, and only and entirely in Christ Jesus. Why, brethren, we should be accepted one day and non-accepted the next; no, more, we might be accepted one minute and non-accepted the next. If it lay in anything whatever in our walk, or in our work, we should be in the covenant and out of the covenant fifty times a day. But I suppose the Arminians have a difference between sin and sin. Surely, they must have the old Romish distinction between venial and mortal sin; for if sin puts a man out of Christ, I wonder when he is in, since we are sinning day by day. Perhaps there is a certain quantity of sin required to do it; then that is only the old Romish dogma revived; some sins, mortal on the Arminian theory, so as to put a man out of grace, and other sins venial, so that they can keep in grace and sin too. I glory in my God that I know-

'Once in Christ in Christ for ever,
Nothing from his love can sever.'

If my good works had put me into Christ, then my bad works might turn me out of him; but since he put me in when I was a sinner, vile and worthless, he will never take me out, though I am a sinner vile and worthless still.

FOR MEDITATION: There is no condemnation for those who are in Christ Jesus (Romans 8:1), because no one can draw them out of his hand (John 10:28–29; Romans 8:35,38–39) and he has promised never to drive them out (John 6:37).

Not now, but hereafter!

'Have ye not asked them that go by the way? and do ye not know their tokens, that the wicked is reserved to the day of destruction? they shall be brought forth to the day of wrath.' Job 21:29–30
SUGGESTED FURTHER READING: Matthew 27:44 & Luke 23:39–43

Edward the Second, one of our kings, was exceedingly enraged against one of his courtiers; out hunting one day, he threatened the courtier with the severest punishment. There was a river between them at the time, and the courtier thinking that he was perfectly safe, ventured to offer some jeering remark against the king—telling him that at any rate he would not be likely to chastise him until he got at him. The king, feeling his anger hot within him, told him that the water should not long divide them, leaped into the middle of the stream, and with some difficulty gained the other side. The courtier in great alarm fled in terror, and the king pursued him with might and main, spurring his horse to the utmost. Nor did his anger cease; he carried his drawn sword in his hand with the intention of killing him. At last the courtier, seeing that there was no hope for any escape, knelt down upon the grass, and laying bare his neck, said, 'I heartily deserve to die; mercy, King, mercy!' The king sent back the sword into the scabbard in a moment, and said, 'Whilst you sought to escape me I determined to destroy you, but when I see you humble at my feet I freely forgive you.' Even so it is with the King of heaven. Sinners, you say there is this life between you and God; but how soon will the white horse of Justice pass the stream, and then, flee as you may today, he will surely overtake you. He now is swift to destroy; let it be yours on your knees to make confession of your sin and say, 'I deserve thy wrath, great King;' and if to this you are enabled to add the plea of the precious blood of Christ, the sword of justice will return into its scabbard, and he will say, 'I am just, and yet the justifier of the ungodly.'

FOR MEDITATION: We can never escape from God (Psalm 139:7–10). He gave us his Son as the way of escape from his judgment (John 5:24), but what hope can there be for those who ignore the escape route (Hebrews 2:3; 12:25)?

SERMON NO. 410

War with Amalek

'Then came Amalek, and fought with Israel in Rephidim.' Exodus 17:8
SUGGESTED FURTHER READING: Genesis 39:1–12

Spiritual fighting must be conducted on most earnest and prudent principles. They were to 'choose out men.' So we must choose out our ways of contending with sin. The best part of a man should be engaged in warfare with his sins. Certain sins can only be fought with the understanding; we ought then to sit down, and deliberately look at the evil, and learn its wickedness, by deliberately judging and considering its motives and its consequences. Perhaps when we clearly see what the sin is, Mr Understanding, as Bunyan calls it, may be able to knock the brains out of it. One peculiar order of sins are only to be overcome by a speedy flight like that of the chaste Joseph. Sins of the flesh are never to be reasoned or parleyed with; there is no more reasoning with them than with the winds; understanding is nonplussed, for lust like a hurricane of sand blinds the eyes. We must fly. It is true valour in such a case to turn the back. 'Resist the devil,' says James, but Paul does not say 'resist lust'; he puts it thus—'Flee also youthful lusts.' When warring with the legions of unrighteousness we shall need all the best powers of our renewed nature, for the conflict will be stern. O believer, you will need to bring your veterans, your pick and your choice thoughts into the fight with Amalek; the faith which has endured the storm must face the foe, the love which endures all things must march to the war. It is no child's play to fight with sin. It needed all the Saviour's strength to tread it in the winepress when he was here on earth, and it will want all your might and more to overcome it—you will only overcome it indeed through the blood of the Lamb.

FOR MEDITATION: Whatever the temptation faced by the Christian, God is certain to have provided a way to escape (1 Corinthians 10:13). Whether that is to turn and flee or to stand and fight (1 Timothy 6:11–12) will depend on the circumstances and the nature of the temptation.

A sermon from a rush

'*Can the rush grow up without mire? can the flag grow without water? Whilst it is yet in his greenness, and not cut down, it withereth before any other herb. So are the paths of all that forget God; and the hypocrite's hope shall perish.*' Job 8:11–13
SUGGESTED FURTHER READING: Matthew 12:22–29; 43–45

You have cleansed the house, you have swept it, you have decorated it, and the evil spirit is gone; but if the Holy Spirit has not driven him out, if this has not been a work of power on the part of God, that evil spirit will come back, and he will take unto himself seven other spirits more wicked than himself, and they shall enter in and dwell there, and your last end will be worse than the first. Better not to have known the way of righteousness than, having known it, to be turned back again. I believe in the doctrine of the final perseverance of every true child of God; but there are in all our churches certain spurious pretenders who will not hold on their way, who will blaze and sparkle for a season, and then they will go out in darkness. They are 'wandering stars, to whom is reserved the blackness of darkness for ever.' Far better to make no pretension of having come to Christ, and of having been born again, unless through divine grace you shall hold fast until the end. Remember the back door to hell. There is a public entrance for the open sinner; but there is a back door for the professed saint; there is a back door for the hoary-headed professor, who has lived many years in apparent sincerity, but who has been a liar before God. There is a back door for the preacher who can talk fast and loudly, but who does not in his own heart know the truth he is preaching: there is a back door to hell for church members, who are amiable and excellent in many respects, but who have not really looked unto the Lord Jesus Christ and found true salvation in him.

FOR MEDITATION: Sometimes those pretending to be Christians are exposed by their present behaviour (1 John 3:10) or by steps they take later (1 John 2:19); at other times the pretence can be maintained (Matthew 7:21–23). But God is not mocked (Galatians 6:7); he knows who his people are (2 Timothy 2:19).

Thus saith the LORD

'Thus saith the LORD.*' Ezekiel 11:5*
SUGGESTED FURTHER READING: Mark 7:1–13

True servants of God demand to see for all church ordinances and doctrines the express authority of the church's only teacher and Lord. They remember that the Lord Jesus bade the apostles to teach believers to observe all things whatsoever he had commanded them. The Holy Spirit revealed much of precious truth and holy precept by the apostles, and to his teaching we would give earnest heed; but when men cite the authority of fathers, and councils, and bishops, we give place for subjection, no, not for an hour. They may quote Irenaeus or Cyprian, Augustine or Chrysostom; they may remind us of the dogmas of Luther or Calvin; they may find authority in Simeon, or Wesley, or Gill. We will listen to the opinions of these great men with the respect they deserve as men, but having so done, we deny that we have anything to do with these men as authorities in the church of God, for there nothing has authority, but 'Thus saith the LORD of hosts.' If you shall bring us the concurrent consent of all tradition, if you shall quote precedents, we burn the whole as so much worthless lumber, unless you put your finger upon the passage of Holy Scripture which warrants the matter to be of God. You may further plead, in addition to all this venerable authority, the beauty of the ceremony and its usefulness to those who partake therein, but this is all foreign to the point, for to the true church of God the only question is this, is there a 'Thus saith the LORD' for it? And if divine authority be not forthcoming, faithful men thrust forth the intruder as the cunning craftiness of men.

FOR MEDITATION: Traditions can be good or bad. Are your doctrine and practice based upon the words of men or the Word of God (Mark 7:7–9; Colossians 2:8)? Having turned from the traditions of men to the revelation of Christ (Galatians 1:11–14), the apostle Paul handed down to others what he had received from the Lord (1 Corinthians 11:23; 15:3). God's Word is the only acceptable authority for our doctrines and practices (2 Thessalonians 2:15; 3:6).

SERMON NO. 591

The chief of sinners

'Sinners; of whom I am chief.' 1 Timothy 1:15
SUGGESTED FURTHER READING: 2 John 7–11

Here I ought to include those who hold views derogatory of the deity and the person of Christ. Faithfulness to you, my hearers, compels me to include the Socinian; I will not call him Unitarian, for we all hold the unity of the Godhead. Trinitarians, but Unitarians are we still. Far otherwise the Socinian and the Arian—I include them here—the men who say that Christ is not God, that the Redeemer of the world was but the son of Mary, that he who walked the waters of the deep, chained the winds, cast out evil spirits, and made even Hades startle with his voice when the soul of Lazarus came back—that he was but a prophet, a creature, a mere man. Surely, sir, you are the chief of sinners to have talked thus of him who is 'very God of very God,' the express image of his Father's person. But even to you is Jesus gracious, and he bids you still believe in him. You shall bow the knee to him one day, and worship him, for 'at the name of Jesus every knee should bow...and every tongue should confess that Jesus Christ is Lord, to the glory of God the Father.' Bow your knee now, and 'kiss the Son lest he be angry, and ye perish from the way, when his wrath is kindled but a little.' He bids you come to him, then will he blot out 'as a thick cloud, thy transgressions, and, as a cloud, thy sins.' The chief of sinners, we are sure, are found among those who directly attack the person of Jehovah's Christ, yet even to these is the gospel of salvation sent.

FOR MEDITATION: Sin is not limited to outward acts; it refers also to inward thoughts, desires and attitudes. If the sixth and seventh commandments can be broken inwardly (Matthew 5:21–22,27–28), so can the first three commandments concerning the character and name of God (Exodus 20:3–7; John 5:22–23). 'Jesus is Jehovah' (Romans 10:9) and Jehovah's Christ saves even 'Jehovah's' Witnesses when they stop denying him and start trusting in him!

Thanksgiving and prayer

'Thou crownest the year with thy goodness; and thy paths drop fatness.'
Psalm 65:11
SUGGESTED FURTHER READING: Psalm 147:7–15

We have here crowning mercies, suggesting special and crowning
thanksgiving. All the year round, every hour of every day, God is richly
blessing us; both when we sleep and when we wake, his mercy waits upon us.
The sun may leave off shining, but our God will never cease to cheer his
children with his love. Like a river his lovingkindness is always flowing, with
a fulness inexhaustible as his own nature, which is its source. Like the
atmosphere which always surrounds the earth, and is always ready to
support the life of man, the benevolence of God surrounds all his creatures;
in it, as in their element they live, and move, and have their being. Yet as the
sun on summer days appears to gladden us with beams more warm and
bright than at other times, and as rivers are at certain seasons swollen with
the rain, and as the atmosphere itself on occasions is fraught with more
fresh, more bracing, or more balmy influences than heretofore, so is it with
the mercy of God: it has its golden hours, its days of overflow, when the Lord
magnifies his grace and lifts high his love before the sons of men. If we begin
with the blessings of the nether springs, we must not forget that for the race
of man the joyous days of harvest are a special season of excessive favour. It
is the glory of autumn that the ripe gifts of providence are then abundantly
bestowed; it is the mellow season of realisation, whereas all before was but
hope and expectation. Great is the joy of harvest. Happy are the reapers
who fill their arms with the liberality of heaven. The psalmist tells us that
the harvest is the crowning of the year.

FOR MEDITATION: Consider the common grace of God to all people (Psalm
145:9,15–16; Matthew 5:45; Acts 14:17). Do you take the gifts and ignore
the Giver? Or do you receive his gifts with thanksgiving as one who believes
and knows the truth (1 Timothy 4:3)?

Believers—lights in the world

'Do all things without murmurings and disputings: that ye may be blameless and harmless, the sons of God, without rebuke, in the midst of a crooked and perverse nation, among whom ye shine as lights in the world; holding forth the word of life; that I may rejoice in the day of Christ, that I have not run in vain, neither laboured in vain.' Philippians 2:14–16

SUGGESTED FURTHER READING: 2 Timothy 1:8–2:5

Christians are soldiers. If our soldiers were to take it into their heads that they never ought to be seen, a pretty pass things would come to; what were the soldiers worth when they shunned parade and dreaded battle? We want not men who dare not show themselves to friend or foe. Christians are runners too, and what sort of runners are men who run in the dark? Not so says the apostle; we are 'compassed about with so great a cloud of witnesses,' and therefore he bids us 'lay aside every weight, and the sin which doth so easily beset us.' What! a running match and no spectators? Hail Emperor! The champion salutes thee! He prays thee to dismiss the spectators. You common herd, retire, or put your fingers to your eyes, here comes a runner who is so dainty that he cannot be looked at, a swift-footed runner who must be scrutinised by no vulgar eye or he will faint and lose the crown. 'Ha! Ha!' the mob laughs. 'These are not the men to make a Roman holiday; these timid fools had better play with babes in the nursery; they are not fit to consort with men.' What think you of Christians who must have the stadium cleared before they can enter the course. Rather, O sons of God, defy all onlookers. Crowd the seats and look on, angels, and men, and devils too, and see what you will. What matters it to the Christian, for he is looking unto Jesus, he runs not for you but for the reward, and whether you look or not, his zeal and earnestness are still the same, for Christ is in him and run he must, look on who will.

FOR MEDITATION: How can others see our good works and glorify our Father who is in heaven, if we are ashamed to let our lights shine before them (Matthew 5:16)?

Infant salvation

'Is it well with the child? And she answered, It is well.' 2 Kings 4:26
SUGGESTED FURTHER READING: 2 Samuel 12:13–23

The child is saved, if snatched away by death as we are, on another ground than that of rites and ceremonies and the will of man. On what ground, then, do we believe the child to be saved? It is saved because it is *elect*. In the compass of election, in the Lamb's book of life, we believe there shall be found written millions of souls who are only shown on earth, and then stretch their wings for heaven. They are saved, too, because they were *redeemed* by the precious blood of Jesus Christ. He who shed his blood for all his people, bought them with the same price with which he redeemed their parents, and therefore they are saved because Christ was sponsor for them, and suffered in their room and stead. They are saved, again, not without *regeneration*, for, 'except a man be born again, he cannot see the kingdom of God.' No doubt, in some mysterious manner the Spirit of God regenerates the infant soul, and it enters into glory made meet to be a partaker of the inheritance of the saints in light. That this is possible is proved from Scripture instances. John the Baptist was filled with the Holy Spirit from his mother's womb. We read of Jeremiah also, that the same had occurred to him; and of Samuel we find that while yet a babe the Lord called him. We believe, therefore, that even before the intellect can work, God, who works not by the will of man, nor by blood, but by the mysterious agency of his Holy Spirit, creates the infant soul a new creature in Christ Jesus, and then it enters into the rest which 'remaineth ... to the people of God.'

FOR MEDITATION: Men cannot affect the eternal destiny of infants, but 'Shall not the judge of all the earth do right?' (Genesis 18:25). Spurgeon asks 'Where did David expect to go? Why, to heaven surely. Then his child must have been there, for he said, "I shall go to him". I do not hear him say the same of Absalom ... He had no hope for that rebellious son.' (Psalm 23:6; 2 Samuel 12:23). He also mentions Ezekiel 16:21 where God describes sacrificed infants as 'my children.'

Soul murder—who is guilty?

'*Deliver me from bloodguiltiness, O God, thou God of my salvation; and my tongue shall sing aloud of thy righteousness.*' Psalm 51:14
SUGGESTED FURTHER READING: 1 Corinthians 8:1–13

Every man, especially in a great city like this, is responsible not only for himself but for his neighbours, and there are some of us who are like the church clock—other people set their watches by us. It becomes such of us as are religious teachers to be particularly careful. There are some things which I feel I might do, as far as I am concerned, which I believe I might do without suffering any personal hurt, but which I would not do for your sakes and which I dare not do for the sake of many who would take license from my example to do a great deal more than I would do, and would make me the horse on which they would put the saddle of their sin. Christian parents, you must not always say, 'I can do this.' Yes, but would you like everybody else to do it, because, if it is unsafe for one, it seems to me, you have no business to touch it. 'If meat make my brother to offend, I will eat no flesh while the world standeth,' is a grand old Christian saying of one who was not a whit behind the very chief of the apostles. We must be careful even of things indifferent, but when it comes to those things which are positively evil, the ill example of a Christian is ten times worse than that of one who is not a Christian, for if I see a sinner commit sin, his example is poison, but it is labelled. The inconsistent life of a Christian is unlabelled poison, and I am very likely to be injured by it. Inconsistent Christians, false professors, you that have a name to live and are dead, take care lest bloodguiltiness lie at your door, and much of it too.

FOR MEDITATION: No man is perfect. Spurgeon was a cigar-smoker. This became the subject of controversy in later years. He did not regard smoking as a sin in itself, but justified his habit on the grounds that it relieved his physical pain, soothed his weary brain and helped him to sleep. However, non-smokers criticised him for setting an example which led others into a body-destroying habit. Do you eat or drink anything or do something else which could cause others to stumble (Romans 14:21)?

SERMON NO 713

Jesus—the Shepherd

'He shall feed his flock like a shepherd.' Isaiah 40:11
SUGGESTED FURTHER READING: John 10:11–29

'And when the chief Shepherd shall appear, ye shall receive a crown of glory that fadeth not away.' So you see Christ is the chief Shepherd at the second advent; then shall the world be astonished to find that though alone in atonement, and alone in justification, he is not alone in service or in glory. Then every minister who has fed his sheep, every teacher who has fed his lambs—all of you, holy men and women, who have in any way whatever contributed under him towards the guidance, and the government, and the feeding, and the protection of his dear, blood-bought flock—you shall appear. He has no crown, you perceive, as the good Shepherd; we do not read of a crown for him as the great Shepherd, but when he comes 'with the crown wherewith his mother crowned him', then shall you also appear with him in glory, having the crown of life that fades not away. I do not know whether this peculiar circumstance interests you, but it did me when I observed it: *Good* in his dying, *great* in his rising, *chief* in his coming. It seems to me to gather such force—*good* to me as a sinner, *great* to me as a saint, *chief* to me as one with him in his glorious reign. I pass, as it were, through three stages—as a sinner I look to the good Shepherd laying down his life for the sheep; I reach higher ground, and as a saint I look to the great Shepherd to make me perfect in every good work to do his will; I mount higher still, I die, I rise again, I walk in resurrection life, and now I look to the chief Shepherd, and hope to receive at his hands the crown of life which he shall give to me, and not to me only, but to all them that love his appearing—the good, great, chief Shepherd.

FOR MEDITATION: Spurgeon gives descriptions of Old Testament types of Christ as a shepherd—Abel, the shepherd slain (Genesis 4:2,4,8); Jacob, the toiling shepherd (Genesis 31:38–41); Joseph, reigning in the world for the good of his own people (Genesis 37:2; 49:22–24); Moses, the shepherd of a separated people (Exodus 3:1; 10:9,24–26); David, the shepherd as king in the midst of his church (Psalm 78:70–71). Are you one of Christ's flock?

The true position of assurance

'In whom ye also trusted, after that ye heard the word of truth, the gospel of your salvation: in whom also after that ye believed, ye were sealed with that holy Spirit of promise.' Ephesians 1:13
SUGGESTED FURTHER READING: 1 John 3:14–24

We know that God is true because we have proved him. Sometimes this comes through the hearing of the Word—as we listen our faith is confirmed. But there is doubtless besides this, a special and supernatural work of the Holy Spirit, whereby men are assured that they are born of God. You will observe in one place the apostle says that the Spirit 'beareth witness with our spirit, that we are the children of God;' so that there are two witnesses— first, our spirit bears witness, that is, by evidences: I look at my faith, and see myself depending upon Christ, and then I know, because I love the brethren, and for other reasons, that I am born of God. Then there comes over and above the witness of evidence, faith and feeling, the Spirit himself bearing witness with our spirit. Have you not felt it? I cannot describe this to you, but you who have felt it know it. Did you not the other day feel a heavenly calm as you meditated upon your state and condition in Christ? You wondered where it came from. It was not the result of protracted devotion, but it stole over you, you knew not how it was, you were bathed in it as in sunlight, and you rejoiced exceedingly. You rejoiced in Christ—that was the basis of confidence, but that confidence came through the Spirit bearing witness with your spirit. And this has occurred sometimes in the midst of sharp conflicts just when dark despair seemed ready to overwhelm you. You may have enjoyed this comfort under peculiar trials, and losses of friends, and you may expect to have it when you come to die. Then, if ever in your life, you should be able to say, 'I will fear no evil: for thou art with me.'

FOR MEDITATION: We must not regard the Holy Spirit as a loose cannon giving us feelings, experiences and revelations which are nothing to do with the Scriptures. But he can confirm personally in our hearts what God has said in his Word and done in our lives (Romans 8:14–16; Galatians 4:6; 1 John 3:24; 4:13).

SERMON NO. 592

The church aroused

'Wherefore he saith, Awake thou that sleepest, and arise from the dead, and Christ shall give thee light.' Ephesians 5:14
SUGGESTED FURTHER READING: Romans 13:8–14

Some people can walk in their sleep, and walk in dangerous places, where waking men would be unsafe. They by some strange influence seem to walk steadily and calmly along the eddies and turn by the dangers beneath; even the howling of winds abroad seems to be inoperative upon their senses; and they therefore have a kind of security which more wakefulness would remove from them. O the fatal security of some professors, and the way in which they will dally with the world, and yet keep up an outwardly consistent character. O the manner in which some Christians will go as near to the fire of sin as well may be, and be scorched by it and yet not burned. O some of you are good, excellent, moral people in the judgment of men, but nevertheless, as Christians you do not seem to be awake to the interest of Christ's kingdom. And as a man can talk in his sleep, and walk in his sleep, there is another thing he can do better than other people, namely, dream in his sleep. He is the man to concoct plans, and find out new inventions. He can sketch out methods for building chapels, he can find ways of bringing out ministers, and doing all sorts of things, and yet he is asleep all the while. The waking man does it, and proves that he is awake by doing it, but the slumbering man only calculates, so many pounds a week, so many subscriptions, and the thing will be done; but there is never a brick to show. He dreams deliciously, but as for activity it is not there. He could always manage a Sunday school, or build a Christian interest better than anybody else, but no Sunday school or Christian interest ever does spring up under his hand, because the man's whole activity shows itself in inventions which are never executed, and in plans which are never carried out.

FOR MEDITATION: If apostles could sleep in the midst of danger (Matthew 26:40–45), and if a half-asleep apostle could dream up foolish plans without knowing what he was saying (Luke 9:32–33), we also need a reminder to be spiritually awake and alert (1 Thessalonians 5:6–8).

SERMON NO. 716

The queen of the south, or the earnest enquirer

'The queen of the south shall rise up in the judgment with this generation, and shall condemn it: for she came from the uttermost parts of the earth to hear the wisdom of Solomon; and behold, a greater than Solomon is here.' Matthew 12:42
SUGGESTED FURTHER READING: 1 Kings 10:1–13

'The Queen of Sheba gave to King Solomon.' And so souls that know the beauty of Christ give him all they have. Nothing gives Christ greater delight than the love of his people. We think our love to be a very poor and common thing, but he does not think so—he has set such a store by us that he gave his heart's blood to redeem us, and now he looks upon us as being worth the price he paid. He never will think that he had a bad bargain of it, and so he looks upon every grain of our love as being even choicer spices than archangels before the throne can render to him in their songs. What are we doing for Christ? Are we bringing him our talents of gold? Perhaps you have not one hundred and twenty, but if you have one bring that; you have not very much spices, but bring what you have—your silent, earnest prayers, your holy consistent life, the words you sometimes speak for Christ, the training up of your children, the feeding of his poor, the clothing of the naked, the visitation of the sick, the comforting of his mourners, the winning of his wanderers, the restoring of his backsliders, the saving of his blood-bought souls—all these shall be like camels laden with spices, an acceptable gift to the Most High. When the Queen of Sheba had done this, Solomon made her a present of his royal bounty. She lost nothing; she gave all she had, and then Solomon gave her quite as much again, for I will be bound to say King Solomon would not be outdone in generosity, such a noble-hearted prince as he, and so rich. I tell you Jesus Christ will never be in your debt. Oh, it is a great gain to give to Christ.

FOR MEDITATION: Giving begins with God; we can never repay him, but we can give back to him what he has given to us (1 Chronicles 29:14). Even then God is no man's debtor (Malachi 3:10; 2 Corinthians 9:7–8; Philippians 4:18–19).

Good news for you

'But a certain Samaritan, as he journeyed, came where he was.' Luke 10:33
SUGGESTED FURTHER READING: John 11:11–44

I do not believe in the way in which some people pretend to preach the gospel. They have no gospel for sinners as sinners, but only for those who are above the dead level of sinnership, and are technically styled *sensible* sinners. Like the priest in this parable, they see the poor sinner, and they say, 'He is not conscious of his need, we cannot invite him to Christ. He is dead; it is of no use preaching to dead souls;' so they pass by on the other side, keeping close to the elect and quickened, but having nothing whatever to say to the dead, lest they make out Christ to be too gracious, and his mercy to be too free. The Levite was not in quite such a hurry as the priest. The priest had to preach, and might be late for the service, and therefore he could not stop to relieve the man; besides he might have soiled his cassock, or made himself unclean; and then he would have been hardly fit for the dainty and respectable congregation over which he officiated. As for the Levite, he had to read the hymns; he was a clerk in the church, and he was somewhat in a hurry, but still he could get in after the opening prayer, so he indulged himself with the luxury of looking on. Just as I have known ministers say, 'Well, you know we ought to describe the sinner's state, and warn him, but we must not invite him to Christ.' Yes, gentlemen, you must pass by on the other side, after having looked at him, for on your own confession you have no good news for the poor wretch. I bless my Lord and Master that he has given to me a gospel which I can take to *dead* sinners, a gospel which is available for the vilest of the vile. I thank my Master that he does not say to the sinner, 'Come half way and meet me,' but he comes 'where he is.'

FOR MEDITATION: Jesus went and raised the dead physically where they were (Mark 5:40–42) without them having to make themselves half-alive first. He works on exactly the same principle when he raises sinners from the dead spiritually (Ephesians 2:1,5). Is he raising you to trust in him now (Ephesians 2:8)?

God's first words to the first sinner

'The LORD *God called unto Adam, and said unto him, Where art thou?'*
Genesis 3:9
SUGGESTED FURTHER READING: Luke 5:1–10; 27–32

Lost, perishing sinners, hear the voice of God, for it speaks to you. "Where art thou?' for I am come to seek thee.' 'Lord, I am in such a place that I cannot do anything for myself.' 'Then I am come to seek thee and do all for thee.' 'Lord, I am in such a place that the law threatens me and justice frowns upon me.' 'I am come to answer the threatenings of the law, and to bear all the wrath of justice.' 'But, Lord, I am in such a place that I cannot repent as I would.' 'I am come to seek thee, and I am exalted on high to give repentance and remission of sins.' 'But, Lord, I cannot believe in thee, I cannot believe as I would.' 'A bruised reed I will not break, and a smoking flax will I not quench; I am come to give thee faith.' 'But, Lord, I am in such a state that my prayers can never be acceptable.' 'I am come to pray for thee, and then to grant thee thy desires.' 'But, Lord, thou dost not know what a wretch I am.' 'Yes, I know thee. Though I asked thee the question, 'Where art thou?' it was that thou mightest know where thou art, for I know well enough.' 'But, Lord, I have been the chief of sinners; none can have so aggravated their guilt as I have.' 'But wherever thou mayest be, I have come to save thee.' 'But I am an outcast from society.' 'But I am come to gather together the outcasts of Israel.' 'O but I have sinned beyond all hope.' 'Yes, but I have come to give hope to hopeless sinners.' 'But, then I deserve to be lost.' 'Yes, but I have come to magnify the law and make it honourable, and so to give thee thy deserts in the person of Christ, and then to give thee my mercy because of his merits.'

FOR MEDITATION: A story which seems to begin with a sinner seeking the Lord Jesus Christ (Luke 19:1–4), ends by emphasising that it was more a case of the Lord Jesus Christ coming and seeking for the lost sinner (Luke 19:5–10).

A Saviour such as you need

'And their sins and iniquities will I remember no more. Now where remission of these is, there is no more offering for sin.' Hebrews 10:17–18
SUGGESTED FURTHER READING: Hebrews 9:23–28

There is no more sacrifice for sin, because Christ supplies all that is needed. Just see what a broom this doctrine is to sweep this country from popery, and to sweep all nations of it. Think of what is called 'the unbloody sacrifice of the mass, for quick and dead.' What becomes of that? The apostle says, 'Where remission of these is, there is no more offering for sin.' Where, then, did the mass come from, and of what avail is it? The Lord's Supper was intended to be the remembrancer to us of our Lord's sufferings; instead of which it has been prostituted by the church of Rome into the blasphemy of a pretended continual offering up of the body of the Lord Jesus Christ, a continual sacrifice. According to the Romish doctrine the offering upon Calvary is not enough; the atonement for sin is not finished; it has to be performed every day, and many times a day, in the divers churches of Christendom, by certain appointed persons, so that that sacrifice is always being offered. Do you notice how strongly the apostle speaks in this matter? He says Christ offered a sacrifice for sin *once*. He declares that while other priests stood ministering at the altar, this man, the Lord Jesus, offered a sacrifice once only, and has by that one offering perfected for ever his set apart ones. Brethren, the mass is a mass of abominations, a mass of hell's own concocting, a crying insult against the Lord of glory. It is not to be spoken of in any terms but those of horror and detestation. Whenever I think of another sacrifice for sin being offered, by whoever it may be presented, I can only regard it as an infamous insult to the perfection of the Saviour's work.

FOR MEDITATION: The Lord's Supper was not the first picture of salvation through faith in Christ crucified (Numbers 21:8–9; John 3:14–15), nor was it the first to be abused in false worship (2 Kings 18:4). Satan cannot damage Christ's work, but he does vandalise pictures of it.

A blow for Puseyism

'It is the spirit that quickeneth; the flesh profiteth nothing: the words that I speak unto you, they are spirit, and they are life.' John 6:63
SUGGESTED FURTHER READING: 1 Corinthians 11:23–26

Do not men receive the body and blood of Christ in the Lord's Supper? Yes, spiritual men do, in a real and spiritual sense, but not in a carnal way—not so as to crush it with their teeth, or taste it with their palate, or digest it by the gastric juice; but they receive the Lord Jesus, as incarnate and crucified, into their spirits, as they believe in him, love him, and are comforted by thoughts of him. 'But how is that a real reception of him?' cries one. Alas, this question reveals at once the world's thoughts; you think the carnal alone real, and that the spiritual is unreal. If you can touch and taste, you think it real, but if you can only meditate and love, you dream it to be unreal. How impossible it is for the carnal mind to enter into spiritual things! Yet, hearken once again, I receive the body and blood of Christ when my soul believes in his incarnation, when my heart relies upon the merit of his death, when the bread and wine so refresh my memory that thoughts of Jesus Christ and his agonies melt me to penitence, cheer me to confidence, and purify me from sin. It is not my body which receives Jesus, but my spirit; I believe in him, casting myself upon him alone; trusting him, I feel joy and peace, love and zeal, hatred of sin and love of holiness, and so as to my spiritual nature I am fed upon him. My spiritual nature feeds upon truth, love, grace, promise, pardon, covenant, atonement, acceptance, all of which I find, and much more, in the person of the Lord Jesus. Up to the extent in which my spirit has communion with the Lord Jesus, the ordinance of breaking of bread is living and acceptable.

FOR MEDITATION: There are great spiritual blessings in sharing the Lord's Supper with his people (1 Corinthians 10:16–17), but it is not the Lord's Supper at all when it is eaten unworthily, without discernment and without self-examination (1 Corinthians 11:20,27–29).

N.B. Puseyism was a variety of ritualism within the Church of England that followed many Roman Catholic practices.

SERMON NO. 653

Inward conflicts

'Return, return, O Shulamite; return, return, that we may look upon thee. What will ye see in the Shulamite? As it were the company of two armies.' Song of Solomon 6:13
SUGGESTED FURTHER READING: Romans 7:15–25

The new nature which God implants in his people is directly the opposite of the old one. As the old nature comes of Satan, being defiled and depraved by the fall, so the new nature comes direct from heaven, pure and without spot. As the old nature is sin, essentially sin, so the new nature is essentially grace; it is a living and incorruptible seed which lives and abides for ever, a seed which cannot sin, because it is born of God. When these two, therefore, come into conflict, it is as when fire and water meet; either the one or the other must die. There can be no truce, no parley; the two are deadly foes; the life of the one is the death of the other; the strength of the one is the weakness of the other. Now the old nature has been there beforehand; it is like a tree well rooted—it has been there twenty, thirty, forty, fifty, or sixty years, according to the date of conversion, and it is not easily to be torn up by its roots. Even when grace comes into the heart and makes sin to fall, as Dagon did before the ark of God, yet it is true of sin as it was of Dagon, the stump thereof is left, and there is enough vitality in that old stump still to breed pain and confusion without limit. The reigning power of sin falls dead the moment a man is converted, but the struggling power of sin does not die until the man dies. Bunyan said that unbelief had as many lives as a cat, and sin has the same vitality. Until we are wrapped in our winding-sheets, we shall never have that black thread of depravity drawn out from us; it will, it must continue to be there till God shall sanctify us, spirit, soul, and body, and take us home.

FOR MEDITATION: The new birth (1 Peter 2:2) produces a new creation (2 Corinthians 5:17), a new person (Colossians 3:10), a new life (Romans 6:4) and a new spirit (Romans 7:6), but also results in some new enemies, one of which is the old nature (Galatians 5:17; 1 Peter 2:11).

SERMON NO. 593

The mighty power which creates and sustains faith

'*The exceeding greatness of his power to us-ward who believe, according to the working of his mighty power, which he wrought in Christ, when he raised him from the dead, and set him at his own right hand in the heavenly places, far above all principality, and power, and might, and dominion, and every name that is named.' Ephesians 1:19–21*
SUGGESTED FURTHER READING: 1 Chronicles 29:10–13

Our text twice over uses the strongest words which could be employed, to set forth the almighty power exhibited in bringing a soul to believe in Jesus, and in bringing that believing soul onward till it ascends to heaven. You will carefully notice we have first of all this expression, 'The exceeding greatness of his power;' and then we have on the other side of the word 'Believe,' lest it should escape anyhow from the sacred barrier, these words, 'According to the working of his mighty power.' Now, the first expression is a very amazing one. It might read thus: 'The super-excellent, sublime, overcoming, or triumphing greatness of his power;' and the other is even more singular; it is a Hebrew mode of speech forced to do duty in the Greek tongue: 'The effectual working of the might of his strength;' or 'The energy of the force of his power,'—some such strong expression as that. As if the apostle was not content to say, 'You believe through the power of God,' nor 'through the greatness of that power,' but 'through the *exceeding* greatness of his power;' and not satisfied with declaring that the salvation of man is the fruit of God's might, he must needs put it, his mighty power: and as if that were not enough, he writes, the energy, the efficacious activity of the power of that might. No amount of straining at the passage can ever get rid of the grand doctrine which it contains, namely, that the bringing of the soul to simple faith in Jesus, and the maintenance of that soul in the life of faith, displays an exercise of omnipotence such as God alone could put forth.

FOR MEDITATION: God's almighty power saves and keeps the believer (1 Peter 1:5), but we have to put on the whole armour of God in order to 'be strong in the Lord, and in the power of his might' (Ephesians 6:10–11).

Ben-hadad's escape—an encouragement for sinners

'So they...came to the king of Israel, and said, thy servant Ben-hadad saith, I pray thee, let me live. And he said, is he yet alive? he is my brother ... Then he said, go ye, bring him.' 1 Kings 20:32–33
SUGGESTED FURTHER READING: Luke 18:9–17

How does your child come to you when he wants anything? Does he open a big book, and begin reading, 'My dear, esteemed, and venerated parent, in the effulgence of thy parental beneficence'? Nothing of the kind. He says, 'Father, my clothes are worn out, please buy me a new coat;' or else he says, 'I am hungry, let me have something to eat.' That is the way to pray, and there is no prayer which God accepts but that kind of prayer—right straight from the heart, and right straight to God's heart. We miss the mark when we go about to gather gaudy words. What! gaudy words on the lips of a poor sinner? Fine phrases from a rebel? There is more true eloquence in 'God be merciful to me a sinner,' than in all the books of devotion which bishops, and archbishops, and divines ever compiled. 'Thy servant Ben-hadad saith, I pray thee, let me live.' I feel inclined to stop and ask you to bow your heads, and pray that prayer—'O God, thy servant saith, I pray thee, let me live. O cut me not down as a cumberer of the ground, but let me live; I am dead in trespasses and sins; quicken me, O Lord, and let me live; and when thou comest to slay the wicked on the earth, I pray thee, let me live; and when thou shalt destroy the ungodly, and sweep them with the broom of destruction into the pit that is bottomless, I pray thee, let me live.' You see there is not a word of merit; there is nothing about what man has done; Ben-hadad only calls himself a servant. 'Make me as one of thy hired servants.' 'Thy servant Ben-hadad saith, I pray thee, let me live.'

FOR MEDITATION: There are three kinds of prayers which cut no ice with God—publicity-seeking prayers (Matthew 6:5), padded-out prayers (Matthew 6:7) and pretended prayers (Mark 12:40). Jesus taught His followers to pray privately and pointedly (Matthew 6:6,9–13). Have you truly prayed for your sins to be forgiven (Luke 11:4)?

SERMON NO. 535

Citizenship in heaven

'For our conversation is in heaven; from whence also we look for the Saviour, the Lord Jesus Christ.' Philippians 3:20
SUGGESTED FURTHER READING: 2 Timothy 4:1–8

You know I am no prophet. I do not know anything about 1866; I find quite enough to do to attend to 1862. I do not understand the visions of Daniel or Ezekiel; I find I have enough to do to teach the simple word such as I find in Matthew, Mark, Luke, and John, and the epistles of Paul. I do not find many souls have been converted to God by exquisite dissertations about the battle of Armageddon, and all those other fine things; I have no doubt prophesyings are very profitable, but I rather question whether they are so profitable to the hearers, as they may be to the preachers and publishers. I conceive that among religious people of a certain sort, the abortive explanations of prophecy issued by certain doctors gratify a craving which in irreligious people finds its food in novels and romances. People have a panting to know the future; and certain divines pander to this depraved taste, by prophesying for them, and letting them know what is coming by and by. I do not know the future, and I shall not pretend to know. But I do preach this, because I know it, that Christ will come, for he says so in a hundred passages. The epistles of Paul are full of the advent, and Peter's too, and John's letters are crowded with it. The best of saints have always lived on the hope of the advent. There was Enoch; he prophesied of the coming of the Son of Man. So there was another 'Enoch' who was always talking of the coming, and saying 'Come quickly.' I will not divide the house tonight by discussing whether the advent will be pre-millenial or post-millenial, or anything of that; it is enough for me that he will come, and 'in such an hour as ye think not the Son of man cometh.'

FOR MEDITATION: The 'whens', 'ifs' and 'buts' of the Lord's second coming were no business of the apostles (Matthew 24:36; John 21:22; Acts 1:7) and they are none of our business either. Our business is to serve him and be prepared for his return whenever that may be (Matthew 24:44–46). See also notes for 8 September.

SERMON NO. 476

Faith omnipotent

'Jesus said unto him, If thou canst believe, all things are possible to him that believeth.' Mark 9:23
SUGGESTED FURTHER READING: Romans 4:13–22

Faith studies *what the promise is*—an emanation of divine grace, an overflowing of the great heart of God; and faith says, 'My God could not have given this promise, except from love and grace; therefore it is quite certain that this promise will be fulfilled.' Then faith thinks, '*Who gave* this promise?' She considers not so much its greatness, as 'Who is the author of it?' She remembers that it is God that cannot lie, God omnipotent, God immutable; and therefore she concludes that the promise must be fulfilled; and forward she goes in this firm conviction. Then she remembers, also, *why* the promise was given, namely, for God's glory, and she feels perfectly sure that God's glory is safe, that he will never stain his own character, nor mar the lustre of his own crown; and therefore she concludes that the promise must and will stand. Then faith also considers the amazing *work of Christ* as being a clear proof of the Father's intention to fulfil his word. 'He that spared not his own Son, but delivered him up for us all, how shall he not with him also freely give us all things?' Then faith looks back upon *the past*, for her battles have strengthened her, and her victories have given her courage. She remembers that God never has failed her, that he never did once fail any of his children. She recollects times of great peril, when deliverance came, hours of awful need, when as her day her strength was; and she says, 'No; I never will be led to think that he can now forswear himself, and change his character, and leave his servant.' Faith, moreover, feels that she cannot believe a hard thing of her dear God. Is it wrong to use that expression? I must use it, for he is dear to me.

FOR MEDITATION: The faith of the early Christians was widely spoken about (Romans 1:8; Ephesians 1:15; Colossians 1:4; 1 Thessalonians 1:8; 3:6; Philemon 5). What message does your faith convey to you about God, and to others about your relationship with him?

Children's bread given to dogs

'And she said, Truth, Lord: yet the dogs eat of the crumbs which fall from their masters' table.' Matthew 15:27
SUGGESTED FURTHER READING: Isaiah 64:4–9

Instead of trying to make your case out to be better, believe in its thorough badness, and yet be of good cheer. You cannot exaggerate your sin, and even if you could, it would be wiser to err in that direction than the other. A man called at my house some time ago for charity; an arrant beggar, I have no doubt. Thinking that the man's rags and poverty were real, I gave him a little money, some of my clothes, and a pair of shoes. After he had put them on and gone out, I thought, 'Well, after all, I have done you a bad turn very likely, for you will not get so much money now as before, because you will not look so wretched an object.' Happening to go out a quarter of an hour afterwards, I saw my friend, but he was not wearing the clothes I had given him, not he; why, I should have ruined his business if I could have compelled him to look respectable. He had been wise enough to slip down an archway, take all the good clothes off, and put his rags on again. Did I blame him? Yes, for being a rogue, but not for carrying on his business in a businesslike manner. He only wore his proper livery, for rags are the livery of a beggar. The more ragged he looked, the more he would get. Just so is it with you. If you are to go to Christ, do not put on your good doings and feelings, or you will get nothing; go in your sins, they are your livery. Your ruin is your argument for mercy; your poverty is your plea for heavenly alms; and your need is the motive for heavenly goodness. Go as you are, and let your miseries plead for you.

FOR MEDITATION: The filthy rags of sin are the natural uniform of all human beings (Romans 3:23). The Lord Jesus Christ wore them spiritually on the cross in our place and in return offers you now his spotless robe of righteousness (Isaiah 61:10; Zechariah 3:3–5), which is the Christian's uniform and ticket to heaven. But you won't even be able to gatecrash heaven (John 10:1), if you reject Christ's righteousness and continue to wear the filthy rags of your sin (Matthew 22:11–13).

Memory—the handmaid of hope

'This I recall to my mind, therefore have I hope.' Lamentations 3:21
SUGGESTED FURTHER READING: Psalm 73:1–28

In a lamentable accident which occurred in the North, in one of the coal pits, when a considerable number of the miners were down below, the top of the pit fell in, and the shaft was completely blocked up. Those who were down below sat together in the dark, and sang and prayed. They gathered to a spot where the last remains of air could be breathed. There they sat and sang after the lights had gone out, because the air would not support the flame. They were in total darkness, but one of them said he had heard that there was a connection between that pit and an old pit that had been worked years ago. He said it was a low passage, through which a man might get by crawling all the way, lying flat upon the ground—he would go and see; the passage was very long, but they crept through it, and at last they came out to light at the bottom of the other pit and their lives were saved. If my present way to Christ as a saint gets blocked up, if I cannot go straight up the shaft and see the light of my Father up yonder, there is an old working, the old fashioned way by which sinners go, by which poor thieves go, by which harlots go—come, I will crawl along lowly and humbly, flat upon the ground—I will crawl along till I see my Father, and cry, 'Father, I am no more worthy to be called thy son: make me as one of thy hired servants, so long as I may but dwell in thy house.' In your very worst case you can still come as sinners. 'Christ Jesus came into the world to save sinners;' call this to mind and you may have hope.

FOR MEDITATION: The believer who suffers a fall should remember, repent and return to those first but abandoned works (Revelation 2:4–5). That was Jonah's route back from the pit to the land of the living (Jonah 2:6–10).

Barabbas preferred to Jesus

'Then cried they all again, saying, Not this man, but Barabbas. Now Barabbas was a robber.' John 18:40
SUGGESTED FURTHER READING: Leviticus 14:1–8

Barabbas was a murderer, a felon, and a traitor. This fact is very significant. There is more teaching in it than at first sight we might imagine. Have we not here in this act of the deliverance of the sinner and the binding of the innocent, a sort of type of that great work which is accomplished by the death of our Saviour? You and I may fairly take our stand by the side of Barabbas. We have robbed God of his glory; we have been seditious traitors against the government of heaven: if he who hates his brother be a murderer, we also have been guilty of that sin. Here we stand before the judgment seat; the Prince of life is bound for us and we are suffered to go free. The Lord delivers us and acquits us, while the Saviour, without spot or blemish, or shadow of a fault, is led forth to crucifixion. Two birds were taken in the rite of the cleansing of the leper. The one bird was killed, and its blood was poured into a basin; the other bird was dipped in this blood, and then, with its wings all crimson, it was set free to fly into the open field. The bird slain well pictures the Saviour, and every soul that has by faith been dipped in his blood, flies upward towards heaven singing sweetly in joyous liberty, owing its life and its liberty entirely to him who was slain. It comes to this— Barabbas must die or Christ must die; you the sinner must perish, or Christ Immanuel, the Immaculate, must die. He dies that we may be delivered. Have we all a participation in such a deliverance today? Though we have been robbers, traitors and murderers, yet we can rejoice that Christ has delivered us from the curse of the law, having been made a curse for us.

FOR MEDITATION: What do you prefer to Jesus? Your family (Matthew 10:37), the praise of men (John 12:43), God's creation (Romans 1:25) or your pleasures (2 Timothy 3:4)? The Lord Jesus Christ died to save people like you, but you will have to change your priorities and preferences (Acts 3:14–15,18–19).

Encourage your minister

'Encourage him.' Deuteronomy 1:38
SUGGESTED FURTHER READING: Hebrews 13:17–19

Why do you leave your own minister? If I see one come into my place from the congregation of another brother in the ministry, I would like just to give him a flea in his ear such as he may never forget. What business have you to leave your minister? If everyone were to do so, how discouraged the poor man would be. Just because somebody happens to come into this neighbourhood, you leave your seats. Those who are going from place to place are of no use to anybody; but those are the truly useful men who, when the servants of God are in their places, keep to theirs, and let everybody see that whoever discourages the minister they will not, for they appreciate his ministry. Again, let me say by often being present at the prayer-meeting you can encourage the minister. You can always tell how a church is getting on by the prayer-meetings. I will almost prophesy the kind of sermon on the Sabbath from the sort of prayer-meeting on the Monday. If many come up to the house of God, and they are earnest, the pastor will get a blessing from on high; it cannot but be, for God opens the windows of heaven to believing prayer. Never fail to plead for your pastor in your closet. Dear friends, when you mention a father's name, and a child's name, let the minister's name come forth too. Give him a large share in your heart, and both in private and public prayer, encourage him. Encourage him, again, by letting him know if you have received any good.

FOR MEDITATION: The apostle Paul was greatly encouraged by people who stood by him, like Onesiphorus and Luke (2 Timothy 1:16–17; 4:11). Are you faithful to your minister or do you leave him in the lurch, as Demas and others did to Paul (2 Timothy 4:10,16)?

N.B. This sermon was preached at Cornwall Road Chapel, Bayswater, to the congregation pastored by Spurgeon's brother, James, since the opening of the chapel on 1 July 1863. For sermons assumed to have been preached for the first and third anniversaries, see readings on 3 and 1 July respectively.

Forward! Forward! Forward!

'And the LORD *said unto Moses, Wherefore criest thou unto me? speak unto the children of Israel, that they go forward.'* Exodus 14:15
SUGGESTED FURTHER READING: Matthew 28:16–20

How often I have heard people say, 'Well, yes, the Lord is my gracious Master, and I am his servant, and I believe it is the duty of believers to be baptised; but if the Lord ever reveals it to me, then I will do it.' There is a soldier for you! He is not content to get the same orders as his fellow-soldiers, but he cries, 'When the regiment is on the march, if the captain will come round to my tent and talk to me by myself, I will not mind going.' Why, he deserves to be flogged for a deserter. I will not wish anything hard to my Christian brother, but I do venture to prophesy that he will be beaten with many stripes if he talks in that way. 'Ah,' says one, 'but the Lord must apply it to me.' What for? The thing is clear enough without its being applied. If there is anything in the Bible which is plain at all, it is that he who believes in Christ should be buried with him in baptism. Then, if it is your clear duty, you ought to do it at once. 'Well, I will pray about it.' And do you believe God will hear such a wicked prayer as that? If I tell my child that there is something to do, and he tells me, 'Well, I will think about it,' I shall let him know that I am not to be thus impudently trifled with. If I say to him, 'Now, my child, do so-and-so,' and he replies, 'Father, I will pray about it,' I shall not put up with such hypocritical rebellion; it will not do in one's own house, much less in the house of God. Are you to be permitted to trifle with positive precepts, and then to lay your sin upon God's back? I do not think so.

FOR MEDITATION: There are no loopholes in the command 'Repent and be baptized every one of you' (Acts 2:38). The first step of repentance and faith is essential to salvation (Mark 16:16); the second step of baptism is essential to obedience.

Self-delusion

'Many, I say unto you, will seek to enter in, and shall not be able.' Luke
13:24
SUGGESTED FURTHER READING: Luke 12:15–21

I marvel not that so many are deceived, when I see the careless way in which
you deal with religion. When men have to do with their estates, they are very
careful; they fee a lawyer to go back over the title-deeds perhaps for two or
three hundred years. In trade they will hurry hither and thither to attend to
their commercial engagements; they would not launch into speculations,
nor would they run great risks; but the soul, the poor soul, how men play
with it as a toy, and despise it as if it were worthless earth. Two or three
minutes in the morning when they first roll out of bed, two or three odd
minutes in the evening, when they are nearly asleep—the fag-ends of the day
given to their souls, and all the best part given to the body! And then, the
Sabbath! How carelessly spent by most people! With what indifference do
you lend your ears too often to the preaching of the Word! It is an old song;
you have heard it so many times; heaven has become a trifle to you, hell is
almost a jest, eternity a notion, and death but a bugbear. Alas! it is a marvel
that there are not more deceived. The wonder is that any find the gate, that
any discover eternal life, when we are so, so mad, so foolish, so insane, as to
trifle where we ought to be awfully in earnest, and to play and toy, where the
whole heart is all too little to be given to a work of such dread, such
everlasting importance. God help us, since it is so easy to be deceived, to
search, and watch, and look, and test, and try, that we be not found
castaways at the last!

FOR MEDITATION: Satan does not need to deceive us, when we are doing his
dirty work by deceiving ourselves. Beware of delusions of wisdom
(1 Corinthians 3:18), self-satisfaction (Galatians 6:3), hearing God's Word
without applying it (James 1:22), a loose tongue (James 1:26) and claims to
sinless perfection (1 John 1:8). These are all paths to self-deceit.

The glory of Christ—beheld

'And the Word was made flesh and dwelt among us, (and we beheld his glory, the glory as of the only begotten of the Father,) full of grace and truth.' John 1:14
SUGGESTED FURTHER READING: Exodus 25:1–9

Let me read the text again, giving another translation: 'The Word was made flesh, and tabernacled among us, and we beheld his glory, the glory as of the only begotten of the Father, full of grace and truth.' Now, you remember that in the Jewish church its greatest glory was that God *tabernacled* in its midst: not the tent of Moses, not the various pavilions of the princes of the twelve tribes, but the humble tabernacle in which God dwelt, was the boast of Israel. They had the king himself in the midst of them, a present God in their midst. The tabernacle was a tent to which men went when they would commune with God, and it was the spot to which God came manifestly when he would commune with man. Here they met each other through the sacrifice of an animal, and there was reconciliation between them. Now, Christ's human flesh was God's tabernacle, and it is in Christ that God meets with man, and in Christ that man has dealings with God. The Jew of old went to God's tent, in the centre of the camp, if he would worship: we come to Christ if we would pay our homage. If the Jew would be released from ceremonial uncleanness, after he had performed the rites, he went up to the sanctuary of his God, that he might feel again that there was peace between God and his soul; and we, having been washed in the precious blood of Christ, have access with boldness unto God, even the Father, through Christ, who is our tabernacle and the tabernacle of God among men.

FOR MEDITATION: Some of the things in the tabernacle which point to Christ are the veil (Matthew 27:51; John 14:6; Hebrews 10:19–20), the manna and the shewbread (John 6:31,35,48), the mercy seat (see 29th March) and the lampstand (John 8:12; 9:5; 12:46). There is no need of tabernacle, temple or lamp in heaven where mere pictures are replaced by the actual presence of the Lord and the Lamb (Revelation 21:22–23).

SERMON NO. 414

Pray for Jesus

'Prayer also shall be made for him continually.' Psalm 72:15
SUGGESTED FURTHER READING: Matthew 6:9–13

'Lo, I am with you alway, even unto the end of the world,' is the blessed assurance that Jesus is our Captain in the great fight of faith, and is still present in the battle field. His great cause is here, his enterprise and business are here below. The work which he undertook to accomplish is not yet accomplished in the person of every one of his elect. His blood has been fully shed and his atonement has been perfected, but those for whom the atonement was made are not yet all ingathered. Many sheep he has which are not yet of his fold. We are therefore to pray for him, that the good work which he has undertaken may be prospered, and that one by one those whom his Father gave him may be brought to reconciliation and to eternal life. Brethren, the Lord Jesus Christ describes himself as being still persecuted and still suffering. He said to Saul, 'Saul, Saul, why persecutest thou me?' He calls his people himself; they are his mystical body; and in praying for the church we pray for Christ. He is the head of the body, and you cannot pray for the body except you pray for the head. We must put them all into one prayer. He is still struggling with the hosts of darkness in his church, still striving for the victory over sin in his people, and his people are waiting and longing for his second advent, which shall fulfil their brightest hopes. We must still pray for him, not personally, but relatively; for his cause, for his kingdom, for his gospel, for his people, for his blood-bought ones who as yet are in the ruins of the fall, for his second coming, and glorious reign. In this sense, I take it, the text is meant that 'prayer also shall be made for him continually.'

FOR MEDITATION: In the first half of the Lord's Prayer, the Lord teaches us to pray for the Lord (thy name, thy kingdom, thy will—Matthew 6:9–10); after that we pray for ourselves. Do you pray for him? If you are one of his people, don't forget that he is continually interceding for you (Hebrews 7:25).

SERMON NO. 717

The great itinerant

'Who went about doing good.' Acts 10:38
SUGGESTED FURTHER READING: 1 Peter 2:12–21

God give us to rest implicitly upon the Lord Jesus Christ by a living faith, and so to be cleansed in his precious blood, and then we may resolve to go forth and live for him. Have we any work to do now that we can set about at once? If we have, whatsoever our hand finds to do, let us do it. Let us not be asking for greater abilities than we have. If we can get them, let us do so; but meanwhile let us use what we have. Go, housewife, to your house, and from the lowest chamber to the top, go about doing good: here is range enough for you. Go, teacher, to your little school, and among those boys and girls, let your example tell, and there is range enough for you. Go, worker, to your shop, and amongst your fellow workmen, let fall here and there a word for Christ; above all, let your example shine, and there is work for you. You domestic servants, the kitchen is sphere enough for you. You shall go about doing good from the dresser to the fireplace, and you shall have width enough and verge enough to make it a kingdom consecrated to God. Without leaving your position any one of you, without giving up the plough, or the cobbler's lapstone, or the needle, or the plane, or the saw, without leaving business, without any of you good sisters wanting to be nuns, or any of us putting on the serge and becoming monks, in our own calling let us go about doing good. The best preparation for it will be, renew your dedication to Christ, be much in earnest prayer, seek the sanctifying influences of the Holy Spirit, and then go forth in your Master's strength with this as your resolve—that as portraits of Jesus Christ it shall be said of you, 'He went about doing good.'

FOR MEDITATION: Consider the text 'Thy will be done on earth, as it is in heaven' (Matthew 6:10)—'Thy will' is God's purpose; 'be done' is our part; 'on earth' is our place, and 'as it is in heaven' is our pattern. Do you, like David, delight to do God's will (Psalm 40:8)? Will you join him in praying 'Teach me to do thy will; for thou art my God' (Psalm 143:10)?

SERMON NO. 655

Praying and waiting

'And this is the confidence that we have in him, that, if we ask anything according to his will, he heareth us: and if we know that he hear us, whatsoever we ask, we know that we have the petitions that we desired of him.' 1 John 5:14–15

SUGGESTED FURTHER READING: Psalm 22:1–24

I saw the other day a greyhound coursing a hare. The moment the hare ran through the hedge out of the greyhound's sight, the race was over, for he could not follow where he could not see. The true hound hunts by scent, but the greyhound only by sight. Now there are some Christians too much like the greyhound; they only follow the Lord as far as they can see his manifest mercy; but the true child of God hunts by faith, and when he cannot see the mercy, he scents it and still pursues it, till at last he lays hold upon it. Why, man, you say you have had no answers! How know you? God may have answered you, though you have not seen the answer. This is a riddle, but it is a fact. God has not promised to give you the particular mercy in kind, but he will give it you somehow or other. If I pay my debts in gold, no man can blame me because I do not pay them in silver; and if God gives you spiritual mercies in abundance, instead of temporal ones, he has heard your prayer. You may pray, like Paul, thrice, that the thorn in the flesh may be taken away from you: God's answer is given, and it is, 'My grace is sufficient for thee.' Christ prayed that God might hear him; he was heard in that he feared, but he had not the cup taken from him. No, but he had an angel to comfort and strengthen him; and this was in truth an answer, though not such as the prayer seemed to require. You have had an answer, and if God has heard you but once, pluck up courage and go again.

FOR MEDITATION: It is one thing to ask God for an answer (Job 31:35; Jeremiah 42:1–6), but quite another to recognise it. We either humbly accept God's answer and draw near to him (Job 42:5–6) or proudly reject it and withdraw from him because it doesn't suit us (Jeremiah 43:1–4).

The fulness of Christ—received

'And of his fulness have all we received.' John 1:16
SUGGESTED FURTHER READING: Colossians 2:1–10

The text informs us that there is a fulness in Christ. There is a fulness of essential Deity, 'for in him dwelleth all the fulness of the Godhead.' There is a fulness of perfect manhood, for in him 'bodily' that Godhead was revealed. Partaker of flesh and blood, made in all things like unto his brethren, there was nothing lacking that was necessary to the perfection of human kind in him. There is a fulness of atoning efficacy in his blood, for 'the blood of Jesus Christ his Son cleanseth us from all sin.' There is a fulness of justifying righteousness in his life, for 'there is therefore now no condemnation to them which are in Christ Jesus.' There is a fulness of divine prevalence in his plea, for 'he is able also to save them to the uttermost that come unto God by him, seeing he ever liveth to make intercession for them.' There is a fulness of victory in his death, for 'through death' he destroyed 'him that had the power of death, that is, the devil.' There is a fulness of efficacy in his resurrection from the dead, for by it we are begotten 'again unto a lively hope.' There is a fulness of triumph in his ascension, for 'when he ascended up on high, he led captivity captive, and gave gifts unto men.' There is a fulness of blessings unspeakable, unknown; a fulness of grace to pardon, of grace to regenerate, of grace to sanctify, of grace to preserve, and of grace to perfect. There is a fulness at all times, a fulness by day and a fulness by night; a fulness of comfort in affliction, a fulness of guidance in prosperity, a fulness of every divine attribute, of wisdom, of power, of love; a fulness which it were impossible to survey, much less to explore.

FOR MEDITATION: Praise God that he did not keep his fulness to himself. The church is described as Christ's body and fulness (Ephesians 1:23). We can actually receive of his fulness (John 1:16), be filled with it (Ephesians 3:19) and make progress towards it (Ephesians 4:13).

Jehovah-shammah

'Whereas the LORD *was there.' Ezekiel 35:10*
SUGGESTED FURTHER READING: Jeremiah 17:5–13

Old Adam has given you many a grip in the side, as though he would tear the heart out of you, but you have held on your way despite all that he could do. How is this? Why, God was in you, and if he had not been there, then indeed you would have been a prey unto your adversaries. I went last week into the lighthouse at Holyhead and marked the lights that warn the mariner crossing the sea, or guide him in time of storm into the haven. I noticed in the second storey of the lighthouse many large vats filled with oil laid up in store that the lamps might be constantly trimmed for months to come, and I compared that in my own mind to that gracious provision of divine grace which the Lord lays up in store for his people. The lamps would go out but Jehovah-shammah, the Lord is there—we have the all-sufficiency of God laying up a store of oil, that our lights may be always trimmed. A Christian is something like an express train. On some of our railroads you know there are express trains which do not stop to take water; the water lies in a trench in the middle between the rails, and as the train runs it sucks up its own supply of cold water, and so continues its course without a pause. Our God in grace has forestalled our needs; he prepares supplies for his own people, so that without their stopping to seek the streams of creature confidence, sometimes without the use of means, he is pleased to speed them on their pathway towards heaven, fed by a divine arrangement of grace. O it is blessed to think that if God be there, everything a Christian can want for his final persevering, for his eternal life, is ready at hand.

FOR MEDITATION: The Lord was there with his people in the wilderness and sustained them for forty years (Nehemiah 9:19–21). He can still meet every need that his people face today (Philippians 4:19). Paul had proved that God's grace and strength were sufficient for him (2 Corinthians 12:9; Philippians 4:13).

SERMON NO. 536

Our stronghold

'The name of the LORD *is a strong tower: the righteous runneth into it, and is safe.'* Proverbs 18:10
SUGGESTED FURTHER READING: Psalm 20:1–9

It is useless for me to attempt to describe the various ways in which your trials come; but I am sure they that know Jehovah's name will put their trust in him. Perhaps your trial has been want, and then you have said, 'His name is Jehovah-jireh, the Lord will provide;' or else you have been banished from friends, but you have said, 'His name is Jehovah-shammah, the Lord is there;' or else you have had a disturbance in your family; there has been war within, and war without, but you have run into your strong tower, for you have said, 'His name is Jehovah-shalom, the Lord send peace;' or else the world has slandered you, and you yourself have been conscious of sin, but you have said, 'His name is Jehovah-tsidkenu, the Lord our righteousness,' and so you have gone there, and been safe; or else many have been your enemies; then his name has been 'Jehovah-nissi, the Lord my banner;' and so he has been a strong tower to you. Defy, then brethren, in God's strength, tribulations of every sort and size. Say with the poet,

'There is a safe and secret place	The least and feeblest here may hide
Beneath the wings divine	Uninjured and unawed.
Reserved for all the heirs of grace;	While thousands fall on every side,
That refuge now is mine.	I rest secure in God.'

But, beloved, besides the trials of this life, we have the sins of the flesh, and what a tribulation these are; but the name of our God is our strong tower then. At certain seasons we are more than ordinarily conscious of our guilt; and I would give little for your piety, if you do not sometimes creep into a corner with the poor publican and say, 'God be merciful to me a sinner.'

FOR MEDITATION: The name of the Lord Jesus Christ is a strong tower: the unrighteous run into it, and are saved (Matthew 1:21; Acts 4:12; 10:43; 1 John 5:13). Have you 'fled for refuge' (Hebrews 6:18)? Are you 'in Christ'?

SERMON NO. 491

The shield of faith

'Above all, taking the shield of faith, wherewith ye shall be able to quench all the fiery darts of the wicked.' Ephesians 6:16
SUGGESTED FURTHER READING: 1 Peter 5:8–11

There is a sacred art in being able to handle the shield of faith. Let me explain to you how that can be. You will handle it well if you are able to quote the promises of God against the attacks of your enemy. The devil said 'One day you shall be poor and starve.' 'No,' said the believer, handling his shield well, 'He has said "I will never leave thee, nor forsake thee"; "bread shall be given him; his waters shall be sure".' 'Yes,' said Satan, 'but you will one day fall by the hand of the enemy.' 'No,' said faith, 'for I am persuaded "that he which hath begun a good work in you will perform it until the day of Jesus Christ".' 'Yes,' said Satan, 'but the slander of the enemy will overturn you.' 'No,' said faith, 'Surely the wrath of man shall praise thee: the remainder of wrath shalt thou restrain.' 'Yes,' said Satan, as he shot another arrow, 'you are weak.' 'Yes,' said faith, handling his shield, 'but "my strength is made perfect in weakness". Most gladly therefore will I rather glory in my infirmities, that the power of Christ may rest upon me.' 'Yes,' said Satan, 'but your sin is great.' 'Yes,' said faith, handling the promise, 'but "he is able also to save them to the uttermost that come unto God by him".' 'But,' said the enemy again, drawing his sword and making a tremendous thrust, 'God has cast you off.' 'No,' said faith, '"he hateth putting away"; "the Lord will not cast off his people, neither will he forsake his inheritance".' 'But I will have you, after all,' said Satan. 'No,' said faith, dashing the bosses in the enemy's jaws, 'He has said, "I give unto them eternal life; and they shall never perish, neither shall any man pluck them out of my hand".' This is what I call handling the shield.

FOR MEDITATION: The faith that resists Satan (2 Peter 5:9) and overcomes the world (1 John 5:4) is not faith in faith, but faith in the truth and faithfulness of God (Psalm 91:4). Handling the shield will do us no good, unless we are also wearing God's truth (Ephesians 6:14).

The standard uplifted in the face of the foe

'When the enemy shall come in like a flood, the Spirit of the LORD *shall lift up a standard against him.'* Isaiah 59:19
SUGGESTED FURTHER READING: Ephesians 6:10–18

Christian, you are in the land where foes abound. There are enemies within you; you are not clean delivered from the influence of inbred sin. The new nature is of divine origin, and it cannot sin because it is born of God; but the old nature, the carnal mind, is there too, and it is not reconciled to God, neither indeed can it be; and therefore it strives and struggles with the new nature. The house of Saul in our heart wars against the house of David, and tries to drive it out and despoil it of the crown. This conflict you must expect to have continued with more or less of violence till you enter into rest. Moreover, in the world without there are multitudes of foes. This vain world is no friend to the principle of the work of grace. If you were of the world the world would love its own, but as you are not of the world but of a heavenly race, you may expect to be treated as an alien and foreigner, no, as a hated and detested foe. All sorts of snares and traps will be laid for you; those who sought to entangle the Master in his speech will not be more lenient towards you. Moreover there is one whose name is called 'the enemy,' the 'evil one;' he is the leader among your adversaries; hating God with all his might, he hates that which he sees of God in you. He will not spare the arrows in his infernal quiver; he will shoot them all at you. There are no temptations which he knows of—and he understands the art well from long practice— there are no temptations which he will not exercise upon you. He will sometimes fawn upon you, and at other times will frown; he will lift you up, if possible, with self-righteousness, and then cast you down with despair. You will always find him your fierce, insatiable foe. Know this then, and put on the whole armour of God.

FOR MEDITATION: Self, society and Satan are an unholy trinity to follow (Ephesians 2:2–3) and an unholy trinity to fight, but, in Christ, self (Romans 7:24–25), society (Galatians 1:3–4) and Satan (John 17:15; Hebrews 2:14–15) can all be overcome (Hebrews 2:18).

Satanic hindrances

'*Satan hindered us.*' 1 Thessalonians 2:18
SUGGESTED FURTHER READING: 2 Corinthians 11:1–15

How may I tell when Satan hinders me? I think you may tell thus: first by *the object*. Satan's object in hindering us is to prevent our glorifying God. If anything has happened to you which has prevented your growing holy, useful, humble, and sanctified, then you may trace that to Satan. If the distinct object of the interference to the general current of your life has been that you may be turned from righteousness into sin, then from the object you may guess the author. It is not God who does this, but Satan. Yet know that God does sometimes put apparent hindrances in the way of his own people, even in reference to their usefulness and growth in grace, but then his object is still to be considered: it is to try his saints and so to strengthen them; while the object of Satan is to turn them out of the right road and make them take the crooked way. You may tell the suggestions of Satan, again, by *the method* in which they come: God employs good motives, Satan bad ones. If that which has turned you away from your object had been a bad thought, a bad doctrine, bad teaching, a bad motive—that never came from God, that must be from Satan. Again, you may tell them from *their nature*. Whenever an impediment to usefulness is pleasing, gratifying to you, consider that it came from Satan. Satan never brushes the feathers of his birds the wrong way; he generally deals with us according to our tastes and likings. He flavours his bait to his fish. He knows exactly how to deal with each man, and to put that motive which will fall in with the suggestions of poor carnal nature. Now, if the difficulty in your way is rather contrary to yourself than for yourself, then it comes from God; but if that which now is a hindrance brings you gain, or pleasure, or emolument in any way, rest assured it came from Satan.

FOR MEDITATION: Satan's devices during his attempts to hinder the Lord Jesus Christ (Matthew 4:1–11; 16:21–23). Jesus was aware of Satan's devices (Luke 22:31). You need to be aware of them too, if Satan is not to take advantage of you (2 Corinthians 2:11).

SERMON NO. 657

Preparation for revival

'Can two walk together, except they be agreed?' Amos 3:3
SUGGESTED FURTHER READING: 1 John 2:15–17

Am I guilty of *worldliness?* This is the crying sin of many in the Christian church. Do I put myself into association with men who cannot by any possibility profit me? Am I seen where my Master would not go? Do I love amusements which cannot afford me comfort when I reflect upon them, and which I would never indulge in, if I thought that Christ would come while I was at them? Am I worldly in spirit as to fashion? Am I as showy, as volatile, as frivolous as men and women of the world? If so, if I love the world, the love of the Father is not in me; consequently he cannot walk with me, for we are not agreed.

Again, am I *covetous?* Do I scrape and grind? Is my first thought, not how I can honour God, but how I can accumulate wealth? When I gain wealth, do I forget to make use of it as a steward? If so, then God is not agreed with me; I am a thief with his substance; I have set myself up for a master instead of being a servant, and God will not walk with me till I begin to feel that this is not my own, but his, and that I must use it in his fear.

Again, am I of an *angry spirit?* Am I harsh towards my brethren? Do I cherish envy towards those who are better than myself, or contempt towards those who are worse off? If so, God cannot walk with me, for he hates envy, and all contempt of the poor is abhorrent to him. Is there any *lust* in me? Do I indulge the flesh? Am I fond of carnal indulgences by which my soul suffers? If so, God will not walk with me; for chambering, and wantonness, and gluttony, and drunkenness, separate between a believer and his God: these things are not convenient to a Christian.

FOR MEDITATION: We must not be in agreement with the things which God hates, if he is going to keep his promise to walk with us; we must practice separation from such things (2 Corinthians 6:14–18). The Christian is not supposed to walk in the darkness, but as the Lord walked—in the light (1 John 1:6–7; 2:6,11).

Never! Never! Never!

'He hath said, I will never leave thee, nor forsake thee.' Hebrews 13:5
SUGGESTED FURTHER READING: Revelation 21:1–9

The Lord will not and cannot leave his people, because of his relationship to them. He is your *Father;* will your Father leave you? Has he not said—'Can a woman forget her sucking child, that she should not have compassion on the son of her womb? yea, they may forget, yet will I not forget thee.' Would you, being evil, leave your child to perish? Never, never! Remember, Christ is your *husband.* Would you, a husband, neglect your wife? Is it not a shame to a man, unless he nourishes and cherishes her even as his own body, and will Christ become one of these ill husbands? Has he not said that, 'he hateth putting away'? Will he ever put you away? Remember, you are *part of his body.* No man yet ever hated his own flesh. You may be but as a little finger, but will he leave his finger to rot, to perish, to starve? You may be the least honourable of all the members, but is it not written that upon these he bestows abundant honour, and so our uncomely parts have abundant comeliness? If he be father, if he be husband, if he be head, if he be all-in-all, how can he leave you? Think not so hardly of your God.

Consider, also, that his honour binds him never to forsake you. When we see a house half-built and left in ruins, we say, 'This man began to build and was not able to finish.' Shall this be said of your God, that he began to save you and could not bring you to perfection? Is it possible that he will break his word, and so stain his truth? Shall men be able to cast a slur upon his power, his wisdom, his love, his faithfulness? No! thank God, no! 'I give,' he says 'unto them eternal life; and they shall never perish, neither shall any man pluck them out of my hand.' If you should perish, believer, hell would ring with diabolical laughter against the character of God.

FOR MEDITATION: 'I've started, so I'll finish' may not always be true of us (Luke 14:28–30), but it is true of God (Numbers 23:19; Isaiah 46:10–11), whether we consider his work of creation (Genesis 2:1–3), his work on the cross (John 19:28–30) or his work in the Christian (Philippians 1:6).

Caleb—the man for the times

'But my servant Caleb, because he had another spirit with him, and hath followed me fully, him will I bring into the land whereinto he went; and his seed shall possess it.' Numbers 14:24
SUGGESTED FURTHER READING: 2 Timothy 1:1–7

I would to God that we had all of us that which is the distinguishing mark of a right spirit, the spirit of faith, that spirit which takes God at his word, reads his promise, and knows it to be true. He that has this spirit will soon follow the Lord fully. Unbelief is the mother of sin, but faith is the nurse of virtue. More faith, Lord, may we have more simple childlike faith upon a precious Saviour! Then a faithful spirit always begets a meek spirit, and a meek spirit always begets a brave spirit. It is said of the wood of the elder tree that none is softer, but yet it is recorded of old that Venice was built upon piles of the elder tree because it will never rot; and so the meek-spirited man who is gentle and patient lasts on bravely, holding his own against all the attacks of the destroying adversary. The true believer has also a loving spirit as the result of Jesus' grace. He loves God, therefore he loves God's people and God's creatures, and having this loving spirit he has next a zealous spirit, and so he spends and is spent for God, and this begets in him a heavenly spirit and so he tries to live in heaven and to make earth a heaven to his fellow-men, believing that he shall soon have a heaven for himself and for them too on the other side of the stream. Such a spirit had good Caleb. We cannot imitate him till we get his spirit; we are dead until God quickens us. O that his Holy Spirit would lead us to go to Jesus just as we are, and look up to him and beseech him to fulfil that great covenant promise—'A new heart also will I give you, and a new spirit will I put within you.'

FOR MEDITATION: The Holy Spirit dwells in every truly converted person (Romans 8:9; 2 Timothy 1:14), but Paul still found it necessary to remind Timothy of the kind of spirit God has given us (2 Timothy 1:7). Is the fruit of the Spirit seen in your life (Galatians 5:22–23)?

SERMON NO. 538

Christ—perfect through sufferings

'For it became him, for whom are all things, and by whom are all things, in bringing many sons unto glory, to make the captain of their salvation perfect through sufferings.' Hebrews 2:10
SUGGESTED FURTHER READING: Revelation 7:13–17

We must not say what God could do or could not do, but it does seem to me that by no process of creation could he have ever made such beings as we shall be when we are brought to heaven; for if he had made us perfect, yet then we should have stood through our own holiness; or if he had forgiven us without an atonement, then we should never have seen his justice, nor his amazing love. But in heaven we shall be creatures who feel that we have everything but deserve nothing, creatures that have been the objects of the most wonderful love, and therefore so mightily attached to our Lord that it would be impossible for a thousand Satans ever to lead us astray. Again, we shall be such servants as even the angels cannot be, for we shall feel under deeper obligation to God than even they. They are but created happy; we shall be redeemed by the blood of God's dear Son, and I am sure, brethren, day without night we shall circle God's throne rejoicing, having more happiness than the angels, for they do not know what evil is, but we shall have known it to the full, and yet shall be perfectly free from it. They do not know what pain is, but we shall have known pain, and grief, and death, and yet shall be immortal. They do not know what it is to fall, but we shall look down to the depths of hell and remember that these were our portion. How we will sing, how we will chant his praise, and this, I say again, shall be the highest note, that we owe all to that bright one, that Lamb in the midst of the throne. We will tell it over, and over, and over again, and find it an inexhaustible theme for melodious joy and song that he became man, that he sweat great drops of blood, that he died, that he rose again.

FOR MEDITATION: Sinners have received far more attention from God than his holy angels have (Hebrews 2:16). If angels serve him with praise and long to learn more about the gospel of our salvation, how much more should we (Psalm 103:20–22; 1 Peter 1:12–13).

Scourge for slumbering souls

'*Woe to them that are at ease in Zion.*' Amos 6:1
SUGGESTED FURTHER READING: Hebrews 3:7–4:2

I think it was Christmas Evans who used the simile of the blacksmith's dog, which, when his master first set up in trade, was very much frightened with the sparks, but at last he got to be so used to them that he went to sleep under the anvil. 'And so,' said the good preacher, 'there be many that go to sleep under the gospel, with the sparks of damnation flying about their nostrils.' And certainly there are such. I am told that when they are making the great boilers at Bankside, when a man has to go inside for the first time and hold the hammer, the noise is so frightful, that his head aches and his ears seem to have lost all power of hearing for a long time afterwards; but I am also told that after a week or two a person can go to sleep in the midst of these boilers while the workmen are hammering outside, and he would sleep none the less soundly for the noise. So I know there is such a thing as going to sleep under the most thundering ministry. I know that men get used to these things, used to being invited, used to being warned, used to being thundered at. They have been pleaded with until they sleep under it; I doubt not they would sleep even if the world were blazing, if the sun were turned into darkness, and the moon into blood; and I think that even the trumpet of the archangel would not suffice to wake them from their lethargy, if they heard it long enough to be accustomed to it. Shall we give you up as hopeless? I think we almost may. If you have heard so long, and been unblessed, there is no great likelihood that you ever will be blessed; but you will go on as you have been going, till at last you perish.

FOR MEDITATION: Faithful gospel preachers sometimes get accused of hardening the hearts of their unbelieving hearers. That is the equivalent of blaming Moses for repeating a message from God (Exodus 5:1,3; 6:11; 7:2,16; 8:1,20; 9:1,13; 10:3) which led to Pharaoh hardening his heart (Exodus 8:15,32; 9:34). Beware of apportioning blame like this—those who harden their hearts against the gospel will not be able to hide on the day of judgment (Romans 2:4–5).

Praying in the Holy Ghost

'Praying in the Holy Ghost.' Jude 20
SUGGESTED FURTHER READING: Romans 8:26–27

With such prayer it is an absolute certainty that I must succeed with God in prayer. If my prayer were my own prayer, I might not be so sure of it, but if the prayer which I utter be God's own prayer written on my soul, God is always one with himself, and what he writes on the heart is only written there because it is written in his purposes. It is said by an old divine that prayer is the shadow of omnipotence. Our will, when God the Holy Spirit influences it, is the indicator of God's will. When God's people pray, it is because the blessing is coming, and their prayers are the shadow of the coming blessing. Rest assured of this, brethren, God never did belie himself; he never contradicted in one place what he said in another. You and I may contradict ourselves, not only through untruthfulness, but even through infirmity; we may not be able to stand to our word, and we may forget what we did say, and so in another place we may say something that contradicts it, but God is neither infirm as to memory, nor yet changeable as to will; what he promised yesterday he fulfils today, and what he has said in one place, he declares in another. Then if God says in my heart, 'Pray for So-and-so,' it is because he has said it in the book of his decrees. The Spirit of God's writing in the heart always tallies with the writing of destiny in the book of God's eternal purpose. Rest assured that you cannot but succeed when you have laid your soul like a sheet of paper before the Lord, and asked him to write upon it; then it is no more your own prayer merely, but the Spirit making intercession in you according to the will of God.

FOR MEDITATION: We cannot guarantee at any given time that we are praying in the Spirit, but we will be heading in the right direction if we pray in faith (Matthew 21:22), in Jesus' name (John 14:13–14; 16:24) and according to God's revealed will (1 John 5:14–15), while being in a state of fellowship with Christ (John 15:7) and obedience to God (1 John 3:22).

From the dunghill to the throne

'He raiseth up the poor out of the dust, and lifteth the needy out of the dunghill; that he may set him with princes, even with the princes of his people.' Psalm 113:7–8
SUGGESTED FURTHER READING: 1 Peter 1:3–9

O the joy of being a Christian! I know the world's idea is that we are a miserable people. If you read the pages of history, the writers speak of the merry cavaliers as being men of high spirit and overflowing joy; but the poor Puritans, what a wretched set they were, blaspheming Christmas Day, abhorring games and sports, and going about the world, looking so terribly miserable, that it were a pity they should go to hell, for they had enough of torment here! Now this talk is all untrue, or at best is a gross caricature. Hypocrites, then as now, did wear a long face and a rueful countenance, but there were to be found among the Puritans hosts of men whose holy mirth and joy were not to be equalled, not to be dreamed of, or understood by those poor grinning fools who fluttered round the heartless rake whose hypocrisies had lifted him to the English throne. The cavaliers' mirth was the crackling of thorns under a pot, but a deep and unquenchable joy dwelt in the breasts of those men that 'trampled on the haughty who slew the saints of God.' O far above the laughter of the gallants of the court, was the mighty and deep joy of those who rode from the victorious field singing unto the Lord who had made them triumph gloriously. They called them 'Ironsides,' and such they were, but they had hearts of steel, which while they flinched not in the day of danger, forgot not to flash with joy even as steel glitters in the shining of the sun. Believe me, however, whatever they were, that we who trust in Jesus are the happiest of people, not constitutionally, for some of us are much tried and are brought to the utter depths of poverty, but inwardly, truly, our heart's joy is not to be excelled.

FOR MEDITATION: We do not have to choose between purity and joy, as if they were opposites or alternatives; the Christian can experience a pure joy and a joyful purity (Psalm 19:8; Matthew 5:8,12; Philippians 4:4,8,10; 1 Peter 1:6,8,22).

SERMON NO. 658

Two visions

'And they answered ... We have walked to and fro through the earth, and behold, all the earth sitteth still, and is at rest.' Zechariah 1:11
SUGGESTED FURTHER READING: Colossians 1:1–6

'We have walked to and fro through the earth, and behold, all the earth sitteth still, and is at rest.' The mysterious agency of angels is at work together and in unison with the great work of providence. Whatever may be occurring, great or small, is certainly happening for the good of God's church, and for the propagation of God's truth. How singularly does God, in political events, prepare men's minds for the particular phase which his church assumes! There was perfect peace over the whole world at the time when Christ was put to death. The whole world was subject to one dominion, so that the apostle Paul and his assistants could preach everywhere the unsearchable riches of Christ. I cannot go into the question now, but every Christian student of history knows that the circumstances of the outward world have ever been arranged by God so as to prepare the way for the advance of his great cause. How strangely providence works to spread the truth. They said of Martin Luther's writings, that they were scattered by angels. No such distributors were employed; but still they were scattered so widely that it was a perfect mystery how it was done. There was scarcely a little pedlar who went about with jewels, who did not somewhere in his stock keep a copy of the Word of God or Luther's Psalms. It was said that in England, out of every three persons you met with on the road, though they might be but peasants breaking stones, there would be one of the three a Wycliffite; for Wycliffe's translation of the New Testament spread marvellously, though it was continually hunted after, and burnt when discovered. You will find that soon God will broadcast over all lands those testimonies which are most clear and most full of Christ.

FOR MEDITATION: Do twentieth century inventions, like radio broadcasting, exist for a divine purpose? The apostle Paul used all legitimate means to spread the Gospel (1 Corinthians 9:22).

SERMON NO. 598

Heavenly love-sickness!

'I charge you, O daughters of Jerusalem, if ye find my beloved, that ye tell him that I am sick of love.' Song of Solomon 5:8
SUGGESTED FURTHER READING: Psalm 107:17–22

Certain sicknesses are peculiar to the saints: the ungodly are never visited with them. Strange to say, these sicknesses are signs of vigorous health. Who but the beloved of the Lord ever experience that *sin-sickness* in which the soul loathes the very name of transgression, is unmoved by the enchantments of the tempter, finds no sweetness in its besetting sins, but turns with detestation and abhorrence from the very thought of iniquity? Not less is it for these, and these alone, to feel that *self-sickness* whereby the heart revolts from all creature-confidence and strength, having been made sick of self, self-exalting, self-reliance, and self of every sort. The Lord afflicts us more and more with such self-sickness till we are dead to self and its unsanctified desires. Then there is a *twofold love-sickness*. Of the one kind is that love-sickness which comes upon the Christian when he is transported with the full enjoyment of Jesus, even as the bride, elated by the favour, melted by the tenderness of her Lord, says in the fifth verse of the second chapter of the Song, 'Stay me with flagons, comfort me with apples: for I am sick of love.' The soul overjoyed with the divine communications of happiness and bliss which came from Christ, the body scarcely able to bear the excessive delirium of delight which the soul possessed, she was so glad to be in the embraces of her Lord, that she needed to be stayed under the overpowering weight of joy. Another kind of love-sickness widely different from the first, is that in which the soul is sick, not because it has too much of Christ's love, but because it has not enough present consciousness of it; sick, not of the enjoyment, but of the longing for it; sick, not because of excess of delight, but because of sorrow for an absent lover.

FOR MEDITATION: Do you suffer from spiritual sickness? Christ came to call those who are prepared to admit to him that they are spiritually sick (Mark 2:17). As he said of his physically sick friend Lazarus, 'This sickness is not unto death, but for the glory of God' (John 11:4).

The ship on fire—a voice of warning

'Escape for thy life; ... Thou hast magnified thy mercy, which thou hast shewed unto me in saving my life.' Genesis 19:17,19
SUGGESTED FURTHER READING: Luke 17:28–33

This alarm demands of every one of us who are unsaved, an undivided attention. You have fifty things to think about. You tell me you have a thousand cares. O sirs, a man whose life is in danger, has no other care than to save his life. Did those who were rescued from the 'Amazon' have time to save their money and their gold? We are told that they were utterly destitute when they landed at Margate, and what does it matter? Would not a flush of joy be on their cheeks because their lives were preserved? If one said to his fellow, 'Where is your purse?' 'Oh,' would say the other, 'never mind my purse; I am in the lifeboat; my life is saved.' And what is the loss after all, if you lose the world and gain your soul? Those on board the ship had not time to save their clothes. They ran just as they were, half-naked, to the vessel's deck, and so must you. I know you will tell me you are not living to make money; if you could just make ends meet, keep your family—that is all—are you not to think of this? It is well and good; far be it from me to discourage prudent carefulness in all matters; it is your business to see to temporal matters, but still your paramount business must be your soul; even necessaries must not come between your soul and your most serious thoughts. You must see to this first and foremost, and remember there is a promise about it—'Seek ye first the kingdom of God, and his righteousness; and all these things shall be added unto you.'

FOR MEDITATION: We are horrified by fires on earth; how much more should we dread the everlasting fires of hell (Isaiah 33:14). It's far better to have Christ and lose out on earth than to end up in hell without Christ (Mark 9:43–48).

N.B. This sermon was preached following the burning of the ship *Amazon* off Broadstairs on the Kent coast. All the passengers and crew were saved. The captain was in Spurgeon's congregation on this occasion as was his custom when on shore.

SERMON NO. 550

Christian sympathy—a sermon for the Lancashire distress

'Did not I weep for him that was in trouble? was not my soul grieved for the poor?' Job 30:25
SUGGESTED FURTHER READING: James 1:26–2:16

Remember a little more the intimate connection between the body and the soul. Go to the poor man and tell him of the bread of heaven, but first give him the bread of earth, for how shall he hear you with a starving body? It seems an idle tale to a poor man, if you talk to him of spiritual things and cruelly refuse him help as to temporals. Sympathy, thus expressed, may be a mighty instrument for good; and even without this, if you are too poor to be able to carry out the pecuniary part of benevolence, a kind word, a look, a sentence or two of sympathy in trouble, a little loving advice, or an exhortation to your neighbour to cast his burden on the Lord, may do much spiritual service. I do not know, but I think if all our church members were full of love, and would always deal kindly, there would be very few hearts that would long hold out, at least from hearing the Word. You ask a person to hear your preacher; but he knows that you are crotchety, short-tempered, illiberal, and he is not likely to think much of the Word, which, as he thinks, has made you what you are; but if, on the other hand, he sees your compassionate spirit, he will first be attracted to you, then next to what you have to say, and then you may lead him as with a thread, and bring him to listen to the truth as it is in Jesus, and who can tell, but thus, through the sympathy of your tender heart, you may be the means of bringing him to Christ.

FOR MEDITATION: Jesus had compassion on the shepherdless and hungry crowds (Mark 6:34; 8:1–3). His disciples had doubts and wanted to send them away (Mark 6:35–36; 8:4). But it is amazing what God can do with a little willingness on our part (Mark 6:37–44; 8:5–9).

N.B. Due to the failure of the cotton supply, the Lancashire mills had closed, resulting in unemployment and food shortages. Spurgeon was financially supporting one of his former students in his attempts to help those suffering.

SERMON NO. 479

Bread for the hungry

'And he humbled thee, and suffered thee to hunger, and fed thee with manna, which thou knewest not, neither did thy fathers know; that he might make thee know that man doth not live by bread only but by every word that proceedeth out of the mouth of the LORD doth man live.' Deuteronomy 8:3

SUGGESTED FURTHER READING: Psalm 119:1–24

We must open our Bibles every morning with this prayer—'Give us this day our daily bread.' We must get some choice text to fill our homer. If we read a chapter we shall have nothing over; if we read a verse we shall have no lack. Then we put the word in our memories, and we shall surely find, perhaps not the first hour, but some other hour in the day, that it will taste like wafers made with honey to us. It is astonishing how much a man may know of the Bible by learning a text a day, and how much he may know experimentally by watching the events of the day, and interpreting them in the light of the text. If you cannot retain by memory a whole passage, never mind that; take a short text, and let it be under your tongue all day, and be looking out for a commentary upon it. I do not mean Matthew Henry, or Scott, or Gill—I mean your own daily experience. Be looking out to see how the Lord translates that text to you by his own providence, and you will frequently see a striking relation between the text that was given you in the morning, and the trials or the mercies that are given you during the day. At any rate, let the Word of God be the man of your right hand. We are so busy reading the magazines, newspapers, and new books, and so forth that we forget this—this new book, this that is always new, and always old, always having a freshness in it. Like a well, it is always springing up, not with musty, stale water, but with fresh water that has never sparkled in the sun before, and in all its virgin lustre of purity scatters jewels on the right hand and on the left. Let us go to this fountain and drink fresh and fresh.

FOR MEDITATION: It is a blessing to seek God's wisdom daily (Proverbs 8:34). Are you keen to read his Word daily (Acts 17:11)? If not, you are depriving yourself of daily refreshment (Psalm 1:2–3), daily light (Psalm 119:105) and daily bread (Jeremiah 15:16).

SERMON NO. 418

The Gospel's healing power

'And it came to pass on a certain day, as he was teaching, that there were Pharisees and doctors of the law sitting by, which were come out of every town of Galilee, and Judæa, and Jerusalem: and the power of the Lord was present to heal them.' Luke 5:17
SUGGESTED FURTHER READING: Mark 2:13–17

Christian men and women, join together to pray for your friends who cannot or will not pray for themselves; and if you meet with any in deep distress, palsied with despair, who cannot lift the finger of faith, strive to bring them to hear the gospel; bring them where Christ is working miracles. If one of you cannot prevail to lay the case before the Lord, let two of you unite; if two should not be enough, let four blend their petitions; if four should not suffice, tell it to the church, and ask the whole to pray; but do strive to bring dying sinners where Christ is working spiritual miracles. If you read further on in the chapter you will learn how to bring some persons to the Saviour who would otherwise never hear of him. Levi made a great feast, for he thought to himself, 'I should like Jesus to come and preach to the tax collectors. They are such great sinners, just such as I am; if I could but get them to hear him they might be converted. But,' he thought, 'if I ask them they would say they could not afford to give up a day's work; they will not care to listen to a sermon; so,' said he, 'I will get them this way—I will invite them to my house to a feast; they will be sure to come then, and then I will ask Jesus to come and eat with them, and I know he will not let them go without saying a good word.' So you see he used arts, as fowlers do when they are anxious to catch their prey. Now cannot you be as watchful and thoughtful in your generation as Levi was? Cannot you get the outcasts and the neglecters of the Sabbath to your own house or to anybody else's house, and use means to bring them under the sound of God's word?

FOR MEDITATION: If your church or chapel is 'God's house', so is your home! God does not live in man-made buildings (Acts 17:24), but in his people (Hebrews 3:6); fellowship and evangelism are valid wherever his people are, whether in a public place or in private houses (Acts 2:46; 5:42; 20:20–21).

Light, natural and spiritual

'And God said, Let there be light: and there was light. And God saw the light, that it was good: and God divided the light from the darkness. And God called the light Day, and the darkness he called Night. And the evening and the morning were the first day.' Genesis 1:3–5
SUGGESTED FURTHER READING: Ephesians 5:8–14

'God saw the light, that it was good.' Light is good in all respects. The natural light is good. Solomon says, 'Truly the light is sweet, and a pleasant thing it is for the eyes to behold the sun.' But you did not need Solomon to inform you upon that point. Any blind man who will tell you the tale of his sorrows will be quite philosopher enough to convince you that light is good. Gospel light is good. 'Blessed are the eyes which see the things that ye see.' You only need to travel into heathen lands, and witness the superstition and cruelty of the dark places of the earth, to understand that gospel light is good. As for spiritual light, those that have received it long for more of it, that they may see yet more and more the glory of heaven's essential light! O God, thou art of good the unmeasured Sea; thou art of light both soul, and source, and centre. Whether, then, we take natural light, gospel light, spiritual light, or essential light, we may say of it, as God did, that it was good. But we are speaking now of light spiritual. Why is that good? Well, it must be so, from its source. The light emanates from God, in whom is no darkness at all, and, as it comes absolutely and directly from him, it must be good. As every good gift, and every perfect gift is from above, so everything which comes from above is good and perfect. The Lord distributes no alloyed metal: he never gives his people that which is mixed and debased. Thy words, O God, are pure; as silver tried in the furnace of earth purified seven times. The light of the new nature is good when we consider its origin.

FOR MEDITATION: Light is good, because God is light (1 John 1:5) and the Father of lights (James 1:17). Not surprisingly the evildoer hates the light (John 3:19–20). Have you become a child of light by following the light of the world (John 8:12) and trusting in him (John 12:35–36)?

The certainty and freeness of divine grace

'All that the Father giveth me shall come to me; and him that cometh to me I will in no wise cast out.' John 6:37
SUGGESTED FURTHER READING: 1 Timothy 1:12–17

It says, 'Him that cometh,' and this shuts out no comer. John Newton was a blasphemer of so gross a kind, that even the sailors in the vessel in the storm said that they should never get to port with such a sinner as John Newton on board; but he came to Christ and was not cast out, but lived to preach the Word. John Bunyan was so foul a blasphemer, that even a woman of the street, who passed him by and heard him swear, said that he was enough to corrupt the whole parish; and he was astonished that a woman of so bad a character should so rebuke him. John Bunyan came to Jesus, and he was not cast out; he lived to have the honour of suffering for his Master, and to be the winner of multitudes of souls. Saul of Tarsus had stained himself with the blood of saints; he was a very wolf after Christ's sheep. He was not satisfied with worrying them in his own land, so he obtained power to persecute them in Damascus; but when he fell upon his face and cried for mercy, he was not cast out. Manasseh was blood-red with the murder of God's prophets. It is said that he cut the prophet Isaiah in two with a saw; and yet, when out of the low dungeon he cried for mercy, he was not cast out. So that any kind of 'him', though he may have been a persecutor even unto blood, though he may have been exceeding mad against God till he could not speak without blasphemies against the name of Christ, though he hated everything which is good, and despised everything held precious by believing men and women, yet if he comes to Christ, he shall not be cast out.

FOR MEDITATION: Even the most scandalous of past sins will not be held against those who come to Christ for forgiveness and cleansing (1 Corinthians 6:9–11). They are the ones who go to heaven, not those who think that they are good enough as they are (Matthew 21:31–32). Those who assume that their 'goodness' guarantees them a place in heaven are the sinners who will be 'cast out' (Matthew 8:11–12).

SERMON NO. 599

The special call and the unfailing result

'God is faithful, by whom ye were called unto the fellowship of his Son Jesus Christ our Lord.' 1 Corinthians 1:9
SUGGESTED FURTHER READING: 1 Corinthians 15:3–10

Where would you have been but for grace? To repeat the old saying of John Bradford, when he saw a cartful of men going off to Tyburn to be hanged, 'There goes John Bradford but for the grace of God.' When you see the swearer in the street, or the drunkard rolling home at night, there are you, there am I, but for the grace of God. Who am I? What should I have been if the Lord, in mercy, had not stopped me in my mad career? I know there are some of us who can remember the old story of Rowland Hill, when a good Scotsman called to see him, and without saying a word, sat still for some five minutes, looking into the good old gentleman's face. At last, Rowland Hill asked him what engaged his attention. Said he, 'I was looking at the lines of your face.' 'Well, what do you make out of 'em?' 'Why,' said he, 'that if the grace of God hadn't been in you, you would have been the biggest rascal living;' and some of us do feel just that, that if it had not been for the grace of God, we should have been out-and-out ringleaders in every kind of infamy and sin. I know for myself I can never do things by halves. If I had served Baal, I would have built him an altar, and made victims smoke upon it day and night; and if we serve God zealously and earnestly, we have the more reason to be humble and to lay low in the dust; for that very zeal of spirit would have been turned to the very worst account unless grace had been pleased to transform us.

FOR MEDITATION: God's saving grace is his free undeserved favour towards people spiritually dead in sin (Ephesians 2:5,7–8). Where would you be now but for the grace of God? See Ephesians 2:1–3. That is exactly where you are now, if you are still rejecting his grace—and the worst is yet to come (Hebrews 10:29).

The lambs and their Shepherd

'He shall gather the lambs with his arm, and carry them in his bosom.'
Isaiah 40:11
SUGGESTED FURTHER READING: Nehemiah 13:23–27

There is another flock in the world—the devil's flock. It is not easy for a Christian man to associate with the world without feeling the influence of it. The worst form of ill association is ungodly marriage. I do not know anything that gives me more satisfaction than to see our brethren and sisters, who have walked in the faith of God, united in marriage—the husband and wife, both fearing and loving God. It is a delightful spectacle, and bids fair to be the means of building up the church with a generation which shall fear the Lord. But a very fruitful source of ruin to church members is that of a young man or a young woman choosing an ungodly partner in life. They never can expect God's blessing upon it. They tell you sometimes they hope to be the means of their friend's conversion. They have no right to hope such a thing; it so seldom occurs. The much more likely thing is that the ungodly one will drag the other down to his level, than that the godly one shall pull the other up. We are fearful, I say, for the lambs, for we mark some of them that were as earnest as they well could be, and apparently as loving to their Lord and Master, but another love came across their path, and where are they now? Perhaps the house of God sees them no longer, and the theatre or the ballroom is now their delight. When we think of some cases of this kind that have occurred, we tremble for the lambs, and lift up our hearts in prayer to God for them, that they may be kept.

FOR MEDITATION: We say 'As wise as Solomon', but no one was a bigger fool when it came to marriage. He should be a terrible warning to any Christian contemplating marriage to an unbeliever (1 Kings 11:1–11). Some Jews failed to heed the warning (Nehemiah 13:26) and some Christians think they know better than God. 'Be ye not unequally yoked together with unbelievers' (2 Corinthians 6:14).

A message from God for thee

'The punishment of thine iniquity is accomplished, O daughter of Zion.'
Lamentations 4:22
SUGGESTED FURTHER READING: Daniel 9:20–26

In the case of the kingdom of Judah, the people had suffered so much in their captivity that their God, who in his anger had put them from him, considered that they had suffered enough; 'For she hath received of the Lord's hand,' said the prophet Isaiah, 'double for all her sins.' Brethren, in our case we have not been punished at all, for the punishment of our iniquity is accomplished. Remember that sin must be punished. Any theology which offers the pardon of sin without a punishment, ignores part of the character of God. God is love, but God is also just, as severely just as if he had no love, and yet as intensely loving as if he had no justice. To gain a just view of the character of God you must perceive all his attributes as infinitely developed; justice must have its infinity acknowledged as much as mercy. This is the voice which thunders from the midst of the smoke and the fire of Sinai— 'The soul that sinneth it shall die.' 'Sin must be punished' is written on the base of the eternal throne in letters of fire; and as the damned in hell behold it, their hopes are burned to ashes. Sin must be punished, or God must cease to be. The testimony of the gospel is not that the punishment has been mitigated or foregone, or that justice has had a sop given it to close its mouth. The consolation is far more sure and effectual. Christ has for his people borne all the punishment which they deserved; and now every soul for whom Christ died may read with exultation, 'The punishment of her iniquity is accomplished.'

FOR MEDITATION: Christ cried out in agonised separation from his Father as he was punished for our sins (Matthew 27:46), but later in triumph upon the completion of that work (John 19:30). Marvel at the prophecy of his crucifixion which begins with that cry of agony and ends by proclaiming his completed work (Psalm 22:1,31).

SERMON NO. 480

The roaring lion

'Be sober, be vigilant; because your adversary the devil, as a roaring lion, walketh about, seeking whom he may devour: whom resist stedfast in the faith.' 1 Peter 5:8–9
SUGGESTED FURTHER READING: Luke 4:1–13

Here comes Esau, hungry with hunting; there is a mess of pottage ready, that he may be tempted to sell his birthright. Here is Noah, glad to escape from his long confinement in the ark; he is merry, and there is the wine-cup ready for him, that he may drink. Here is Peter; his faith is low, but his presumption is high; there is a maiden ready to say 'Thou also wast with Jesus of Nazareth.' There is Judas, and there are thirty pieces of silver in the priestly hand to tempt him, and there is the rope afterwards for him to hang himself with. No lack of means! If there be a Jonah, wishing to go to Tarshish rather than to Nineveh, there is a ship ready to take him. One of the greatest mercies God bestows upon us is his not permitting our inclinations and opportunities to meet. Have you not sometimes noticed that when you had the inclination to a sin there has been no opportunity, and when the opportunity has presented itself you have had no inclination towards it? Satan's principal aim with believers is to bring their appetites and his temptations together; to get their souls into a dry, seared state, and then to strike the match and make them burn. He is so crafty and wily with all the experience of these many centuries, that man, who is but of yesterday, can scarcely be thought of as a match for him! Did he not drag down the wise man, even Solomon, whose wisdom was more excellent than any of the sons of men? Did he not lay the royal preacher like a helpless victim at his feet? Did he not cast down the strong man, Samson, who could slay a thousand Philistines, but who could not resist the dallyings of Delilah? Did he not bring down even the man after God's own heart?

FOR MEDITATION: Be thankful for the temptation-resistant inclinations of the indwelling Holy Spirit (Galatians 5:17), but beware of Satan's opportunity-seizing devices (2 Corinthians 2:11; Galatians 6:1). He left Jesus for a season (Luke 4:13), only to return (Luke 22:2–6).

SERMON NO. 419

The last enemy destroyed

'The last enemy that shall be destroyed is death.' 1 Corinthians 15:26
SUGGESTED FURTHER READING: Romans 8:35–39

To live well is the way to die well. Death is not our first foe but the last; let us then fight our adversaries in order, and overcome them each in its turn, hoping that he who has been with us even until now will be with us until the end. Notice, dear friends—for herein lies the savour of the thought—it is the last enemy. Picture in your mind's eye our brave soldiers at the battle of Waterloo; for many weary hours they had been face to face with the foe; the fight had lasted so long and been so frequently renewed that they seemed to have encountered successive armies, and to have fought a dozen battles; charge after charge had they borne like walls of stone: imagine then that the commander is able to announce that they have only to endure one more onslaught of the foe. How cheerfully do the ranks close! How gallantly are the squares formed! How firmly their feet are planted! 'Now,' say they, 'let us stand like a wall of rock; let no man shrink for a moment, for it is the last the enemy can do. He will do his worst; but soon he will be able to do no more but sound to boot and saddle, and leave the field to us.' The last enemy! Soldiers of Christ, do not the words animate you? Courage, Christian, courage; the tide must turn after this; it is the highest wave that now dashes over you; courage, man, the night must close; you have come to its darkest hour; the day star already dawns! Now that you are dying, you are beginning to live. The last enemy conquered! Does it not bring tears to your eyes to think of bearing your last temptation? Little care we who the foe may be, if he be but conquered and be but the last.

FOR MEDITATION: Christ's veteran soldiers were calm as they prepared to do battle with the last enemy (2 Timothy 4:6–8; 2 Peter 1:12–15). 'Thanks be to God, which giveth us the victory through our Lord Jesus Christ' (1 Corinthians 15:57). Do we have a similar attitude to our own death?

SERMON NO. 721

Are you prepared to die?

'How wilt thou do in the swelling of Jordan?' Jeremiah 12:5
SUGGESTED FURTHER READING: 2 Corinthians 5:1–10

You that are in Christ, 'How will you do in the swelling of Jordan?' Why, you will do as a man does who has had a long day's walk, and he can see his home. You will clap your hands. You will sit down upon the next milestone with the tears in your eyes, and wipe the sweat from your face and say, 'It is well, it is over. O how happy it is to see my own roof-tree, and the place where my best friends, my kindred dwell. I shall soon be at home, at home for ever with the Lord.' How will you do? Why, we will do as a soldier does when the battle is fought; he takes off his armour and stretches himself out at length to rest. The battle is all over. He forgets his wound, and reckons up the glory of the victory and the reward which follows. So will we do. We will begin to forget the wounds, and the garments rolled in blood, and we will think of the 'crown of glory that fadeth not away.' How will we do in the swelling of Jordan? We will do as men do when they launch for a foreign country. They look back upon those they leave behind, and wave their handkerchiefs as long as they can get sight of them; but they are soon gone. And we will bid adieu to dear ones; they shall have the tears, but we shall have the joy, for we go to the islands of the blessed, the land of the hereafter, the home of the sanctified, to dwell with God for ever. Who will weep when he starts on such a voyage, and launches on such a blessed sea? What will we do when we come into the swelling of Jordan? Why, dear friends, we shall then begin to see through the veil, and to enjoy the paradise of the blessed which is ours for ever.

FOR MEDITATION: Naturally we look upon death in a negative light, but Christ's death makes all the difference for the believer (Hebrews 2:14–15). The Christian can adopt a positive attitude and use words such as 'conquerors' (Romans 8:37), 'present with the Lord' (2 Corinthians 5:8), 'gain … far better' (Philippians 1:21,23), 'blessed' and 'rest' (Revelation 14:13).

The smoke of their torments

'And Abraham gat up early in the morning ... and he looked toward Sodom and Gomorrah ... and beheld, and, lo, the smoke of the country went up as the smoke of a furnace.' Genesis 19:27–28
SUGGESTED FURTHER READING: Jude 5–18

The assurance that God is just, even in the midst of his hot displeasure, must ever be cherished. The Judge of all the earth cannot but do right. Though he is terrible and dreadful in his anger, as a consuming fire, yet he is still our God for ever and ever, full of goodness and full of truth. There is a deep-seated unbelief among Christians just now, about the eternity of future punishment. It is not outspoken in many cases, but it is whispered; and it frequently assumes the shape of a spirit of benevolent desire that the doctrine may be disproved. I fear that at the bottom of all this there is a rebellion against the dread sovereignty of God. There is a suspicion that sin is not, after all, so bad a thing as we have dreamed. There is an apology, or a lurking wish to apologise for sinners, who are looked upon rather as objects of pity than as objects of indignation, and really deserving the condign punishment which they have wilfully brought upon themselves. I am afraid it is the old nature in us putting on the specious garb of charity, which thus leads us to discredit a fact which is as certain as the happiness of believers. Shake the foundations upon which the eternity of hell rests, and you have shaken heaven's eternity too. 'These shall go away into everlasting punishment; but the righteous into life eternal.' There is precisely the same word in the original. We have it translated a little more strongly in our version, but the word stands the same; and if the one be not eternal, the other is not. Brethren, this is a fearful thing. Who can meditate upon the place appointed for the wicked without a shudder?

FOR MEDITATION: 'For ever' sounds wonderful when applied to heaven, but appalling when applied to hell. If devils believe and tremble when they think about God (James 2:19), we should tremble and ensure we are trusting in Christ when we contemplate the suffering of the unsaved, which will never end (Mark 9:48; 2 Thessalonians 1:9; Revelation 14:11).

A solemn enquiry concerning our families

'And the men said unto Lot, Hast thou here any besides? son in law, and thy sons, and thy daughters, and whatsoever thou hast in the city, bring them out of this place.' Genesis 19:12
SUGGESTED FURTHER READING: Romans 9:1–5 & 10:1–4

If you do not care for the souls of others, you do not know the value of your own. God's people are a tender-hearted people. Like their Saviour, they cannot look upon Jerusalem without weeping over it: they cannot view with complacency the destruction of any; much less can they be careless concerning the condition of those who spring from their own loins, who are united to them by ties of blood. We love the souls of men. Like Doddridge, we dare say in the sight of God: 'My bowels yearn o'er dying men.'

I set you down as nearer akin to a devil than to a saint, if you can go your way and look into the face of your friend or child, and know him to be on the downward road, and yet never pray for him nor use any means for his conversion. May God grant that no doctrinal belief may ever dry up the milk of human kindness in our souls! Certainly the doctrines of divine grace, such as election and effectual redemption, will not do so. Error may petrify, but truth melts. May we feel that no dogma can be scriptural which is not consistent with a sincere love to men. Truth must be consistent with its Author's character; and he who has revealed saving truth is the God of love; he is love itself; and that cannot be true which naturally and legitimately would lead men to be unloving! May we be such parents, such brothers, such sisters, such children, that it shall be the first anxiety of our spirits that our children, our parents, our husband, our wife, our brothers and our sisters, should be brought to partake with us of the things of God!

FOR MEDITATION: At best human love can only long to perish in the place of others (Exodus 32:32; 2 Samuel 18:33; Romans 9:3), but it's the thought that counts. Are you really concerned for others (Romans 9:1–2; Philippians 3:18–19)? The best way to show it is to pray for them (Romans 10:1) and point them to the Saviour who died in the place of others (1 Peter 2:24).

Direction in dilemma

'Stand still, and see the salvation of the Lord.' Exodus 14:13
SUGGESTED FURTHER READING: Psalm 37:1–9

In what way are we to stand still, dear friends? Surely it means among other things, that we are to *wait awhile*. Time is precious, but there are occasions when the best use we can make of it, is to let it run on. If time flies, that is no reason why I am always to fly. Every experienced man knows that by being wrongly busy for one hour, he may make mischief which a lifetime would hardly rectify. If I run without waiting to enquire the way, I may run upon my ruin. Many who have been very busy in helping themselves, would have done better waiting upon their Lord. Prayer is never a waste of time. A man who would ride post-haste, had better wait till he is perfectly mounted, or he may slip from the saddle. He who glorifies God by standing still, is better employed than he who diligently serves his own self-will. Wait awhile then. *Wait in prayer*, however. Call upon God, and spread the case before him; tell him your difficulty, and plead his promise of aid. Express your unstaggering confidence in him; *wait in faith*, for unfaithful, untrusting waiting, is but an insult to the Lord. Believe that if he shall keep you tarrying even till midnight, yet he will come at the right time; the vision shall come and shall not tarry. *Wait in quiet patience*, not murmuring because you are under the affliction, but blessing God for it; never murmuring against the second cause, as the children of Israel did against Moses; never wish you could go back to the world again, but accept the case as it stands, and put it as it stands simply and with your whole heart, without any self-will, into the hand of your covenant God.

FOR MEDITATION: There is a time to be swift and a time to be slow (James 1:19). The Christian should be active, but not an activist; advancing in faith, but not rushing ahead (Proverbs 21:5). 'Why should I wait for the Lord any longer?' (2 Kings 6:33) is the language of unbelief. 'He that believeth shall not make haste' (Isaiah 28:16). Does your busy timetable allow for you to be still and know that the Lord is God (Psalm 46:10)?

A drama in five acts

'But this I say, brethren, the time is short: it remaineth, that both they that have wives be as though they had none; And they that weep, as though they wept not; and they that rejoice, as though they rejoiced not; and they that buy, as though they possessed not; And they that use this world, as not abusing it: for the fashion of this world passeth away.' 1 Corinthians 7:29–31

SUGGESTED FURTHER READING: Matthew 19:3–12

When the apostle declares that 'they that have wives be as though they had none,' he does not teach us to despise the marriage state, but not to seek our heaven in it, nor let it hinder our serving the Lord. It is supposed that there are some things which a man without a wife and family can do—those things the man with a wife and family should do. It is supposed that a man without a wife can give his time to the cause of God: the man with a wife should do the same, and he will not find it difficult to do if God has blessed him with one who will second all his holy endeavours. It is supposed that a man without a wife has no care: a man with a wife should have none, for he should cast all his cares on God who cares for him. 'If any provide not for his own, and specially for those of his own house, he hath denied the faith, and is worse than an infidel;' and yet the apostle says, in the verse following my text, 'But I would have you without carefulness;' for we should learn to live by faith. The man who has a large family, and many things to exercise his mind, should yet, through the teaching of the Holy Spirit, live as quietly and comfortably as though he had none, depending and resting by simple faith upon the providence and goodness of God. Then, again, it is supposed that an unmarried man will find it easier to die, for there will be none of that sorrow at leaving his beloved family: the man with a wife and family should, by faith, find it just as easy since the promise runs, 'Leave thy fatherless children, I will preserve them alive; and let thy widows trust in me.'

FOR MEDITATION: 'I have married a wife, and therefore I cannot' (Luke 14:20) is not a good excuse to give to God. A godly wife can reduce worldly cares (Proverbs 31:10–11,25) and provide support in the Lord's work (Acts 18:2,26; Romans 16:3–4; 1 Corinthians 9:5).

SERMON NO. 481

Abram and the ravenous birds

'And when the fowls came down upon the carcases, Abram drove them away.' Genesis 15:11
SUGGESTED FURTHER READING: Isaiah 58:13–14

I am not under the law, and therefore I keep this day, not the seventh, but the *first* day of the week, on which my Saviour rose again from the dead—keep it not of law, but of grace—keep it not as a slavish bondage, not as a day on which I am chained and hampered with restraints against my will, but a day in which I may take holy pleasure in serving God, and in adoring before his throne. The sabbath of the Jew is to him a task; the Lord's Day of the Christian, the first day of the week, is to him a joy, a day of rest, of peace, and of thanksgiving; and if you Christian men can earnestly drive away all distractions, so that you can really rest today, it will be good for your bodies, good for your souls, good mentally, good spiritually, good temporally, and good eternally. Let me give you a second reason. You will find, if you are able to take a perfect rest, by driving away these evil thoughts when you are worshipping God, that you will do your work during the other days of the week far better ... If you have a bad Lord's Day, you will have a bad week; but if you have a good day of rest, you will find it good with your souls the whole week long; not that you will be without trouble all the week; that would not be good for you; but you shall never be without grace during the week; nor if you have peace on the Sunday shall you be without peace on the Monday; the old Puritans used to say the first day of the week was the market-day; ... This is our market-day, and if we gain but little today, we shall have slender diet during the other days; but if we get the basket loaded well, if we have reason to say, 'The Lord has satisfied my soul with fatness, and caused my spirit to delight in his word,' you will find that during the week your peace shall be like a river, and your righteousness like the waves of the sea.

FOR MEDITATION: The Lord's Day is the one day in the week when Christians should feel free to do what they most want to do. What does a spiritual person really want to do (Psalm 27:4; 84:2,10)? Do you, like Abraham, drive away the things that interfere with your worship of God? Jesus did (John 2:13–17).

SERMON NO. 420

The captive Saviour freeing his people

'Jesus answered, I have told you that I am he: if therefore ye seek me, let these go their way: that the saying might be fulfilled, which he spake, Of them which thou gavest me have I lost none.' John 18:8–9
SUGGESTED FURTHER READING: Hebrews 12:5–11

When you suffer tribulation, affliction and adversity, do not think that God is punishing you for your sins, for no child of God can be punished for sin penally. Let me not be misunderstood. A man is brought before God first of all as a criminal before a judge. You and I have stood there. Through Christ's blood and righteousness we have been absolved and acquitted as before God the Judge, and it is not possible for the law to lay so much as the weight of a feather upon us since we have been perfectly acquitted. In all the pains and sufferings which a Christian may endure, there is not so much as a single ounce of penal infliction. God cannot punish a man whom he has pardoned and who is then adopted into God's family. Now, if he shall as a child offend against his father's rule, he will be chastened for it. Everyone can see the distinction between chastening by a father and punishment by a judge. If your child were to steal, you would not think of punishing that child in the light in which the judge would do it, who would commit him to imprisonment for having broken the law; but you chasten your child yourself, not so much to avenge the law as for the child's good, that he may not do this evil thing again. So our heavenly Father chastens his people with the rod of the covenant, but he never punishes them with the sword of vengeance. There is a difference between chastening and punishing. Punishing is from a judge; Christ has suffered all such punishment, so that no penal infliction can fall upon a soul that believes in him; but we may have chastisement which comes to us as the result of a father's love, and not as the result of a judge's anger; we have felt such chastisement, and have reason to bless God for it.

FOR MEDITATION: If God becomes our Father, he will sometimes judge that we need disciplining now (Hebrews 12:6–7). If he remains our Judge, he will one day condemn us for ever. Faith in Christ is the only way to have a Father instead of a Judge in heaven (John 5:24).

Consolation in the furnace

'He answered and said, Lo, I see four men loose, walking in the midst of the fire, and they have no hurt; and the form of the fourth is like the Son of God.' Daniel 3:25
SUGGESTED FURTHER READING: Acts 13:44–52

Luther, I dare say, like other men, had some respect for his own character, and some reverence for public opinion, and might have been willing to pay some deference to the learning and authority of the age, both of which lent their aid to the ancient system of Rome, but in a happy hour the Pope excommunicated the German troubler. All is well for Luther now. He must henceforth never conciliate or dream of peace. Now his bonds are broken. He burns the Pope's bull and thunders out, 'The Pope of Rome excommunicates Martin Luther, and I, Martin Luther, excommunicate the Pope of Rome. The world hates me, and there is no love lost between us, for I esteem it as much as it esteems me. War to the knife,' says he. The man was never clear till the world thrust him out. It is a splendid thing to run the gauntlet of so much contempt, that the soul is hardened to it under a strong consciousness that the right is none the more contemptible because its friend may be despised. 'Why,' you say, 'is this how I am treated for the statement of truth? I was inclined to conciliate and yield, but after this never! You have loosed my bonds.' When man has done his worst, as Nebuchadnezzar did in this case, why then Shadrach, Meshach, and Abednego could say, 'What more could he do? He has thrown us into a fiery furnace heated seven times hotter; he has done his worst and now what have we to fear?' When persecution rages, it is wonderful what liberty it gives to the child of God. Remember Luther, Knox, Calvin, Wycliffe, Bradford, Latimer, and many others! Under God these men owed their liberty of speech and liberty of conscience to the fact that the world thrust them out from all hope of its favour, and so loosed their bonds.

FOR MEDITATION: Consider the increasing boldness of one man while being cast out for Christ's sake by the Pharisees (John 9:24–38). One plus God is always a majority.

SERMON NO. 662

The voice from heaven

'And they heard a great voice from heaven, saying unto them, Come up hither.' Revelation 11:12

SUGGESTED FURTHER READING: John 13:36–14:3

'Come up hither.' The Father seems to say this to every adopted child. We say, 'Our Father which art in heaven.' The Father's heart desires to have his children round his knee, and his love each day beckons us with a tender 'Come up hither.' Nor will your Father and my Father ever be content till every one of his children shall be in the many mansions above. And Jesus whispers this in your ear too. Hearken! Do you not hear him say, 'I will that they also, whom thou hast given me, be with me where I am; that they may behold my glory, which thou hast given me;'—'the glory which I had with thee before the world was.' Jesus beckons you to the skies, believer. Lay not fast hold upon the things of earth. He who is but a lodger in an inn must not live as though he were at home. Keep your tent ready for striking. Be ever prepared to draw up your anchor, and to sail across the sea and find the better port, for while Jesus beckons, here we have no continuing city. No true wife has rest save in the house of her husband. Where her consort is, there is her home, a home which draws her soul towards it every day. Jesus, I say, invites us to the skies. He cannot be completely content until he brings his body, the church, into the glory of its Head, and conducts his elect spouse to the marriage feast of her Lord. Besides the desires of the Father and the Son, all those who have gone before, seem to be leaning over the battlements of heaven, and calling, 'Courage, brothers! Eternal glory awaits you. Fight your way, stem the current, breast the wave, and come up hither. We without you cannot be made perfect: there is no perfect church in heaven till all the chosen saints be there; therefore come up hither.'

FOR MEDITATION: God calls us to himself on earth first (Matthew 11:28) and to heaven afterwards. Others have added their voices to that call (Revelation 22:17). Having come to Christ on earth, we should be calling him to come again from heaven (Revelation 22:20) to receive us, as his people, to himself (John 14:3).

SERMON NO. 488

28 NOVEMBER (UNDATED SERMON)

Christians kept in time and glorified in eternity

'*Now unto him that is able to keep you from falling, and to present you faultless before the presence of his glory with exceeding joy, to the only wise God our Saviour, be glory and majesty, dominion and power, both now and ever. Amen.*' Jude 24–25

SUGGESTED FURTHER READING: Psalm 56:1–13

Here and there is an enemy who is in ambush, who comes out when we least expect him, and labours to trip us up, or hurl us down a precipice. I suppose you never did see a man fall from a precipice. Some of you may have been fools enough to go and see a man walk on a rope, in which case, I believe, you have incurred the guilt of murder; because if the man does not kill himself, you encourage him to put himself where he probably might do so. But if you have ever really seen a man fall over a precipice, your hair must surely have stood on end, your flesh creeping on your bones, as you saw the poor human form falling off the edge, never to stand in mortal life again: surely as you left the place where you stood, and fled away from the edge of the precipice, you cried, 'O bless the God that made me stand, and kept my feet from falling.' How alarmed you would be, if you were in such a position and had seen one fall, and that same monster who had pushed him over, should come to hurl you over also, and especially if you felt that you were as weak as water, and could not resist the gigantic demon. Now, just such is your case; you cannot stand against Satan; even your own flesh will be able to get the mastery over your spirit. A little maid made Peter deny his Master, and a little maid may make the strongest among us tremble sometimes. Oh, if you are preserved in spite of such mighty enemies, who are ever waiting to destroy you, you shall have great cause to sing praise 'unto him that is able to keep you from falling.'

FOR MEDITATION: God has the ability to keep his people from falling (Romans 14:4), and exercises that ability (Psalm 116:8), but we are not to abuse that fact as an excuse for failing in our responsibilities to take all sensible precautions (1 Corinthians 10:12; Hebrews 4:11).

SERMON NO. 634

Paul—his cloak and his books

'The cloke that I left at Troas with Carpus, when thou comest, bring with thee, and the books, but especially the parchments.' 2 Timothy 4:13
SUGGESTED FURTHER READING: Ecclesiastes 12:9–12

A man who comes up into the pulpit, professes to take his text on the spot, and talks any quantity of nonsense, is the idol of many. If he will speak without premeditation, or pretend to do so, and never produce what they call a dish of dead men's brains—that is the preacher. How rebuked are they by the apostle! He is inspired, and yet he wants books. He has been preaching for at least thirty years, and yet he wants books! He had seen the Lord, and yet he wants books! He had had a wider experience than most men, and yet he wants books! He had been caught up into the third heaven, and had heard things which it was unlawful for a man to utter, yet he wants books! The apostle says to Timothy and so he says to every preacher, 'Give attendance to reading.' The man who never reads will never be read; he who never quotes will never be quoted. He who will not use the thoughts of other men's brains, proves that he has no brains of his own. Brethren, what is true of ministers is true of all our people. *You* need to read. Renounce as much as you will all light literature, but study as much as possible sound theological works, especially the Puritan writers, and expositions of the Bible. We are quite persuaded that the very best way for you to be spending your leisure, is to be either reading or praying. You may get much instruction from books which afterwards you may use as a true weapon in your Lord and Master's service. Paul cries, 'Bring the books'; join in the cry.

FOR MEDITATION: What Christian books are in your library? God's Word must come first (2 Timothy 3:16–17), but every Christian will benefit from having at least a concordance, commentaries, a cyclopaedia or Bible dictionary, a Christian theology and a church history. Remember that, unlike the inspired writers of Scripture, all authors make mistakes (James 3:1–2). If you borrow books from others, don't forget that there are biblical principles relating to borrowing (Exodus 22:14; 2 Kings 6:5; Psalm 37:21).

The royal rider in his glorious chariot

'Who is this that cometh out of the wilderness?' Song of Solomon 3:6
SUGGESTED FURTHER READING: Acts 17:16–23

'Who is this that cometh out of the wilderness?' The equipage excites the attention of the onlooker; his curiosity is raised, and he asks, 'Who is this?' Now, in the first progress of the Christian church, in her very earliest days, there were persons who marvelled greatly: and though they put down the wonders of the day of Pentecost to drunkenness, yet 'they were all amazed, and were in doubt, saying one to another, What meaneth this?' In after years many a heathen philosopher said, 'What is this new power which is breaking the idols in pieces, changing old customs, making even thrones unsafe? What is this?' By and by, in the age of the Reformation, there were hooded monks, cardinals in their red hats, and bishops, and princes, and emperors, who all said, 'What is this? What strange doctrine has come to light?' In the times of the modern reformation, a century ago, when God was pleased to revive his church through the instrumentality of Whitefield and his brethren, there were many who said, 'What is this new enthusiasm, this Methodism? Whence came it, and what power is this which it wields?' And, doubtless, whenever God shall be pleased to bring forth his church in power, and to make her mighty among the sons of men, the ignorance of men will be discovered breaking forth in wonder, for they will say, 'Who is this?' Spiritual religion is as much a novelty now as in the day when Greek sages scoffed at it on Mars' hill. The true church of God is a stranger and pilgrim still; an alien and a foreigner in every land; a speckled bird; a dove in the midst of ravens, a lily among thorns.

FOR MEDITATION: The church will not arouse any worthwhile curiosity unless it is preaching the Lord Jesus Christ as he really is. Pray that Christ will be preached in truth (Philippians 1:18) in these days, and that men and women will be caused to ask, as when he was on earth, 'Who is this?' (Matthew 21:10; Luke 5:21; 7:49; 9:9; 19:3).

It is finished

'When Jesus therefore had received the vinegar, he said, It is finished: and he bowed his head, and gave up the ghost.' John 19:30
SUGGESTED FURTHER READING: Revelation 14:6–13

When Christ said 'It is finished,' the words had effect on *heaven*. Before, the saints had been saved as it were on credit. They had entered heaven, God having faith in his Son Jesus. Had not Christ finished his work, surely they must have left their shining spheres, and suffered in their own persons for their own sins. I might represent heaven, if my imagination might be allowed a moment, as being ready to totter if Christ had not finished his work; its stones would have been unloosed; massive and stupendous though its bastions are, yet had they fallen as earthly cities reel under the throes of earthquakes. But Christ said, 'It is finished,' and oath, and covenant, and blood set fast the dwelling-place of the redeemed, made their mansions safely and eternally their own, and bade their feet stand immovably upon the rock. Moreover, that word 'It is finished!' took effect in the gloomy caverns and depths of *hell*. Then Satan bit his iron bands in rage, howling, 'I am defeated by the very man whom I thought to overcome; my hopes are blasted; never shall an elect one come into my prison house, never a blood-bought one be found in my abode.' Lost souls mourned that day, for they said, 'It is finished! and if Christ himself, the substitute, could not be permitted to go free till he had finished all his punishment, then we shall never be free.' It was their double death-knell, for they said, 'Alas for us! Justice, which would not allow the Saviour to escape, will never allow us to be at liberty. It is finished with him, and therefore it shall never be finished for us.'

FOR MEDITATION: Heaven and hell are the only places where it can be said 'It's started, so it will never finish' (Matthew 25:46; Luke 16:26). We, who are by nature God's enemies (Romans 5:10), can be delivered from the prison of hell only by the full payment of the penalty for our sins—either we accept now that Christ has fully paid that penalty, or we commit ourselves to the never-ending task of paying the penalty ourselves (Matthew 5:25–26).

SERMON NO. 421

The root that beareth wormwood

'Lest there should be among you a root that beareth gall and wormwood.'
Deuteronomy 29:18
SUGGESTED FURTHER READING: 2 Peter 2:4–9

Ask Noah, as he looks out of his ark, 'Does sin bring bitterness?' and he points to the floating carcases of innumerable thousands that died because of sin. Turn to Abraham: does sin bring bitterness? He points to the smoke of Sodom and Gomorrah that God destroyed because of their wickedness. Ask Moses, and he reminds you of Korah, Dathan and Abiram, who were swallowed up alive. Turn to Paul, and you do not find Paul speaking with the honeyed phrases of these modern deceivers, who would make people believe that sin will not be punished. 'He that despised Moses' law died without mercy under two or three witnesses: of how much sorer punishment, suppose ye, shall he be thought worthy, who hath trodden under foot the Son of God, and hath counted the blood of the covenant, wherewith he was sanctified, an unholy thing, and hath done despite unto the Spirit of grace?' Listen to James or Jude, or Peter, and you hear them speak of chains of darkness and flaming fire. Hear John as he writes of the wrath of God and of the winepress of it, out of which the blood flows up to the horse's bridles. Let the Saviour himself speak to you. He cries, 'These shall go away into everlasting punishment.' He is the author of those words, 'Where their worm dieth not, and the fire is not quenched.' It is he who speaks of the outer darkness, where there is weeping and wailing and gnashing of teeth. The Bible tells you (and O that you might hear it as God's own voice to you!), not that sin will end in pleasure and joy, but that the wrath of God will abide upon you if you do not turn from sin; that the soul that sinneth, it shall die; that God's curse is upon the wicked, and that everlasting punishment is the portion of the impenitent.

FOR MEDITATION: A life of pleasure and sin which has no room for the Lord Jesus Christ can be great fun in the short term, but it will all end in everlasting tears (Ecclesiastes 11:8–9; Luke 12:19–21; 16:19,25). The wise person takes eternity into account (Ecclesiastes 12:1; Hebrews 11:24–26).

SERMON NO. 723

Walking in the light and washed in the blood

'But if we walk in the light, as he is in the light, we have fellowship one with another, and the blood of Jesus Christ his Son cleanseth us from all sin.' 1 John 1:7

SUGGESTED FURTHER READING: John 12:20–36

Whereas there are some who urge you to look to your doctrinal intelligence as a ground of comfort, I beseech you beloved, look only to the blood; whereas there are others who would set up a standard of Christian experience and urge that this is to be the channel of your consolation, I pray you, while you prize both doctrine and experience, rest nowhere your soul's weight but in the precious blood. Some would lead you to high degrees of fellowship; follow them, but not when they would lead you away from the simple position of a sinner resting upon the blood. There be those who could teach you mysticism, and would have you rejoice in the light within; follow them as far as they have the warrant of God's Word, but never take your foot from that Rock of Ages, where the only safe standing can be found. Certain of my brethren are very fond of preaching Christ in his second advent—I rejoice wherein they preach the truth concerning Christ glorified, but my beloved, I entreat you to build your hope not on Christ glorified, nor on Christ to come, but on 'Christ crucified.' Remember that in the matter of taking away sin, the first thing is not the throne, but the cross, not the reigning Saviour, but the bleeding Saviour, not the King in his glory, but the Redeemer in his shame. Care not to be studying dates of prophecies if burdened with sin, but seek your chief, your best comfort in the blood of Jesus Christ which 'cleanseth us from all sin.' Here is the pole star of your salvation; sail by it and you shall reach the port of peace.

FOR MEDITATION: Blessings spring from our reliance on 'nothing but the blood of Jesus'—eternal life (John 6:53), propitiation (Romans 3:25), justification (Romans 5:9), redemption and forgiveness (Ephesians 1:7; Colossians 1:14), peace (Colossians 1:20), access (Hebrews 10:19), and cleansing (1 John 1:7; Revelation 1:5). Why look elsewhere?

SERMON NO. 663

Now

'For he saith, I have heard thee in a time accepted, and in the day of salvation have I succoured thee: behold, now is the acceptable time; behold, now is the day of salvation.' 2 Corinthians 6:2

SUGGESTED FURTHER READING: Matthew 7:13–14

When the express trains first began to run to Scotland, there was seen at the station one morning a gentleman tall and thin, whose cheek had the consumptive mark upon it. The porters asked him several questions about his luggage, and when he had been asked several times by different persons, another came up, and said, 'Where are you going, sir?' Being of short temper, and in great haste, he said, 'To hell!' A servant of Christ passed by that moment and heard the answer. He sought to get in the same carriage, and did so; and this gentleman was talking freely to others upon common topics, and the man thought, 'I will get a word in if I can.' So he joined in the conversation till they alighted at a refreshment station, when, taking the opportunity, he said to the gentleman, 'When do you expect to get to the end of your journey?' 'O,' said he, 'I am going to cross at such-and-such a town by the boat tonight, and hope to get to my journey's end about twelve o'clock tomorrow morning.' The man said, 'I think you misunderstand my question. You said when the porter asked you just now where you were going to, that you were going to a very different place.' 'O yes, I recollect I did,' said the gentleman, 'but I am sometimes very hasty.' The other said to him, 'Was it true? Are you going to hell? If so, when do you expect to get there?' And he began to talk to him about that sickness which he could see so certainly in his cheek, and warned him that unless he sought another road, and fled to Christ, the only refuge, he would certainly reach that dreadful end. There are some who, if they were labelled this morning as to where they are going, would have to be directed 'to hell.'

FOR MEDITATION: Where are you going? There is a way to death and destruction (Proverbs 14:12; Matthew 7:13). To continue on it, all you have to do is neglect or reject the only way to life, the Lord Jesus Christ (John 14:6).

The weeding of the garden

'But he answered and said, Every plant, which my heavenly Father hath not planted, shall be rooted up.' Matthew 15:13
SUGGESTED FURTHER READING: John 6:52–71

We have often a number of good and affectionate but very weak hearers. They are always afraid that we shall offend other hearers. Hence, if the truth be spoken in a plain and pointed manner, and seems to come close home to the conscience, they think that surely it ought not to have been spoken, because So-and-so took offence at it. Truly, my brethren, we are not slow to answer in this matter. If we never offended, it would be positive proof that we did not preach the gospel. They who can please men will find it quite another thing to have pleased God. Do you suppose that men will love those who faithfully rebuke them? If you make the sinner's heart to groan, and waken his conscience, do you think he will pay you court and thank you for it? Not so; in fact, this ought to be one aim of our ministry, not to offend, but to test men and make them offended with themselves, so that their hearts may be exposed to their own inspection. Their being offended will reveal of what sort they are. A ministry that never uproots will never water; a ministry that does not pull down will never build up. He who knows not how to pluck up the plants which God has not planted, scarcely knows how to be a worker of God in his vineyard. Our ministry ought always to be a killing as well as a healing one—a ministry which kills all false hopes, blights all wrong confidences, and weeds out all foolish trusts, while at the same time it trains up the feeblest shoot of real hope, and tends comfort and encouragement even to the weakest of the sincere followers of Christ.

FOR MEDITATION: Over the past few days the readings have concentrated on serious matters of eternal life and death. Have they offended you? While the Christian should avoid giving unnecessary offence (Matthew 17:27; 1 Corinthians 10:32), the Lord Jesus Christ offended others when it was necessary (Matthew 13:57; 15:10; John 6:61). Christians have no reason to feel ashamed, if others take offence at Christ (1 Peter 2:8) and his cross (Galatians 5:11).

SERMON NO. 423

Once a curse but now a blessing

'And it shall come to pass, that as ye were a curse among the heathen, O house of Judah, and house of Israel; so will I save you, and ye shall be a blessing: fear not, but let your hands be strong.' Zechariah 8:13
SUGGESTED FURTHER READING: Romans 11:13–24

In the dark ages, to be a Jew was to be deserving of all scorn and cruelty, and of no pity or consideration. To what exactions, to what fines, to what imprisonments and tortures, have not the sons of Jacob been subjected by the professed followers of the Messiah? It is perhaps the greatest of all modern miracles, that there should be one Jew upon earth who is a Christian, for the treatment they have received from pretended Christians has been enough to make them hate the name of Jesus; it has not been simply villainous, but diabolical. Devils in hell could not be more cruel to their victims than professed Christians have been to the sons of Abraham. They have been a curse indeed. Among all nations they have been a hissing and a byword. But the day is coming, and is dawning already, when the whole world shall discern the true dignity of the chosen seed, and shall seek their company, because the Lord has blessed them. In that day when Israel shall look upon him whom they have pierced, and shall mourn for their sins, the Jew shall take his true rank among the nations as an elder brother and a prince. The covenant made with Abraham, to bless all nations by his seed, is not revoked; heaven and earth shall pass away, but the chosen nation shall not be blotted out from the book of remembrance. The Lord has not cast away his people; he has never given their mother a bill of divorcement; he has never put them away; in a little wrath he has hidden his face from them, but with great mercies will he gather them.

FOR MEDITATION: We should thank God for the Jews; through them he gave us his Word (Romans 3:2; 9:4) and his Son (Romans 9:5); he still has blessings to give to the world through them (Romans 11:12). If you blame them for Christ's death, remember that he died for sinners, and that you, as a sinner, were also responsible.

SERMON NO. 543

Life and walk of faith

'As ye have therefore received Christ Jesus the Lord, so walk ye in him.'
Colossians 2:6
SUGGESTED FURTHER READING: 1 John 2:3–11

There are many Christians whose lives really are not consistent. I cannot understand this if they are walking in Christ; in fact, if a man could completely walk in Christ he would walk in perfect holiness. We hear an instance, perhaps, of a little shopkeeper who puffs and exaggerates as other shopkeepers do; he does not exactly tell a lie, but something very near it. Now I want to know whether that man was walking in Christ when he did that. If he had said to himself, 'Now I am in Christ,' do you think he would have done it? We hear of another who is constantly impatient, always troubled, fretting, mournful. I want to know whether that man is really walking in Christ as he walked at first, when he is doubting the goodness, the providence, the tenderness of God. Surely he is not. I have heard of hard-hearted professors who take a Christian brother by the throat with, 'Pay me that thou owest.' Do you think they are walking in Christ when they do that? We hear of others who, when their brothers have need, shut up the bowels of their compassion and are mean and stingy; are they walking in Christ when they do that? Why, if a man walks in Christ, then he acts as Christ would act; for Christ being in him, his hope, his love, his joy, his life, he is the reflex of the image of Christ; he is the glass into which Christ looks; and then the image of Christ is reflected, and men say of that man, 'He is like his Master; he lives in Christ.' O dear brethren, if we live now as we did the first day we came to Christ, we should live very differently from what we do.

FOR MEDITATION: Christ gave us a perfect example—in service (Mark 10:43–45; John 13:14–15), in kindness, forgiveness and love (Ephesians 4:32–5:2), and in suffering (1 Peter 2:21–23). Could you honestly encourage other Christians to imitate you, as you imitate Christ (1 Corinthians 11:1)?

The peacemaker—a sermon for the times

'Blessed are the peacemakers: for they shall be called the children of God.'
Matthew 5:9
SUGGESTED FURTHER READING: Romans 12:14–21

This is the seventh of the beatitudes. There is a mystery always connected with the number seven. It was the number of perfection among the Hebrews, and it seems as if the Saviour had put the peacemaker there, as if he was nearly approaching to the perfect man in Christ Jesus. He who would have perfect blessedness, so far as it can be enjoyed on earth, must labour to attain to this seventh benediction, and become a peacemaker. The preceding verse speaks of the blessedness of 'the pure in heart: for they shall see God.' It is well that we should understand this. We are to be 'first pure, then peaceable.' Our peaceableness is never to be a compact with sin, or an alliance with that which is evil. That being in our souls a settled matter, we can go on to peaceableness towards men. Not less does the verse that follows my text seem to have been put there on purpose. However peaceable we may be in this world, yet we shall be misrepresented and misunderstood; and no marvel, for even the Prince of Peace, by his very peacefulness, brought fire upon the earth. He himself, though he loved mankind, and did no ill, was 'despised and rejected of men; a man of sorrows, and acquainted with grief.' Lest, therefore, the peaceable in heart should be surprised when they meet with enemies, it is added in the following verse, 'Blessed are they which are persecuted for righteousness' sake: for their's is the kingdom of heaven.' Thus the peacemakers are not only pronounced to be blessed, but they are compassed about with blessings. Lord, give us grace to climb to this seventh beatitude!

FOR MEDITATION: Are you a peacemaker or a troublemaker (James 3:16–18)? While peacemaking doesn't depend entirely on the individual Christian (Romans 12:18), we should all make the effort (Romans 14:19).

N.B. This sermon's subtitle related to the recently commenced American Civil War (1861–5) amongst other conflicts.

SERMON NO. 422

His name—the everlasting Father

'The everlasting Father.' Isaiah 9:6
SUGGESTED FURTHER READING: John 10:30–38

God is called the Father of the fatherless, and Job says of himself that he became a father to the poor. You know what it means, of course, at once; it means that he exercised a father's part. Now, albeit that the Spirit of adoption teaches us to call God our Father, yet it is not straining truth to say that our Lord Jesus Christ exercises to all his people a Father's part. According to the old Jewish custom the elder brother was the father of the family in the absence of the father; the firstborn took precedence of all, and took upon himself the father's position; so the Lord Jesus, the firstborn among many brethren, exercises to us a Father's office. Is it not so? Has he not succoured us in all time of our need as a father succours his child? Does he not daily protect us? Did he not yield up his life that we his little ones might be preserved? Will he not say at the last, 'Behold I and the children which God hath given me;' 'those that thou gavest me I have kept, and none of them is lost'? Does he not chastise us by hiding himself from us, as a father chastens his children? Do we not find him instructing us by his Spirit and leading us into all truth? Has he not told us to call no man father upon earth in the sense that he is to be our true guide and instructor, but to sit at his feet and make him our authoritative Teacher? Is he not the head in the household to us on earth, abiding with us, and has he not said, 'I will not leave you comfortless' (the Greek word is 'orphans'): 'I will come to you,' as if his coming was the coming of a father?

FOR MEDITATION: Think on Christ's fatherly words to his 'children' (Mark 10:24; John 13:33; 14:18; 21:5). If he is fatherlike towards us, we should be childlike (not childish) towards him (Matthew 18:1–4).

N.B. Spurgeon had preached on the previous three titles of Christ to be found in Isaiah 9:6 at the Royal Surrey Gardens Music Hall in 1858–9 (see New Park Street Pulpit nos. 214, 215, 258—all represented in the previous volume of daily readings *365 days with Spurgeon*).

SERMON NO. 724

Early and late

'The kingdom of heaven is like unto a man ... which went out early in the morning to hire labourers ... And he went out about the third hour, and saw others standing idle ... Again he went out, about the sixth and ninth hour, and did likewise. And about the eleventh hour he went out, and found others standing idle.' Matthew 20:1,3,5–6

SUGGESTED FURTHER READING: 2 Chronicles 33:1–13; 34:1–3

Some of us in time and in eternity will have to utter a special song of thankfulness to the love which took us in our days of folly and simplicity, and conducted us into the family of God. Look at the grace which calls man at the age of *twenty*, when the passions are hot, when there is strong temptation to plunge into the vices and the so-called pleasures of life. To be delivered from the charms of sin, when the world's cheek is ruddy, when it wears its best attire, and to be taught to prefer the reproach of Christ to all the riches of Egypt, this is mighty grace for which God shall have our sweetest song. To be called of the Lord at *forty*, in the prime of life, is a wonderful instance of divine power, for worldliness is hard to overcome, and worldliness is the sin of middle age. With a family about you, with much business, with the world eating into you as does a canker, it is a wonder that God should in his mercy have visited you then, and made you a regenerate soul. You are a miracle of grace, and you will have to feel it and to praise God for it in time and eternity. *Sixty* again. 'Can the Ethiopian change his skin, or the leopard his spots? then may ye also do good, that are accustomed to do evil.' And yet you have learned; you have had a blessed schoolmaster who sweetly taught you, and you have learned to do well. Though your vessel had begun to rot in the waters of the Black Sea of sin, you have got a new owner, and you will run up a new flag, and you will sail round the Cape of Good Hope to the Islands of the Blessed, in the Land of the Hereafter. But what shall I say of you that are called when you are *aged?* You will have to love much, for you have had much forgiven.

FOR MEDITATION: Best to come to Christ early (Ecclesiastes 12:1), but better late than never (Luke 23:39–43).

The man with the measuring line

'I...looked, and behold a man with a measuring line in his hand. Then said I, Whither goest thou? And he said unto me, To measure Jerusalem, to see what is the breadth thereof, and what is the length thereof. ' Zechariah 2:1–2
SUGGESTED FURTHER READING: Mark 9:38–41

You know, brethren, that there is no soul living who holds more firmly to the doctrines of grace than I do, and if any man asks me whether I am ashamed to be called a Calvinist, I answer, I wish to be called nothing but a Christian; but if you ask me, do I hold the doctrinal views which were held by John Calvin, I reply, I do in the main hold them, and rejoice to admit it. But, my dear friends, far be it from me even to imagine that Zion contains none within her walls but Calvinistic Christians, or that there are none saved who do not hold our views. Most atrocious things have been spoken about the character and spiritual condition of John Wesley, the modern prince of Arminians. I can only say concerning him, that, while I detest many of the doctrines which he preached, yet for the man himself I have a reverence second to no Wesleyan; and if there were wanted two apostles to be added to the number of the twelve, I do not believe that there could be found two men more fit to be so added than George Whitefield and John Wesley. The character of John Wesley stands beyond all imputation for self-sacrifice, zeal, holiness, and communion with God; he lived far above the ordinary level of common Christians, and was one of whom the world was not worthy. I believe there are multitudes of men who cannot see these truths, who nevertheless have received Christ into their hearts, and are as dear to the heart of the God of grace as the soundest Calvinist out of heaven. I thank God we do not believe in the measuring line of any form of bigotry.

FOR MEDITATION: Christ said 'He that is not with me is against me' (Luke 11:23); separation from such is commanded (2 John 7–11). But Christ also said 'He that is not against us is for us' (Luke 9:50); schism from such is condemned (3 John 9–10).

Too good to be true

'They yet believed not for joy.' Luke 24:41
SUGGESTED FURTHER READING: 2 Corinthians 4:1–6

If you should see tomorrow a heavy shower of rain, you would not believe, I suppose, that it was made with a watering-can; and if you saw the Thames swollen to its banks from a great flood, you would not believe that the London waterworks had filled it to the brim. 'No,' say you, 'this is God at work in nature. The greatness of the work proves that God is here.' If you were ever in Cambridge, you might have seen a little mountain which is so small nobody knows how it was made. Some say it is artificial; some say it is natural. Now, I have never heard any dispute about the Alps; nobody ever said that they were artificial. I never heard of any disputation about the Himalayas; no one ever conjectured that human hands piled them up to the skies and clothed them with their hoary snows. So, when I read of the mercies of God in Christ, reaching up like mountains to heaven, I am sure they must be divine. I am certain the revelation must come from God; it must be true; it is self-evidential. I might enlarge this argument by showing that God's works in creation are very great, and therefore it would be idle to think that there would be no great works in grace. Two works which have been made by the same artist always have some characteristics which enable you to see that the same artist made them. In like manner, to us there is one God; creation and redemption have but one author; the same eternal power and Godhead are legibly inscribed on both. Now when I look at the sea, and hear it roaring in the fulness thereof, I see a great artist there. And when my soul surveys the ocean of grace, and listens to the echoes of its motion as the sound of many waters, I see the same Almighty artist. When I see a great sinner saved, then I think I see the same Master-hand which first formed man.

FOR MEDITATION: The wonderful works of the one and only God (Isaiah 44:6–8), both in creation (Isaiah 45:5–7) and in salvation (Isaiah 43:10–11; 45:21–22) are fully evident. Have you experienced the second as well as the first?

SERMON NO. 425

Lessons from Lydia's conversion

'And a certain woman named Lydia, a seller of purple, of the city of Thyatira, which worshipped God, heard us; whose heart the Lord opened, that she attended unto the things which were spoken of Paul.' Acts 16:14
SUGGESTED FURTHER READING: Acts 2:37–47

All who believe shall be saved, but still for our part, when we see baptism put in so close connection with believing, we would not be disobedient to our Master's command. We think it to be a sweet sign of a humble and broken heart, when the child of God is willing to obey a command which is not essential to his salvation and which is not forced upon him by a selfish fear of damnation: we say it is no mean sign of grace, when, as a simple act of obedience and of communion with his Master in his burial to the world and resurrection to a new life, the young convert yields himself to be baptised. Lydia was baptised, but her good works did not end at the water; she then would have the apostles come to her house. She will bear the shame of being thought to be a follower of the crucified Jew, a friend of the despised Jewish apostle, the renegade, the turncoat; she will have him in her house; and though he says 'No,' out of his bashfulness to receive anything, yet she constrains him, for love is in her heart, and she has a generous spirit; and while she has a crust it shall be broken with the man who brought her to Christ; she will give not only the cup of cold water in the prophet's name, but her house shall shelter him. Brethren, I do not think much of a conversion where it does not touch a man's substance; and those people who pretend to be Christ's people, and yet live only for themselves, and do nothing for him or for his church, give but sorry evidence of having been born again. A love to the people of God has ever been a distinguishing mark of the true convert. Look, then, at Lydia.

FOR MEDITATION: Baptism is a once-for-all command; hospitality to one another (Romans 12:13; 1 Peter 4:9) and to strangers (Hebrews 13:2; 3 John 5–8) is the Christian's ongoing responsibility, especially in leadership (1 Timothy 3:2; Titus 1:8). Lydia didn't need telling to be hospitable (Acts 16:15).

SERMON NO. 544

The LORD—the Liberator

'The LORD looseth the prisoners.' Psalm 146:7
SUGGESTED FURTHER READING: Psalm 107:10–16

When preaching last Tuesday in Dover, the mayor of the town very courteously lent the ancient town hall for the service, and in passing along to reach a private entrance, I noticed a large number of grated windows upon a lower level than the great hall. These belonged to the prison cells where persons committed for offences within the jurisdiction of the borough were confined. It at once struck me as a singular combination, that we should be preaching the gospel of liberty in the upper chamber, while there were prisoners of the law beneath us. Perhaps when we sang praises to God, the prisoners, like those who were in the same jail with Paul and Silas, heard us; but the free word above did not give them liberty, nor did the voice of song loose their bonds. Alas! what a picture is this of many in our congregations. We preach liberty to the captives; we proclaim the acceptable year of the Lord; but how many remain year after year in the bondage of Satan, slaves to sin. We send up our notes of praise right joyously to our Father who is in heaven, but our praises cannot give them joy, for alas! their hearts are unused to gratitude. Some of them are mourning on account of unpardoned sin, and others are deploring their blighted hopes, for they have looked for comfort where it is never to be found. Let us breathe a prayer this morning, 'Lord, break the fetters, and set free the captives. Glorify thyself this morning by proving thyself to be Jehovah, who 'looseth the prisoners'.'

FOR MEDITATION: Dover Old Town Gaol is now a prison museum. Spurgeon's allegorical guided tour of Victorian and earlier prisons included the common prison (sin), the solitary cell (penitence), the silent cell (prayerlessness), the cell of ignorance (unbelief), the ball and chain (habit), the hard labour room (self-righteousness), the low dungeon (despondency), the inner prison (despair), the torture chamber (Satanic temptation) and the condemned cell (self-condemnation). Are you in spiritual prison? Christ was sent to set the prisoners free (Isaiah 42:7; 61:1; Luke 4:18; John 8:36), but nothing can be done for those who choose to stay in prison.

SERMON NO. 484

The true apostolical succession

'Instead of thy fathers shall be thy children, whom thou mayest make princes in all the earth.' Psalm 45:16
SUGGESTED FURTHER READING: 2 Kings 2:1–15

The fathers must depart. We will not dwell on that, lest we indulge in dreary apprehensions as to our church's future, though that would be folly and sin, for in looking back on the past, we have seen such a marvellous succession in the ministry, and also in all the offices of the church, that we cannot but thank God that he does walk still among the golden candlesticks and trim the lamps! But let us turn to the pleasing reflection, 'Instead of thy fathers shall be thy children.' When the fathers die, God shall find other men who, trained while their fathers yet lived, shall be ready and ripe to take their places. Very often we hear the question, 'If such-and-such a minister should die, who could occupy his pulpit? What would be the use of such-and-such a building, if So-and-so were taken to his rest?' Ah! you know not what you ask, nor what you say—'Instead of thy fathers shall be thy children.' Men of faith are followed by men of faith. They who trust God, when they die, shall be succeeded by others who shall walk in the same divine life, and shall see the same promises fulfilled. The love which burned in the heart of one, when quenched there by death, shall burn in the breast of another; the hope that gleamed from one joyous eye, shall soon gleam from the eyes of another whom God has raised up to be his successor. The work shall not stop for want of a workman; supplication shall not cease for want of righteous men to pray; the offering of praise shall not be stayed from the absence of grateful hearts to offer joyous songs. God shall be pleased to raise up one after another, as he said to Joshua, 'Moses my servant is dead; now therefore arise, go over this Jordan, thou, and all this people.'

FOR MEDITATION: It is God's right to appoint successors to his servants (Numbers 27:18–20), but they still need training (Deuteronomy 1:38; 3:28; 31:7–8). The trainee soon becomes the trainer (2 Timothy 2:1–2).

A message from God to his church and people

'O LORD, I have heard thy speech, and was afraid: O LORD, revive thy work in the midst of the years, in the midst of the years make known; in wrath remember mercy.' Habakkuk 3:2
SUGGESTED FURTHER READING: Psalm 85:1–13

O God, have mercy upon thy poor church, and visit her, and revive her. She has but a little strength; she has desired to keep thy word; refresh her; restore to her thy power, and give her yet to be great in this land. Mercy is also wanted for the land itself. This is a wicked nation, this England; its wickedness belongs to all classes. Sin runs down our streets; we have a fringe of elegant morality, but behind it we have a mass of rottenness. There is not only the immorality of the streets at night, but look at the dishonesty of business men in high places. Cheating and thieving upon the grandest scale are winked at. Little thieves are punished, and great thieves are untouched. This is a wicked city, this city of London, and the land is full of drunkenness, fornication, theft, and popish idolatry. I am not the proper prophet to take up this burden; my temperament is not that of Jeremiah; but I may at least, with Habakkuk, having heard the Lord's speech concerning it, be afraid, and exhort you to pray for this land, and be asking that God would revive his work, in order that this drunkenness may be given up, that this dishonesty may be purged out, that this great social evil may be cut out from the body politic, as a deadly cancer is cut out by the surgeon's knife. O God, for mercy's sake, cast not off this island of the seas, give her not up to internal distraction, leave her not in darkness and blackness for ever, but 'revive thy work in the midst of the years, in the midst of the years make known; in wrath remember mercy.'

FOR MEDITATION: Despite the 1859 revival, the late nineteenth century in Britain was clearly not 'the good old days'; the early twenty first century is certainly 'the bad new days.' Sin is still a reproach to any people (Proverbs 14:34). Pray that God will revive us again, that his people may rejoice in him (Psalm 85:6) and that righteousness may again exalt a nation (Proverbs 14:34).

SERMON NO. 725

Open house for all comers

'This man receiveth sinners, and eateth with them.' Luke 15:2
SUGGESTED FURTHER READING: John 15:8–17

'This man receiveth sinners.' Whatever other men may do, this man, this one, this one alone if no other with him, this one beyond all other teachers, however gentle and compassionate—'this man receiveth sinners.' He will speak and tell out his mysteries too, even when sinful ears are listening, for he receives sinners *as disciples,* as well as his hearers. If they come casually into the throng, his eye glances upon them, and he has a word of gentle rebuke, and wooing love; but if they will come and join the class who cluster constantly about him, they shall be thoroughly welcome, and the deeper and higher truths reserved for disciples shall be revealed to them, and they shall know the mystery of the kingdom. When he has cleansed sinners, he receives them not only as disciples, but *as companions.* This man permits the guilty, the once profane, the lately debauched, and formerly dissolute, to associate themselves with him, to wear his name, to sit in his house, to be written in the same book of life as himself. He makes them here partakers with him in his affliction, and hereafter they shall be partakers with him in his glory. This man receives pardoned sinners into companionship. More, he receives them *as friends.* The head that leaned upon him was a sinner's head, and those who sat at the table with him, to whom he said, 'Henceforth I call you not servants; ... I have called you friends,' were all of them sinners, as they felt themselves to be. She who bore him, she who ministered to him of her substance, she who washed his feet with tears, she who was first at his empty sepulchre, all these were sinners, and some of them sinners emphatically. Into his heart's love he receives sinners.

FOR MEDITATION: The humility of the Lord Jesus Christ in receiving sinners is in stark contrast to the pride of sinners who refuse to receive him, the sinless Lord of glory (Luke 9:53; John 1:11). What a difference mutual receiving makes (John 1:12).

SERMON NO. 665

Good works in good company

'Come, my beloved, let us go forth into the field; let us lodge in the villages. Let us get up early to the vineyards; let us see if the vine flourish, whether the tender grape appear, and the pomegranates bud forth: there will I give thee my loves.' Song of Solomon 7:11–12
SUGGESTED FURTHER READING: Luke 10:38–42

Some persons imagine that one cannot serve Christ actively and yet have fellowship with him. I think they are very much mistaken. I confess it is very easy to get into Martha's position, and to be cumbered with much serving; you may have to preach here and there so many times a week, to attend committees, to visit sick people, and to do so many other things, that you may really, unless you are careful, fritter away your own inward life in outward exercises. I do not think, however, that there is any reason why this should be the case except through our own folly. Certain is it that a person may do nothing at all, and yet grow quite lifeless in spiritual things. Mary was not praised for sitting still; no, but for sitting still at Jesus' feet. And so, Christians are not to be praised, if they neglect duties, merely because they live in retirement, and keep much at home: it is not sitting, I say, but sitting at Jesus' feet. Had Martha been sitting still, or had Mary been sitting anywhere else, I doubt not that the Master would have given a word of rebuke: he would never had said that mere sitting still was choosing the good part. Indeed, I know some of you who are none the better for doing nothing, but a great deal the worse; for those who do nothing grow sour, and are always willing to find fault with the way in which others serve Christ. Do not think, therefore, that mere activity is in itself an evil: I believe it is a blessing. Taking a survey of Christ's church, you will find that those who have most fellowship with Christ, are not the persons who are recluses or hermits, who have much time to spend with themselves, but they are the useful indefatigable labourers who are toiling for Jesus.

FOR MEDITATION: Devotion to God and his Word is not an alternative to Christian service. Devotion should lead to action; action should spring from devotion (Joshua 1:8; Daniel 11:32; 2 Timothy 3:16–17).

The royal death bed

'Shall there be evil in a city, and the Lord hath not done it?' Amos 3:6
SUGGESTED FURTHER READING: 1 Samuel 5:6–6:9

There are still some found foolish enough to believe that events happen without divine predestination, and that different calamities transpire without the overruling hand, or the direct agency of God. What would we be, brethren, if chance had done it? We should be like poor mariners, at sea in an unsafe vessel, without a chart or a helm; we should know nothing of the port to which we might ultimately come; we should only feel that we were now the sport of the winds, the captives of the tempest, and might soon be the victims of the deep. Alas! poor orphans would we all be, if we were left to chance. No Father's care to watch over us, but left to the fickleness and fallibility of mortal things! What would all that we see about us be, but a great sandstorm in the midst of a desert, blinding our eyes, preventing us from ever hoping to see the end through the darkness of the beginning. We would be travellers in a pathless waste, where there would be no roads to direct us, travellers who might be overwhelmed at any moment, and our bleached bones left the victims of the tempest, unknown, or forgotten of all. Thank God, it is not so with us. Chance exists only in the hearts of fools; we believe that everything which happens to us is ordered by the wise and tender will of him who is our Father and our Friend; and we see order in the midst of confusion; we see purposes accomplished where others discern fruitless wastes; we believe that, 'the Lord hath his way in the whirlwind and in the storm, and the clouds are the dust of his feet.'

FOR MEDITATION: God is never the author of sin, but he himself claims responsibility not only for pleasant things which we welcome, but also for unpleasant events which we may call 'evil' (Isaiah 45:7). The English language even calls them 'acts of God' rather than 'acts of chance'.

N.B. This was a memorial sermon for Albert, the Prince Consort, who died on 14 December 1861.

The holy child, Jesus

'That signs and wonders may be done by the name of thy holy child, Jesus.' Acts 4:30

SUGGESTED FURTHER READING: Luke 2:1–20

Let us marvel at his condescension. It is the greatest miracle that was ever heard or read of, that 'the Word was made flesh, and dwelt among us.' That God should make a creature out of nothing is certainly a marvellous manifestation of power, but that God should enter into that creature, and should take it into intimate union with his own nature—this is the strangest of all acts of condescending love. Indeed, so marvellous is it, that in all the heathen mythologies—strange freaks though imagination has there played—though we do find instances of 'gods' appearing in the likeness of men, yet never do we find anything like the mystical union of the two natures in the person of Christ. Human wisdom in its most happy moments has never risen to anything like the thought of deity espousing manhood, that man might be redeemed. To you and to me the marvel lies in the motive which prompted the incarnation. What unrivalled, indescribable, unutterable love was this that made Christ leave his Father's glory, that he might be made a man like ourselves, to suffer, to bleed, to die? He was 'seen of angels,' says the apostle, and this was a great wonder, for the angels had worshipped at his throne, but their created eyes could not bear to look upon the brightness of his person. They veiled their faces with their wings when they cried 'Holy! Holy! Holy!' But angels saw the Son of God lying in a manger! The Lord of all wrestling with a fallen spirit in the wilderness! The Prince of Peace hanging upon the tree on Calvary!

FOR MEDITATION: Consider the wonder of Jesus Christ 'in carne' (in the flesh):—'Incomprehensibly made man' (Wesley). In his flesh deity was seen (John 1:14), death was suffered (Romans 8:3; 1 Peter 2:24; 4:1) and deliverance was secured for believing sinners (Colossians 1:21–22; Hebrews 2:14–15; 1 Peter 3:18).

SERMON NO. 545

No room for Christ in the inn

'And she brought forth her firstborn son, and wrapped him in swaddling clothes, and laid him in a manger; because there was no room for them in the inn.' Luke 2:7
SUGGESTED FURTHER READING: 1 Peter 4:1-5

If you have room for Christ, then from this day forth remember the world has no room for you; for the text says not only that there was no room for him, but look—'There was no room for them,' no room for Joseph, nor for Mary, any more than for the babe. Who are his father, and mother, and sister, and brother, but those that receive his word and keep it? So, as there was no room for the blessed virgin, nor for the reputed father, remember henceforth there is no room in this world for any true follower of Christ. There is no room for you to take your ease; no, you are to be a soldier of the cross, and you will find no ease in all your life-warfare. There is no room for you to sit down contented with your own attainments, for you are a traveller, and you are to forget the things that are behind, and press forward to that which is before; no room for you to hide your treasure in, for here the moth and rust corrupt; no room for you to put your confidence, for 'Cursed be the man that trusteth in man, and maketh flesh his arm.' From this day there will be no room for you in the world's good opinion; they will count you to be an offscouring; no room for you in the world's polite society; you must go outside the camp, bearing his reproach. From this time forth, I say, if you have room for Christ, the world will hardly find room of sufferance for you; you must expect now to be laughed at; now you must wear the fool's cap in men's esteem; and your song must be at the very beginning of your pilgrimage—'Thou from hence my all shall be'. There is no room for you in the worldling's love.

FOR MEDITATION: Do you find that you are the odd one out even at Christmas? So was the Lord Jesus Christ—'He came unto his own, and his own received him not' (John 1:11). Since sin entered the world, God's people have always been out of place in it (Hebrews 11:13,38).

SERMON NO. 485

The two advents of Christ

'And as it is appointed unto men once to die, but after this the judgment:
So Christ was once offered to bear the sins of many; and unto them that
look for him shall he appear the second time without sin unto salvation.'
Hebrews 9:27–28
SUGGESTED FURTHER READING: Philippians 2:5–11

In the prophecy of his coming the first and the second time there was disparity as well as correspondence. It is true in both cases he will come attended by angels, and the song shall be, 'Glory to God in the highest, And on earth peace, good will toward men.' It is true in both cases, shepherds who keep watch over their flocks even by night shall be among the first to hail him with their sleepless eyes—blessed shepherds who watch Christ's folds and therefore shall see the Great Shepherd when he comes. Still, how different, I say, will be his coming. At first he came an infant; now he shall come—'In rainbow-wreath and clouds of storm', the glorious One. Then he entered into a manger, now he shall ascend his throne. Then he appeared the infant, now the infinite. Then he was born to trouble as the sparks fly upward, now he comes to glory as the lightning from one end of heaven to the other. A stable received him then; now the high arches of earth and heaven shall be too little for him. Horned oxen were then his companions, but now the chariots of God which are twenty thousand, even thousands of angels, shall be at his right hand. Then in poverty his parents were glad to receive the offerings of gold and frankincense and myrrh; but now in splendour, King of kings, and Lord of lords, all nations shall bow before him, and kings and princes shall pay homage at his feet. Still he shall need nothing at their hands.

FOR MEDITATION: At his first coming the Lord Jesus Christ 'descended first into the lower parts of the earth' and finished by 'ascending up far above all heavens' (Ephesians 4:9–10). No one has ever descended lower; no one can ever ascend higher. His heavenly glory was interrupted by his first coming, but will be extended and acknowledged throughout the new creation at his second coming (Philippians 2:7–11).

God incarnate, the end of fear

'And the angel said unto them, Fear not.' Luke 2:10
SUGGESTED FURTHER READING: Isaiah 9:2–7

Observe the angel's word, 'Unto you is *born*.' Our Lord Jesus Christ is in some senses more man than Adam. Adam was not born; Adam never had to struggle through the risks and weaknesses of infancy; he knew not the littleness of childhood; he was full grown at once. Father Adam could not sympathise with me as a babe and a child. But how man-like is Jesus! He is cradled with us in the manger; he does not begin with us in mid-life, as Adam, but he accompanies us in the pains and feebleness and infirmities of infancy, and he continues with us even to the grave. Beloved, this is such sweet comfort. He that is God this day was once an infant: so that if my cares are little and even trivial and comparatively infantile, I may go to him, for he was once a child. Though the great ones of the earth may sneer at the child of poverty, and say, 'You are too mean, and your trouble is too slight for pity,' I recollect with humble joy, that the King of heaven did hang upon a woman's breast, and was wrapped in swaddling bands, and therefore I tell him all my griefs. How wonderful that he should have been an infant, and yet should be God over all, blessed for ever! I am not afraid of God now; this blessed link between me and God, the holy child Jesus, has taken all fear away. Observe, the angel told them somewhat of his office, as well as of his birth. 'Unto you is born this day *a Saviour*.' The very object for which he was born and came into this world was that he might deliver us from sin. What was it that made us afraid? Were we not afraid of God because we felt that we were lost through sin? Well then, here is joy upon joy.

FOR MEDITATION: Adam was created, but never born; he identifies with us only as a creature and a sinner (Romans 5:12). Christ, the second Adam (Romans 5:14), was never created, but his birth was an important part of his identification with us, so that believers could be identified with him as sons of God (Galatians 4:4–5).

Holy work for Christmas

'And when they had seen it, they made known abroad the saying which was told them concerning this child. And all they that heard it wondered at those things which were told them by the shepherds. But Mary kept all these things, and pondered them in her heart. And the shepherds returned, glorifying and praising God for all the things that they had heard and seen, as it was told unto them.' Luke 2:17–20
SUGGESTED FURTHER READING: Luke 4:14–22

Begin with the eighteenth verse—*wondering!* Wondering that you are spared, wondering that you are not in hell, wondering that his good Spirit still strives with the chief of sinners. Wonder that this morning the gospel should have a word for you after all your rejections of it and sins against God. I should like you to begin there, because then I should have good hope that you would go on to the next verse and change the first letter, and so go from wondering to *pondering.* Oh sinner, I wish you would ponder the doctrines of the cross. Think of your sin, God's wrath, judgment, hell, your Saviour's blood, God's love, forgiveness, acceptance, heaven—think on these things. Go from wondering to pondering. And then I would to God you could go on to the next verse, from pondering to *glorifying.* Take Christ, look to him, trust him. Then sing 'I am forgiven,' and go your way a believing sinner, and therefore a sinner saved, washed in the blood, and clean. Then go back after that to the seventeenth verse and begin to *tell to others.* But as for you Christians who are saved, I want you to begin this very afternoon at the seventeenth and tell of your Saviour. Then when the day is over, get up to your chambers and wonder, admire and adore; go on tonight, tomorrow, and all the days of your life, glorifying and praising God for all the things that you have seen and heard.

FOR MEDITATION: Wondering, pondering, glorifying and telling are admirable things to do on Christmas Eve as we prepare to celebrate Christ's first coming; they are also appropriate ways in which to prepare for his second coming (1 Corinthians 15:51–58).

SERMON NO. 666

Mary's song

'And Mary said, My soul doth magnify the Lord, and my spirit hath rejoiced in God my Saviour.' Luke 1:46–47
SUGGESTED FURTHER READING: Matthew 2:1–12

When we meet with our kinsfolk and acquaintances, let it be our prayer to God that our communion may be not only pleasant, but profitable; that we may not merely pass away time and spend a pleasant hour, but may advance a day's march nearer heaven, and acquire greater fitness for our eternal rest. Observe the sacred joy of Mary that you may imitate it. This is a season when all men expect us to be joyous. We compliment each other with the desire that we may have a 'Merry Christmas.' Some Christians who are a little squeamish, do not like the word 'merry.' It is a right good old Saxon word, having the joy of childhood and the mirth of manhood in it; it brings before one's mind the old song of the waits, and the midnight peal of bells, the holly and the blazing log. This is the season when we are expected to be happy; and my heart's desire is, that in the highest and best sense, you who are believers may be 'merry'. Mary's heart was merry within her; but here was the mark of her joy, it was all holy merriment, it was every drop of it sacred mirth. It was not such merriment as worldlings will revel in today and tomorrow, but such merriment as the angels have around the throne, where they sing, 'Glory to God in the highest,' while we sing 'On earth peace, good will toward men.' Such merry hearts have a continual feast. I want you, children of the bride-chamber, to possess today and tomorrow, and all your days, the high and consecrated bliss of Mary, that you may not only read her words, but use them for yourselves, ever experiencing their meaning: 'My soul doth magnify the Lord, and my spirit hath rejoiced in God my Saviour.'

FOR MEDITATION: The reasons why Mary's soul magnified the Lord were— God's might and majesty (Luke 1:49), God's mercy (Luke 1:50) and God's memory (Luke 1:54–55). Such holy mirth is good for the soul (2 Chronicles 7:10; Proverbs 15:13,15; 17:22; James 5:13) and makes for a truly 'Merry Christmas'.

SERMON NO. 606

Open house for the great Saviour

'But as many as received him, to them gave he power to become the sons of God, even to them that believe on his name: Which were born, not of blood, nor of the will of the flesh, nor of the will of man, but of God.'
John 1:12–13
SUGGESTED FURTHER READING: Luke 9:18–36

My Master will not be satisfied with the acknowledgment that his character is lovely, his doctrine pure, and his moral teaching super-excellent; he will not be content with your admission that he is a prophet greater than any prophet that ever came before or after him; he will not rest satisfied with your admission that he is a teacher sent from heaven, and a being who on account of his virtues is now peculiarly exalted in heaven: all this is well, but it is not enough; you must also believe that he who as man was born of the virgin, and was dandled upon her lap at Bethlehem, was as God none other than the everlasting Lord, without beginning of days or end of years. You do not receive Christ in very deed and truth unless you believe in his proper humanity and actual Godhead. Indeed, what is there for you to receive if you do not receive this? A Saviour who is not divine can be no Saviour for us. How can a mere man, however eminent, deliver his fellows from sins such as yours and mine? How can he bear the burden of our guilt any more than we can ourselves bear it, if there be no more about him than about any other singularly virtuous man? An angel would stagger beneath the load of human criminality, and much more would this be the case with even a perfect man. It needed those mighty shoulders—'Which bear the earth's huge pillars up', to sustain the weight of human sin, and carry it into the wilderness of forgetfulness. You must receive Christ, in order to be saved by him, as being God though man.

FOR MEDITATION: 'What think ye of Christ?' (Matthew 22:42); consider the second person of the Godhead—Christ in eternity before creation (John 1:1–2; Colossians 1:16–17; 1 Peter 1:18–20), Christ in Old Testament history (John 8:56–58; 12:41–42), Christ in the womb before Christmas (Matthew 1:18,20,23; Luke 1:31,35).

Alpha and Omega

'I am Alpha and Omega, the beginning and the end, the first and the last.'
Revelation 22:13
SUGGESTED FURTHER READING: Ecclesiastes 12:13–14

Our Lord should be the Alpha and Omega of our life's end and aim. What is there worth living for but Christ? What is there in the whole earth that is worth a thought but Jesus? Well did an old writer say, 'If God be the only Eternal, then all the rest is but a puff of smoke, and shall I live to heap up puffs of smoke, and shall I toil and strive merely to aggrandise myself with smoky treasures that the wind of death shall dissipate for ever?' No, beloved, let us live for eternal things, and what is there of eternal things that can be chosen but our Lord? O let us give him next year the Alpha of our labour. Let us begin the year by working in his vineyard, toiling in his harvest field. This year is almost over. There is another day or two left—let us serve him till the year is ended, going forward with double haste because the days are now so few. Lord, 'teach us to number our days, that we may apply our hearts unto wisdom.' Let your time and your talents, your substance and your energies, all be given to my Master, who is worthy to be your soul's Alpha and Omega. Jesus crucified should also be the Alpha and Omega of all our preaching and teaching. Woe to the man who makes anything else the main subject of his ministry. 'God forbid that I should glory, save in the cross of our Lord Jesus Christ, by whom the world is crucified unto me, and I unto the world.' Do not tell me you preach sound doctrine; you preach rotten doctrine, if you do not preach Christ—preach nothing up but Christ, and nothing down but sin. Preach Christ; lift him up high on the pole of the gospel, as Moses lifted up the serpent in the wilderness, and you will accomplish your life's end.

FOR MEDITATION: The Lord Jesus Christ is the A to Z of creation and should be acknowledged by us as the A to Z of our lives (Romans 11:36; 2 Corinthians 5:15). Behaving as if he is only Alpha and Iota (A to I) falls far short of obeying the commandment to love the Lord our God with all our heart, soul, mind and strength (Mark 12:30).

The sinner's end

'Until I went into the sanctuary of God; then understood I their end. Surely thou didst set them in slippery places: thou castedst them down into destruction.' Psalm 73:17–18
SUGGESTED FURTHER READING: Jude 20–25

This subject should teach Christians to be in earnest about the salvation of others. If the punishment of sin were some slight pain we need not exercise ourselves diligently to deliver men from it; but if 'eternity' be a solemn word, and if the wrath to come be terrible to bear, how should we be instant in season and out of season, striving to win others from the flames! What have you done this year, some of you? I fear, brother Christians, some of you have done very little. Blessed be God, there are many earnest hearts among you; you are not all asleep; there are some of you who strive with both your hands to do your Master's work, but even you are not as earnest as you should be. The preacher puts himself here in the list, mournfully confessing that he does not preach as he desires to preach. Had I the tears and cries of Baxter, or the fervent seraphic zeal of Whitefield, my soul would be well content, but, alas! we preach coldly upon burning themes and carelessly upon matters which ought to make our hearts like flames of fire. But I say, brethren, are there not men and women here, members of this church, doing nothing for Christ? No soul saved this year by you, Christ unhonoured by you, no gems placed in his crown? What have you been living for, you cumber-ground? For what stand you in the church, you fruitless trees? God make you—you that do little for him—to humble yourselves before him, and to begin the next year with this determination, that knowing the terrors of the Lord, you will persuade men, and labour, and strive to bring sinners to the cross of Christ.

FOR MEDITATION: 'What shall the end be of them that obey not the gospel of God?' (1 Peter 4:17); the Bible on many occasions teaches us the dreadfulness of the sinner's end (Psalm 37:38; Proverbs 14:12; Romans 6:21; 2 Corinthians 11:15; Philippians 3:19). Can you thank God for delivering you from it? If so, what part are you playing in the deliverance of others?

SERMON NO. 486

The new song

'*O sing unto the* LORD *a new song; for he hath done marvellous things: his right hand, and his holy arm, hath gotten him the victory.*' *Psalm* 98:1
SUGGESTED FURTHER READING: Galatians 5:19–24

'What is your war-cry?' There has been a good deal of wickedness these last few days in London. I love to see holy mirth; I delight to see men well feasted. I like Christmas. I like the generosity of those who give to the poor. I would not stop a smile. God forbid me! But cannot men be happy without drunkenness? Cannot they be mirthful without blasphemy? Are there no other ways of finding true pleasure besides selling your soul to the devil? O sirs! I say there have been thousands in this huge city who have been going about the streets, and whose cry has been, 'Sin, and the pleasures thereof! Where is the music-hall? Where is the casino? Where is the tavern? Where is the ballroom? Sin, and the pleasures thereof.' O Satan! you have many soldiers, and right brave soldiers they are, and never are they afraid of your cause, nor ashamed of your name nor of your unholy work. Yes, you are well served, O prince of hell! And rich will be your wages when your drudges earn the fire for which they have laboured. But I hope and trust there are some who will change their watch-note. You have not nailed your colours to the mast, have you? Even if you have, by God's grace I would pull the nails out. Are you determined to die? Will you serve the black prince for ever, and perish with him? Jesus Emmanuel, the captain of our salvation, bids me cry to you, 'Enlist beneath my banner.' Believe in him, trust in him, and live. Oh! trust the merit of the cross, the virtue of the blood, the tears, and the dying groans. This it is to be a Christian, and ever afterwards this shall be your war-note—'Holiness, and the cross thereof!'

FOR MEDITATION: The cry 'What have I to do with thee, Jesus?' (Luke 8:28) can quickly be replaced by an eagerness to follow Jesus and witness for Him (Luke 8:38–39). Under conviction of sin, even the cry 'Crucify him' (Luke 23:21,23) was within weeks drowned by the question 'What shall we do?' (Acts 2:36–37). Have you changed your tune and called upon the Lord to save you (Acts 2:21)?

SERMON NO. 496

A triumphal entrance

'Lift up your heads, O ye gates; even lift them up, ye everlasting doors; and the King of glory shall come in.' Psalm 24:9
SUGGESTED FURTHER READING: John 1:9–13

The year is fast drawing to a close. We call it 'the year of grace, one thousand eight hundred and sixty-six.' Oh! that it may indeed be 'the year of grace' to some unconverted persons here. It may be that I am not casting my net tonight where there are many such to be found. Most of you, my hearers, are members of the church of Christ: you are saved, I trust. Still there are sure to be here and there, like weeds growing in a garden of flowers, some who are still strangers to the Lord Jesus Christ. I would to God that the Holy Spirit would move them to say, 'Come in, Saviour! Let the King of glory come in!' Oh! let this true saying of the faithful and true witness be your encouragement: 'Behold, I stand at the door, and knock: if any man hear my voice, and open the door, I will come in to him, and will sup with him, and he with me.' What a blessed thing! You breakfasted with the devil, and dined with the world: what a mercy if you should sup with Christ; and what a blessed supper you would have! Why, when you woke tomorrow it would be to breakfast with Christ; it would be to hear him say, 'Come and dine,' and then to sup with him again, and so on until you come to eat bread at the marriage supper of the Lamb. May the Lord bless you; and if he grants me my heart's desire, you will each of you say to your souls, 'Lift up your heads, O ye gates; even lift them up, ye everlasting doors; and the King of glory shall come in.'

FOR MEDITATION: The marriage supper of the Lamb (Revelation 19:7,9)— the reception has been planned, the invitations have been sent out, the catering has been laid on (Matthew 22:2–4). How have you replied to God's RSVP? By ignoring it (Matthew 22:5–6) or by glad acceptance of the free invitation (Matthew 22:9–10)?

Last things

'At the last.' Proverbs 5:11
SUGGESTED FURTHER READING: Isaiah 46:8–47:7

I can only compare my text in its matchless power to Ithuriel's spear, with which, according to Milton (Paradise Lost 4:810), he touched the toad and straightway Satan appeared in his true colours. If I can apply my text to certain things today, they will come out in their true light; 'At the last,' shall be the rod in my hand with which I shall touch tinsel, and it shall disappear and you will see it is not gold, and I will touch varnish and paint and graining, and you shall understand that they are really what they are, and not what they profess to be: the light of 'At the last' shall be the light of truth, the light of wisdom to our souls. It seems to me a fitting occasion for holding up this light this morning, when we have come to the end of the year, and shall in a few short hours be at the beginning of another. This period, like the Roman 'god' Janus, has two faces, looking back on the year that is past, and looking forward on the year that is to come, and my four-sided lamp will perhaps gleam afar. I wish that you may have courage enough to look down the vista of the years that you have already lived, and think of everything that you have thought, and spoken, and done, in the light of the beams of this lamp 'At the last,' and then I hope you will have holy daring enough to let the same light shine forward on the years yet to come, when your hair shall be grey and the grinders shall fail, and they that look out of the windows shall be darkened. Let us, then, examine the past and the future of life in the light of 'At the last.' May it teach us wisdom, and make us walk as in the fear of God.

FOR MEDITATION: Spurgeon asked his hearers to examine themselves in the light of his imaginary lantern's four sides, namely death, then judgment (Hebrews 9:27), heaven and hell. 'Happy New Year' is no more than sentimental wishful thinking for those who are still without Christ; but those whose eternal prosperity is guaranteed by their trust in Christ's sacrifice (Hebrews 9:28) can look forward to a 'Happy New Year' whatever happens to them during it.

SERMON NO. 667

Subject Index

II

Subject Index

Section 5   **The Christian life**

Scripture Index

Scripture Index

Scripture Index

Scripture Index

Scripture Index

1. Location of numbers (in order of appearance)

The Metropolitan Tabernacle, Newington (355 numbers; 354 readings)
369, 373–375, 379, 382–388, 391–454, 456–536, 538–568, 570–577, 579–623, 625–658, 661–680, 682–697, 699–714, 716–741, 750, 862

Surrey Chapel, Blackfriars Road (2)
455 (Wednesday 18/6/1862), 756 (Thursday 21/3/1867)

Cornwall Road Chapel, Bayswater (4)
537 (18/10/1863—see 17/10), 578 (3/7/1864), 660 (12/11/1865), 698 (1/7/1866)

Upton Chapel, Lambeth (2—opening & first anniversary)
569 (Tuesday 22/3/1864—see 13/3), 624 (Wednesday 22/3/1865—see 14/3)

No location or date (1)
659 (published 1865 and originally issued 'some years ago')

Westbourne Grove Chapel, Bayswater (1)
681 (18/3/1866)

The Free Tabernacle, Notting Hill (1)
715 (14/10/1866)

2. Time of numbers
The time of most sermons is given on the title page; that of the undated sermons is in most cases indicated by internal references. Most of the sermons were preached on the **Lord's Day** in the **morning;** the exceptions are as follows:—

Time unclear (4)—516, 636, 659, 661 (undated sermons)

Evening (day unclear; probably Sunday, possibly Thursday) (30)—499, 510, 526, 530, 556, 559, 561, 576, 586, 594, 600, 610, 616, 629–634, 640, 646, 656, 677, 686, 693, 702, 726, 731, 736, 741

Sunday evening (29)—375, 413, 415, 423, 425, 426, 430, 440, 446, 452, 456, 470, 476, 488, 491, 496, 505, 523, 535, 548, 550, 584, 602, 669, 672, 691, 706, 710, 716

Monday afternoon (1)—369

Tuesday evening (1)—569

Wednesday evening (2)—455, 624

Thursday afternoon & evening day-meeting (4 numbers, 3 readings)—385–388

Thursday evening (6)—432, 582, 696, 750, 756, 862

Good Friday — morning (1) — 373; **evening** (1)—374

3. Sermons preached on behalf of societies

Baptist Missionary Society — 383 (21/4/1861)

British Society for the propagation of the Gospel amongst the Jews — 582 (16/6/1864—see 13/6)

Baptist Irish Society—629 (Undated—see 25/6)

4. Notably used sermons

In the Prefaces to volumes 7 & 9 Spurgeon selects the following numbers which were particularly used of God:— 373, 374, 391, 403, 404, 412, 416, 417, 488, 492, 505, 508, 518, 519, 522

The Baptismal Regeneration controversy raged around nos. 573, 577, 581 & 591 (all in volume 10) and numerous publications appeared at the time either to support or oppose the position taken by Spurgeon.

5. Details of numbers omitted from this volume

No. 370 (25/3/1861—Rev. W. Brock— 'Evangelical congratulation'—Philippians 1:18)

No. 371 (26/3/1861—Meeting of over 3,000 contributors to the Building Fund)

No. 372 (27/3/1861—Meeting of the neighbouring churches)

No. 376 (2/4/1861—Public meeting of our London Baptist brethren)

No. 377 (3/4/1861—Public meeting of the various denominations—Christian unity)

No. 378 (4/4/1861—Rev. Octavius Winslow—'Christ's finished work'—John 19:30)

No. 380 (8/4/1861—Meeting of our own church—independency, harmony & family)

No. 381 (9/4/1861—Rev. Hugh Stowell Brown—'Christian baptism'—Colossians 2:12)

Nos. 389–390 (12/4/1861—Henry Vincent—'Nonconformity'—an oration)

The speakers at the Exposition of the Doctrines of Grace (385–388), chaired by Spurgeon, were:—Rev. John Bloomfield (Election), Rev. Evan Probert (Human Depravity), Rev. J.A. Spurgeon (Particular Redemption), Rev. James Smith (Effectual calling), Rev. William O'Neill (The Final Perseverance of Believers in Christ Jesus).

6. Contents of Volumes used in this compilation

Vol. 7	nos. 369–426 (following conclusion of the New Park Street Pulpit)
Vol. 8	nos. 427–486
Vol. 9	nos. 487–546
Vol. 10	nos. 547–606
Vol. 11	nos. 607–667
Vol. 12	nos. 668–727
Vol. 13	nos. 728–741, 750, 756 (to 21 March 1867)
Vol. 15	no. 862 (17 January 1867)

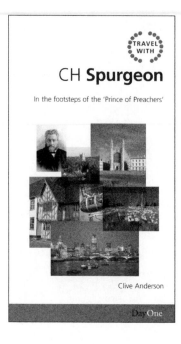

TRAVEL WITH

CH Spurgeon

In the footsteps of the 'Prince of Preachers'

Clive Anderson

Day One

Here is a unique gift idea which combines the concept of a biography with a travel guide. Not only do you have the story of notable Christians from history, but you have a series of travel notes and maps to help you to explore the areas where they lived and worked. John Bunyan, author of *Pilgrim's Progress;* and Charles Haddon Spurgeon, the 'Prince of Preachers', are the first two in this exciting series.

★ **THESE BOOKS ARE UNIQUE**

★ **LEARN ABOUT SOME OF THE MAJOR FIGURES IN CHRISTIAN HISTORY**

★ **PLACES OF INTEREST TO VISIT**

★ **OVER 100 COLOUR PHOTOS**

★ **CLEAR ILLUSTRATED MAPS**

★ **QUICK REFERENCE TRAVEL FACTS**

★ **GREAT GIFT IDEA**

★**BUY THE FIRST TWO IN THIS SERIES**

Travel with John Bunyan

Travel with CH Spurgeon

UK   £9.99
US $14.99
CAN $19.99

365 days with **Spurgeon**

Volume

1

A unique collection of 365 sermons preached by Charles H. Spurgeon from his Park Street Pulpit

Day One

'I recommend this without hesitation'

ENGLISH CHURCHMAN

365 days with Spurgeon   Volume 1

A selection of daily readings taken from the lesser known Park Street years.

Spurgeon was only nineteen when he first preached at New Park Street on December 18th 1853. As we read these daily notes abridged from the New Park Street era (long before his well known days at London's more famous Metropolitan Tabernacle), we can sense the extraordinary vitality which characterised his preaching, together with the wonderful unction attending his ministry in those early years.

Because Spurgeon treated every occasion as a unique opportunity for evangelism, an outstanding feature of these extracts chosen by Terence Crosby is the amazing diversity of the subjects covered, and their relevance to the ears of the contemporary Christian. Spurgeon understood only too well the sinful nature and motives of contemporary society in search of meaning. More than that, he provides insight into the contemporary 'worldly-wise' mind and its wearying, pressurising effect on the soul of the believing Christian living in its midst.

Unusually for a daily devotional, 365 days with Spurgeon also contains a useful Scripture and subject index section, together with a unique guide to where and when Spurgeon preached.

If you are wanting food for the soul, you will find ample in these pages.

HARDBACK (REF 365 HB)
ISBN 0 902548 84 0

UK	£11.99
US	$16.99
CAN	$23.99

PAPERBACK VERSION (REF 365 PB)
ISBN 0 902548 83 2

UK	£9.99
US	$14.99
CAN	$19.99

365 days with Spurgeon

Volume 1

A unique collection of 365 sermons preached by Charles H. Spurgeon from his Park Street Pulpit

Day One

'I recommend this without hesitation'

ENGLISH CHURCHMAN

365 days with Spurgeon   Volume 1

A selection of daily readings taken from the lesser known Park Street years.

Spurgeon was only nineteen when he first preached at New Park Street on December 18th 1853. As we read these daily notes abridged from the New Park Street era (long before his well known days at London's more famous Metropolitan Tabernacle), we can sense the extraordinary vitality which characterised his preaching, together with the wonderful unction attending his ministry in those early years.

Because Spurgeon treated every occasion as a unique opportunity for evangelism, an outstanding feature of these extracts chosen by Terence Crosby is the amazing diversity of the subjects covered, and their relevance to the ears of the contemporary Christian. Spurgeon understood only too well the sinful nature and motives of contemporary society in search of meaning. More than that, he provides insight into the contemporary 'worldly-wise' mind and its wearying, pressurising effect on the soul of the believing Christian living in its midst.

Unusually for a daily devotional, 365 days with Spurgeon also contains a useful Scripture and subject index section, together with a unique guide to where and when Spurgeon preached.

If you are wanting food for the soul, you will find ample in these pages.

HARDBACK (REF 365 HB)
ISBN 0 902548 84 0

UK	£11.99
US	$16.99
CAN	$23.99

PAPERBACK VERSION (REF 365 PB)
ISBN 0 902548 83 2

UK	£9.99
US	$14.99
CAN	$19.99